Cornerstones of Psychology

Readings in the History of Psychology

R. John Huber, Ph.D.

Cynthia Edwards, Ph.D,

David Heining-Boynton, Ph.D.

Editors

Harcourt Brace College Publishers

Fort Worth   Philadelphia   San Diego   New York   Orlando
Austin   San Antonio   Toronto   Montreal   London
Sydney   Tokyo

Publisher	Earl McPeek
Executive Editor	Carol Wada
Strategist	Kathleen Sharp
Project Editor	Michele Tomiak
Art Director	Carol Kincaid
Project Manager	Andrea E. Archer

ISBN: 0-15-505457-D

Address for Domestic Orders
Harcourt College Publishers, 6277 Sea Harbor Drive, Orlando, FL 32887 – 6777
800 – 782 – 4479

Address for International Orders
International Customer Service
Harcourt College Publishers, 6277 Sea Harbor Drive, Orlando, FL 32887 – 6777
407 – 345 – 3800
(fax) 407 – 345 – 4060
(e-mail) hbintl@harcourtbrace.com

Address for Editorial Correspondence
Harcourt College Publishers, 301 Commerce Street, Suite 3700, Fort Worth, TX 76102

Web Site Address
http://www.harcourtcollege.com

Printed in the United States of America
0 1 2 3 4 5 6 7 8 9   039   9 8 7 6 5 4 3 2 1
Harcourt College Publishers

This book is dedicated to the memory of Robert I. Watson.

The production of a book of any kind is impossible without the support of a great many individuals. The authors particularly want to thank their families who have endured the inevitable disruption a project like this would cause. The first author is particularly indebted to his wife, Polly, who has been an invaluable editor and guide for many years.

Meredith College and its staff have proven to be of invaluable help. The college provided sabbatical leaves to the first two authors thus making the project possible. In addition, many individuals have been of great help. Without the help of Dianne Andrews, interlibrary loan specialist, Jaxie Morton and Connie Ahrendsen, departmental assistants to the department of psychology, and several student assistants, Angela Grady, Nellie Navarro, and Samantha Plume, this project would not have been possible.

The authors wish to thank G. Alfred Forsyth of Millersville University for his support and critical reading of the project. We also would like to thank Lisa Hensley, our editor through most of the project, for her active support. Her willingness to be flexible and her quick response to questions certainly made our lives much easier. To all of you and to many not mentioned we are truly grateful.

RJH
CAE
DHB

Raleigh, North Carolina
2000

TABLE OF CONTENTS

Chapter 1
The Study of the History of Psychology   1

Watson, R. I. (1967). Psychology: A prescriptive science.
American Psychologist, 22, 435–443.   3

Chapter 2
Philosophical Influences on Psychology   19

Descartes, R. (1931). The passions of the soul. In E. S. Haldane &
G. R. T. Ross (Trans.). *Philosophical works of Descartes* (Rev. ed.)
(Vol. 1, pp. 329–427 excerpted). New York: Dover. (Originally
published in 1649).   22

Locke, J. (1964). *An essay concerning human understanding.* Cleveland:
World, pp. 63–78. (Originally published in 1690).   29

Chapter 3
Physiological Influences on Psychology   38

Helmholtz, H. (1948). On the rate of transmission of the nerve impulse.
In W. Dennis (Ed.) *Readings in the history of psychology*
(pp. 197–198). New York: Appleton-Century. (Originally published
in 1850).   41

Helmoltz, H. (1912). A manual of physiological optics. In B. Rand (Ed.)
The classical psychologists (pp. 571–581). (Originally published
in 1898).   42

Fechner, G. (1966). *Elements of psychophysics.* New York: Holt,
pp. 1–11. (Originally published in 1859).   48

Chapter 4
The New Psychology   56

Wundt, W. (1907). *Outlines of psychology.* Leipzig: Engelmann,
pp.1–8.   59

Ebbinghaus, H. (1964). *Memory: A contribution to experimental psychology*. H. A. Ruger & E. E. Bussenius (Trans.). New York: Dover. (Originally published in 1885).   71

Chapter 5
Structuralism   83

Titchener, E. B. (1897). *An outline of psychology* (2nd ed.). New York: Macmillan. (Pp. 1–25 are excerpted).   86

Boring, E. G. (1953). A history of introspection. *Psychological Bulletin, 50,* 169–189. (Pp 171–175 are excerpted).   90

Chapter 6
Functionalism: Antecedent Influences   94

Darwin, C. (1936). *The origin of the species.* New York: Modern Library, pp. 1–10. (Originally published in 1859).   98

Galton, F. (1888). Co-relations and their measurement, chiefly from anthropometric data. *Proceedings of the Royal Society of London, 15,* 135–145.   104

Chapter 7
Functionalism: Development and Founding   113

James, W. *Principles of psychology.* New York: Holt, pp. 1–11.   116

Angell, J. R. The province of Functional Psychology. *Psychological Review,* 14. (Pp. 61–91 are excerpted).   123

Chapter 8
The Legacy of Functionalism: Applied Psychology   131

Binet, A. & Simon, T. (1905). *Sur la necissite a etablis un diagnostic scientific des etate inferieurs de l'intelligence. L'Anee Psychologique,* 11, 163–190.   134

Binet, A. & Simon. T. (1908). *La developpment de l'intelligence chez les infants. L'Anee Psychologique,* 14, 1–94.[1]

Cattell, J. M. (1904). The conceptions and methods of psychology. *Popular Science Monthly,* 66, 176–186.   145

Chapter 9
Behaviorism: Antecedent Influences   154

Pavlov, I. P. (1927). *Conditioned reflexes.* New York: Dover.   158

Thorndike, E. L. (1898). *Some experiments on animal intelligence,* 2(8). *Science,* 7, 818–824.   170

---

[1] The first reading is the editors' abridgment of Binet and Simon (1905, 1908). The translation is by Kite (1916). *The development of intelligence.* Baltimore: Williams and Wilkins.

Chapter 10
Behaviorism: The Beginning   177

Watson, J. B. (1913). Psychology as the Behaviorist views it.
Psychological Review, 20, 158–177.   180

Watson, J. B. & Rayner, R. (1920). Conditioned emotional reactions.
Journal of Experimental Psychology, 3, 1–14.   191

Chapter 11
Behaviorism: After the Founding   201

Skinner, B. F. (1948). *Walden two.* New York: Macmillan,
pp. 36–53.   204

Bandura, A., Ross, D., & Ross, S. A. (1963). Imitation of film mediated
aggressive models. *Journal of Abnormal and Social Psychology,*
66, 3–11.   215

Chapter 12
Gestalt Psychology   228

Wertheimer, M. (1938). Gestalt theory. In W. D. Ellis (Ed.) *A source
book of Gestalt psychology* (pp. 1–11). New York: Harcourt Brace.
(Talk originally given in 1924/1925).   230

Köhler, W. (1925). *The mentality of apes.* E. Winter (Trans.). New York:
Harcourt Brace, pp. 1–5, 7–10, 139–140, 198, 276–279.   238

Chapter 13
Psychoanalysis: The Beginnings   245

Freud, S. (1910). The origin and development of psychoanalysis. *The
American Journal of Psychology,* 21 (pp. 181–197, are
excerpted).   248

Freud, S. (1960). The psychopathology of everyday life. In *Standard
Edition* (Vol. 6). London: Hogarth. (First German edition,
1901).   260

Chapter 14
Psychoanalysis: Dissenters and Descendants   265

Jung, C. G. (1950). The Tavistock lectures. In *Collected works.* (Vol. 18).
Princeton: Princeton University Press. (Pp. 5–45 are excerpted).
(Originally published in 1935).   269

Adler, A. (1956). *The Individual Psychology of Alfred Adler.* H. L. &
R. R. Ansbacher (Eds.). New York: Basic Books, pp. 103–108,
179–183, 127–142. (Originally published between 1914 and
1931).   277

Chapter 15
The Current Science   291

Neisser, U. (1967). *Cognitive psychology.* New York: Appleton-Century-Crofts, pp. 3–11.   294

Maslow, A. H. (1970). *Motivation and personality* (2nd ed.). New York: Harper & Row. (Pp. 149–180 are excerpted).   302

PREFACE

An elegant building without a firm foundation would fall. The same is true about science; no thinker, no matter how great an intellect, can create anything of significance without the intellectual cornerstones laid by his or her forbearers. In this collection of readings, we have endeavored to bring together the writings of those in the field of psychology who have provided foundational works, that is, cornerstones. One might logically wonder how the particular psychologists were selected for this volume. Did not someone like James or Watson, for example, build on the work of others? One can demonstrate the influence of Aristotle on both individuals by citing James's interest in function and Watson's emphasis on association.

With the exception of Descartes and Locke, psychologists from the late 19th and early 20th centuries have been selected because psychology became a science during this period. The 1870s is the commonly accepted decade marking the beginning of psychology as a science since it is during this period that William James formally requested funds (the grand sum of $300) to establish a laboratory at Harvard, and Wilhelm Wundt established the first laboratory of magnitude in Leipzig, Germany. We psychologists are quite close to our roots. While psychology was in its infancy during the late 19th and early 20th centries, the founders of the various schools and approaches took great pains in defining the content of and the method to be used in the study of psychology. It is because of their proximity to the birth of psychology that these thinkers were plucked from the flow of history.

By studying these pioneers, the reader and student of psychology gains a perspective and wisdom provided by time. I have a friend who is a skilled family therapist. One of his special skills involves the use of family stories, the kind of story passed down from generation to generation within a family. He and many family theorists believe that these stories contain the kernel of a family's functional psychology. The viewpoints and attitudes of individuals who lived several generations ago still affect the functioning of the contemporary family. This, too, is true of psychology. The seminal definitions of the field by the great thinkers of the past still affect the functioning of the psychological family today. We have tried to show the origin of this influence by including in each set of readings such a seminal statement. As the family can better understand its functioning by looking at the great stories of the past, you, the student of psychology, will better understand the functioning of the psychological family by looking at the great stories of its past.

C H A P T E R 1

The Study of the History of Psychology

Scientific Progress

Currently, there is a chain of stores called "Great Mistakes." In many ways, this would be a fitting title for the history of psychology and all of science. The ideas of all the great psychologists cited in this book are just that, great mistakes. Does this mean that we now have the truth? No! In a profound book concerning the history of science, T. S. Kuhn (1970) indicated that all scientific knowledge is ultimately flawed and that progress in science occurs when observations are made that indicate the ultimate invalidity of any idea. Scientific revolutions occur when, by necessity, a rethinking of any approach is necessitated. Such was the case with Ptolemaic astronomy. Certain difficulties with the calendar made the geocentric (the idea that the sun revolves around the earth) theory an untenable assumption. These difficulties necessitated the revolution in astronomic thinking led by Copernicus with his heliocentric (the idea that the earth revolves around the sun) theory. Most of you were taught during elementary school that Ptolemy was wrong and Copernicus was right. This is not true. From the vantage point of a properly positioned space shuttle, you could clearly see that the earth revolves around the sun. Yet, from

1

most Atlantic beaches, you can clearly see that the sun rises in the east and sets in the west. In this sense, Ptolemy was correct. In fact, his mistake is ultimately useful. Several years ago, I was hiking in New Hampshire and became disoriented. As the sun began to set and the early fall air became chilly, I became quite anxious to find the road and my car. I remembered that the road was somewhere to the west and followed the setting sun until, much to my relief, the road appeared. Ptolemy's great but partially true mistake helped me find my car. In this instance, Copernican theory might have been a hindrance. Can you imagine being lost in some thick woods as it got colder and colder and thinking, "Wait, Ptolemy was wrong! The earth actually revolves around the sun. I need to figure out the relative position of the planets to find my way back to the car." This would be extremely foolish. The point of this anecdote is that scientific ideas are neither correct nor incorrect. They are merely useful or not useful. In fact, Kuhn suggests that all theories are ultimately falsifiable; that is, they are great mistakes. This may seem like a preposterous idea, but can you think of any area of your life where you know everything you possibly could? The same is true in science; all knowledge has limits. When these limits are pushed, there is opportunity for great progress. Roughly speaking, the history of scientific progress can be charted by great shifts in ideas (Kuhn calls these paradigmatic shifts) as one generally accepted theory gives way to another. Greatly simplified, the history of physics can be summarized as a shift from Aristotelian, to Newtonian, to Einsteinian thinking.

Would it be that the history of psychology were so simple! In the aforementioned examples concerning astronomy and physics, there were prevailing models (paradigms) embraced by most scientists within the field. In 1860, virtually all physicists were Newtonians. Physics could be described as a paradigmatic science since most physicists embraced a common theoretical viewpoint. This was not and is not the case with psychology since there never has been a prevailing paradigm in psychology. Thus, it is necessary every time one reads a psychological theory to understand the philosophical assumptions upon which that theory is built. In your reading, for instance, you will find that E. B. Titchener and the structuralists made consciousness the cornerstone of their approach, whereas J. B. Watson and the behaviorists doubted the very existence of consciousness.

R. I. Watson's (1967) paper, "Psychology: A Prescriptive Science," provides a useful tool for analyzing psychological theories. Watson indicates that since psychology is a science without a prevailing paradigm, that is, a viewpoint, one must assess every psychological theory to determine upon what philosophical assumptions (prescriptions) the theory is founded. This is important because these prescriptions affect each theorist's approach to psychology and thus the subsequent research conducted by that theorist's followers. The same is true with the practice of psychotherapy. If, on the one hand, a therapist is a Freudian and thus a strict determinist, he or she will most likely be historically oriented and quite interested in the client's past. If, on the other hand, a therapist is a humanist and thus an indeterminist, he or she will be ahistorical in orientation and show little interest in the client's past. One can, therefore, understand the directions a theory will take by understanding its philosophical assumptions about the nature of reality (metaphysical assumptions). Watson's paper is an excellent guide in how to go about this analysis. Following Watson's article is a table you can use to compare and contrast psychological theories using Watson's prescriptive theory.

In summary, I have suggested the following: (1) Theories are never proven but are only falsified; (2) progress occurs in science when scientists out of necessity develop better theories, that is, better mistakes; (3) many sciences, such as physics, are paradigmatic sciences; (4) psychology is not a paradigmatic science; and (5) it is necessary to examine every psychological theory to see what prescriptions each theorist uses.

REFERENCES

Kuhn, T. S. (1970). *The structure of scientific revolution* (2nd ed.). Chicago: University of Chicago Press.

Watson, R. I. (1967). Psychology: A prescriptive science. *American Psychologist, 22,* 435–443.

Psychology: A Prescriptive Science[1]

Robert I. Watson
Northwestern University

In a recent analysis of the dynamics of the history of the older, more mature sciences Kuhn (1962, 1963) holds that each of them has reached the level of guidance by a paradigm. In one of its meanings a paradigm is a contentual model, universally accepted by practitioners of a science at a particular temporal period in its development. With this agreement among its practioners, the paradigm defines the science in which it operates. In a science where a paradigm prevails, one recognizes that a particular paradigm concerns chemistry, astronomy, physics, or the biological science. Illustrative in astronomy is the Ptolemaic paradigm which gave way to the Copernican paradigm, and in physics is the Aristotelian paradigm which gave way to the Newtonian dynamic paradigm, which, in the relatively recent past, was superseded by the paradigm provided by Einstein and Bohr. The great events of science which occur when a new paradigm emerges Kuhn calls a revolution.

The historical sequence Kuhn holds to be as follows: As scientists go about the tasks of normal science, eventually an anomaly, i.e., a research finding, which does not fit the prevailing paradigm, is obtained. A normal science problem that ought to be solvable by the prevailing procedures refuses to fit into the paradigm or a piece of equipment designed for normal research fails to perform in the anticipated

---

[1]Address of the President of the Division of the History of Psychology at its charter meeting at the American Psychological Association in New York City, September 1966. During 1966 earlier versions of the paper were given at colloquia at Cornell University and Knox College.

manner. Failures in science to find the results predicted in most instances are the result of lack of skill of the scientist. They do not call into question the rules of the game, i.e., the paradigm, that the scientist is following. Reiterated efforts generally bear out this commitment to the accepted paradigm that Kuhn calls a dogmatism. Only repeated failure by increasing numbers of scientists results in questioning the paradigm which, in turn, results in a "crisis" (Kuhn, 1963). The state of Ptolemaic astronomy was a recognized scandal before Copernicus proposed a basic change, Galileo's contribution arose from recognized difficulties with medieval views, Lavoisier's new chemistry was the product of anomalies created both by the proliferation of new gases found and the first quantitative studies of weight relations. When the revealed anomaly no longer can be ignored, there begin the extraordinary investigations that lead to a scientific revolution. After sufficient acceptance of this anomaly is achieved from the other workers in the field, a new paradigm takes the place of the one overthrown and a period of normal science begins. Since a paradigm is sufficiently open-ended it provides a host of problems still unsolved. In this period of normal science the task of the scientist is to fill out the details of the paradigm to determine what facts, perhaps already known, that may be related to the theory, to determine what facts are significant for it, to extend to other situations, and in general to articulate the paradigm. In short, it would appear that the activities of normal science are a form of "working through" in a manner somewhat akin to that task which occupies so much time in psychoanalytic psychotherapy.

When a new anomaly appears and is given support, the cycle then repeats.

The bulk of Kuhn's monograph is taken up with a historical account of the events leading up to scientific revolutions, the nature of these revolutions, and the paradigmatic developments thereafter, with many familiar facts of the history of astronomy, physics, and chemistry cast in this particular perspective. It is here that the persuasiveness of his point of view is to be found. The test of the correctness of Kuhn's views rests upon the fit of his data with the available historical materials. Kuhn uses the key concept of paradigm in several degrees of breadth other than contentually defining and it is difficult to know precisely what differentiates each of the usages. Fortunately, I can leave to the specialist in the history of the physical sciences the evaluation of the correctness of his reading the details of their history and the various meanings of paradigm, for I am more concerned with what can be drawn from what he has to say about other sciences that he contends lack a contentually defining paradigm.

In all of its meanings, a paradigm has a guidance function. It functions as an intellectual framework, it tells them what sort of entities with which their scientific universe is populated and how these entities behave, and informs its followers what questions may legitimately be asked about nature.

What are the consequences in those sciences that lack a defining paradigm? Foremost is a noticeable lack of unity within a science, indications of which Kuhn acknowledges as one of the sources for his paradigmatic concept, which arose in part from his being puzzled about "the number and extent of the overt disagreement between social scientists about the nature of legitimate scientific methods and problems [1962, p. X]" as compared to the relative lack of such disagreement among natural scientists.

That psychology lacks this universal agreement about the nature of our contentual model that is a paradigm, in my opinion, is all too readily documented.[2] In psychology there is still debate over fundamentals. In research, findings stir little argument but the overall framework is still very much contested. There is still disagreement about what is included in the science of psychology. In part, at least, it is because we lack a paradigm that one psychologist can attack others who do not agree with him as being "nonscientific" or "not a psychologist," or both. Schools of psychology still have their adherents, despite wishful thinking. And an even more telling illustration, because it is less controversial, is the presence of national differences in psychology to such an extent that in the United States there is an all too common dismissal of work in psychology in other countries as quaint, odd, or irrelevant. National differences, negligible in the paradigmatic sciences such as physics and chemistry, assume great importance in psychology. A provincialism in psychology in the United States is the consequence, provincialism on a giant scale, to be sure, but still a provincialism which would and could not be present if a paradigm prevailed.

Before its first paradigm had served to unify it and while still in "the preparadigmatic stage" each physical science was guided by "something resembling a paradigm," says Kuhn. Since it was outside his scope, Kuhn said hardly more than this about the matter.

Psychology has not experienced anything comparable to what atomic theory has done for chemistry, what the principle of organic evolution has done for biology, what laws of motion have done for physics. Either psychology's first paradigm has not been discovered or it has not yet been recognized for what it is. Although the presence of an unrecognized paradigm is not ruled out completely, it would seem plausible to proceed on the assumption that psychology has not yet had its initial paradigmatic revolution. The present task is to answer the question—if psychology lacks a paradigm, what serves to take its place?

It would seem that it follows from Kuhn's position that whatever provides the guidance could not have the all-embracing unifying effect of defining the field in question since if it did so, a paradigm would exist. What seems to be required is some form of trends or themes, numerous enough to deal with the complexity of psychology and yet not so numerous as to render each of them only narrowly meaningful. Those which I have isolated follow:

---

[2]Others have expressed themselves about the lack of unity in psychology. If one were asked what is the most comprehensive treatment of psychology since Titchener's *Manual*, the answer must be the multivolumed *Psychology: A Study of a Science*, edited by Sigmund Koch (1959). Its general introduction makes considerable capital of the diversity of tongues with which psychologists speak and the preface comments that psychology proceeds along "several quite unsure directions, [p. V]." To turn to but one other source, Chaplin and Krawiec (1960) close their recent book on systems and theories with the prophecy that the task of the future is "to integrate all points of view into one. . . .": to provide "a comprehensive theoretical structure with the integrating force of atomic theory. . . . [pp. 454–455]."

THE PRESCRIPTIONS OF PSYCHOLOGY ARRANGED IN CONTRASTING PAIRS

Conscious mentalism-Unconscious mentalism *(emphasis on awareness of mental structure or activity—unawareness)*

Contentual objectivism-Contentual subjectivism *(psychological data viewed as behavior of individual—as mental structure or activity of individual)*

Determinism-Indeterminism *(human events completely explicable in terms of antecedents—not completely so explicable)*

Empiricism-Rationalism *(major, if not exclusive source of knowledge is experience—is reason)*

Functionalism-Structuralism *(psychological categories are activities—are contents)*

Inductivism-Deductivism *(investigations begun with facts or observations—with assumed established truths)*

Mechanism-Vitalism *(activities of living beings completely explicable by physiochemical constituents—not so explicable)*

Methodological objectivism-Methodological subjectivism *(use of methods open to verification by another competent observer—not so open)*

Molecularism-Molarism *(psychological data most aptly described in terms of relatively small units—relatively large units)*

Monism-Dualism *(fundamental principle or entity in universe is of one kind—is of two kinds, mind and matter)*

Naturalism-Supernaturalism *(nature requires for its operation and explanation only principles found within it—requires transcendent guidance as well)*

Nomotheticism-Idiographicism *(emphasis upon discovering general laws—upon explaining particular events or individuals)*

Peripheralism-Centralism *(stress upon psychological events taking place at periphery of body—within the body)*

Purism-Utilitarianism *(seeking of knowledge for its own sake—for its usefulness in other activities)*

Quantitativism-Qualitativism *(stress upon knowledge which is countable or measurable—upon that which is different in kind or essence)*

Rationalism-Irrationalism *(emphasis upon data supposed to follow dictates of good sense and intellect—intrusion or domination of emotive and conative factors upon intellectual processes)*

Staticism-Developmentalism *(emphasis upon cross-sectional view—upon changes with time)*

Staticism-Dynamicism *(emphasis upon enduring aspects—upon change and factors making for change)*

The overall function of these themes is orientative or attitudinal; they tell us how the psychologist-scientist must or should behave. In short, they have a directive function. They help to direct the psychologist-scientist in the way he selects a problem, formulates it, and the way in which he carries it out.

The other essential characteristic is that of being capable of being traced historically over some appreciable period of time. On both counts, the term *prescription* seems to have these connotations.[3] It is defined in the dictionaries as the act of prescribing, directing, or dictating with an additional overtone of implying long usage, of being hallowed by custom, extending over time.[4]

It is for the reason of persisting over relatively long periods of time that prescriptions can be of historical moment. In fact, in choosing the particular prescriptions with which I deal the presence of historical continuity over at least most of the modern period was a major decisive factor. If an instance of some conception serving a directive function was of relatively short temporal dimension, it was not considered a prescription. It is for this reason that some prominent trends in psychology today do not appear as prescriptions. Physicalism and operationalism are very much part of the current *Zeitgeist* in psychology but because they are relatively new upon the psychological scene, they are not considered prescriptions. Instead, they serve as challenges to utilize the prescriptions for their explanation. It is characteristic of prescriptions that modern, more specifically formulated versions of the more general historically rooted ones may appear. Empiricism-rationalism have modern descendents in environmentalism-nativism.

---

[3]A fortunate historical precedent for using prescriptions in this way is to be found in a quotation from Leibniz in his *New Essays Concerning Human Understanding* (1949). It may help to make clear what is meant. "The discussions between Nicole[1] and others on the *argument from the great number* in a matter of faith may be consulted, in which sometimes one defers to it too much and another does not consider it enough. There are other similar *prejudgments* by which men would very easily exempt themselves from discussion. These are what Tertullian, in a special treatise, calls *Prescriptiones* . . . availing himself of a term which the ancient jurisconsults (whose language was not unknown to him) intended for many kinds of exceptions or foreign and predisposing allegations, but which now means merely the temporal prescription when it is intended to repel the demand of another because not made within the time fixed by law. Thus there was reason for making known the *legitimate prejudgments* both on the side of the Roman Church and on that of the Protestants [Book IV, Ch. 14, pp. 530–531]."

[4]Something akin to the prescriptive approach has been suggested in the past. In the early part of the last century Victor Cousin (1829) followed by J. D. Morell (1862) developed a synthetical system of the history of philosophy based upon a division into the four aspects of sensationalism, idealism, scepticism, and mysticism.

In the '30s, Kurt Lewin (1935) was groping toward something similar in his discussion of the conflict between the Aristotelian and Galilean modes of thought. Lewin's shift of modes of thought from the Aristotelian to Galilean, although admitting of partial overlap, impress me as too saltatory, too abrupt in movement from qualitative appearance to quantitative reality, from search for phenotypes to search for genotypes, from surface to depth, from disjointed descriptions to nomothetic search for laws. They are, in my opinion, not so much a matter of qualitative leaps as they are gradual changes with the older views still very much operative. Lewin's conceptualizing in relation to the historic facts seems similar in spirit to Piaget's brilliant strokes on the process of development. I suspect that if we were to take Lewin as seriously, as did the American investigators who followed the leads of Piaget into painstaking detailed research, we would find that there was much blurring and overlap of these Lewinian shifts, as there seems to be at the Piagetian levels. *(Footnote 4 continued on next page.)*

To arrive at a reasonably complete and appropriate categorization of the prescriptions, I carried out two separable, although actually intertwined steps. I considered the present scene, for example, in a paper on national trends in psychology in the United States (1965), in order to ascertain what seemed to characterize psychology today, and then turned to the very beginning of the modern period in the history of psychology in the seventeenth century to see if these themes were then discernible in recognizable form. In the 300-page manuscript that I have so far prepared, I can say that I find encouraging indications of the historical roots of these prescriptions somewhere in the contributions of Bacon, Descartes, Hobbes, Spinoza, Leibniz, Locke, and Newton, and in those of the lesser figures of the seventeenth century.

Turning to its directive-orientative function, it will be remembered that this theory of prescriptions is more than a classificatory system, more than a convenient means for a particular historian to order his account. These prescriptions were and are part of the intellectual equipment of psychologists. Psychologists are always fac-

---

(Footnote 4 continued)

In applying the shift in modes of classification from the Aristotelian to Galilean syndrome, Brunswik (1956) placed psychology as showing the shift between Titchener in 1901 and Lewin in 1935. It is unfortunate that an arbitrary impression of finality emerges. Prescriptions, at any rate, are not conceived as emerging with such definitiveness; they appear gradually and tentatively to disappear and then to reappear.

Brunswik (1955, 1956) also casually used the term, "Thema" in somewhat the same broad sense that I use prescription, but without working out its meaning or scope. He also used the same term to apply to the seeking of analogical similarity to the content of another science (1955) and even to psychological content, as such (1956).

In his *Historical Introduction to Modern Psychology* through the 1932 revision but not his 1949 revision, Murphy (1932) in his summing up of the decades of 1910 and 1920 utilized quantification as the integrating theme to unify psychology but gave previous consideration to problem trends over the time expressed such as from structural to functional, from part to whole, from qualitative to quantitative and experimental to genetic-statistical. It is important to reiterate that these were used as guiding themes only for a summary of 2 decades, and not for the earlier history of psychology. When Murphy faced the task of summarizing from the vantage point of the late '40s, he abandoned this form of summarization.

Bruner and Allport (1940) analyzed the contents of psychological periodicals for the 50-year period, 1888–1938, in terms of individual "author's problem, his presupposition procedure, explanatory concepts and outlook in psychological science [p. 757]." The material provided the basis for Allport's 1939 Presidential Address to the American Psychological Association. In his summarization, Allport (1940) indicated that his survey showed an agreement with an earlier one by Bills and not only stated that psychology is "increasingly empirical, mechanistic, quantitative, nomothetic, analytic and operational," but also pleaded that should not psychology be permitted to be "rational, teological, qualitative, idiographic, synoptic, and even nonoperational [p. 26]?" Thus, Allport and I show substantial agreement since five out of six "presuppositions" as he calls them, are among those in my schema of prescriptions. The reason that one exception, operational-nonoperational presuppositions, is not included in my schema is that I consider it, as explained before, historically rooted in other older prescriptions.

Allport and Bruner's work cries out for follow-up and I hope to have someone working on it in the near future. Allport did, however, use something akin to his schema in a comparison of American and European theories of personality published in 1957.

A more recent related publication is that of Henry Murray, who in the course of an overview of historical trends in personality research, made a plea for "a comprehensive and fitting classification of elementary trends" (1961, pp. 15–16), which he then classified as regional, populational, theoretical, technique, data ordering, intentional (pure or applied), and basic philosophical assumptional trends. This last, the basic philosophical assumption, was not in any way spelled out so there is no way of knowing what he had in mind.

ing problems, novel and otherwise. They do so with habits of thought, methodological and contentual, which they have taken from the past. This applies today with just as much force as it ever did in the past. In short, they are dynamic because psychologists accept, reject and combine prescriptions, thus thinking in certain ways, and not in others.

In the above list, prescriptions have been presented in one of the ways they function—as contrasting or opposing trends.[5] At some point in their history most of these prescription pairings have been considered as opposed, even irreconcilable for example, naturalism as opposed to supernaturalism, and empiricism as opposed to rationalism.

A summarization, such as the list gives, inevitably distorts its subject matter. Especially pertinent here is the false impression of tidiness this arrangement of antithetical isolated pairs gives. Consider the dichotomy, mechanism-vitalism. Does this oppositional way of presenting them exhaust the matter? By no means, mechanism bears relation to molecularism, and molecularism may come in conflict with supernaturalism, which in turn, relates to certain forms of dualism.

Prescriptions are by no means simple, dominant, isolated themes moving monolithically through history. In a recent analysis of the history of mathematical concepts in psychology, George Miller (1964) warns expressly against this kind of oversimplification. His treatment of what he calls the "varieties of mathematical psychology" (p. 1), that I consider to bear considerable relation to the quantitavistic prescription, is further subdivided into several categories and subcategories. As he indicates, a more extensive treatment would require still others.

Their oppositional character does lead to explication of another characteristic of prescriptions. At a time, past or present, when both of the opposed prescriptions had or have supporters, it is possible to make some sort of an estimate of their relative strength; in other words, we may speak of dominant and counterdominant prescriptions. Rationalism dominated in seventeenth-century England; Locke was nearly alone in advocating empiricism. Nomotheticism dominates today in the United States; an idiographic prescription is sufficiently viable to make itself heard in protest against the prevailing state of affairs. Hence, idiography is counterdominant.

---

[5]There is a precedent for considering the trends studies in terms of antithetical pairs. In his critical study, *Biological Principles*, J. H. Woodger (1929) considered the problems of biological knowledge to center on six antitheses: vitalism and mechanism, structure and function, organism and environment, preformation and epigenesis, teleology and causation, and mind and body. His emphasis was upon examining the current views circa 1929. Although he showed a lively appreciation of their historical roots, his task was not essentially historical.

W. T. Jones (1961) also has developed a means of evaluation of so-called "axes of bias" of order-disorder, static-dynamic, continuity-discreteness, inner-outer, sharp focus–soft focus, this world–other world, and spontaneity-process. Content high on the order axis shows a strong preference for system, clarity and conceptual analysis while that for disorder shows a strong preference for fluidity, muddle, and chaos. Illustrative applications to samples of poetry, painting, and documents in the social and physical sciences were made. Syndromes for the medieval, the Renaissance, the enlightenment, and the romantic periods were developed. The last, receiving the most attention, was characterized as showing soft-focus, inner-disorder, dynamic, continuity, and other-world biases. The results so far reported show it to be a promising technique.

Brunswik (1956) also speaks of the survival of dichotemizing doctrines, such as the four temperaments as illustrative of a prescientific syndrome in psychology.

The presence of dominant and counterdominant prescriptions helps us to see how competitions and conflict may result. Whether purism or utilitarianism dominates in American psychology today, I would be hard put to say, but we can be sure of one thing—both prescriptions have sufficient protagonists to make for a prominent conflict. Dominance may shift with time; at one time supernaturalism dominated decisively, there followed centuries of conflict and today naturalism dominates almost completely.

Although important, their oppositional nature is not always present. Empiricism-rationalism has been presented as a contrasting pair, yet at least to the satisfaction of some psychologists and philosophers of science, they have been reconciled today at a higher level of synthesis. Induction and deduction were also considered antithetical once. In actual practice today, the scientist often sees them as aspects of an integrated method which permits him to weave them together. Sometimes prescriptions, rather than being contradictory, are contrary; there may be gradations, or relationships of degree as seems to be the case with methodological subjectivity-objectivity.

Reinforcing its directive character is the fact that prescriptions sometimes are "prejudgments," presuppositions or preconceptions that are acted upon without examination, that are taken for granted.[6] Some prescriptions are characterized by their being tacit presuppositions taken as a matter of course and even operating without explicit verbalization. What psychologist today says to himself that the problem he is considering is one that I must decide whether I should or should not quantify; instead he immediately starts to cast the problem in quantitative terms without further ado. Similarly, most psychologists are monists. That many psychologists would react to being called monists with a sense of incredulity and even resentment nicely illustrates my point. We think monistically without using the term. Similarly we are apt to follow empiricistic and naturalistic prescriptions without much thought to the fact that we do so. But there was a time when the issues of quantitativeness-qualitativeness, of monism-dualism, of empiricism-rationalism, and of naturalism-supernaturalism were very much explicit issues, occupying the center of the psychological stage. Often their implicit character seems to have come about when one became so dominant that the other no longer stirred argument. Sometimes no clean-cut agreed-on solution was verbalized, instead they were allowed to slide into implicitness. A shift of interest, rather than resolution with a clear-cut superiority of one over the other seems characteristic. Old prescriptions never die, they just fade away. Naturally, at some times and to some extent a prescription became less relevant to psychology, but these are matters of degree.

---

[6]Of course, implicitness of historical trends is not a novel idea. Whitehead (1925) remarked that when one is attempting to examine the philosophy of a period, and by implication to examine the philosophy of a period, and by implication to examine a science as well, one should not chiefly direct attention to those particular positions adherents find it necessary to defend explicitly but to the assumptions which remain *unstated*. These unverbalized presuppositions appear so obvious to their adherents that it may even be that no way to state them has occurred to them. In similar vein, Lovejoy (1936) has observed that implicit or incompletely explicit assumptions operate in the thinking of individuals and ages.

Much of psychology's early history is, of course, a part of philosophy. Many of these prescriptions had their roots in philosophical issues, and are even still stated in what is current philosophical terminology as in monism-dualism and empiricism-rationalism to mention the two most obvious. I do not hesitate to use philosophical terminology because psychology cannot be completely divorced from philosophy either in its history or in its present functioning. This state of affairs is cause for neither congratulation nor commiseration. Psychology is not the more scientific by trying to brush this sometimes embarrassing fact under the rug as do some of our colleagues by teaching and preaching psychology as if it had no philosophically based commitments. They are psychology's Monsieur Jourdaines who deny they talk philosophical prose. Denying there is need to consider philosophical questions does not solve the problem. The very denial is one form of philosophical solution.

Since they were originally philosophical issues, it will be convenient to refer to some prescriptions as "contentual" problems. To bring home this point, the areas of philosophy in which certain of the prescriptions fall might be identified. Rationalism and empiricism have their origins in epistemology, monism and dualism in ontology (nature of reality), and molarism and molecularism in cosmology (structure of reality).

A major task in the history of psychology is to trace how the field individuated from the philosophical matrix. In this process, the prescriptions that served as major guidelines in the emergence of psychology as a separate discipline originally had a philosophical character, which took on a general scientific character with the emergence of the physical sciences in general, and psychological science in particular. It is in this sense that they can be referred to as philosophically contentual in character. Moreover, consideration by psychologists and others in the sciences transformed them sometimes in ways that only by tracing their history can one see the relation to their parentage.

Often the traditional terminology used herewith, for example, its dualistic and mentalistic locus has had to give way to objectivistic and monistic terminology. Confused and confusing though these terms might be, they still referred to something relevant to psychology. As they are formulated, psychologists may be repelled by "old-fashioned" air of the statement of many of the prescriptions. Justification is found in the fact that these are the terms in psychology's long history until a short 50 years ago.

Lacking a paradigm has meant that psychology looked to other scientific fields for guidance. It is characteristic of prescriptions that borrowing from other fields has taken place. Psychology's heritage from philosophy could be viewed in this manner. But there are other forms of borrowing which have entered into prescription formation. There has been noteworthy borrowing from biology, physiology in particular, signalized by Wundt's calling his work "physiological psychology" in deference to the methodological inspiration it was to him. But physics, highest in the hierarchy of the sciences, has just as often served as the model science. Psychology has had its dream of being a changeling prince. The rejected child of drab philosophy and low-born physiology, it has sometimes persuaded itself that actually it was the child of high-born physics. It identified with the aspiration of the physical sciences, and, consequently, acquired an idealized version of the parental image as a superego, especially concerning scientific morality, i.e., the "right" way for a scientist to behave.

Psychologists looked to these other sciences for methodological guidance.[7] This methodological cast is particularly evident in the prescriptions concerned with nomothetic law, inductivism-deductivism, quantitativism-qualitativism, methodological objectivism and subjectivism, and determinism-indeterminism. It follows that these prescriptions apply in varying degrees to other sciences. So, too, does the puristic-utilitarian prescription, and working through the naturalistic-supernaturalistic problem.

Some of the centential prescriptions have counterparts in other sciences. Salient to all biological sciences are developmentalism-statisticism, functionalism-structuralism, mechanism in its various guises, and molecularism-molarism. It is also at least possible that many of these prescriptions would be found to have counterparts in other nonscientific areas of knowledge, such as literature, religion, and politics. After all, man's reflective life, as the "Great Ideas" of Adler and Hutchins and their cohorts show, has much more interpenetration into the various compartmentalization of knowledge than is customarily recognized. But to explore this further would be to extend discussion beyond the scope of the paper.

In the preparadigmatic stage of a science, a scientist may also become an adherent to a school, that is to say, he may accept a set of interlocking prescriptions espoused by a group of scientists generally with an acknowledged leader. Functionalism, behaviorism, Gestalt psychology, and psychoanalysis are representative.

The orientative character of prescriptions is also present in a school. As Marx and Hillex (1963) recognize, each school seems to follow a directive—you should be primarily concerned with the study of the functions of behavior in adapting to the environment and the formulation of mathematical functions relating behavior to antecedent variables: *functionalism*—you ought to study the stimulus-response connections through strict methodological objectivism; *behaviorism*—you can arrive at useful formulations of psychological principles through consideration of molar units of both stimulus and response, i.e., configurations or fields; *Gestalt*—you should be concerned with the interplay and conflict of the environment and native constituents of the disturbed personality with special attention to its unconscious aspect, *psychoanalysis*.

Salience or nonsalience of particular prescriptions characterize schools. Behaviorism is both contentually objectivistic and environmentalistic (empirical). However, the former is salient; the latter is nonsalient. Contentual objectivism is central and indispensable, environmentalism is not crucial to its central thesis. Behaviorism would still be behaviorism even if all behaviorists were nativistic in orientation.

In broad strokes based on salient prescriptions, functionalism is functionalistic, empiricistic, quantitativistic and molecularistic. Behaviorism has as salient orientative prescriptions, contentual objectivism, and molecularism. Gestalt psychol-

---

[7]It should be noted that this looking to other sciences and finding evidences for prescriptions implies that paradigmatic sciences are not denied the presence of prescriptions. Exploration is, however, outside of the scope of this paper.

ogy may be said to make salient molarism, subjectivism, and nativism. The salient directive prescriptions of psychoanalysis seem to be dynamicism, irrationalism, unconscious mentalism, and developmentalism.

The differing patterns of salient prescriptions of the schools serves also to make more intelligible their differing research emphases upon particular contentual problems—the functionalists with their empiricistic salience upon learning; the behaviorists with their peripheralism upon motor activity (including learning); Gestalt psychology with its molarism and nativism upon perception; and psychoanalysis with its dynamicism and irrationalism upon motivation.

There is an even broader level of prescriptions, that of national trends exemplified by the Symposium on National Trends at the XVIIth International Congress to which reference already has been made (Watson, 1965). Here greater diversity than that of the schools is expected. Instead of patterns, it is most meaningful to couch their discussion in terms of dominance and counterdominance.

Immersion in the current scene as a participant-observer, adds immeasurably to the already complicated task of the historian who is apt therefore to approach the present with a great deal of trepidation. What will be hazarded is inclusive broad, therefore, crude overall characterization of the current scene of psychology in the United States. It will serve as another exercise in the application of the prescriptive approach. Although couched in terms of a somewhat different array of prescriptions than now is being used, for reasons explained earlier, I will quote from the concluding summary of my paper on this Symposium:

> It has been seen that national trends in modern American psychology follow certain dominant prescriptions. Determinism, naturalism, physicalism and monism, although very much operative, are judged to incite relatively little opposition. Functionalism, operationalism, quantification, hypothetico-deductivism, environmentalism, and nomotheticism are likewise dominant, but there are counterprescriptions which tend to oppose them. As for the schools of psychology, psychoanalysis, very obviously, and Gestalt psychology, less firmly, still stand apart. Serving as counterprescriptions to those dominant in psychology are those calling for increased complexity in theorizing, for an increased attention to philosophical matters, for general acceptance of phenomenology, for increased attention to existential psychology and in a somewhat amorphous way almost all of the areas of personality theory calls for counterprescriptions of one sort or another [p. 137].

It is important to note that most national prescriptive trends have been stated in terms of dominance and counterdominance, which reflects diverseness, not integration. Indeed, the highest level of integration in psychology is still that of the schools, not that of the nation. Different patterns of dominance and counterdominance are present in different countries. For the sake of brevity, but at the risk of oversimplification, methodological and contentual objectivity, particularly in the form of operationalism prevails in the United States, while methodological and contentual subjectivity, especially in the form of phenomenalism, does so in large segments of Continental Europe.

It follows that patterns of dominant prescriptions characterize a given temporal period and geographical area. When we wish to emphasize the then current intertwined pattern to dominant prescriptions as having a massive cumulative effect, we refer to the *Zeitgeist*. The *Zeitgeist* in itself is empty of content until we describe that which we assign to a particular *Zeitgeist*. The strands that enter into the *Zeitgeist* include the dominant prescriptions of that time. So the *Zeitgeist* and prescriptive concepts are considered complementary. One of the puzzling facets of the *Zeitgeist* theory is just how to account for differential reaction to the same climate of opinion. The prescriptive approach may be helpful in this connection. Plato and Aristotle, Hobbes and Spinoza, Hume and Rousseau, each experienced the same *Zeitgeist* but also had idiosyncratic, nondominant prescriptive allegiances.

What I have said about prescriptions by no means exhausts this complexity. Prescriptive trends fall and rise again, combine, separate, and recombine, carry a broader or narrower scope of meaning, and enter into different alliances with other prescriptions, change from implicitness to explicitness and back again, and concern with different psychological content and its related theories. Beyond this, I hesitate to go, except to say I am confident there are probably other as yet unrecognized ramifications. Prescriptions endure while the psychological facts, theories, and areas which influenced their acceptance are ephemeral and ever changing.

If I have stressed the directing and guiding phase of the effect of prescriptions on a scientist's thinking, it is not because of blindness to the other side of the coin, the originality of the scientist. A scientist not only is guided by but also exploits both paradigms and prescriptions. He does so in terms of his originality, and other factors that make for individuality.

My enthusiasm for prescriptions may have left you wondering whether this is all that I can see in the history of psychology. Let me reassure you at this point. The usual contentual topics of psychology, most broadly summarized as sensation, learning, motivation, and personality and the hypotheses, laws, and theories to which their investigations give rise are still considered very much a part of its history. As differentiated from philosophically oriented contentual prescriptions, it is these and related contentual topics which show that a concern for psychology is the subject matter of historical investigation. These contentual topics are the vehicles with which all historians of psychology must work. Even here there is another point about prescriptions that I might mention. There seems to be some historical evidence of an affinity between certain prescriptions and certain contentual topics, e.g., dynamicism with motivation, developmentalism with child and comparative psychology, personalism, idiographicism, and irrationalism with personality, and empiricism with learning. Individual psychologists who have been strongly influenced by particular prescriptions are apt to reflect them in their work. Although the evidence has not yet been sought, it is quite plausible to believe that, reciprocally, choice of problem area may influence allegiance to certain prescriptions. In similar vein, I suspect that prescriptions tend to cluster in nonrandom fashion. Off hand, acceptance of supernaturalism seems to have an affinity for teleology, indeterminism, and qualtitativism; nomothesis with determinism; rationalism with deduction; empiricism with induction.

To return to extraprescriptive aspects of psychology, the methods of psychologist—observation and experiment—cannot be neglected in a historical account. Psychologists' use of these methods are an integral part of that history. However, certain prescriptions, particularly those identified earlier as methodological in nature, allow casting considerable historical material in the way that has been sketched.

Any adequate history of psychology must reconsider the personality characteristics of individual psychologists and the extrapsychological influences, such as social circumstance, which have been brought to bear upon each psychologist. Can one imagine that Hobbes' psychological views were independent of his detestation of organized religion, adoration of a strong central government, and fear of the consequence of political disorders?

I would like to summarize briefly some of the functions that I consider prescriptions to serve. They provide classification and summarization through a conceptual framework which can be applied historically. Prescriptions provide principles of systematization which are related to, and yet to some extent are independent of, the particular contentual or methodological problem of the individual psychologist. They are also mnemonic devices which make it possible to summarize and convey a maximum of meaning with a minimum of words. Going beyond anything even hinted at in the paper, prescriptive theory might also help to make history a tool for investigation of the psychology of discovery, and also serve as a framework for studies using content analysis applied to historical documents.

Prescriptions are characterized by an oppositional character manifested in dominance and counterdominance, an implicit as well as explicit nature, a philosophically based contentual character, a methodological character borrowed from the other sciences, a presence in other fields, an interlocking in schools of psychology with some salient and others nonsalient, a clash of prescriptions at the national level and a participation of prescriptions at the national level, and a participation of prescriptions in the *Zeitgeist*. Since psychology seems to lack a unifying paradigm, it would seem that as a science it functions at the level of guidance by prescriptions.

REFERENCES

Allport, G. W. The psychologist's frame of reference. *Psychological Bulletin*, 1940, 37, 1–28.

Allport, G. W. European and American theories of personality. In H. P. David & H. von Bracken (Eds.), *Perspectives in personality theory*. New York: Basic Books, 1957. Pp. 3–24.

Bruner, J. S., & Allport, G. W. Fifty years of change in American Psychology. *Psychological Bulletin*, 1940, 37, 757–776.

Brunswik, E. The conceptual framework of psychology. In O. Neurath et al. (Eds.), *International encyclopedia of unified science*. Chicago: University of Chicago Press, 1955. Pp. 655–760.

Brunswik, E. Historical and thematic relations of psychology to other sciences. *Scientific Monthly*, 1956, 83, 151–161.

Chaplin, J. P., & Krawiec, T. S. *Systems and theories of psychology*. New York: Holt, Rinehart & Winston, 1960.

Cousin, V. *Cours de l'histoire de la philosophie*. 2 vols. Paris: Pichon & Didier, 1829.

Jones, W. T. *The romantic syndrome: Toward a new method in cultural anthropology and history of ideas*. The Hague: Nijhoff, 1961.

Koch, S. (Ed.) *Psychology: A study of a science*. Study 1. *Conceptual and systematic*. New York: McGraw-Hill, 1959.

Kuhn, T. S. *The structure of scientific revolutions*. Chicago: University of Chicago Press, 1962.

Kuhn, T. S. The function of dogma in scientific research. In A. C. Crombie (Ed.), *Scientific change*. New York: Basic Books, 1963. Pp. 347–369.

Leibniz, G. W. *New essays concerning human understanding*.

(Trans. by A. G. Langley) La Salle, Ill.: Open Court, 1949.

Lewin, K. The conflict between Aristotelian and Galilean modes of thought in contemporary psychology. In, *A dynamic theory of personality.* New York: McGraw-Hill, 1935. Pp. 1–42.

Lovejoy, A. O. *The great chain of being.* Cambridge: Harvard University Press, 1936.

Marx, M. H., & Hillix, W. A. *Systems and theories in psychology.* New York: McGraw-Hill, 1963.

Miller, G. A. (Ed.) *Mathematics and psychology.* New York: Wiley, 1964.

Morell, J. D. *An historical and critical view of the speculative philosophy in Europe in the nineteenth century.* New York: Carter, 1862.

Murphy, G. *An historical introduction to modern psychology.* (3rd rev. ed.) New York: Harcourt Brace, 1932.

Murray, H. A. Historical trends in personality research. In H. P. David & J. C. Brengelmann (Eds.), *Perspective in personality research.* New York: Springer, 1961. Pp. 3–39.

Watson, R. I. The historical background for national trends in psychology: United States. *Journal of the History of the Behavioral Sciences,* 1965, 1, 130–138.

Whitehead, A. N. *Science and the modern world.* New York: Mentor, 1925.

Woodger, J. H. *Biological principles: A critical study.* New York: Harcourt, Brace, 1929.

A Chart to Compare the Psychological Theories Presented in This Book

	Locke	Descartes	Helmholtz	Fechner	Wundt	Ebbinghaus	Titchener	Darwin	Galton	James	Angell	Cattell	Binet	Thorndike
Conscious Unconscious Mentalism														
Contentual Objectivism Subjectivism														
Determinism Indeterminism														
Empiricism Rationalism														
Functionalism Structuralism														
Inductivism Deductivism														
Mechanism Vitalism														
Methodological Objectivism Subjectivism														
Molecularism Molarism														
Naturalism Supernaturalism														
Nomotheticism Idiographicism														
Purism Utilitarianism														
Quantitativism Qualitativism														
Rationalism Irrationalism														
Staticism Dynamicism														

	Pavalov	Watson	Skinner	Bandura	Wertheimer	Köhler	Freud	Adler	Jung	Neisser	Maslow
Conscious Unconscious Mentalism											
Contentual Objectivism Subjectivism											
Determinism Indeterminism											
Empiricism Rationalism											
Functionalism Structuralism											
Inductivism Deductivism											
Mechanism Vitalism											
Methodological Objectivism Subjectivism											
Molecularism Molarism											
Naturalism Supernaturalism											
Nomotheticism Idiographicism											
Purism Utilitarianism											
Quantitativism Qualitativism											
Rationalism Irrationalism											
Staticism Dynamicism											

C H A 2 P T E R

PHILOSOPHICAL INFLUENCES ON PSYCHOLOGY

RENE DESCARTES (1596–1650)

Rene Descartes, the son of a provincial councilor in Brittany and one of the leading mathematicians of France, was born in 1596.[1][2] In 1606, he entered a Jesuit school in Anjou where he stayed until 1614. In frail health, he convinced the school rector that he should be able to stay in bed until noon, a habit he maintained most of his life. This gave him time to reflect on his intellectual pursuits and may have influenced him to believe that through reason one could arrive at bedrock principles. The eminent philosopher, Bertrand Russell (1945), contends that Descartes may have done his best thinking in bed. In Anjou, Descartes was trained in the humanities and mathematics, and after leaving Anjou he received his bachelor's degree in law at the University of Poitiers in 1616.

The young Descartes joined a group of mercenaries in 1618 and went to Holland. This may seem an odd choice for a budding intellectual with a penchant to spend a good deal of the day in bed. Nevertheless, Descartes was a man of the world as evidenced by the facts that he was an excellent swordsman and a suc-

---

[1]Descartes' first intellectual *tour de force* was the development of analytical geometry, i.e., geometric properties expressed in algebraic terms.

[2]For biographical material concerning Descartes, see Gaukroger, S. (1995), Mahaffey (1880), and Russell (1945).

cessful gambler (his mathematical skills were of no small help) and that he fathered a child with his paramour.

In 1619, he had a series of dreams that pricked his intellectual conscience. In one "The Spirit of Truth" visited and rebuked him for his life of idleness. From this point on, Descartes devoted his life to the pursuit of truth that resulted in the production of several monumental works.

Descartes moved to Paris in 1623 but found city life too distracting and so returned to Holland, where he stayed from 1628 to 1649. To protect his solitude, he moved constantly, living in 24 houses in 13 towns in a little more than 20 years. It is in Holland during this period that he wrote most of his significant works, including *The Discourse on Method* (1637) and his final work, *The Passions of the Soul* (1649). It is in *The Discourse* where one can find Descartes' (1637) famous statement concerning the one ultimate truth upon which he felt all other truth could be built, "*. . . I think, therefore I am . . .*" (p. 101).[3] To arrive at this axiom, Descartes proceeded by doubting everything, including the existence of God, thus bringing him the displeasure of the church; the authorities even brought him before a court to answer to charges of atheism (Newman, 1956).

In line with Catholic doctrine, Descartes believed that the mind (soul) and body were of two essences: He believed the mind was immaterial and free, whereas the body was material and controlled by mechanical principles. Descartes, however, stated that the mind and body influenced each other by interacting through the pineal gland. In his (1649) *The Passions of the Soul*, Descartes describes how this interaction takes place and how the body can influence the function of the mind. Thus, he helped lay a substrate for the development of neuropsychology. It is from *The Passions* that one of the readings for this chapter is drawn.

Descartes' writings drew wide attention, including that of Queen Christina of Sweden, and in 1649 she summoned him to court to be her tutor. An eager but not an apt pupil, she insisted on having her lessons at 5:00 in the morning. Descartes succumbed, only four months after arriving, dying on February 11, 1650.

JOHN LOCKE (1632 – 1704)

John Locke, the son of a Puritan country lawyer, was born in Wrington, England, on August 29, 1632. At the age of 15, he entered the Westminster School next to the abbey of the same name; there, he was privy to the dramatic political events of the day. He, for example, may very likely have witnessed the execution of Charles I as a traitor. He lived during a time of significant political unrest, and this may have influenced his lifelong emphasis on and interest in the nature of government and the potency of the environment. In 1689, he published his *Two Treatises on*

---

[3]At this point, the influence of Descartes' geometric study is clear. Subsequent truths, corollaries, are derived from one ultimate truth, a postulate.

Government, in which he advocated human rights and a governmental structure based on checks and balances. This writing had an influence on the likes of Washington, Franklin, Hamilton, and Madison as they struggled to develop a new government.[4]

In 1652, he took a junior studentship at Christchurch at Oxford, receiving his B.A. in 1656 and his M.A. in 1658. Locke found the philosophy taught at Oxford dull, but the writing of Descartes intellectually stimulated him. It was not until 1689, when he was 56, that Locke published anything of note; he had been, however, mentally alive during this time, having been elected to the Royal Society of Oxford and having met some leading intellectuals of the day such as Isaac Newton and Robert Boyle.

After 1689, Locke's output was prolific, including the previously mentioned *Two Treatises on Government* (1689), *An Essay Concerning Human Understanding* (1690), *Some Thoughts Concerning Education* (1693), and the posthumously published *The Conduct of Human Understanding* (1706). Because of poor health, Locke moved to his country manor in Essex; however, the books and revisions published after his relocation suggest that he was intellectually busy. Locke died in 1704, leaving behind a legacy of ideas that would dramatically affect the development of psychology.

His (1690) text *Concerning Human Understanding* is considered his chief work, and it is here where he describes the mind as a blank slate, or to be more specific, as ". . . white Paper, void of all Characters . . ." (p. 89). The "paper," however, was written on by experience, and thus the mind was filled. Reacting against Descartes, Locke had taken a radically empirical stand. It is from *An Essay Concerning Human Understanding* that the second reading for this chapter is taken. In this selection, Locke sets forth several arguments against the existence of innate ideas. In his writing, Locke also explained that complex ideas consisted of the amalgamation of several simple ideas.[5]

Locke's ideas were to affect psychology as it emerged as a science in the late 19th and early 20th centuries. In the 1890s at Cornell, for example, Edward Bradford Titchener (Chapter 5), believing all conscious experience consisted of the combination of several elements, set about trying to develop something akin to a psychological table of periodic elements. Later, in the midteens, John Watson of Johns Hopkins University was to insist there was no such thing as instinct and given the right environment, he could make any child into anything (Watson, 1930).[6] Later, Skinner stated much the same thing in his 1948 novel *Walden Two* and his later book, *Beyond Freedom and Dignity.*[7]

---

[4]He was even influential in helping draft a constitution for the fledgling Carolina Colony (Watson, 1962).

[5]Here Locke displays the influence of noted physicist and chemist Robert Boyle.

[6]Watson (1930) is a second revision of some of his lecture notes from Johns Hopkins.

[7]Wolpe's (1973) description of the acquisition and elimination of phobias is in accord with that of Locke (1693).

REFERENCES

Descartes, R. (1931). Discourse on method. In E. S. Haldane & G. R. T. Ross (Trans.) *Philosophical works of Descartes* (Rev. ed.) (Vol. 1, pp. 79–30). New York: Dover. (Originally published in 1637).

Descartes, R. (1931). The passions of the soul. In E. S. Haldane & G. R. T. Ross (Trans.) *Philosophical works of Descartes* (Rev. ed.) (Vol. 1, pp. 329–427). New York: Dover. (Originally published in 1649).

Gaukroger, S. (1995). *Descartes: An intellectual biography.* Oxford: Clarendon.

Locke, J. (1960). *Two treatises on government.* Cambridge: Cambridge University Press. (Originally published in 1689).

Locke, J. (1964). *An essay concerning human understanding.* Cleveland: World. (Originally published in 1690).

Locke, J. (1912). Some thoughts concerning education. In J. W. Adamson (Ed.) *The educational writings of John Locke* (pp. 21–179). London: Longmans. (Originally published in 1693).

Locke, J. (1912). Of the conduct of human understanding. In J. W. Adamson (Ed.) *The educational writings of John Locke* (pp. 181–265). London: Longmans. (Originally published in 1706).

Mahaffey, J. P. (1880). *Descartes.* London: Blackwood.

Russell, B. (1945). *A history of Western philosophy.* New York: Simon & Schuster.

Skinner, B. F. (1948). *Walden Two.* New York: Macmillan.

Watson, J. B. (1930). *Behaviorism* (Rev. ed.). New York: Norton.

Watson, R. I. (1962). *The great psychologists.* Philadelphia: Lippincott.

Wolpe, J. (1973). *The practice of behavior therapy* (2nd ed.). Elmsford, NY: Pergamon.

The Passions of the Soul (1649)

Rene Descartes

ARTICLE VIII.

What Is the Principle of All These Functions?

But it is not usually known in what way these animal spirits and these nerves contribute to the movements and to the senses, nor what is the corporeal principle which causes them to act. That is why, although I have already made some mention of them in my other writings, I shall not here omit to say shortly that so long as we live there is a continual heat in our heart, which is a species of fire which the blood of the veins there maintains, and that this fire is the corporeal principle of all the movements of our members.

ARTICLE IX.

How the Movement of the Heart Is Carried on.

Its first effect is to dilate the blood with which the cavities of the heart are filled; that causes this blood, which requires a greater space for its occupation, to pass impetuously from the right cavity into the arterial vein, and from the left into the great artery; then when this dilation ceases, new blood immediately enters from the vena cava into the right cavity of the heart, and from the venous artery into the left; for there are little membranes at the entrances of these four vessels, disposed in such a manner that they do not allow the blood to enter the heart but by the two last, nor to issue from it but by the two others. The new blood which has entered into the heart is then immediately afterwards rarefied, in the same manner as that which preceded it; and it is just this which causes the pulse, or beating of the heart and arteries; so that this beating repeats itself as often as the new blood enters the heart. It is also just this which gives its motion to the blood, and causes it to flow ceaselessly and very quickly in all the arteries and veins, whereby it carries the heat which it acquires in the heart to every part of the body, and supplies them with nourishment.

ARTICLE X.

How the Animal Spirits are Produced in the Brain.

But what is here most worthy of remark is that all the most animated and subtle portions of the blood which the heat has rarefied in the heart, enter ceaselessly in large quantities into the cavities of the brain. And the reason which causes them to go there rather than elsewhere, is that all the blood which issues from the heart by the great artery takes its course in a straight line towards that place, and not being able to enter it in its entirety, because there are only very narrow passages there, those of its parts which are the most agitated and the most subtle alone pass through, while the rest spreads abroad in all the other portions of the body. But these very subtle parts of the blood form the animal spirits; and for this end they have no need to experience any other change in the brain, unless it be that they are separated from the other less subtle portions of the blood; for what I here name spirits are nothing but material bodies and their one peculiarity is that they are bodies of extreme minuteness and that they move very quickly like the particles of the flame which issues from a torch. Thus it is that they never remain at rest in any spot, and just as some of them enter into the cavities of the brain, others issue forth by the pores which are in its substance, which pores conduct them into the nerves, and from there into the muscles, by means of which they move the body in all the different ways in which it can be moved.

ARTICLE XI.

How the Movements of the Muscles Take Place.

For the sole cause of all the movements of the members is that certain muscles contract, and that those opposite to them elongate, as has already been said; and the sole cause of one muscle contracting rather than that set against it, is that there comes from the brain some additional amount of animal spirits, however little it may be, to it rather than to the other. Not that the spirits which proceed immediately from the brain suffice in themselves to move the muscles, but they determine the other spirits which are already in these two muscles, all to issue very quickly from the one of them and to pass into the other. By this means that from which they issue becomes longer and more flaccid, and that into which they enter, being rapidly distended by them, contracts, and pulls the member to which it is attached. This is easy to understand provided that we know that there are but very few animal spirits which continually proceed from the brain to each muscle, but that there are always a quantity of others enclosed in the same muscle, which move there very quickly, sometimes by only turning about in the place where they are,—that is, when they do not find any passage open from which to issue forth from it—and sometimes by flowing into the opposite muscle; and inasmuch as there are little openings in each of these muscles by which the spirits can flow from one to the other, and which are so arranged that when the spirits that come from the brain to one of them have ever so little more strength than those that proceed to the other, they open all the entrances by which the spirits of the other muscle can pass into this one, and at the same time close all those by which the spirits of this last can pass into the other. By this means all the spirits formerly contained in these two muscles very quickly collect in one of them and then distend and shorten it, while the other becomes elongated and flaccid.

ARTICLE XVI.

How All the Members May be Moved By the Objects of the Senses and By the Animal Spirits Without the Aid of the Soul.

We must finally remark that the machine of our body is so formed that all the changes undergone by the movement of the spirits may cause them to open certain pores in the brain more than others, and reciprocally that when some one of the pores is opened more or less than usual (to however small a degree it may be) by the action of the nerves which are employed by the senses, that changes something in the movement of the spirits and causes them to be conducted into the muscles which serve to move the body in the way in which it is usually moved when such an action takes place. In this way all the movements which we make without our will contributing thereto (as frequently happens when we breathe, walk, eat, and in fact perform all those actions which are common to us and to the brutes), only depend on the conformation of our members, and on the course which the spirits, excited by the heat of the heart, follow naturally in the brain, nerves, and muscles, just as the movements of a watch are produced simply by the strength of the springs and the form of the wheels.

ARTICLE XVII.

What the Functions of the Soul Are.

After having thus considered all the functions which pertain to the body alone, it is easy to recognise that there is nothing in us which we ought to attribute to our soul excepting our thoughts, which are mainly of two sorts, the one being the actions of the soul, and the other its passions. Those which I call its actions are all our desires, because we find by experience that they proceed directly from our soul, and appear to depend on it alone: while, on the other hand, we may usually term one's passions all those kinds of perception or forms of knowledge which are found in us, because it is often not our soul which makes them what they are, and because it always receives them from the things which are represented by them.

ARTICLE XXX.

That the Soul Is United To all the Portions of the Body Conjointly.

But in order to understand all these things more perfectly, we must know that the soul is really joined to the whole body, and that we cannot, properly speaking, say that it exists in any one of its parts to the exclusion of the others, because it is one and in some manner indivisible, owing to the disposition of its organs, which are so related to one another that when any one of them is removed, that renders the whole body defective; and because it is of a nature which has no relation to extension, nor dimensions, nor other properties of the matter of which the body is composed, but only to the whole conglomerate of its organs, as appears from the fact that we could not in any way conceive of the half or the third of a soul, nor of the space it occupies, and because it does not become smaller owing to the cutting off of some portion of the body, but separates itself from it entirely when the union of its assembled organs is dissolved.

ARTICLE XXXI.

That There is a Small Gland in the Brain in Which the Soul Exercises its Functions More Particularly Than in the Other Parts.

It is likewise necessary to know that although the soul is joined to the whole body, there is yet in that a certain part in which it exercises its functions more particularly than in all the others; and it is usually believed that this part is the brain, or possibly the heart: the brain, because it is with it that the organs of sense are connected, and the heart because it is apparently in it that we experience the passions. But, in examining the matter with care, it seems as though I had clearly ascertained that the part of the body in which the soul exercises its functions immediately is in nowise the heart, nor the whole of the brain, but merely the most inward of all its parts, to wit, a certain very small gland which is situated in the middle of its substance and so suspended above the duct whereby the animal spirits in its anterior cavities have communication with those in the posterior, that the slightest movements which take place in it may alter very greatly the course of these spirits; and reciprocally that the smallest changes which occur in the course of the spirits may do much to change the movements of this gland.

ARTICLE XXXII.

How We Know That This Gland Is the Main Seat of the Soul.

The reason which persuades me that the soul cannot have any other seat in all the body than this gland wherein to exercise its functions immediately, is that I reflect that the other parts of our brain are all of them double, just as we have two eyes, two hands, two ears, and finally all the organs of our outside senses are double; and inasmuch as we have but one solitary and simple thought of one particular thing at one and the same moment, it must necessarily be the case that there must somewhere be a place where the two images which come to us by the two eyes, where the two other impressions which proceed from a single object by means of the double organs of the other senses, can unite before arriving at the soul, in order that they may not represent to it two objects instead of one. And it is easy to apprehend how these images or other impressions might unite in this gland by the intermission of the spirits which fill the cavities of the brain: but there is no other place in the body where they can be thus united unless they are so in this gland.

ARTICLE XXXIII.

That the Seat of the Passions Is Not in the Heart.

As to the opinion of those who think that the soul receives its passions in the heart, it is not of much consideration, for it is only founded on the fact that the passions cause us to feel some change taking place there; and it is easy to see that this change is not felt in the heart excepting through the medium of a small nerve which descends from the brain towards it, just as pain is felt as in the foot by means of the nerves of the foot, and the stars are perceived as in the heavens by means of their light and of the optic nerves; so that it is not more necessary that our soul should exercise its functions immediately in the heart, in order to feel its passions there, than it is necessary for the soul to be in the heavens in order to see the stars there.

ARTICLE XXXIV.

How the Soul and the Body Act on One Another.

Let us then conceive here that the soul has its principal seat in the little gland which exists in the middle of the brain, from whence it radiates forth through all the remainder of the body by means of the animal spirits, nerves, and even the blood, which, participating in the impressions of the spirits, can carry them by the arteries into all the members. And recollecting what has been said above about the machine of our body, i.e. that the little filaments of our nerves are so distributed in all its parts, that on the occasion of the diverse movements which are there excited by sensible objects, they open in diverse ways the pores of the brain, which causes the animal spirits contained in these cavities to enter in diverse ways into the muscles, by which means they can move the members in all the different ways in which they are capable of being moved; and also that all the other causes which are capable of moving the spirits in diverse ways suffice to conduct them in diverse muscles; let us here add that the small gland which is the main seat of the soul is so suspended between the cavities which contain the spirits that it can be moved by them in as many different ways as there are sensible diversities in the object, but that it may also be moved in diverse ways by the soul, whose nature is such that it receives in itself as many diverse impressions, that is to say, that it possesses as many diverse perceptions as there are diverse movements in this gland. Reciprocally, likewise, the machine of the body is so formed that from the simple fact that this gland is diversely moved by the soul, or by such other causes, whatever it is, it thrusts the spirits which surround it towards the pores of the brain, which conduct them by the nerves into the muscles, by which means it causes them to move the limbs.

ARTICLE XL.

The Principal Effect of the Passions.

For it is requisite to notice that the principal effect of all the passions in men is that they incite and dispose their soul to desire those things for which they prepare their body, so that the feeling of fear incites it to desire to fly, that of courage to desire to fight, and so on.

ARTICLE XLI.

The Power of the Soul in Regard To the Body.

But the will is so free in its nature, that it can never be constrained; and of the two sorts of thoughts which I have distinguished in the soul (of which the first are its actions, i.e. its desires, the others its passions, taking this word in its most general significance, which comprises all kinds of perceptions), the former are absolutely in its power, and can only be indirectly changed by the body, while on the other hand the latter depend absolutely on the actions which govern and direct them, and they can only indirectly be altered by the soul, excepting when it is itself their cause. And the whole action of the soul consists in this, that solely because it desires something, it causes the little gland to which it is closely united to move in the way requisite to produce the effect which relates to this desire.

ARTICLE XLII.

How We Find in the Memory the Things Which We Desire To Remember.

Thus when the soul desires to recollect something, this desire causes the gland, by inclining successively to different sides, to thrust the spirits towards different parts of the brain until they come across that part where the traces left there by the object which we wish to recollect are found; for these traces are none other than the fact that the pores of the brain, by which the spirits have formerly followed their course because of the presence of this object, have by that means acquired a greater facility than the others in being once more opened by the animal spirits which come towards them in the same way. Thus these spirits in coming in contact with these pores, enter into them more easily than into the others, by which means they excite a special movement in the gland which represents the same object to the soul, and causes it to know that it is this which it desired to remember.

ARTICLE XLIII.

How the Soul Can Imagine, Be Attentive, and Move the Body.

Thus when we desire to imagine something we have never seen, this desire has the power of causing the gland to move in the manner requisite to drive the spirits towards the pores of the brain by the opening of which pores this particular thing may be represented; thus when we wish to apply our attention for some time to the consideration of one particular object, this desire holds the gland for the time being inclined to the same side. Thus, finally, when we desire to walk or to move our body in some special way, this desire causes the gland to thrust the spirits towards the muscles which serve to bring about this result.

An Essay Concerning Human Understanding (1690)

John Locke

BOOK ONE
OF INNATE NOTIONS

Chapter I
Introduction

I. *An Inquiry into the Understanding pleasant and useful.*   Since it is the *understanding* that sets man above the rest of sensible beings, and gives him all the advantage and dominion which he has over them, it is certainly a subject, even for its nobleness, worth our labour to inquire into. The understanding, like the eye, whilst it makes us see and perceive all other things, takes no notice of itself; and it requires art and pains to set it at a distance and make it its own object. But whatever be the difficulties that lie in the way of this inquiry, whatever it be that keeps us so much in the dark to ourselves, sure I am that all the light we can let in upon our own minds, all the acquaintance we can make with our own understandings, will not only be very pleasant, but bring us great advantage, in directing our thoughts in the search of other things.

2. *Design.*   This, therefore, being my *purpose*—to inquire into the original, certainty, and extent of *human knowledge,* together with the grounds and degrees of *belief, opinion,* and *assent*—I shall not at present meddle with the physical consideration of the mind; or trouble myself to examine wherein its essence consists; or by what motions of our spirits or alterations of our bodies we come to have any *sensation* by our organs, or any *ideas* in our understandings; and whether those ideas do in their formation, any or all of them, depend on matter or no. These are speculations which, however curious and entertaining, I shall decline, as lying out of my way in the design I am now upon. It shall suffice to my present purpose to consider the discerning faculties of a man, as they are employed about the objects which they have to do with. And I shall imagine I have not wholly misemployed myself in the thoughts I shall have on this occasion, if, in this historical, plain method, I can give any account of the ways whereby our understandings come to attain those notions of things we have, and can set down any measures of the certainty of our knowledge, or the grounds of those persuasions which are to be found amongst men, so various, different, and wholly contradictory; and yet asserted somewhere or other with such assurance and confidence that he that shall take a view of the opinions of mankind, observe their opposition, and at the same time con-

sider the fondness and devotion wherewith they are embraced, the resolution and eagerness wherewith they are maintained, may perhaps have reason to suspect that either there is no such thing as truth at all, or that mankind hath no sufficient means to attain a certain knowledge of it.

3. *Method.*   It is therefore worth while to search out the *bounds* between opinion and knowledge, and examine by what measures, in things whereof we have no certain knowledge, we ought to regulate our assent and moderate our persuasions. In order whereunto I shall pursue this following method:—

First, I shall inquire into the *original* of those *ideas,* notions, or whatever else you please to call them, which a man observes, and is conscious to himself he has in his mind; and the ways whereby the understanding comes to be furnished with them.

Secondly, I shall endeavour to show what *knowledge* the understanding hath by those *ideas;* and the certainty, evidence, and extent of it.

Thirdly, I shall make some inquiry into the nature and grounds of *faith* or *opinion:* whereby I mean that assent which we give to any proposition as true, of whose truth yet we have no certain knowledge. And here we shall have occasion to examine the reasons and degrees of *assent.*

4. *Useful to know the Extent of our Comprehension.*   If by this inquiry into the nature of the understanding, I can discover the powers thereof, how far they reach, to what things they are in any degree proportionate, and where they fail us, I suppose it may be of use to prevail with the busy mind of man to be more cautious in meddling with things exceeding its comprehension; to stop when it is at the utmost extent of its tether; and to sit down in a quiet ignorance of those things which, upon examination, are found to be beyond the reach of our capacities. We should not then perhaps be so forward, out of an affectation of an universal knowledge, to raise questions, and perplex ourselves and others with disputes about things to which our understandings are not suited, and of which we cannot frame in our minds any clear or distinct perceptions, or whereof (as it has perhaps too often happened) we have not any notions at all. If we can find out how far the understanding can extend its view, how far it has faculties to attain certainty, and in what cases it can only judge and guess, we may learn to content ourselves with what is attainable by us in this state.

6. *Knowledge of our Capacity a Cure of Scepticism and Idleness.*   When we know our own strength, we shall the better know what to undertake with hopes of success; and when we have well surveyed the *powers* of our own minds, and made some estimate what we may expect from them, we shall not be inclined either to sit still, and not set our thoughts on work at all, in despair of knowing anything, nor, on the other side, question everything, and disclaim all knowledge, because some things are not to be understood. It is of great use to the sailor to know the length of his line, though he cannot with it fathom all the depths of the ocean. It is well he knows that it is long enough to reach the bottom at such places as are necessary to direct his voyage, and caution him against running upon shoals that may ruin him. Our business here is not to know all things, but those which concern our conduct. If we can find out those measures, whereby a rational creature,

put in that state which man is in this world, may and ought to govern his opinions, and actions depending thereon, we need not to be troubled that some other things escape our knowledge.

E.C.H.U.   C

Chapter II
No Innate Principles in the Mind

1. *The way shown how we come by any Knowledge, sufficient to prove it not innate.*   It is an established opinion amongst some men that there are in the understanding certain *innate principles,* some primary notions, κοιναι εννοιαι, characters, as it were stamped upon the mind of man, which the soul receives in its very first being, and brings into the world with it. It would be sufficient to convince unprejudiced readers of the falseness of this supposition, if I should only show (as I hope I shall in the following parts of this Discourse) how men, barely by the use of their natural faculties, may attain to all the knowledge they have, without the help of any innate impressions, and may arrive at certainty, without any such original notions or principles.

2. *General Assent the great Argument.*   There is nothing more commonly taken for granted than that there are certain *principles,* both *speculative* and *practical* (for they speak of both), universally agreed upon by all mankind: which therefore, they argue, must needs be constant impressions which the souls of men receive in their first beings, and which they bring into the world with them, as necessarily and really as they do any of their inherent faculties.

3. *Universal Consent proves nothing innate.*   This argument, drawn from universal consent, has this misfortune in it, that, if it were true in matter of fact that there were certain truths wherein all mankind agreed, it would not prove them innate, if there can be any other way shown how men may come to that universal agreement in the things they do consent in, which I presume may be done.

4. *"What is, is,"* and *"It is impossible for the same Thing to be and not to be" not universally assented to.*   But, which is worse, this argument of universal consent, which is made use of to prove innate principles, seems to me a demonstration that there are none such, because there are none to which all mankind give an universal assent. I shall begin with the speculative, and instance in those magnified principles of demonstration, "Whatsoever is, is," and "It is impossible for the same thing to be and not to be," which, of all others, I think have the most allowed title to innate. These have so settled a reputation of maxims universally received that it will no doubt be thought strange if anyone should seem to question it. But yet I take liberty to say that these propositions are so far from having an universal assent, that there are a great part of mankind to whom they are not so much as known.

5. *Not on the Mind naturally imprinted, because not known to Children, Idiots, & c.*   For, first, it is evident, that all children and idiots have not the least apprehension or thought of them. And the want of that is enough to destroy that

universal assent which must needs be the necessary concomitant of all innate truths; it seeming to me near a contradiction to say, that there are truths imprinted on the soul, which it perceives or understands not: imprinting, if it signify anything, being nothing else but the making certain truths to be perceived. For to imprint anything on the mind without the mind's perceiving it seems to me hardly intelligible. If therefore children and idiots have souls, have minds, with those impressions upon them, they must unavoidably perceive them, and necessarily know and assent to these truths; which since they do not, it is evident that there are no such impressions. For if they are not notions naturally imprinted, how can they be innate? And if they are notions imprinted, how can they be unknown? To say a notion is imprinted on the mind, and yet at the same time to say that the mind is ignorant of it and never yet took notice of it, is to make this impression nothing. No proposition can be said to be in the mind which it never yet knew, which it was never yet conscious of. For if any one may, then, by the same reason, all propositions that are true, and the mind is capable ever of assenting to, may be said to be in the mind, and to be imprinted; since, if any one can be said to be in the mind, which it never yet knew, it must be only because it is capable of knowing it; and so the mind is of all truths it ever shall know. Nay, thus truths may be imprinted on the mind which it never did, nor ever shall know; for a man may live long, and die at last in ignorance of many truths which his mind was capable of knowing, and that with certainty. So that if the capacity of knowing be the natural impression contended for, all the truths a man ever comes to know will, by this account, be every one of them innate; and this great point will amount to no more, but only to a very improper way of speaking; which, whilst it pretends to assert the contrary, says nothing different from those who deny innate principles. For nobody, I think, ever denied that the mind was capable of knowing several truths. The capacity, they say, is innate, the knowledge acquired. But then to what end such contest for certain innate maxims? If truths can be imprinted on the understanding without being perceived, I can see no difference there can be between any truths the mind is capable of knowing in respect of their original: they must all be innate or all adventitious; in vain shall a man go about to distinguish them.

6. *That men know them when they come to the Use of Reason answered.*   To avoid this, it is usually answered that all men know and assent to them, *when they come to the use of reason;* and this is enough to prove them innate.

7. This answer must signify one of these two things: either that as soon as men come to the use of reason these supposed native inscriptions come to be known and observed by them; or else, that the use and exercise of men's reasons assists them in the discovery of these principles, and certainly makes them known to them.

8. *If Reason discovered them, that would not prove them innate.*   If they mean that by the use of reason men may discover these principles, and that this is sufficient to prove them innate, their way of arguing will stand thus, viz. that whatever truths reason can certainly discover to us, and make us firmly assent to, those are all naturally imprinted on the mind; since that universal assent, which is made the mark of them, amounts to no more but this,—that by the use of reason we are capable to come to a certain knowledge of and assent to them; and, by this means, there will be no difference between the maxims of the mathematicians and theo-

rems they deduce from them: all must be equally allowed innate, they being all discoveries made by the use of reason, and truths that a rational creature may certainly come to know, if he apply his thoughts rightly that way.

9. *It is false that Reason discovers them.* But how can these men think the use of reason necessary to discover principles that are supposed innate, when reason (if we may believe them) is nothing else but the faculty of deducing unknown truths from principles or propositions that are already known? That certainly can never be thought innate which we have need of reason to discover, unless, as I have said, we will have all the certain truths that reason ever teaches us to be innate. We may as well think the use of reason necessary to make our eyes discover visible objects, as that there should be need of reason, or the exercise thereof, to make the understanding see what is originally engraven in it, and cannot be in the understanding before it be perceived by it. So that to make reason discover those truths thus imprinted, is to say that the use of reason discovers to a man what he knew before; and if men have those innate impressed truths originally, and before the use of reason, and yet are always ignorant of them till they come to the use of reason, it is in effect to say, that men know and know them not at the same time.

10. It will here perhaps be said that mathematical demonstrations, and other truths that are not innate, are not assented to as soon as proposed, wherein they are distinguished from these maxims and other innate truths. I shall have occasion to speak of assent upon the first proposing more particularly by and by.[1] I shall here only, and that very readily, allow that these maxims and mathematical demonstrations are in this different: that the one has need of reason, using of proofs, to make them out and to gain our assent; but the other, as soon as understood, are, without any the least reasoning, embraced and assented to.

11. Those who will take the pains to reflect with a little attention on the operations of the understanding will find that this ready assent of the mind to some truths depends not either on native inscription or the use of reason, but on a faculty of the mind quite distinct from both of them, as we shall see hereafter.[2] Reason, therefore, having nothing to do in procuring our assent to these maxims, if by saying that "men know and assent to them, when they come to the use of reason" be meant that the use of reason assists us in the knowledge of these maxims, it is utterly false; and, were it true, would prove them not to be innate.

12. *The coming to the Use of Reason not the time we come to know these Maxims.* If by knowing and assenting to them "when we come to the use of reason" be meant that this is the time when they come to be taken notice of by the mind; and that, as soon as children come to the use of reason, they come also to know and assent to these maxims; this also is false and frivolous. First, it is false, because it is evident these maxims are not in the mind so early as the use of reason; and therefore the coming to the use of reason is falsely assigned as the time of their discovery. How many instances of the use of reason may we observe in children, a long time before they have any knowledge of this maxim, "That it is

---

[1] §§ 17–21.

[2] IV ii l; vii 19; xvii 14.

impossible for the same thing to be and not to be"? And a great part of illiterate people and savages pass many years, even of their rational age, without ever thinking on this and the like general propositions. I grant, men come not to the knowledge of these general and more abstract truths, which are thought innate, till they come to the use of reason; and I add, nor then neither. Which is so, because, till after they come to the use of reason, those general abstract ideas are not framed in the mind, about which those general maxims are, which are mistaken for innate principles, but are indeed discoveries made and verities introduced and brought into the mind by the same way, and discovered by the same steps, as several other propositions, which nobody was ever so extravagant as to suppose innate.

14. *If coming to the Use of Reason were the time of their discovery, it would not prove them innate.*   But, secondly, were it true that the precise time of their being known and assented to were when men come to the use of reason, neither would that prove them innate. This way of arguing is so frivolous as the supposition of itself is false. For, by what kind of logic will it appear that any notion is originally by nature imprinted in the mind in its first constitution, because it comes first to be observed and assented to when a faculty of the mind, which has quite a distinct province, begins to exert itself?

15. *The Steps by which the Mind attains several Truths.*   The senses at first let in *particular* ideas, and furnish the yet empty cabinet, and, the mind by degrees growing familiar with some of them, they are lodged in the memory, and names got to them. Afterwards, the mind proceeding further abstracts them, and by degrees learns the use of general names. In this manner the mind comes to be furnished with ideas and language, the materials about which to exercise its discursive faculty. And the use of reason becomes daily more visible, as these materials that give it employment increase. But, though the having of general ideas and the use of general words and reason usually grow together, yet I see not how this any way proves them innate. The knowledge of some truths, I confess, is very early in the mind; but in a way that shows them not to be innate. For, if we will observe, we shall find it still to be about ideas, not innate, but acquired; it being about those first which are imprinted by external things, with which infants have earliest to do, which make the most frequent impressions on their senses. In ideas thus got the mind discovers that some agree and others differ, probably as soon as it has any use of memory, as soon as it is able to retain and receive distinct ideas. But whether it be then or no, this is certain, it does so long before it has the use of words, or comes to that which we commonly call "the use of reason". For a child knows as certainly before it can speak the difference between the ideas of sweet and bitter (i.e. that sweet is not bitter), as it knows afterwards (when it comes to speak) that wormwood and sugarplums are not the same thing.

16. A child knows not that three and four are equal to seven, till he comes to be able to count to seven, and has got the name and idea of equality; and then, upon explaining those words, he presently assents to, or rather perceives the truth of, that proposition. But neither does he then readily assent because it is an innate truth, nor was his assent wanting till then because he wanted the use of reason; but the truth of it appears to him as soon as he has settled in his mind the clear and distinct ideas that these names stand for. And then he knows the truth of that propo-

sition upon the same grounds and by the same means, that he knew before that a rod and cherry are not the same thing; and upon the same grounds also that he may come to know afterwards "That it is impossible for the same thing to be and not to be". So that the later it is before anyone comes to have those general ideas about which those maxims are, or to know the signification of those general terms that stand for them, or to put together in his mind the ideas they stand for, the later also will it be before he comes to assent to those maxims;—whose terms, with the ideas they stand for, being no more innate than those of a cat or a weasel, he must stay till time and observation have acquainted him with them; and then he will be in a capacity to know the truth of these maxims, upon the first occasion that shall make him put together those ideas in his mind, and observe whether they agree or disagree, according as is expressed in those propositions.

17. *Assenting as soon as proposed and understood, proves them not innate.* This evasion therefore of general assent when men come to the use of reason, failing as it does, and leaving no difference between those supposed innate and other truths that are afterwards acquired and learnt, men have endeavoured to secure an universal assent to those they call maxims, by saying they are generally assented to as soon as proposed, and the terms they are proposed in understood; seeing all men, even children, as soon as they hear and understand the terms, assent to these propositions, they think it is sufficient to prove them innate.

18. *If such an Assent be a mark of innate, then "that One and Two are equal to three, that Sweetness is not Bitterness" and a thousand the like, must be innate.* In answer to this I demand whether ready assent given to a proposition, upon first hearing and understanding the terms, be a certain mark of an innate principle? If it be not, such a general assent is in vain urged as a proof of them; if it be said that it is a mark of innate, they must then allow all such propositions to be innate which are generally assented to as soon as heard, whereby they will find themselves plentifully stored with innate principles. For upon the same ground, viz. of assent at first hearing and understanding the terms, that men would have those maxims pass for innate, they must also admit several propositions about numbers to be innate. Even natural philosophy, and all the other sciences, afford propositions which are sure to meet with assent as soon as they are understood. That "two bodies cannot be in the same place" is a truth that nobody any more sticks at than at this maxim, that "it is impossible for the same thing to be and not to be," that "white is not black," that "a square is not a circle," that "yellowness is not sweetness". But, since no proposition can be innate unless the *ideas* about which it is be innate, this will be to suppose all our ideas of colours, sounds, tastes, figure, &c., innate, than which there cannot be anything more opposite to reason and experience. Universal and ready assent upon hearing and understanding the terms is, I grant, a mark of self-evidence; but self-evidence, depending not on innate impressions but on something else, belongs to several propositions which nobody was yet so extravagant as to pretend to be innate.

19. *Such less general Propositions known before these universal Maxims.* Nor let it be said that those more particular self-evident propositions, which are assented to at first hearing, as that "one and two are equal to three," that "green is not red," &c., are received as the consequences of those more universal propositions

which are looked on as innate principles, since anyone, who will but take the pains to observe what passes in the understanding, will certainly find that these, and the like less general propositions, are certainly known and firmly assented to by those who are utterly ignorant of those more general maxims; and so, being earlier in the mind than those (as they are called) first principles, cannot owe to them the assent wherewith they are received at first hearing.

21. *These Maxims not being known sometimes till proposed, proves them not innate.* Men grow first acquainted with many of these self-evident truths upon their being proposed; but it is clear that whosoever does so finds in himself that he then begins to know a proposition, which he knew not before, and which from thenceforth he never questions, not because it was innate, but because the consideration of the nature of the things contained in those words would not suffer him to think otherwise, how, or whensoever he is brought to reflect on them.

22. *Implicitly known before proposing, signifies that the Mind is capable of understanding them, or else signifies nothing.* If it be said the understanding hath an *implicit* knowledge of these principles, but not an *explicit,* before this first hearing (as they must who will say that they are in the understanding before they are known), it will be hard to conceive what is meant by a principle imprinted on the understanding implicitly, unless it be this,—that the mind is capable of understanding and assenting firmly to such propositions. And thus all mathematical demonstrations, as well as first principles, must be received as native impressions on the mind.

23. *The Argument of assenting on first hearing, is upon a false supposition of no precedent teaching.* There is, I fear, this further weakness in the foregoing argument, that men are supposed not to be taught nor to learn anything *de novo,* when, in truth, they are taught, and do learn something they were ignorant of before. For, first, it is evident that they have learned the terms, and their signification, neither of which was born with them. But this is not all the acquired knowledge in the case: the ideas themselves, about which the proposition is, are not born with them, no more than their names, but got afterwards. For, though a child quickly assent to this proposition, "that an apple is not fire," when by familiar acquaintance he has got the ideas of those two different things distinctly imprinted on his mind, and has learnt that the names 'apple' and 'fire' stand for them, yet it will be some years after, perhaps, before the same child will assent to this proposition, "that it is impossible for the same thing to be and not to be"; because that, though perhaps the words are as easy to be learnt, yet the signification of them being more large, comprehensive, and abstract than of the names annexed to those sensible things the child hath to do with, it is longer before he learns their precise meaning, and it requires more time plainly to form in his mind those general ideas they stand for.

25. *These Maxims not the first known.* But that I may not be accused to argue from the thoughts of infants, which are unknown to us, and to conclude from what passes in their understandings before they express it, I say next that these two general propositions are not the truths that first possess the minds of children, nor are antecedent to all acquired and adventitious notions; which, if they were innate, they must needs be. Whether we can determine it or no, it matters not, there is cer-

tainly a time when children begin to think, and their words and actions do assure us that they do so. When therefore they are capable of thought, of knowledge, of assent, can it rationally be supposed they can be ignorant of those notions that nature has imprinted, were there any such? The child certainly knows that the nurse that feeds it is neither the cat it plays with, nor the blackamoor it is afraid of, that the wormseed or mustard it refuses is not the apple or sugar it cries for; this it is certainly and undoubtedly assured of; but will anyone say, it is by virtue of this principle, "That it is impossible for the same thing to be and not to be," that it so firmly assents to these and other parts of its knowledge?

26. *And so not innate.*   Though therefore there be several general propositions that meet with constant and ready assent, as soon as proposed to men grown up, who have attained the use of more general and abstract ideas, and names standing for them, yet, they not being to be found in those of tender years, who nevertheless know other things, they cannot pretend to universal assent of intelligent persons, and so by no means can be supposed innate; it being impossible that any truth which is innate (if there were any such) should be unknown, at least to anyone who knows anything else. Since, if they are innate truths, they must be innate thoughts, there being nothing a truth in the mind that it has never thought on. Whereby it is evident, if there be any innate truths, they must necessarily be the first of any thought on, the first that appear there.

27. *Not innate, because they appear least, where what is innate shows itself clearest.*   There is this further argument in it against their being innate: that these characters, if they were native and original impressions, should appear fairest and clearest in those persons in whom yet we find no footsteps of them; and it is, in my opinion, a strong presumption that they are not innate, since they are least known to those in whom, if they were innate, they must needs exert themselves with most force and vigour. For children, idiots, savages, and illiterate people, being of all others the least corrupted by custom, or borrowed opinions; learning and education having not cast their native thoughts into new moulds, nor by superinducing foreign and studied doctrines, confounded those fair characters nature had written there; one might reasonably imagine that in *their* minds these innate notions should lie open fairly to everyone's view, as it is certain the thoughts of children do. But he that from a child untaught, or a wild inhabitant of the woods, will expect these abstract maxims and reputed principles of science, will, I fear, find himself mistaken. Such kind of general propositions are seldom mentioned in the huts of Indians; much less are they to be found in the thoughts of children, or any impressions of them on the minds of naturals. They are the language and business of the schools and academies of learned nations, accustomed to that sort of conversation or learning, where disputes are frequent; these maxims being suited to artificial argumentation and useful for conviction, but not much conducing to the discovery of truth or advancement of knowledge. But of their small use for the improvement of knowledge I shall have occasion to speak more at large, IV vii.

CHAPTER 3

PHYSIOLOGICAL INFLUENCES ON PSYCHOLOGY

HERMANN HELMHOLTZ (1821–1894)

Hermann Ludwig Helmholtz was born in the German town of Potsdam on August 31, 1821. He has been described as one of the greatest physiologists of the 19th century.[1] He was the son of an intellectual school teacher whose own drive influenced his son. Both father and son were influenced by the works of the German philosopher Immanuel Kant. Physics became a passion very early in Helmholtz's life, and he reportedly experimented with optics, chemistry, and other scientific endeavors when he should have been doing other work. Nonetheless, he graduated early from his gymnasium (the European equivalent of an advanced high school or junior college for seniors and academically able students). Pure science was, however, a costly pursuit during this historical period, and Helmholtz chose to pursue a more practical educational future. He entered the military medical school and immersed himself in the discipline afforded by the Prussian government. While dedicated to this strenuous program, he also found time for music and other social pursuits, indications of his intellectual brilliance. He also had an opportunity to study at Müller's institute of physiology. After graduation, he served his mandatory years as an army surgeon in the Prussian military. In 1849, right after he left the military, he was appointed a professor of physiology at the University of Königsberg.

---

[1]See Boring (1950), Fancher (1979), and Koenigsberger (1965) for more complete bibliographic material.

This appointment brought several changes to his life. He was able to marry his fiancée of several years and to pursue more scientific pursuits. He had already published several works, some at his own expense. Indeed, it was one of these papers that had influenced his obtaining the university position. He is credited with developing the opthalmosope during his first year as a professor. His time at Königsberg was rich and varied, and he made contributions to physics, chemistry, physiology, and mathematics. Here Helmholtz researched and published the article on the measurement of the speed of transmission of impulses along the nerve fiber included in your reading for this section (Helmholtz, 1850). Here, too, as well as at the Universities of Bonn and Heidelberg, he carried out experiments in vision and hearing. A theory of color vision had been developed earlier; and Helmholtz incorporated parts into his own work while giving credit to its originator, the English scientist Thomas Young (1773–1829). This theory, the Young–Helmholtz theory, is also presented in part as a selected reading for this section (Helmholtz, 1896). It is a theory still in use at the end of the 20th century!

Helmholtz finally realized his life's ambition and was appointed professor of physics at the University of Berlin in 1871. In 1882, the German emperor granted him the status of a noble and he became *von Helmholtz*. About this time, the government established an entire lab for his use. Although Helmholtz denied being a psychologist and spent his entire life identifying himself as practitioner of physics and physiology, his influence on the field and on many of the important figures who were junior to him can be felt in this text and beyond.

GUSTAV THEODOR FECHNER (1801–1887)

Gustav Fechner was born in 1801 in a small village in southeastern Germany. Fechner's father was the village minister, as had been his father before him. Fechner's father passed away when the boy was 5 years old and the young Gustav went, with his mother and brother, to live with an uncle who was yet another minister. Despite his heritage, Fechner considered himself an atheist for much of his student life. As his translater notes, H.E Adler he did experience a sort of conversion in 1820 upon reading the first chapter of Lorenz Oken's *Philosophy of Nature,* which inspired in him a "point of view for a great unifying conception of the world" (Howes & Boring, p. xx). Fechner remained interested in the unity of the spiritual and physical for the rest of his life.

At the age of 16, after a brief stint in a medical and surgical academy, Fechner enrolled in the university in Leipzig to study medicine. He reportedly attended few lectures, preferring instead to study from books. He made an exception for E. H. Weber's course in physiology and a course in algebra. He received his medical degree in 1822 by passing the examinations but never completed the doctorate, which would have enabled him to practice medicine.

After finishing his medical studies, Fechner turned to an interest in the physical sciences and mathematics. He began translating physics and chemistry handbooks from French to German in order to support himself. This work eventually brought him some prominence as a physicist. He was appointed in 1824 as a lecturer at the university, at which time he began conducting research of his own. Over the next decade, he published extensively, eventually earning an appointment as a professor of physics, and then as chair of the physics department. This was an impressive achievement for a young man of 33, and it appeared Fechner was set for life.

Unfortunately, Fechner's health began to deteriorate seriously at this point. It is unclear how much of his ailment was physical and how much was psychological. He had injured his eyes by looking at the sun through colored glasses while conducting research on afterimages. He became extremely sensitive to light and stopped, for a time, venturing out in daylight at all. In addition, he appears to have suffered from some variety of anxiety disorders, leaving him unable to sleep or eat, exhausted and with little will to live. Fechner attempted to battle his illnesses with exercise and activity, and then with a variety of medical treatments, some of them bizarre. None was effective, and Fechner spent a dozen years as a virtual invalid (from about 1839 to 1851), with the first three of those years as the most intense. He resigned his post at the university and, in 1844, was awarded a small pension. Suddenly, as mysteriously as the illness had come, it began to lift.

The rejuvenated Fechner turned his interest to philosophy—particularly to the problem of the relationship between the mental and the physical. Fechner published several volumes laying out his views on mind, matter, and consciousness, but none was well received by the scientific or philosophical communities. It was in the midst of this philosophical enterprise that Fechner made the discovery for which he is best known. While lying in bed on the morning of October 22, 1850, Fechner had a revelation. He realized that the way to quantify the relationship between mind and body was to make "the relative increase of bodily energy the measure of the increase of the corresponding mental intensity" (Boring, p. 280). He reasoned that an arithmetic description of mental intensity (the perception) could be made to correspond to a geometric description of the physical intensity (the stimulus). Literally, in this moment, Fechner founded the field of psychophysics and laid the foundation for experimental psychology. Unfortunately for Fechner, this is not the accomplishment for which he would have liked to be remembered. Fechner, in his heart, was a philosopher. Psychophysics, to him, was merely a means of proving his philosophical point. The reading, which is the introduction to Fechner's best known book, *Elements of Psychophysics,* shows his fascination with the mind–body problem.

REFERENCES

Boring, E. G. (1950). *A history of experimental psychology* (2nd ed.). New York: Appleton-Century.

Fechner, G. (1966). Translator's foreword. In D. H. Howes & E. G. Boring (Ed.) & H. E. Adler (Trans.) *Elements of psychophysics* (Vol. 1, pp. xix–xxvi). New York: Holt, Rinehart & Winston. (Originally published in 1860).

Francher, R. (1979). *Pioneers of psychology.* New York: Norton.

Helmholtz, H. (1948). On the rate of transmission of the nerve impulse. In W. Dennis (Ed.) *Readings in the history of psychology* (pp. 197–198). New York: Appleton-Century.

Helmholtz, H. (1912). A manual of physiological optics. In B. Rand (Ed.) *The classical psychologists* (pp. 571–581). (Originally published in 1898).

Hothersall, D. (1995). *History of psychology* (3rd ed.). New York: McGraw-Hill.

Kahl, R. (1971) *Selected writings of Hermann von Helmholtz.* Middletown, CT: Wesleyan University Press.

Koenigsberger, L. (1965) *Hermann von Helmholtz* F. A. Welby (Trans.). New York: Dover.

On the Rate of Transmission of the Nerve Impulse[*] 1850

Hermann von Helmholtz

I have found that there is a measurable period of time during which the effect of a stimulus consisting of a momentary electrical current applied to the iliac plexus of a frog is transmitted to the calf muscles at the entrance of the crural nerve. In the case of large frogs with nerves 50–60 mm. in length, which I preserved at a temperature of 2–6° C. while the temperature of the observation chamber was 11–15°, this period of time amounted to 0.0014 to 0.0020 of a second.

The stimulation of the nerve was given by means of an induction coil. By means of a special mechanical device, a second electrical current was transmitted to a galvanometer at the moment the original current was transmitted to the induction coil. I convinced myself that the error of measurement amounted to considerably less than 1/10 of the period of time with which we are here concerned. The current flowed through the induction coil until the stimulated gastrocnemius muscle had contracted sufficiently to lift a weight which was suspended by a platinum point on a gold-plated support. The lifting of the weight interrupted the current to the induction coil and to the galvanometer. The duration of the current, therefore, was exactly equal to the period elapsing from the application of the stimulation to the nerve to the commencement of the mechanical reaction of the muscle. The effect produced by the current on the galvanometer is proportional to the duration of the current. The time period may be calculated from the oscillation of the galvanometer when the oscillation which would result from known current is also known. I measured the deviation with mirror and telescope. In its essentials the procedure coincides with that of Pouillet for measurements of short periods of time.

The results are the following:

After a standard stimulus the time required for the muscle to lift the attached weight is longer the heavier the weight.

---

[*]This is Helmholtz's first brief report on the speed of the nerve impulse. It appeared in *Monatsberichten der Akademie der Wissenschaften zu Berlin,* January 21, 1850. Mrs. Alfred G. Dietze has made the translation.

Time is modified by varying the intensity of stimulation or sensitivity of the muscle, also the height to which the muscle lifts the weight.

Usually, but not always, the weight is lifted less high when the upper end of the sciatic nerve is stimulated than when the area adjacent to the muscle is stimulated. This fact coincides with the well-known findings of nerve degeneration, when the nerve is severed from the nerve center. In any case, an equal height of lifting may be brought about by reducing the force of the induction currents in the distal area. The galvanometer then indicates that, in stimulating the distal end of the nerve, the same mechanical effect regularly occurs earlier, than by stimulation of the proximal end. In the case of the same specimens, this difference is constant and is independent of the attached weights. In a series of observations with different specimens, the difference varied between 0.0014 and 0.0020 sec. The higher figures occurred on colder days. In experiments with smaller weights, the individual twitches are somewhat less regular, and the constant amount of difference must be calculated from the averages of the experimental series, while, in the case of 100 to 180 gr. weights, this amount may be found directly from a comparison of the individual recordings.

A Manual of Physiological Optics

Translated from the German* by Benjamin Rand

THEORY OF COLOR VISION

Hypotheses

The facts to be deduced from the laws of color-mixture, that three constituents of sensation which proceed independently of one another are produced by external stimulation, have received their more definite and more significant expression in the hypotheses, which assume, that these different constituents are excited and transmitted in different portions of the optic nerve; but that they simultaneously attain to consciousness, and thereby, so far as they have become excited from the same place of the retina, they are also localized in the same place of the field of vision.

---

*From H. von Helmholtz's *Handbuch der Physiologischen Optik*. Leipzig, 1856–66; 2te. umgearb. Aufl. Hamb. u. Lpz. 1896.

Such a theory was first proposed by Thomas Young.[1] The more detailed development of it is essentially conditioned by the fact, that its author would ascribe to the sensitive nerves of the eye only the properties and capacities, which we positively know as belonging to the motor nerves of men and of animals. We have a much more favorable opportunity to discover these latter by experiment than is the case with the nerves of sensation, since we are able comparatively easily and definitely both to discern and to measure the finest changes of their excitation and excitability by means of the contractions occurring in the muscles, and their changes. What we furthermore have been able to ascertain concerning the structure, the chemical constitution, the excitability, the conductivity, and the electrical behavior of the sensitive nerves, harmonises so perfectly with the corresponding behavior of the motor nerves, that fundamental differences in the nature of their activity are extremely improbable, at least so far as these do not depend upon the other organic apparatus connected with them, upon which they exert their influence.

Now we know in regard to motor nerves only the contrast between the state of rest and of activity. In the former state the nerve can remain unaltered a long time without important chemical change or development of heat; and at the same time the muscle dependent upon the nerve remains lax. If we stimulate the nerve, heat develops in it material changes, electrical oscillations are shown, and the muscle is contracted. In a cut nerve-preparation the sensitiveness is quickly lost, probably on account of the expansion of the chemical constituents necessary for activity. Under the action of atmospheric oxygen, or better still of the arterial blood containing oxygen, the sensitiveness is wholly or partially slowly restored, save that these processes of restoration excite contractions of the muscle, or changes of electrical relation in nerve and muscle coincident with the activity. We are acquainted also with no external means which can produce this process of restoration so quickly and intensively, and which can permit it at the same time so suddenly to appear and again to cease, as would be necessary, if this process were to serve as the physiological basis of a powerful sensation occurring with precision.

If we confine our assumptions concerning the development of a theory of color vision to the properties belonging with certainty to the nerves, there is presented in fairly secure outline the theory of Thomas Young.

The sensation of dark corresponds to the state of rest of the optic nerve, that of colored or white light to an excitement of it. The three simple sensations which correspond to the excitement only of a single one of the three nerve systems, and

---

[1]Thomas Young's theory of color vision is as follows: "From three simple sensations, with their combinations, we obtain seven primitive distinctions of colours; but the different proportions, in which they may be combined, afford a variety of traits beyond all calculation. The three simple sensations being red, green, and violet, the three binary combinations are yellow, consisting of red and green; crimson, of red and violet; and blue, of green and violet; and the seventh in order is white light, composed by all three united. But the blue thus produced, by combining the whole of the green and violet rays, is not the blue of the spectrum, for four parts of green and one of violet make a blue differing very little from green; while the blue of the spectrum appears to contain as much violet as green: and it is for this reason that red and blue usually make a purple, deriving its hue from the predominance of the violet." Thomas Young's *A Course of Lectures on Natural Philosophy.* Lond. 1807, vol. I, p. 440.

Figure 3.1

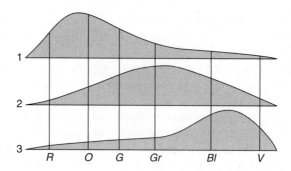

from which all the others can be composed, must correspond in the table of colors to the three angles of the color triangle.

In order to assume the finest possible color sensations not demonstrable by objective stimulus, it appears appropriate so to select the angles of the color triangle that its sides include in the closest possible way the curves of the colors of the spectrum.

Thomas Young has therefore assumed:

1. There are in the eye three kinds of nerve fibres. The excitation of the first produces the sensation of red; the excitation of the second, the sensation of green; the excitation of the third, the sensation of violet.

2. Objective homogeneous light excites these three kinds of fibres with an intensity which varies according to the length of the wave. The fibres sensitive to red are excited most strongly by light of the greatest wave-length; and those sensitive to violet by light of the smallest wave-length. Nevertheless, it is not precluded, but rather to be assumed, for the explanation of a series of phenomena, that each color of the spectrum excites all the kinds of fibres, but with different intensity. If we suppose in *Fig. 1* the spectrum colors placed horizontally and in their natural order, beginning from red R up to violet V, the three curves may represent more or less exactly the strength of the excitation of the three kinds of fibres: no. 1 those sensitive to red; no. 2 those sensitive to green; and no. 3 those sensitive to violet.

The simple red excites strongly the fibres sensitive to red, and weakly the two other kinds of fibres; sensation: red.

The simple yellow excites moderately the fibres sensitive to red and green, weakly the violet; sensation: red.

The simple green excites strongly the fibres sensitive to green, much more weakly the two other kinds; sensation: green.

The simple blue excites moderately the fibres sensitive to green and violet, weakly the red; sensation: blue.

The simple violet excites strongly the fibres which belong to it, and weakly the others; sensation: violet.

The excitation of all the fibres of nearly equal strength gives the sensation of white, or of whitish colors.

Perhaps it may be objected at first view to this hypothesis, that three times the number of nerve fibres and nerve endings must be presumed than in the older assumption, according to which each separate nerve fibre was thought capable of transmitting all kinds of chromatic excitations. But I do not believe, that in this connection the supposition of Young is in contradiction with the anatomical facts. An hypothesis was previously discussed,[1] which explains the accuracy of sight by the aid of a much smaller number of visual nerve fibres, than the number of distinguishable places in the field of vision.

The choice of the three fundamental colors seems at first, as we have observed, somewhat arbitrary. Any other three colors might be chosen from which white can be composed. Young was guided probably by the consideration that the colors at the end of the spectrum appear to claim a privileged position. If we were not to select these it would be necessary to take for one of the fundamental colors a purple shade, and the curve which corresponds to it in the foregoing figure (*Fig. I*), would have two maxima: one in red, and the other in violet.

The single circumstance, which is of direct importance in the mode of sensation and appears to give a clue for the determination of the fundamental colors, is the apparent greater color-saturation of the red and violet; a thing which also manifests itself, although indeed less markedly, for green. Since we style colors the more saturated the farther they are removed from white, we must expect that great saturation must belong particularly to those colors of the spectrum which produce most purely the simplest sensations of color. In fact, these colors, if they are very pure, have even with inferior brilliancy, something of an intensively glowing, almost dazzling quality. There are especially red, violet, or blue violet flowers, e.g. of the cameraria, whose colors display this characteristic blending of darkness and brilliancy. Young's hypothesis affords for this a simple explanation. A dark color can cause an intensive excitation of one of the three nerve systems, while the corresponding bright white causes a much weaker excitation of the same. The difference appears analogous to that between the sensation of very hot water upon a small portion of the skin and lukewarm water striking a greater surface.

In particular violet makes upon me this impression of a deeply saturated color. But inasmuch as the strictly violet rays, even when they occur in sunlight, are of slight intensity and are modified by fluorescence, ultramarine blue, which has far the advantage of greater intensity of light, produces an effect approximately equal to it. The strictly pure violet of the spectrum is very little known among the laity, since the violet pigments give nearly always the effect of a slight admixture of red, or appear very dark. For that very reason, the shades of the ultramarine blue coming near to the violet excite the general attention much more, are much better known, and are designated by a much older name,—that of blue,—than the violet strictly so called. In addition one has in the deep ultramarine blue of the cloudless sky a highly imposing, well known, and constant example of this color.

---

[1]Helmholtz's *Hdb. d. Physiol. Optik.* 2 Aufl., S. 264.

In this fact I seek the reason why in former times blue has always been regarded as the one fundamental color. And the more recent observers, like Maxwell and A. König, who have sought to determine the composition of color, have also in part returned to it. For both of these had, to be sure, a more definite reason in the above mentioned elevation of the curve of the colors of the spectrum in violet.

It should still be mentioned that the Venetian school of painters, which creates effects chiefly by the intense richness of its color, is especially fond of putting in juxtaposition the three colors, red, green, and violet.

Furthermore, I decidedly question the opinion expressed by various investigators, that the need of designating primary sensations has manifested itself in the names of the colors, and that these might therefore give a clue for the determination of colors. Our forefathers had before them in colors a domain of vague distinctions. If they wanted to determine sharp degrees of difference they had first of all to look for good old examples of striking shade, which were everywhere known, and anywhere observable. The names for red led back to the Sanscrit *rudhira* = blood, and also "red." From this ἐρυθρός, rufus, ruber, roth, red, etc. For "blue" the Greeks have πορφύρεος and κυάνεος, which appear to refer to the sea; the Latins coeruleus, from coelum, the sky; the Germans "blau"; the English, blue; the Dutch, blau; the old German, blaw; which appear to lead to the English "blow," that is, the color of the air. Then names for green may be traced back to vegetation, πράσινος (leek-green), ποώδες (grass-green), viridis from vis, virescere (to grow strong); German: green, English: green, refer to "grow".

The oldest designations of color were very vague: ξανθός appears to have extended from golden yellow to blue green. It was clearly a difficult task to fix in sharp degrees of difference this vague domain. To-day even it is difficult for gifted children to learn the names of colors. One should not infer from these facts that the ancients were color blind.

That from the series of colors which may be stimulated by objective light, it is impossible to select three which can be regarded as fundamental sensations, has already been discussed. For this very reason A. König and C. Dieterici have distinguished a middle section of the spectrum, the colors of which we can no longer obtain by the mixture of the end-colors and one of the spectrum colors lying within it. The table of colors drawn according to the measurements of the same observers reveals the same fact in graphic representation. Just on this account the supposition is necessary for Thomas Young's theory, that every color of the spectrum excites simultaneously, even though in different intensity, not merely one, but two or all three, of the three nerve systems which are sensitive to color. At best the hypothesis of simplicity would be permissible for the end-colors of the spectrum, red and violet. But precisely in the case of violet we know, that the fluorescence of the retina produced by the violet rays must vitiate the sensation, and it appears to me not improbable, that the height of the curve between F and Y, found even by Maxwell, is conditioned by the fluorescence of the retina.

It further follows, that it must appear theoretically possible to produce sensations of more saturated colors through other conditions of excitation. That this is also practically possible, and that this demand can be actually fulfilled by Young's theory, I shall have to explain in the description of after-images.

The color theory of Thomas Young, above outlined, is, as compared with the general theory of nervous activity as it was worked out by Johannes Müller, a more special application of the law of specific sensations. Corresponding to its hypotheses the sensations of red, green, and violet would be regarded as determined by the specific energy of sensation of the corresponding three nerve systems. Any sort of excitation whatever, which can in any degree excite the nerve system aforesaid, would always be able to produce in it only its specific sensation. As for the cause of the particular quality of these sensations we hardly need look for it in the retina or the constitution of its fibres, but in the activity of the central parts of the brain associated with them.

I have up to the present kept the analysis of this theory relatively abstract in order to keep it as free as possible from farther hypothetical additions. Nevertheless, there are as great advantages for the certain understanding of such abstractions, if one tries to imagine for oneself pictures as concrete as possible, even though these occasion many a presupposition that is not directly necessary for the nature of the case. In this sense I permit myself to set forth Young's theory in the following somewhat more manifest form. That objections to these additions do not contradict the essence of Young's hypothesis, I have no need to explain.

1. Three kinds of photochemically decomposable substances are deposited in the end organs of the visual nerve fibres, which have different sensitiveness for the different parts of the spectrum. The three color values of the colors of the spectrum depend essentially upon the photochemical reaction of these three substances to the light. In the eyes of birds and reptiles besides colorless cones there occur in fact rods with red, and rods with yellow-green, drops of oil, which might produce a favoring of some simple light in their action upon the back element of these formations. In the case of human beings and other mammals nothing similar has up to the present time been found.

2. By the disintegration of all the substances sensitive to light, the nerve fibre laden therewith, is set into a state of excitation. There is only one kind of activity capable of exciting sensation in every nerve fibre which accompanies the disintegration of the organic substance and the development of heat, as we know from our study of the nerves of muscles. These phenomena in the three systems of fibres are probably also thoroughly similar one to the other. They act differently in the brain only for the reason that they are united to different functioning parts of the brain. The nerve fibres need here as everywhere to play only the part of conducting wires, by which entirely similar electric currents which pass through them can precipitate or call forth the most various activities in the apparatus connected with the ends. These excitations of the three systems of fibre form the above separated three elementary excitations, provided always that the intensity of excitation, for which we still have no universally valid measure, is thereby made proportional to the strength of light. This does not prevent the intensity of the elementary excitation being any involved function whatever of the use of material or of the negative variation of the current in the nerves, which latter phenomena might occasionally be employed as a measure of excitation.

3. In the brain the three systems of fibres stand in alliance with the three different functioning systems of ganglionic cells, which are perhaps spatially so close to one another, that those corresponding to the same parts of the retina lie close together. This appears to follow from recent investigations concerning the influence of lesions of the brain upon the field of vision.

Elements of Psychophysics
Gustav Fechner

I. GENERAL CONSIDERATIONS ON THE RELATION OF BODY AND MIND

While knowledge of the material world has blossomed in the great development of the various branches of natural science and has benefited from exact principles and methods that assure it of successful progress, and while knowledge of the mind has, at least up to a certain point, established for itself a solid basis in psychology and logic, knowledge of the relation of mind and matter, of body and soul, has up to now remained merely a field for philosophical argument without solid foundation and without sure principles and methods for the progress of inquiry.

The immediate cause of this less favorable condition is, in my opinion, to be sought in the following factual circumstances, which admittedly only make us seek their more remote origins. The relationships of the material world itself we can pursue directly and in accord with experience, as no less the relationships of the inner or mental world. Knowledge of the former, of course, is limited by the reach of our senses and their amplifications, and of the latter by the limitations of everyone's mind; still, these researches go on in such a way that we are able to find basic facts, basic laws, and basic relationships in each of the fields, information which can serve us as a secure foundation and starting point for inference and further progress. The situation is not the same in relating material and mental worlds, since each of these two inextricably associated fields enters into immediate experience only one at a time, while the other remains hidden. At the moment when we are conscious of our feelings and thoughts, we are unable to perceive the activity of the brain that is associated with them and with which they are in turn associated—the material side is then hidden by the mental. Similarly, although we are able to examine the bodies of other people, animals, and the whole of nature directly in anatomical, physiological, physical, and chemical terms, we are not able to know anything directly about the minds that belong to the former nor of God who belongs to the latter,[1] for the spiritual side is here hidden by the material. There thus remains great

---

[1]Trans. Note: A typical Fechner notion. God is the soul of the universe.

latitude for hypothesis and disbelief. Is there really anything revealed, we may ask, once the covers are lifted, and if so, what?

The uncertainty, the vacillation, the argument over these factual issues has so far not allowed us to gain a solid foothold or to find a point of attack for a theory of these relationships, whose factual basis is still in dispute.

And what can be the reason for this singular condition, in which body and mind can be observed, each for itself but never together, in spite of the fact that they belong to each other? Usually we can best observe things which belong together when they occur together. The inviolability of this aspect of the relationship between the mental and material worlds makes us suspect that it is fundamental, that it is rooted in their basic natures. Is there nothing similar that can at least illustrate these facts even though it cannot get to the root of the matter?

Admittedly, we can point to one thing or another. For example, when standing inside a circle, its convex side is hidden, covered by the concave side; conversely, when outside, the concave side is covered by the convex. Both sides belong together as indivisibly as do the mental and material sides of man and can be looked upon as analogous to his inner and outer sides. It is just as impossible, standing in the plane of a circle, to see both sides of the circle simultaneously as it is to see both sides of man from the plane of human existence. Only when we change our standpoint is the side of the circle we view changed, so that we now see the hidden side behind the one we had seen before. The circle is, however, only a metaphor and what counts is a question of fact.

Now, it is not the task or the intention of this work to enter into deep or penetrating discussions on the basic question of the relationship of body and mind. Let everyone seek to solve this puzzle—insofar as it appears to him as such—in his own way. It will therefore be without prejudice for what follows, if I state my opinion here in a few words, in order not to leave unanswered some possible questions about the general beliefs that formed the starting point of this inquiry and that for me, at least, still form the background. At the same time I am providing something to go by in this field of fluctuating ideas for those who are still seeking a point of view rather than believing that they have found one, even though what I say will not contain anything essential for further progress of this work. In view of the great temptation in starting a work such as this to lose oneself in voluminous and extensive discussions of this sort, and of the difficulty, by no means slight, of avoiding them completely, I hope that I will be forgiven if I limit myself here to the following brief exposition of my position.

To begin with, however, let me add a second illustrative example to the first. The solar system offers quite different aspects as seen from the sun and as observed from the earth. One is the world of Copernicus, the other the world of Ptolemy. It will always be impossible for the same observer to perceive both world systems simultaneously, in spite of the fact that both belong quite indivisibly together and, just like the concave and convex sides of the circle, are basically only two different modes of appearance of the same matter from different standpoints. Here again one needs but to change the point of view in order to make evident the one world rather than the other.

The whole world is full of such examples, which prove to us that what is in fact one thing will appear as two from two points of view; one cannot expect to find things the same from one standpoint and from the other. Who would not admit that it is always thus and cannot be otherwise? Only with respect to the greatest and most decisive example does one deny it or fail to think of it. That is the relationship of the mental and material worlds.

What will appear to you as your mind from the internal standpoint, where you yourself are this mind, will, on the other hand, appear from the outside point of view as the material basis of this mind. There is a difference whether one thinks with the brain or examines the brain of a thinking person.* These activities appear to be quite different, but the standpoint is quite different too, for here one is an inner, the other an outer point of view. The views are even more completely different than were the previous examples, and for that reason the differences between the modes of their appearance are immensely greater. For the twofold mode of appearance of the circle or the planetary system was after all basically gained by taking two different external standpoints; whether within the circle or on the sun, the observer remained outside the sweep of the circles outside the planets. The appearance of the mind to itself, on the other hand, is gained from the truly inner point of view of the underlying being regarding itself, as in coincidence with itself, whereas the appearance of the material state belonging to it derives from a standpoint that is truly external, and not in coincidence.

Now it becomes obvious why no one can ever observe mind and body simultaneously even though they are inextricably united, for it is impossible for anyone to be inside and outside the same thing at one time.

Here lies also the reason why one mind cannot perceive another mind as such, even though one might believe it would be easiest to become aware of the same kind of entity. One mind, insofar as it does not coincide with the other, becomes aware only of the other's material manifestations. A mind can, therefore, gain awareness of another only through the aid of its corporeality, for the mind's exterior appearance is no more than its material nature.

For this reason, too, the mind appears always as unitary, because there exists only the one inner standpoint, whereas every body appears different according to the multitude of external standpoints and the differences among those occupying them.

The present way of looking at these phenomena thus covers the most fundamental relationships between body and mind, as any basic point of view should seek to do.

One more item: body and mind parallel each other; changes in one correspond to changes in the other. Why? Leibniz says: one can hold different opinions. Two clocks mounted on the same board adjust their movement to each other by means of their common attachment (if they do not vary too much from each other); this

---

*Examination in this case is equivalent to forming, from deductions based on external observations, an adequate concept of how the internal condition would appear upon removal of barriers to direct examination.

is the usual dualistic notion of the mind-body relation. It could also be that someone moves the hands of both clocks so that they keep in harmony; this view is oc-
casionalism, according to which God creates the mental changes appropriate to the
bodily changes and vice versa, in constant harmony. The clocks could also be adjusted so perfectly from the beginning that they keep perfect time, without ever
needing adjustment; that is the notion of prestabilized harmony. Leibniz has left
out one point of view—the most simple possible. They can keep time harmo-
niously—indeed never differ—because they are not really two different clocks.
Therewith we can dispense with the common board, the constant adjustment, the
artificiality of the original setting. What appears to the external observer as the organic clock with its movement and its works of organic wheels and levers (or as
its most important and essential part), appears to the clock itself quite differently,
as its own mind with its works of feelings, drives, and thoughts. No insult is meant,
if man here be called a clock. If he is called that in one respect, yet he will not be
so called in every respect.

The difference of appearance depends not only on the difference of standpoint,
but also on the differences among those that occupy it. A blind person does not see
any of the exterior world from an external standpoint, though his position is just
as favorable as that of a seeing person; and a nonliving clock does not see its interior in spite of its standpoint of coincidence, which is just as favorable as that of
a brain. A clock can exist only as external appearance.

The natural sciences employ consistently the external standpoint in their considerations, the humanities the internal. The common opinions of everyday life are
based on changes of the standpoints, and natural philosophy on the identity of what
appears double from two standpoints. A theory of the relationship of mind and
body will have to trace the relationship of the two modes of appearance of a single thing that is a unity.

These are my fundamental opinions. They will not clear up the ultimate nature
of body and mind, but I do seek by means of them to unify the most general factual relationships between them under a single point of view.

However, as I mentioned before, it remains open to everyone to seek to effect
the same end by another approach, or not to seek to accomplish it at all. Everyone's chosen approach will depend on the context of his other opinions. By arguing backwards, he will have to determine the possibility or impossibility of finding
a suitable general relationship himself. At this point it is not important whether he
wants to consider body and mind as only two different modes of appearance of the
same entity or as two entities brought together externally, or to consider the soul
as a point in a nexus of other points of essentially the same or of a different nature, or to dispense entirely with a fundamentally unitary approach. Insofar as an
empirical relationship between body and mind is acknowledged and its empirical
pursuit is allowed, there is no objection to trying even the most complicated kind
of representation. In what follows we shall base our inquiry only on the empirical
relationships of body and mind, and in addition adopt for use the most common
expressions for the designation of these facts, though they are expressed more in
the terms of a dualistic approach than my own monistic one. Translation from one
to the other is easy.

This does not mean, however, that the theory which will be developed here will be altogether indifferent to the points of view on the basic relationships of body and mind and without influence upon them, for the contrary is true. Still, one must not confuse the effects that this theory may have some day—and that are partially beginning to take form even now—with the basis of this theory. This basis is indeed purely empirical, and every assumption is to be rejected from the start.

One may well ask whether the possibility of such a basis does not directly contradict the fact, with which we started, that the relationships of body and mind are outside the realm of experience. They are not, however, beyond experience altogether, for only the immediate relationships are beyond immediate experience. Our own interpretation of the general relation of body and mind already has had the support of common experiences with these relationships, even if they do not strike everyone who comes to this work with preconceived notions as necessary. What follows will show how we can draw quite as much on special experiences, which can serve us partly to orient ourselves in the area of mediated relationships and partly to provide a foundation for deductions regarding immediate relationships.

Indeed, we could not rest content with this general point of view, even if it were generally accepted. The proof, the fertility, and the depth of a universal law do not depend on the general principles but on the elementary facts. The law of gravitation and the molecular laws (which undoubtedly include the former) are elementary laws; were they thoroughly known and the whole range of their implications exhausted, we would have a theory of the material world in its most general form. Similarly we must seek to form elementary laws of the relationship of the material and the mental world in order to gain a durable and developed theory instead of a general opinion, and we will only be able to do this, here as elsewhere, by building on a foundation of elementary facts.

Psychophysics is a theory that must be based on this point of view. More details follow in the next chapter.

II. THE CONCEPT AND THE TASK OF PSYCHOPHYSICS

Psychophysics should be understood here as an exact theory of the functionally dependent relations of body and soul or, more generally, of the material and the mental, of the physical and the psychological worlds.

We count as mental, psychological, or belonging to the soul, all that can be grasped by introspective observation or that can be abstracted from it; as bodily, corporeal, physical, or material, all that can be grapsed by observation from the outside or abstracted from it. These designations refer only to those aspects of the world of appearance, with whose relationships psychophysics will have to occupy itself, provided that one understands inner and outer observation in the sense of everyday language to refer to the activities through which alone existence becomes apparent.

In any case, all discussions and investigations of psychophysics relate only to the apparent phenomena of the material and mental worlds, to a world that either appears directly through introspection or through outside observation, or that can be deduced from its appearance or grasped as a phenomenological relationship, category, association, deduction, or law. Briefly, psychophysics refers to the *physical* in the sense of physics and chemistry, to the *psychical* in the sense of experiential psychology, without referring back in any way to the nature of the body or of the soul beyond the phenomenal in the metaphysical sense.

In general, we call the psychic a dependent function of the physical, and vice versa, insofar as there exists between them such a constant or lawful relationship that, from the presence and changes of one, we can deduce those of the other.

The existence of a functional relationship between body and mind is, in general, not denied; nevertheless, there exists a still unresolved dispute over the reasons for this fact, and the interpretation and extent of it.

With no regard to the metaphysical points of this argument (points which concern rather more the so-called essence than the appearance), psychophysics undertakes to determine the actual functional relationships between the modes of appearance of body and mind as exactly as possible.

What things belong together quantitatively and qualitatively, distant and close, in the material and in the mental world? What are the laws governing their changes in the same or in opposite directions? These are the questions in general that psychophysics asks and tries to answer with exactitude.

In other words, but still with the same meaning: what belong together in the inner and outer modes of appearance of things, and what laws exist regarding their respective changes?

Insofar as a functional relationship linking body and mind exists, there is actually nothing to prevent us from looking at it and pursuing it from the one direction rather than from the other. One can illustrate this relationship suitably by means of a mathematical function, an equation between the variables x and y, where each variable can be looked upon at will as a function of the other, and where each is dependent upon the changes of the other. There is a reason, however, why psychophysics prefers to make the approach from the side of the dependence of the mind on the body rather than the contrary, for it is only the physical that is immediately open to measurement, whereas the measurement of the psychical can be obtained only as dependent on the physical—as we shall see later. This reason is decisive; it determines the direction of approach in what follows.

The materialistic reasons for such a preference we need not discuss, nor are they meaningful in psychophysics, and the dispute between materialism and idealism over the essential nature of the dependency of one on the other remains alien and immaterial to psychophysics, since it concerns itself only with the phenomenal relationships.

One can distinguish immediate and mediated relationships of dependency or direct and indirect functions relating body and mind. Sensations are in a directly dependent relationship to certain processes in our brains as far as the one is determined by the other or has the other as its immediate consequence; but sensations are merely in a mediated relationship to the external stimulus, which initiates these processes only via the intervention of a neural conductor. All our mental activity has dependent upon it an immediate activity in our brain, or is accompanied immediately by brain activity, or else directly causes the activity, of which the effects then are transmitted to the external world via the medium of our neural and effector organs.

The mediated functional relationships of body and mind fulfill completely the concept of a functional relationship only under the supposition that the mediation enters into the relationship, since omission of the mediation leads to the absence of the constancy or lawfulness of the relationship of body and mind, which exists by virtue of this mediation. A stimulus then releases proper sensations only when a living brain does not lack the living nerves to transmit the effect of the stimulus to the brain.

As far as the psychic is to be considered a direct function of the physical, the physical can be called the carrier, the factor underlying the psychical. Physical processes that accompany or underlie psychical functions, and consequently stand in a direct functional relationship to them, we shall call psychophysical.

Without making any assumptions about the nature of psychophysical processes, the question of their substrate and form we may leave undecided from the start. There is a twofold reason why we may dispense with this question right away: first, because the determination of the general principles of psychophysics will involve the handling only of quantitative relations, just as in physics, where qualitative depend on earlier quantitative relationships; and second, because we will have to give no special consideration to psychophysical processes in the first part, under the plan of work which follows immediately.

By its nature, psychophysics may be divided into an outer and an inner part, depending on whether consideration is focused on the relationship of the psychical to the body's external aspects, or on those internal functions with which the psychic are closely related. In other words, the division is between the mediated and the immediate functional relationships of mind and body.

The truly basic empirical evidence for the whole of psychophysics can be sought only in the realm of outer psychophysics, inasmuch as it is only this part that is available to immediate experience. Our point of departure therefore has to be taken from outer psychophysics. However, there can be no development of outer psychophysics without constant regard to inner psychophysics, in view of the fact that the body's external world is functionally related to the mind only by the mediation of the body's internal world.

Moreover, while we are considering the regular relations of external stimulus and sensation, we must not forget that the stimulus, after all, does not awaken our sensations directly, but only via the awakening of those bodily processes within us that stand in direct relation to sensation. Their nature may still be quite unknown, the inquiry regarding their nature may be neglected for the present (as already stated), but the fact that they do exist must be affirmed and referred to often, whenever it comes to the point of taking dead aim and following up those lawful relationships which are our immediate concern in outer psychophysics. Similarly, even though the body's activities, which are directly subject to the activity of our will and obey it, are still totally unknown, we should not forget that the effect of the will on the outer world can only be achieved via just such activities. We thus have implicitly to interpolate everywhere the unknown intermediate link that is necessary to complete the chain of effects.

Psychophysics, already related to psychology and physics by name, must on the one hand be based on psychology, and on the other hand promises to give psychology a mathematical foundation. From physics outer psychophysics borrows aids and methodology; inner psychophysics leans more to physiology and anatomy, particularly of the nervous system, with which a certain acquaintance is presupposed. Unfortunately, however, inner psychophysics has not profited so far from recent painstaking, exact, and valuable investigations in this field to the extent it should. Inner psychophysics undoubtedly will do this one day, once these investigations (and those from the different kind of attack on which this work is based) have succeeded to the point of reaching a common meeting ground, where they will be able to cross-fertilize each other. That this is not yet the case to any extent indicates only the incomplete state in which our theory finds itself.

The point of view from which we plan to attack our task is as follows:

Even before the means are available to discover the nature of the processes of the body that stand in direct relation to our mental activities, we will nevertheless be able to determine to a certain degree the quantitative relationship between them. Sensation depends on stimulation; a stronger sensation depends on a stronger stimulus; the stimulus, however, causes sensation only via the intermediate action of some internal process of the body. To the extent that lawful relationships between sensation and stimulus can be found, they must include lawful relationships between the stimulus and this inner physical activity, which obey the same general laws of interaction of bodily processes and thereby give us a basis for drawing general conclusions about the nature of this inner activity. Indeed, later discussion will show that, in spite of all our ignorance of the detailed nature of psychophysical processes there exists, for those aspects which are concerned with the more important relationships of ordinary mental life, a basis which within limits already allows us to form certain and sufficient conceptions of the fundamental facts and laws which define the connection of outer to inner psychophysics.

Quite apart from their import for inner psychophysics, these lawful relationships, which may be ascertained in the area of outer psychophysics, have their own importance. Based on them, as we shall see, physical measurement yields a psychic measurement, on which we can base arguments that in their turn are of importance and interest.

CHAPTER 4

THE NEW PSYCHOLOGY

WILHELM WUNDT (1832–1920)

Wilhelm Wundt was born in 1832 near Mannheim, Germany, the youngest child of a Lutheran pastor.[1] Both of his families had a history of intellectual achievement. His brother, eight years older, was away at school, so Wilhelm grew up as an only child. At age 8, his father placed him under the tutelage of a young rector, and his next four years were spent in private education. He entered the gymnasium, an advanced high school and junior college, in his family's small village, but he failed his first year. He was sent away to Heidelberg, a large university town where his older brother and a cousin were enrolled in college, and he restarted his secondary education.

After graduation from the gymnasium, he enrolled in the premedical program at the University of Tübingen. There, he had an unremarkable first academic year. However, his father had recently died, and at the end of this year, he was forced to make some difficult choices since there was limited money for schooling. He transferred to the University of Heidelberg, where his intellectual abilities finally emerged and he became the top medical student in his class. This also heralded the beginning of his interest in research and writing.

Wundt published his first research in 1853, an experiment with himself as the sole subject. Over the next 60 plus years, he was to publish more than 500 books and articles. He graduated *summa cum laude* with a medical degree in 1855. Immediately after graduation, he went to study for several months at the same labo-

---

[1]More biographic material on Wundt may be found in Boring (1950), Fancher (1979), Hothersall (1995), & Titchener (1921).

ratory that influenced Helmholtz. This experience led him to decide on a career in physiology and academics rather to practice medicine, a decision that was to have immense impact on psychology. Wundt returned to Heidelberg to obtain a certificate in teaching.

His first book on muscle movement was published in 1858, and he began another book the same year, which was published in 1862, *Beitrage zur Theorie der Sinneswahrnehmung (Contributions Toward a Theory of Sense Perception)*, which marked the beginning of his interest in psychological issues and research. This important work outlined three new scientific disciplines: experimental psychology, social psychology, and scientific metaphysics.

In 1858, he was given the position as assistant to Herman Helmholtz, who had just been appointed as professor of physiology at Heidelberg. Wundt continued some small studies and classes of his own and gradually increased his interest in psychology while teaching physiology classes for Helmholtz. In 1864, he was appointed to a higher rank (more like associate professor) and was able to resign his position as Helmholtz's assistant and pursue his own interests. By 1867, he actively taught a course named physiological psychology. In 1874, he was appointed professor of inductive philosophy at the University of Zurich. A year later, he was offered the chair of philosophy at Leipzig were he represented the "scientific philosophy." During this time, he established a psychological laboratory. His teaching and laboratory attracted students from around the world, and Wundt increased his publications. Edward B. Titchener was one of his students and later an ardent supporter in the United States. In 1897, an entire building that he helped design was dedicated as a psychological laboratory. He retired in 1917, having served 42 years at Leipzig. He died in 1920. The reading included in this chapter is form the third English translation (1970, from the 7th revised German edition) of his *Outlines of Psychology,* first published in Leipzig in 1896. It is the introduction to his book, setting out a more detailed look at the basic principles and areas of what he viewed as experimental psychology.

HERMANN EBBINGHAUS (1850–1909)

Hermann Ebbinghaus was born in the town of Barmen, near Bonn, Germany. Little has been written about his early life.[1] He was the son of a merchant and attended the local secondary school (gymnasium). At the age of 17 he entered the University of Bonn to study history and philology (classical scholarship). Ebbinghaus attended more than one university, drifting to Halle and Berlin (universities he was to join later as a faculty member). He attended university from 1867 to 1870 and then joined the army and served in the Franco-Prussian War. Following this, he returned to Bonn and received his doctoral degree in philosophy in 1873. He spent the next several years of his life traveling, studying, and working for a short

---

[1]Basic bibliographic material about Ebbinghaus can be found in Boring (1950), Hothersall (1995), Shakow (1930), and Woodworth (1909).

period as a teacher in England and France. On one of his trips to France, he chanced upon a copy of Fechner's *Elemente der Psychophysik* (*Elements of Psychophysics,* 1860) in a used bookstore. He was immediately struck by the application of this work to psychology.

Ebbinghaus set out in 1877 to develop the procedures that would apply this new science to the study of memory. Unlike many of the other psychologists we have studied and will study, he first did this without a university appointment and without being the student of one of the early pioneers. With himself as the sole subject and without a laboratory, he began experiments in memory, using poetry and nonsense syllables that he developed himself. Even when he was appointed to a position at the University of Berlin, he spent the next several years replicating the experiments he had done on himself, before publishing the results in a work entitled *Über das Gedächtnis* (*Concerning Memory*), published in Leipzig in 1885. The selection by Ebbinghaus for this section is taken from the 1964 edition of the English translation of this book. Early in his studies, Ebbinghaus realized that preestablished associations of ordinary words would confound his research. To control these effects, he developed consonant–vowel–consonant combinations—nonsense syllables—reportedly some 2,300 of them.

Shortly after the publication of his *Gedächtnis,* he was made professor "extraordinaire" at the University of Berlin, thanks in no small part to the significance of this work to the new science of psychology! In 1886, the same year as this appointment, he opened a psychological laboratory at the University of Berlin and turned his attention from memory research to sensory perception, and in 1893, he published a theory of color vision.[2] Along with Arthur König, he established the *Zeitschrift für Psychologie und Physiologie der Sinnesorgane* (*Journal of Psychology and Physiology of Sense Organs*). He founded the journal so that work emerging from places other than Wundt's Leipzig laboratory would have an outlet. He moved to the University of Breslau in 1894. There he published *Grundzüge der Psychologie* (*Fundamentals of Psychology,* 1897). In 1905, he moved to the University of Halle, where he died suddenly in 1909 of pneumonia. Experiments 100 years later continue to demonstrate his early contributions to the study of memory.[3]

REFERENCES

Boring, E. G. (1950) *A history of experimental psychology* (2nd ed.). New York: Appleton-Century-Crofts.

Ebbinghaus, H. (1964) *Memory: A contribution to experimental psychology.* H. A. Ruger & E. E. Bussenius (Trans.). New York: Dover. (Originally published in 1885; translated work first published in 1913 by Teachers College, New York).

Ebbinghaus, H. (1902) *Grundzüge der Psychologie.* Leipzig: Veit & Co.

Fancher, R. (1979) *Pioneers of psychology.* New York: Norton.

---

[2]It should be noted that Hermann von Helmholtz, the recognized leader in the study of sensory physiology, was at the University of Berlin at this time.

[3]See Tulving (1985).

Hothersall, D. (1995) *History of psychology* (3rd. ed.). New York: McGraw-Hill.

Shakow, D. (1930) Herman Ebbinghaus. *American Journal of Psychology*, 42, 505–518.

Titcherner, E. B. (1921) Wilhelm Wundt. *American Journal of Psychology*, 32, 161–178.

Tulving, E. (1985). Ebbinghaus's memory: What did he learn and remember? *Journal of Experimental Psychology: Learning, Memory, and Cognition*, 11(3), 485–490.

Woodworth, R. S. (1909) Herman Ebbinghaus. *Journal of Philosophy*, 6, 253–256.

Wundt, W. (1904) *Principles of physiological psychology* (5th ed.). E. Titchener (Ed.). New York: Macmillan. (Originally published in 1874).

Wundt, W. (1907) *Outlines of psychology* (3rd English ed.). C. Judd (Trans.). Leipzig: Engelmann.

Wundt, W. (1912) *An introduction to psychology* (2nd ed.). New York: Macmillan.

Introduction From Outlines Of Psychology

Wilhelm Wundt

1. PROBLEM OF PSYCHOLOGY.

1. Two definitions of psychology have been the most prominent in the history of this science. According to *one*, psychology is the *"science of mind"*, psychical processes being regarded as phenomena from which it is possible to infer the nature of an underlying metaphysical mind-substance. According to the *other*, psychology is the *"science of inner experience"*, psychical processes are here looked upon as belonging to a specific form of experience, which is readily distinguished by the fact that its contents are known through *"introspection"*, or through the *"inner sense"* as it is called if one uses the phrase which has been employed to distinguish introspection from sense-perception through the outer senses.

Neither of these definitions, however, is satisfactory to the psychology of to-day. The first or metaphysical definition belongs to a period of development that lasted longer in this science than in others, but is here, too, forever left behind, since psychology has developed into an *empirical discipline,* operating with methods of its own; and since the *discipline,* operating with methods of its own; and since the "mental sciences" have gained recognition as a great department of scientific investigation, distinct from the sphere of the natural sciences, and requiring as a general groundwork an independent psychology, free from all metaphysical theories.

The second or empirical definition, which sees in psychology a "science of inner experience", is inadequate because it may give rise to the misunderstanding that psychology has to do with objects totally different from the objects of so-called "outer experience". It is, indeed, true that there are certain contents of experience which belong in the sphere of psychological investigation, and are not to be found among the objects and processes studied by natural science; such are our feelings, emotions, and decisions. On the other hand, there is not a single natural phenomenon that may not, from a different point of view, become an object of psychology. A stone, a plant, a tone, a ray of light, are, when treated as natural phenomena, objects of mineralogy, botany, physics, etc. In so far, however, as they are at the same time *ideas*, they are objects of psychology, for psychology seeks to account for the genesis of these ideas, and for their relations, both to other ideas and to those psychical processes, such as feelings, volitions, etc., which are not referred to external objects. There is, then, no such thing as an "inner sense" which can be regarded as an organ of introspection, and as distinct from the outer senses, or organs of objective perception. The ideas of which psychology seeks to investigate the attributes, are identical with those upon which natural science is based; while the subjective activities of feeling, emotion, and volition, which are neglected in natural science, are not known through special organs, but are directly and inseparably connected with the ideas referred to external objects.

2. It follows, then, that the expressions outer experience and inner experience do not indicate different objects, but *different points of view* from which we take up the consideration and scientific treatment of a unitary experience. We are naturally led to these points of view, because **every concrete experience** immediately divides into **two factors:** into a **content** presented to us, and our **apprehension** of this content. We call the first of these factors *objects of experience,* the second, *experiencing subject*. This division indicates two directions for the treatment of experience. One is that of the *natural sciences,* which concern themselves with the *objects* of experience, thought of as independent of the subject. The other is that of *psychology,* which investigates the whole content of experience in its relations to the subject and also in regard to the attributes which this content derives directly from the subject. The point of view of natural science may, accordingly, be designated as that of *mediate experience,* since it is possible only after abstracting from the subjective factor present in all actual experience; the point of view of psychology, on the other hand, may be designated as that of *immediate experience,* since it purposely does away with this abstraction and all its consequences.

3. The assignment of this problem to psychology, making it a general, empirical science coordinate with the natural sciences, and supplementary to them, is justified by the method of all the *mental sciences,* for which psychology furnishes the basis. All of these sciences, philology, history and political and social science, have as their subject-matter, immediate experience as determined by the interaction of objects with knowing and acting subjects. None of the mental sciences employs the abstractions and hypothetical supplementary concepts of natural science; quite otherwise, they all accept ideas and the accompanying subjective activities as immediate reality. The effort is then made to explain the single components of this reality through their mutual interconnections. This method of psychological interpretation employed in *each of the special mental sciences,* must also be the mode of procedure in psychology itself. . . .

2. GENERAL FORMS OF PSYCHOLOGY.

1. The view that psychology is an empirical science which deals, not with a limited group of specific contents of experience, but with the immediate contents of all experience, is of recent origin. It encounters even in the science of today hostile views,

which are to be looked upon, in general, as the survivals of earlier stages of development, and which are in turn arrayed against one another according to their attitudes on the question of the relations of psychology to philosophy and to the other sciences. On the basis of the two definitions mentioned above (§1, I) as being the most widely accepted, two chief forms of psychology may be distinguished: *metaphysical psychology* and *empirical psychology.* Each is further divided into a number of special tendencies.

Metaphysical psychology generally values very little the empirical analysis and causal interpretation of psychical processes. Regarding psychology as a part of philosophical metaphysics, the chief effort of such psychology is directed toward the discovery of definition of the "nature of mind" which shall be in accord with the metaphysical system to which the particular form of psychology belongs. After a metaphysical concept of mind has thus been established, the attempt is made to deduce from it the actual content of psychical experience. The characteristic which distinguishes metaphysical psychology from empirical psychology is, then, to be found in the attempt of metaphysical psychology to deduce psychical processes, not from other psychical processes, but from some substratum entirely unlike these processes themselves: either from the manifestations of a special mind-substance, or from the attributes and processes of matter. According as the substratum of psychical processes is defined in the one way or the other, metaphysical psychology branches off in *two* directions. In the first place, it may become *spiritualistic psychology,* in which case it considers psychical processes as the manifestations of a *specific* mind-substance and regards this mind-substance either as essentially different from matter (*dualism*), or as related in nature to matter (*monism* or *monadology*). The metaphysical tendency of spiritualistic psychology is expressed in the assumption of the *supersensible* nature of mind, and in connection with this, the assumption of the immortality of the mind. Sometimes the further notion of pre-existence is also added. In the second place metaphysical psychology may become *materialistic psychology.* It then refers psychical processes to the *same* material substratum as that which natural science employs for the hypothetical explanation of natural phenomena. According to this view, psychical processes, like physical vital processes, are connected with certain organizations of material particles which are formed during the life of the individual and broken up at the end of that life. The metaphysical character of this form of psychology is determined by its denial that the mind is supersensible in its nature as is asserted by spiritualistic psychology. In order to make good its position such a materialistic form of psychology resorts to one of the two following devices. It may explain the content of psychological experience by means of a vague and inexact theory of molecular processes in the brain (*mechanical* materialism); or it may regard sensation as a necessary attribute, either of all material particles, or else of brain molecules in particular, in which case it treats all complex mental processes as combinations of such sensations, and explains their rise as the result of various combinations of physical brain processes (*psycho-physical* materialism). Materialism in its various forms and spiritualistic psychology in its various forms, agree in that they do not seek to interpret psychical experience by experience itself, but rather attempt to derive this experience from some kind of presuppositions in regard to hypothetical processes which are assumed to take place in some metaphysical substratum.

2. From the strife that followed these attempts at metaphysical explanation, *empirical psychology* arose. Wherever empirical psychology is consistently carried out, it either strives to arrange psychical processes under general concepts derived directly from the interconnection of these processes themselves, or it begins with certain of these processes, as a rule with the simpler ones, and then explains the more complicated processes as the results of the interaction of those with which it began. There may be various fundamental principles upon which to base such an empirical interpretation, and thus it becomes possible to distinguish several varieties of empirical psychology. In general, these may be classified according to *two* principles of division. The *first principle* has reference to the relation of inner and outer experience and to the attitude which the two branches of empirical science, namely natural science and psychology, take toward each other. The *second principle* refers to the facts themselves, or to the derived concepts which are employed in the interpretation of mental processes. Every system of empirical psychology takes its place under both of these principles of classification.

3. On the *general question as to the nature of psychical experience* there stand over against each other the two forms of psychology already mentioned (§1) on account of their decisive significance in determining the problem of psychology: *psychology of the inner sense*, and *psychology as the science of immediate experience*. The first treats psychical processes as contents of a *special* sphere of experience coordinate with the sphere of experiences which are derived through the outer senses and are assigned to the natural sciences. It also holds that the two spheres of experience though coordinate are totally different from each other. The second form of psychology, namely psychology as the science of immediate experience, recognizes no real difference between inner and outer experience, but finds the distinction only in the different *points of view* from which unitary experience is considered in the two cases.

The first of these two varieties of empirical psychology is the older. It arose primarily through the effort to establish the independence of psychological observation in the face of the encroachments of natural philosophy. In thus coordinating natural science and psychology, it sees the justification for the equal recognition of both spheres of science in the fact that they have entirely different objects and modes of perceiving these objects. This view has influenced empirical psychology in two ways. First, it favored the opinion that psychology should employ empirical methods, at the same time holding that these methods, like psychological experience, should be fundamentally different from those of natural science. Second, it gave rise to the necessity of showing some connection or other between these two kinds of experience, which were supposed to be different. In response to the first demand, it was chiefly the psychology of the inner sense that developed the method of *pure introspection* (§ 3, 2). In attempting to solve the second problem, this psychology was necessarily driven back to a metaphysical basis, because of its assumption of a difference between the physical and the psychical contents of experience. For, from the very nature of the case, it is impossible, from the position here taken, to explain the relations of inner to outer experience, or the so-called "interaction between body and mind", except through metaphysical presuppositions. These presuppositions must then, in turn, affect the psychological investigation itself in such a way as to result in the importation of metaphysical hypotheses into it.

4. Essentially distinct from the psychology of the inner sense is the form of psychology which defines itself as "the science of immediate experience". Regarding, as it does, outer and inner experience, not as different parts of experience, but as different ways of looking at one and the same experience, this form of psychology can not admit any fundamental difference between the methods of psychology and those of natural science. It has, therefore, sought above all to cultivate *experimental* methods which shall lead to just such an exact analysis of psychical processes as that which the explanatory natural sciences undertake in the case of natural phenomena, the only differences being those which arise from the diverse points of view. This form of psychology holds, futhermore, that the special mental sciences which have to do with concrete mental processes and creations, stand on the same basis as itself, that is, on the basis of a scientific consideration of the immediate contents of experience and of their relations to acting subjects. It follows, then, that psychological analysis of the most general mental products, such as language, mythological ideas, and laws of custom, is to be regarded as an aid to the understanding of all the more complicated psychical processes. In its methods, accordingly, this form of psychology stands in close relation to other sciences: as *experimental* psychology, to the natural sciences; as *social psychology,* to the special mental sciences.

Finally, from this point of view, the question of the relation between psychical and physical objects disappears entirely. They are not different objects at all, but one and the same content of experience. This content is examined in the one case, that is, in the natural sciences, after abstracting from the subject. In the other case, that is, in psychology, it is examined in its immediate character and its complete relation to the subject. All metaphysical hypotheses as to the relation of psychical and physical objects are, when viewed from this position, attempts to solve a problem which never would have existed if the case had been correctly stated. Psychology must then dispense with metaphysical supplementary hypotheses in regard to the interconnection of psychical processes, because there processes are the immediate contents of experience. Another method of procedure, however, is open since inner and outer experience are supplementary points of view. Wherever breaks appear in the interconnection of psychical processes, it is allowable to carry on the investigation according to the physical methods of considering these same processes, in order to discover whether the absent link can be thus supplied. The same holds for the reverse method of filling up the breaks in the continuity of our physiological knowledge, by means of elements derived from psychological investigation. Only on the basis of such a view, which sets the two forms of knowledge in their true relation, is it possible for psychology to become in the fullest sense an empirical science. Only in this way, too, can physiology become the true supplementary science of psychology, and psychology, on the other hand, the auxiliary of physiology.

5. Under the *second* principle of classification mentioned above (2), that is, the *principle based on the facts or concepts with which the investigation of psychical processes begins,* there are *two* varieties of empirical psychology to be distinguished. They are, furthermore, **successive stages** in the development of psychological interpretation. The first corresponds to a **descriptive,** the second to an **explanatory** stage. The attempt to present a discriminating description of the different psychical processes, gave rise to the need of an appropriate *classification.* Class-concepts were

formed, under which the various processes were grouped; and the attempt was made to satisfy the need of an interpretation in each particular case, by subsuming the components of a given compound process under their proper class-concepts. Such concepts are, for example, sensation, knowledge, attention, memory, imagination, understanding, and will. They correspond to the general concepts of physics which are derived from the immediate perception of natural phenomena, such as weight, heat, sound, and light. Like those concepts of physics, the derived psychical concepts mentioned may serve as a first means of grouping the facts, but they contribute nothing whatever to the explanation of these facts. Empirical psychology has, however, often been guilty of confounding description with explanation. Thus, the *faculty-psychology* considered these class-concepts as psychical forces or faculties, and referred psychical processes to their separate or united activity.

6. Opposed to this method of treatment found in descriptive faculty-psychology, is that of *explanatory* psychology. When consistently empirical, the latter must base its interpretations on certain facts which themselves belong to psychical experience. These facts may, however, be taken from different spheres of psychical activity, and so it comes that explanatory treatment may be further divided into *two* varieties which correspond respectively to the two factors, objects and subject, which go to make up immediate experience. When the chief emphasis is laid on the *objects* of immediate experience, **intellectualistic psychology** results. This type of psychology attempts to derive all psychical processes, especially the subjective feelings, impulses, and volitions, from ideas, or intellectual processes as they may be called on account of their importance for knowledge of the objective world. If, on the contrary, the chief emphasis is laid on the way in which immediate experience arises in the subject, there results a variety of explanatory psychology which attributes to those subjective activities which are not referred to external objects, a position as independent as the assigned to ideas. This variety has been called *voluntaristic psychology,* because of the importance which must be conceded to volitional processes in comparison with other subjective processes.

Of the two varieties of psychology which result from the different general attitudes on the question of the nature of inner experience (3), that form which we have called psychology of the inner sense commonly tends towards intellectualism. This is due to the fact that, when the inner sense is coordinated with the outer senses, the contents of psychical experience which first attract consideration are those which are presented as objects to this inner sense in a manner analogous to that in which natural objects are presented to the outer senses. It is assumed, accordingly, that the character of objects can be attributed to *ideas* alone of all the contents of psychical experience, because ideas are regarded as *images* of the external objects presented to the outer senses. Ideas are, thus, looked upon as the only real objects of the inner sense, while all processes not referred to external objects, as for example the feelings, are interpreted as obscure ideas, or ideas related to one's own body, or, finally, as effects arising from combinations of ideas.

The psychology of immediate experience (4), on the other hand, tends toward voluntarism. It is obvious that here, where the chief problem of psychology is held to be the investigation of the subjective rise of all experience, special attention will be devoted to those factors from which natural science abstracts.

7. *Intellectualistic* psychology has in the course of its development separated into *two* forms. In one form; the *logical* processes of judgment and reasoning are regarded as the typical forms of all psychoses; in the other, certain combinations of successive memory images distinguished by their frequency, the so-called *associations of ideas,* are accepted as typical. The *logical theory* is most clearly related to the popular method of psychological interpretation and is, therefore, the older. It finds some acceptance even in modern times. The *association theory* arose from the philosophical empiricism of the eighteenth century. The two theories stand, to a certain extent, in antithesis, since the first attempts to reduce the totality of psychical processes to higher processes, while the latter seeks to reduce this same totality of processes to lower and, as it is assumed, simpler forms of intellectual activity. Both are one-sided, and not only fail to explain affective processes and volitional processes on the basis of the assumption with which they start, but are not able to give a complete interpretation even of the intellectual processes.

8. The union of psychology of the inner sense with the intellectualistic view has led to a peculiar assumption which has been in many cases fatal to psychological theory. We may define this assumption briefly as the *erroneous and intellectualistic attribution of the nature of things, to ideas.* Not only was an analogy assumed between the objects of the so-called inner sense and those of the outer senses, but the former were regarded as the images of the latter; and so it came that the attributes which natural science ascribes to external objects, were also transferred to the immediate objects of the "inner sense". The assumption was made, accordingly, that ideas are themselves permanent things, just as much as the external objects to which we refer them; that these ideas disappear from consciousness and come back unchanged into it; that they may, indeed, be more or less intensely and clearly perceived, according as the inner sense is stimulated through the outer senses or not, and according to the degree of attention concentrated upon them, but that on the whole they remain constant in qualitative character.

9. In all these respects *voluntaristic psychology* is opposed to intellectualism. While the latter assumes an inner sense and specific objects of inner experience, voluntarism is related to the view that inner experience is identical with *immediate* experience. According to this doctrine, the content of psychological experience does not consist of a sum of objects presented to the subject, but it consists of all that which makes up the process of experience, that is, of all the experiences of the subject in their immediate character, unmodified by abstraction or reflection. It follows of necessity that the contents of psychological experience are here regarded as an *interconnection of processes.* Psychical facts are *occurrences,* not objects; they take place, like all occurrences, in time and are never the same at a given point in time as they were during the preceding moment. In this sense *volitions* are *typical* for the understanding of all mental experiences. Voluntaristic psychology, accordingly, does not by any means assert that volition is the only real form of psychosis, but merely that, with its closely related feelings and emotions, volition is just as essential a component of psychological experience as are sensations and ideas. It holds, further, that all other psychical processes are to be thought of after the analogy of volitions, they too being a series of continuous changes in time, not a sum of permanent objects, as intellectualism generally assumes in consequence of its erroneous

attribution to ideas of those properties which we attribute to external objects. The recognition of the *immediate* reality of psychological experience renders impossible any attempt to derive the particular components of psychical phenomena from processes specifically different from the experiences themselves. It also makes it obvious that the analogous attempts of metaphysical psychology to derive all conscious processes from imaginary processes of an hypothetical substratum, are inconsistent with the real problem of psychology. While psychology concerns itself, accordingly, with immediate experience, it nevertheless assumes from the first that all psychical contents contain objective as well as subjective factors. These are to be distinguished only through deliberate abstraction, and can never appear as really separate processes. In fact, observation teaches that there are no ideas which do not arouse in us feelings and impulses of different intensities, and also that a feeling or a volition which does not refer to some ideated object is altogether impossible.

10. The governing principles of the psychological position maintained in the following chapters may be summed up in *three* general statements.

1. Inner, or psychological experience is not a special sphere of experience apart from others, but is *immediate experience* in its totality.

2. This immediate experience is not made up of unchanging contents, but of an *interconnected system of occurrences;* not of objects, but of *processes,* of *universal human experiences* and their relations in accordance with certain laws.

3. Each of these processes contains an *objective content* and a *subjective process,* thus including the general conditions both of all knowledge and of all practical human activity.

Corresponding to these three general principles, we have a *threefold relation of psychology* to the other sciences.

1. As the science of immediate experience, it is *supplementary* to the *natural sciences,* which, in consequence of their abstraction from the subject, have to do only with the objective, *mediate* contents of experience. Any particular fact can, strictly speaking, be understood in its full significance only after it has been subjected to the analyses of both natural science and psychology. In this sense, then, physics and physiology are auxiliary to psychology, and the latter is, in turn, supplementary to the natural sciences.

2. As the science of the universal forms of immediate human experience and their combination in accordance with certain laws, it is the *foundation of the mental sciences.* These sciences treat in all cases of the activities issuing from immediate human experiences, and of the effects of such activities. Since psychology has for its problem the investigation of the forms and laws of these activities, it is at once the most general mental science, and the foundation of all the others, that is, of philology, history, political economy, jurisprudence, etc.

3. Since psychology pays equal attention to *both* the subjective and objective conditions which underlie not only theoretical knowledge, but practical activity as well, and since it seeks to determine the interrelation of these subjective and objective conditions, it is the empirical discipline the results of which are most immediately useful in the investigation of the general problems of the *theory of knowledge* and *ethics,* the two foundations of *philosophy.* Thus, psychology is, in relation to the natural sciences, the *supplementary science;* in relation to the mental sciences it is the *fundamental science;* and in relation to philosophy it is the *propaedeutic empirical science. . . .*

10a. The following tabular summary presents in their systematic relation, the chief forms of psychology above described (1–3).

METAPHYSICAL PSYCHOLOGY.

Spiritualistic psychology.		Materialistic psychology.	
Dualistic psychology.	Monistic psychology. (Monadological systems)	Mechanical materialism.	Psycho-physical materialism.

EMPIRICAL PSYCHOLOGY.

Psychology of inner sense. (Pure introspection)	Psychology as science of immediate experience. (Experimental and Social psychology)	
Descriptive psychology. (Faculty-psychology)	Explanatory psychology.	
	Intellectualistic psychology.	Voluntaristic psychology.
	Logical Interpretation.	Association psychology.

3. METHODS OF PSYCHOLOGY.

1. Since psychology has for its object, not specific contents of experience, but *general experience in its immediate character,* it can make use of no methods except such as the empirical sciences in general employ for the determination, analysis, and causal interpretation of facts. The fact that natural science abstracts from the subject, while psychology does not, can be no ground for modifications in the essential character of the methods employed in the two fields, though this fact does modify the way in which the methods are applied.

The natural sciences may serve, because they matured earlier, as *an example for psychology* in the matter of method. These sciences *make use of two chief methods,* namely *experiment* and *observation. Experiment* is observation under the condition of purposive control by the observer of the rise and course of the phenomena observed. *Observation,* in the narrower sense of the term, is the investigation of phenomena without such control, the occurrences being accepted just as they are naturally presented to the observer in the course of experience. Wherever experiment is possible, it is always used in the natural sciences; for under all circumstances, even when the phenomena is themselves present the conditions for sufficiently exact observation, it is an advantage to be able to control at will the rise and progress of these phenomena, or to isolate the various components of a composite phenomenon. Yet, even in the natural sciences, the two methods have been distinguished according to their spheres of application. It is held that the experimental methods are indispensable for certain problems, while in others the desired end may not infrequently be reached through mere observation. If we neglect a few exceptional cases due to special relations, these two classes of problems correspond to the general division of natural phenomena into *processes* and *objects.*

Experimental control is required in the exact determination of the course, and in the analysis of the components, of any *natural process,* such for example as light vibration, sound vibration, and electric discharge, or the contraction of a muscle. As a rule such control is desirable because exact observation is possible only when the observer can determine the moment at which the process shall commence. It is also indispensable in separating the various components of a complex phenomenon from one another. As a rule, this is possible only through the addition or subtraction of certain conditions, or through a quantitative variation of them. The case is different with *objects of nature.* They are relatively constant and are always at the observer's disposal and ready for examination. In dealing with such constant objects, experimental investigation is really necessary only when the production and modification of the objects are the subjects to be investigated. When, on the contrary, the only question is the actual nature of these objects, mere observation is generally enough. Thus, mineralogy, botany, zoology, anatomy, and geography, are pure sciences of observation so long as they are kept free from the physical, chemical, and physiological problems which are, indeed, frequently brought into them, but which have to do with processes of nature, not with the objects in themselves.

2. If we apply these considerations to psychology, it is obvious at once, from the very nature of its subject-matter, that exact observation is here possible only in the form of *experimental* observation. The contents of this science are exclusively *processes,* not permanent objects. In order to investigate with exactness the rise and progress of these processes, their composition out of various components, and the interrelations of these components, we must first of all control their beginnings, and we must also vary their conditions at will. This possible here, as in all cases, only through experiment. Besides this general reason there is another reason which is peculiar to psychology, and does not apply at all to natural phenomena. In the case of the natural sciences we purposely abstract from the perceiving subject, and

under circumstances, especially when favored by the phenomena, as in astronomy, mere observation may succeed in determining with adequate certainty the objective contents of the processes. Psychology, on the contrary, is debarred from this abstraction by its fundamental principles; and proper conditions for chance observation can appear only when the same objective components of immediate experience are frequently repeated in connection with the same subjective states. It is hardly to be expected, in view of the great complexity of psychical processes, that this will ever be the case. Such chance coincidence is especially improbable since the very *intention to observe,* which is a necessary condition of all exact investigation, modifies essentially the rise and progress of psychical processes. The chief problem of psychology, however, is the exact investigation of the rise and progress of subjective processes, and it can readily be seen that in such investigations the intention to observe either essentially modifies the facts to be observed, or completely suppresses them, at least if the observation is of the ordinary introspective type unaided by experimental devices of any sort. If, on the other hand, we consider the experimental methods, we see that psychology is led, through the very nature of the origin of the processes with which it deals, to employ, just as do physics and physiology, the experimental mode of procedure. A sensation arises under the most favorable conditions for observation when it is aroused by an external sense stimulus. The *idea* of an *object* is always produced *originally* by the more or less *complicated cooperation* of *sense stimuli.* If we wish to study the way in which an idea is formed, we can choose no method other than that of imitating this natural way in which an idea arises. In doing this, we have at the same time the great advantage of being able to modify the idea itself by changing at will the combination of the impressions that cooperate to form it, and of thus learning what influence each single condition exercises on the product. Memory images, it is true, can not be directly aroused through external sense impressions, but follow these impressions after a longer or shorter interval. Yet, it is obvious that the attributes even of memory images can be most accurately learned, not by waiting for their chance arrival, but by using such memory ideas as may be aroused in a systematic, experimental way, through immediately preceding impressions. The same is true of feelings and volitions; they will be presented in the form best adapted to exact investigation when those impressions are purposely produced which experience has shown to be regularly connected with affective and volitional reactions. There is, then, no fundamental psychical process to which experimental methods can not be applied, and therefore none in the investigation of which such methods are not logically required.

3. *Pure observation,* such as is possible in many departments of natural science, is, from the very character of psychical phenomena, impossible in *individual* psychology. The possibility of pure observation would be conceivable only under the condition that there existed permanent psychical objects, independent of our attention, similar to the relatively permanent objects of nature, which remain unchanged by our observation. There are, however, certain facts at the disposal of psychology, which, although they are not real objects, nevertheless, have the character of psychical objects, inasmuch as they possess the attributes of relative per-

manence and independence of the observer, and are unapproachable by means of experiment in the common acceptance of the term. These facts are the *mental products* which have developed in the course of history, such as language, mythological ideas, and customs. The origin and development of these products depend in every case on general psychical conditions which may be inferred from the objective attributes of the products. All such mental products of a general character presuppose the existence of a mental *community* composed of many individuals, though, of course, their deepest sources are the psychical attributes of the individual. Because of this dependence on the community, in particular on the social community, the whole department of psychological investigation here involved is designated as *social psychology,* and is distinguished from individual psychology, or *experimental* psychology as it may be called because of its predominating method. In the present stage of the science these two branches of psychology are generally taken up in different treatises, although they are not so much different departments as different *methods*. So-called social psychology corresponds to the method of pure observation, the objects of observation in this case being the mental products. The necessary connection of these products with social communities, which has given to social psychology its name, is due to the fact that the mental products of the individual are of too variable a character to be the subjects of objective observation. The phenomena gain the necessary degree of constancy only when they become collective.

Thus psychology has, like natural science, *two* exact methods: the experimental method, serving for the analysis of simpler psychical processes, and the observation of general mental products, serving for the investigation of the higher psychical processes and developments.

3a. The introduction of the experimental method into psychology was originally due to the modes of procedure in physiology, especially in the physiology of the sense-organs and the nervous system. For this reason experimental psychology is also commonly called "physiological psychology"; and works treating it under this title regularly contain those supplementary facts from the physiology of the nervous system and of the sense-organs, which require special discussion with a view to the interests of psychology, though in themselves these facts belong to physiology alone. "Physiological psychology" is accordingly, an intermediate discipline which is, however, as the name indicates, primarily *psychology,* and is, apart from the supplementary physiological facts that it presents, essentially the same as "experimental psychology" in the sense above defined. The attempt sometimes made, to distinguish psychology proper from physiological psychology, by assigning to the first the psychological interpretation of inner experience, and to the second the derivation of this experience from physiological processes, is to be rejected as inadmissible. There is only *one* kind of casual explanation in psychology, and that is the derivation of more complex psychical processes from simpler ones. In this method of interpretation, physiological elements can be used only as supplementary aids, because of the relation between natural science and psychology as above defined (§2, 4).

Memory a Contribution to Experimental Psychology

Hermann Ebbinghaus

CHAPTER 1
OUR KNOWLEDGE CONCERNING MEMORY

Section 1. Memory in its Effects

The language of life as well as of science in attributing a memory to the mind attempts to point out the facts and their interpretation somewhat as follows:

Mental states of every kind,—sensations, feelings, ideas,—which were at one time present in consciousness and then have disappeared from it, have not with their disappearance absolutely ceased to exist. Although the inwardly-turned look may no longer be able to find them, nevertheless they have not been utterly destroyed and annulled, but in a certain manner they continue to exist, stored up, so to speak, in the memory. We cannot, of course, directly observe their present existence, but it is revealed by the effects which come to our knowledge with a certainty like that with which we infer the existence of the stars below the horizon. These effects are of different kinds.

In a first group of cases we can call back into consciousness by an exertion of the will directed to this purpose the seemingly lost states (or, indeed, in case these consisted in immediate sense-perceptions, we can recall their true memory images): that is, we can reproduce them *voluntarily*. During attempts of this sort,—that is, attempts to recollect—all sorts of images toward which our aim was not directed, accompany the desired images to the light of consciousness. Often, indeed, the latter entirely miss the goal, but as a general thing among the representations is found the one which we sought, and it is immediately recognized as something formerly experienced. It would be absurd to suppose that our will has created it anew and, as it were, out of nothing; it must have been present somehow or somewhere. The will, so to speak, has only discovered it and brought it to us again.

In a second group of cases this survival is even more striking. Often, even after years, mental states once present in consciousness return to it with apparent spontaneity and without any act of the will; that is, they are reproduced *involuntarily*. Here, also, in the majority of cases we at once recognize the returned mental state as one that has already been experienced; that is, we remember it. Under certain conditions, however, this accompanying consciousness is lacking, and we know only indirectly that the "now" must be identical with the "then"; yet we receive in this way a no less valid proof for its existence during the intervening time.

As more exact observation teaches us, the occurrence of these involuntary reproductions is not an entirely random and accidental one. On the contrary they are brought about through the instrumentality of other, immediately present mental images. Moreover they occur in certain regular ways which in general terms are described under the so-called 'laws of association.'

Finally there is a third and large group to be reckoned with here. The vanished mental states give indubitable proof of their continuing existence even if they themselves do not return to consciousness at all, or at least not exactly at the given time. Employment of a certain range of thought facilitates under certain conditions the employment of a similar range of thought, even if the former does not come before the mind directly either in its methods or in its results. The boundless domain of the effect of accumulated experiences belongs here. This effect results from the frequent conscious occurrence of any condition or process, and consists in facilitating the occurrence and progress of similar processes. This effect is not fettered by the condition that the factors constituting the experience shall return *in toto* to consciousness. This may incidentally be the case with a part of them; it must not happen to a too great extent and with too great clearness, otherwise the course of the present process will immediately be disturbed. Most of these experiences remain concealed from consciousness and yet produce an effect with is significant and which authenticates their previous existence.

Section 2. Memory in its Dependence

Along with this bare knowledge of the existence of memory and its *effects*, there is abundant knowledge concerning the *conditions* upon which depend the vitality of that inner survival as well as the fidelity and promptness of the reproduction.

How differently do different *individuals* behave in this respect! One retains and reproduces well; another, poorly. And not only does this comparison hold good when different individuals are compared with each other, but also when different phases of the existence of the same individual are compared: morning and evening, youth and old age, find him different in this respect.

Differences in the *content* of the thing to be reproduced are of great influence. Melodies may become a source of torment by the undesired persistency of their return. Forms and colors are not so importunate; and if they do return, it is with noticeable loss of clearness and certainty. The musician writes for the orchestra what his inner voice sings to him; the painter rarely relies without disadvantage solely upon the images which his inner eye presents to him; nature gives him his forms, study governs his combinations of them. It is with something of a struggle that past states of feeling are realized; when realized, and this is often only through the instrumentality of the movements which accompanied them, they are but pale shadows of themselves. Emotionally true singing is rarer than technically correct singing.

If the two foregoing points of view are taken together—differences in individuals and differences in content—an endless number of differences come to light. One individual overflows with poetical reminiscences, another directs symphonies from memory, while numbers and formulae, which come to a third without effort, slip away from the other two as from a polished tone.

Very great is the dependence of retention and reproduction upon the intensity of the *attention* and *interest* which were attached to the mental states the first time they were present. The burnt child shuns the fire, and the dog which has been beaten runs from the whip, after a single vivid experience. People in whom we are interested we may see daily and yet not be able to recall the color of their hair or of their eyes.

Under ordinary circumstances, indeed, frequent repetitions are indispensable in order to make possible the reproduction of a given content. Vocabularies, discourses, and poems of any length cannot be learned by a single repetition even with the greatest concentration of attention on the part of an individual of very great ability. By a sufficient number of repetitions their final mastery is ensured, and by additional later reproductions gain in assurance and ease is secured.

Left to itself every mental content gradually loses its capacity for being revived, or at least suffers loss in this regard under the influence of time. Facts crammed at examination time soon vanish, if they were not sufficiently grounded by other study and later subjected to a sufficient review. But even a thing so early and deeply founded as one's mother tongue is noticeably impaired if not used for several years.

Section 3. Deficiencies in our Knowledge concerning Memory

The foregoing sketch of our knowledge concerning memory makes no claim to completeness. To it might be added such a series of propositions known to psychology as the following: "He who learns quickly also forgets quickly," "Relatively long series of ideas are retained better than relatively short ones," "Old people forget most quickly the things they learned last," and the like. Psychology is wont to make the picture rich with anecdote and illustration. But—and this is the main point—even if we particularise our knowledge by a most extended use of illustrative material, everything that we can say retains the indefinite, general, and comparative character of the propositions quoted above. Our information comes almost exclusively from the observation of extreme and especially striking cases. We are able to describe these quite correctly in a general way and in vague expressions of more or less. We suppose, again quite correctly, that the same influences exert themselves, although in a less degree, in the case of the inconspicuous, but a thousandfold more frequent, daily activities of memory. But if our curiosity carries us further and we crave more specific and detailed information concerning these dependencies and interdependencies, both those already mentioned and others,—if we put questions, so to speak, concerning their inner structure—our answer is silence. How does the disappearance of the ability to reproduce, forgetfulness, depend upon the length of time during with no repetitions have taken place? What proportion does the increase in the certainty of reproduction bear to the number of repetitions? How do these relations vary with the greater or less intensity of the interest in the thing to be reproduced? These and similar questions no one can answer.

This inability does not arise from a chance neglect of investigation of these relations. We cannot say that tomorrow, or whenever we wish to take time, we can investigate these problems. On the contrary this inability is inherent in the nature of the questions themselves. Although the conceptions in question—namely, degrees of forgetfulness, of certainty and interest—are quite correct, we have no means for establishing such degrees in our experience except at the extremes, and even then we cannot accurately limit those extremes. We feel therefore that we are not at all in a condition to undertake the investigation. We form certain conceptions during striking experiences, but we cannot find any realization of them in the similar but less striking experiences of everyday life. *Vice versa* there are probably many conceptions which we have not as yet formed which would be serviceable and indispensable for a clear understanding of the facts, and their theoretical mastery.

The amount of detailed information which an individual has at his command and his theoretical elaborations of the same are mutually dependent; they grow in and through each other. It is because of the indefinite and little specialised character of our knowledge that the theories concerning the processes of memory, reproduction, and association have been up to the present time of so little value for a proper comprehension of those processes. For example, to express our ideas concerning their physical basis we use different metaphors—stored up ideas, engraved images, well-beaten paths. There is only one thing certain about these figures of speech and that is that they are not suitable.

Of course the existence of all these deficiencies has its perfectly sufficient basis in the extraordinary difficulty and complexity of the matter. It remains to be proved whether, in spite of the clearest insight into the inadequacy of our knowledge, we shall ever make any actual progress. Perhaps we shall always have to be resigned to this. But a somewhat greater accessibility than has so far been realised in this field cannot be denied to it, as I hope to prove presently. If by any chance a way to a deeper penetration into this matter should present itself, surely, considering the significance of memory for all mental phenomena, it should be our wish to enter that path at once. For at the very worst we should prefer to see regeneration arise from the failure of earnest investigations rather than from persistent, helpless astonishment in the face of their difficulties.

CHAPTER 11
THE POSSIBILITY OF ENLARGING
OUR KNOWLEDGE OF MEMORY

Section 4. The Method of Natural Science

The method of obtaining exact measurements—*i.e.*, numerically exact ones—of the inner structure of causal relations is, by virtue of its nature, of general validity. This method, indeed, has been so exclusively used and so fully worked out by the natural sciences that, as a rule, it is defined as something peculiar to them, as *the* method of natural science. Top repeat, however, its logical nature makes it generally applicable to all spheres of existence and phenomena. Moreover, the possibility of defining accurately and exactly the actual behavior of any process whatever, and thereby of giving a reliable basis for the direct comprehension of its connections depends above all upon the possibility of applying this method.

We all know of what this method consists: an attempt is made to keep constant the mass of conditions which have proven themselves causally connected with a certain result; one of these conditions is isolated from the rest and varied in a way that can be numerically described; then the accompanying change on the side of the effect is ascertained by measurement of computation.

Two fundamental and insurmountable difficulties, seem, however, to oppose a transfer of this method to the investigation of the causal relations of mental events in general and of those of memory in particular. In the first place, how are we to keep even approximately constant the bewildering mass of causal conditions which, in so far as they are of mental nature, almost completely elude our control, and which, moreover, are subject to endless and incessant change? In the second place, by what possible means are we to measure numerically the mental processes which flit by so quickly and which on introspection are so hard to analyse? I shall first discuss the second difficulty in connection, of course, with memory, since that is our present concern.

Section 5. Introduction of Numerical Measurements for Memory Contents

If we consider once more the conditions of retention and reproduction mentioned above (§2), but now with regard to the possiblity of computation, we shall see that with two of them, at least, a numerical determination and a numerical variation are possible. The different times which elapse between the first production and the reproduction of a series of ideas can be measured and the repetitions necessary to make these series reproducible can be counted. At first sight, however, there seems to be nothing similar to this on the side of the effects. Here there is only one alternative, a reproduction is either possible or it is not possible. It takes place or it does not take place. Of course we take for granted that it may approach, under different conditions, more or less near to actual occurrence so that in its subliminal existence the series possesses graded differences. But as long as we limit our observations to that which, either by chance or at the call of our will, comes out from this inner realm, all these differences are for us equally non-existent.

By somewhat less dependence upon introspection we can, however, by indirect means force these differences into the open. A poem is learned by heart and then not again repeated. We will suppose that after a half year it has been forgotten: no effort of recollection is able to call it back again into consciousness. At best only isolated fragments return. Suppose that the poem is again learned by heart. It then becomes evident that, although to all appearances totally forgotten, it still in a certain sense exists and in a way to be effective. The second learning requires noticeably less time or a noticeably smaller number of repetitions than the first. It also requires less time or repetitions than would now be necessary to learn a similar poem of the same length. In this difference in time and number of repetitions we have evidently obtained a certain measure for that inner energy which a half year after the first learning still dwells in that orderly complex of ideas which make up the poem. After a shorter time we should expect to find the difference greater; after a longer time we should expect to find it less. If the first committing to memory is a very careful and long continued one, the difference will be greater than if it is desultory and soon abandoned.

In short, we have without doubt in these differences numerical expressions for the difference between these subliminally persistent series of ideas, differences which otherwise we would have to take for granted and would not be able to demonstrate by direct observation. Therewith we have gained possession of something that is at least like that which we are seeking in our attempt to get a foothold for the application of the method of the natural sciences: namely, phenomena on the side of the effects which are clearly ascertainable, which vary in accordance with the variation of conditions, and which are capable of numerical determination. Whether we possess in them correct measures for these inner differences, and whether we can achieve through them correct conceptions as to the causal relations into which this hidden mental life enters—these questions cannot be answered *a priori*. Chemistry is just as little able to determine *a priori* whether it is the electrical phenomena, or the thermal, or some other accompaniment of the process of chemical union, which gives it its correct measure of the effective forces of chemical affinity. There is only one way to do this, and that is to see whether it is possible to obtain, on the presupposition of the correctness of such an hypothesis, well classified, uncontradictory results, and correct anticipations of the future.

Instead of the simple phenomenon—occurrence or non-occurrence of a reproduction—which admits of no numerical distinction, I intend therefore to consider from the experimental standpoint a more complicated process as the effect, and I shall observe and measure its changes as the conditions are varied. By this I mean the artificial bringing about by an appropriate number of repetitions of a reproduction which would not occur of its own accord.

But in order to realise this experimentally, two conditions at least must be fulfilled.

In the first place, it must be possible to define with some certainty the moment when the goal is reached—*i.e.*, when the process of learning by heart is completed. For if the process of learning by heart is sometimes carried past that moment and sometimes broken off before it, then part of the differences found under the varying circumstances would be due to this inequality, and it would be incorrect to attribute it solely to inner differences in the series of ideas. Consequently among the different reproductions of, say, a poem, occurring during the process of its memorisation, the experimenter must single out one as especially characteristic, and be able to find it again with practical accuracy.

In the second place the presupposition must be allowed that the number of repetitions by means of which, the other conditions being unchanged, this characteristic reproduction is brought about would be every time the same. For if this number, under conditions otherwise equivalent, is now this and not that, the differences arising from varied conditions lose, of course, all significance for the critical evaluation of those varying conditions.

Now, as far as the first condition is concerned, it is easily fulfilled wherever you have what may properly be called learning by heart, as in the case of poems, series of words, tonesequences, and the like. Here, in general, as the number of repetitions increases, reproduction is at first fragmentary and halting; then it gains in certainty; and finally takes place smoothly and without error. The first reproduction in which this last result appears can not only be singled out as especially characteristic, but can also be practically recognised. For convenience I will designate this briefly as the *first possible reproduction.*

The question now is:—Does this fulfill the second condition mentioned above? Is the number of repetitions necessary to bring about this reproduction always the same, the other conditions being equivalent?

However, in this form, the question will be justly rejected because it forces upon us, as if it were an evident supposition, the real point in question, the very heart of the matter, and admits of none but a misleading answer. Anyone will be ready to admit without hesitation that this relation of dependence will be the same if perfect equality of experimental conditions is maintained. The much invoked freedom of the will, at least, has hardly ever been misunderstood by anybody so far as to come in here. But this theoretical constancy is of little value: How shall I find it when the circumstances under which I am actually forced to make my observations are never the same? So I must rather ask:—Can I bring under my control the inevitably and ever fluctuating circumstances and equalise them to such an extent that the constancy presumably existent in the causal relations in question becomes visible and palpable to me?

Thus the discussion of the one difficulty which opposes an exact examination of the causal relations in the mental sphere has led us of itself to the other (§4). A numerical determination of the interdependent changes of cause and effect appears indeed possible if only we can realise the necessary uniformity of the significant conditions in the repetition of our experiments.

Section 6. The Possibility of Maintaining the Constancy of Conditions Requisite for Research

He who considers the complicated processes of the higher mental life or who is occupied with the still more complicated phenomena of the state and of society will general be inclined to deny the possibility of keeping constant the conditions for psychological experimentation. Nothing is more familiar to us than the capriciousness of mental life which brings to nought all foresight and calculation. Factors which are to the highest degree determinative and to the same extent changeable, such as mental vigor, interest in the subject, concentration of attention, changes in the course of thought which have been brought about by sudden fancies and resolves—all these are either not at all under our control or are so only to an unsatisfactory extent.

However, care must be taken not to ascribe too much weight to these views, correct in themselves, when dealing with fields other than those of the processes by the observation of which these views were obtained. All such unruly factors are of the greatest importance for higher mental processes which occur only by an especially favorable concurrence of circumstances. The more lowly, commonplace, and constantly occurring processes are not in the least withdrawn from their influence, but we have it for the most part in our power, when it is a matter of consequence, to make this influence only slightly disturbing. Sensorial perception, for example, certainly occurs with greater or less accuracy according to the degree of interest; it is constantly given other directions by the change of external stimuli and by ideas. But, in spite of that, we are on the whole sufficiently able to see a house just when we want to see it and to receive practically the same picture of it ten times in succession in case no objective change has occurred.

There is nothing *a priori* absurd in the assumption that ordinary retention and reproduction, which, according to general agreement, is ranked next to sensorial perception, should also behave like it in this respect. Whether this is actually the case or not, however, I say now as I said before, cannot be decided in advance. Our present knowledge is much too fragmentary, too general, too largely obtained from the extraordinary to enable us to reach a decision on this point by its aid; that must be reserved for experiments especially adapted to that purpose. We must try in experimental fashion to keep as constant as possible those circumstances whose influence on retention and reproduction is known or suspected, and then ascertain whether that is sufficient. The material must be so chosen that decided differences of interest are, at least to all appearances, excluded; equality of attention may be promoted by preventing external disturbances; sudden fancies are not subject to control, but, on the whole, their disturbing effect is limited to the moment, and will be of comparatively little account if the time of the experiment is extended, etc.

When, however, we have actually obtained in such manner the greatest possible constancy of conditions attainable by us, how are we to know whether this is sufficient for our purpose? When are the circumstances, which will certainly offer differences enough to keen observation, sufficiently constant? The answer may be made:—When upon repetition of the experiment the results remain constant. The latter statement seems simple enough to be self-evident, but on closer approach to the matter still another difficulty is encountered.

Section 7. Constant Averages

When shall the results obtained from repeated experiments under circumstances as much alike as possible pass for constant or sufficiently constant? Is it when one result has the same value as the other or at least deviates so little from it that the difference in proportion to its own quantity and for our purposes is of no account?

Evidently not. That would be asking too much, and is not necessarily obtained even by the natural sciences. Then, perhaps it is when the averages from larger groups of experiments exhibit the characteristics mentioned above?

Again evidently not. That would be asking too little. For, if observation of processes that resemble each other from any point of view are thrown together in sufficiently large numbers, fairly constant mean values are almost everywhere obtained which, nevertheless, possess little or no importance for the purposes which we have here. The exact distance of two signal poles, the position of a star at a certain hour, the expansion of a metal for a certain increase of temperature, all the numerous coefficients another constants of physics and chemistry are given us as average values which only approximate to a high degree of constancy. On the other hand the number of suicides in a certain month, the average length of life in a given place, the number of teams and pedestrians per day at a certain street corner, and the like, are also noticeably constant, each being an average from large groups of observations. But both kinds of numbers, which I shall temporarily denote as *constants of natural science* and *statistical constants,* are, as everybody knows, constant from different causes and with entirely different significance for the knowledge of causal relations.

These differences can be formulated as follows:—

In the case of the constants of the natural sciences each individual effect is produced by a combination of causes exactly alike. The individual values come out somewhat differently because a certain number of those causes do not always join the combination with exactly the same values (*e. g.,* there are little errors in the adjustment and reading of the instruments, irregularities in the texture or composition of the material examined or employed, etc.). However, experience teaches us that this fluctuation of separate causes does not occur absolutely irregularly but that as a rule it runs through or, rather, tries out limited and comparatively small circles of values symmetrically distributed around a central value. If several cases are brought together the effects of the separate deviations must more and more compensate each other and thereby be swallowed up in the central value around which they occur. And the final result of combining the values will be approximately the same as if the actually changeable causes had remained the same not only conceptually but also numerically. Thus, the average value is in these cases the adequate numerical representative of a conceptually definite and well limited system of causal connections; if one part of the system is varied, the accompanying changes of the average value again give the correct measure for the effect of those deviations on the total complex.

On the other hand, no matter from what point of view statistical constants may be considered it cannot be said of them that each separate value has resulted from the combination of causes which by themselves had fluctuated within tolerably narrow limits and in symmetrical fashion. The separate effects arise, rather, from an oftimes inextricable multiplicity of causal combinations of very different sorts, which, to be sure, may share numerous factors with each other, but which, taken as a whole, have no conceivable community and actually correspond only in some one characteristic of the effects. That the value of the separate factors must be very different is, so to say, self evident. That, nevertheless, approximately constant values appear even here by the combing of large groups—this fact we may make intelligible by saying that in equal and tolerably large intervals of time or extents of space the separate causal combinations will be realised with approximately equal frequency; we do this without doing more than to acknowledge as extant a peculiar and marvellous arrangement of nature. Accordingly these constant mean values represent no definite and separate causal systems but combinations of such which are by no means of themselves transparent. Therefore their changes upon variation of conditions afford no genuine measure of the effects of these variations but only indications of them. They are of no direct value of the setting up of numerically exact relations of dependence but they are preparatory to this.

Let us now turn back to the question raised at the beginning of this section. When may we consider that this equality of conditions which we have striven to realise experimentally has been attained? The answer runs as follows: When the average values of several observations are approximately constant and when at the same time we may assume that the separate cases belong to the same causal system, whose elements, however, are not limited to exclusively constant values, but may run through small circles of numerical values symmetrical around a middle value.

Section 8. The Law of Errors

Our question, however, is not answered conclusively by the statement just made. Suppose we had in some way found satisfactorily constant mean values for some psychical process, how would we go about it to learn whether we might or might not assume a homogeneous causal condition, necessary for their further utilisation? The physical scientist generally knows beforehand that he will have to deal with a single causal combination, the statistician knows that he has to deal with a mass of them, ever inextricable despite all analysis. Both know this from the elementary knowledge they already posses of the nature of the processes before they proceed with the more detailed investigations. Just as, a moment ago, the present knowledge of psychology appeared to us too vague and unreliable to be depended upon for decision about the possibility of constant experimental conditions; so now it may prove insufficient to determine satisfactorily whether in a given case we have to deal with a homogeneous causal combination or a manifold of them which chance to operate together. The question is, therefore, whether we may throw light on the nature of the causation of the results we obtain under conditions as uniform as possible by the help of some other criterion.

The answer must be: This cannot be done with absolute certainty, but can, nevertheless, be done with great probability. Thus, a start has been made from presuppositions as similar as possible to those by which physical constants have been obtained and the consequences which flow from them have been investigated. This has been done for the distribution of the single values about the resulting central value and quite independently of the actual concrete characteristics of the causes. Repeated comparisons of these calculated values with actual observations have shown that the similarity of the suppositions is indeed great enough to lead to an agreement of the results. The outcome of these speculations closely approximates to reality. It consists in this,—that the grouping of a large number of separate val-

FIGURE 4.1

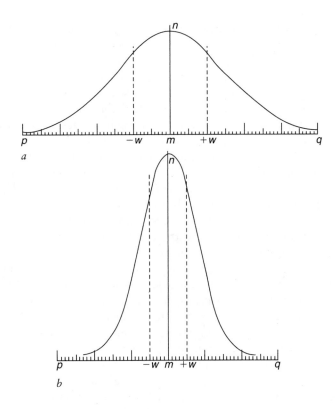

ues that have arisen from causes of the same kind and with the modifications repeatedly mentioned, may be correctly represented by a mathematical formula, the
so-called Law of Errors. This is especially characterised by the fact that it contains
but one unknown quantity. This unknown quantity measures the relative compactness of the distribution of the separate values around their central tendency. It
therefore changes according to the kind of observation and is determined by calculation from the separate values.

Note. For further information concerning this formula, which is not here our
concern, I must refer to the text-books on the calculation of probabilities and on
the theory of errors. For readers unfamiliar with the latter a graphic explanation
will be more comprehensible than a statement and discussion of the formula. Imagine a certain observation to be repeated 1,000 times. Each observation as such is
represented by a space of one square millimeter, and its numerical value, or rather
its deviation from the central value of the whole 1,000 observations, by its position on the horizontal line *p q* of the adjoining Figure 1.

For every observation which exactly corresponds with the central value one
square millimeter is laid off on the vertical line *m n*. For each observed value which
deviates by one unit from the central value upward one square millimeter is laid
off on a vertical line to right of *m n* and distant one millimeter from it, etc. For
every observed value which deviates by *x* units above (or below) the central value,
one sq. mm. is placed on a vertical line distant from *m n* by *x* mms., to the right

(or left, for values below the central value). When all the observations are arranged in this way the outer contour of the figure may be so compacted that the projecting corners of the separate squares are transformed into a symmetrical curve. If now the separate measures are of such a sort that their central value may be considered as a constant as conceived by physical science, the form of the resulting curve is of the kind marked a and b in Fig. 1. If the middle value is a statistical constant, the curve may have any sort of a form. (The curves a and b with the lines p q include in each case an area of 1,000 sq. mms. This is strictly the case only with indefinite prolongation of the curves and the lines p q, but these lines and curves finally approach each other so closely that where the drawing breaks off only two or three sq. mms. at each end of the curve are missing from the full number.) Whether, for a certain group of observations, the curve has a more steep or more flat from depends on the nature of those observations. The more exact they are, the more will they pile up around the central value; and the more infrequent the large deviations, the steeper will the curve be and *vice versa*. For the rest the law of formation of the curve is always the same. Therefore, if a person, in the case of any specific combination of observations, obtains any measure of the compactness of distribution of the observations, he can survey the grouping of the whole mass. He could state, for instance, how often a deviation of a certain value occurs and how many deviations fall between certain limits. Or—as I shall show in what follows—he may state what amount of variation includes between itself and the central value a certain per cent of all the observed values. The lines $+w$ and $-w$ of our figure, for instance, cut out exactly the central half of the total space representing the observations. But in the case of the more exact observations of 1 b they are only one half as far from m n as in 1 a. So the statement of their relative distances gives also a measure of the accuracy of the observations.

C H A 5 P T E R

STRUCTURALISM

EDWARD BRADFORD TITCHENER (1867–1927)

Edward Bradford Titchener was born about 70 miles south of London in the town of Chichester, and old Roman site complete with its ancient walls.[1] Titchener came from an old and distinguished, yet financially insecure family. His father, a schoolmaster, died when Titchener was quite young, leaving his wife and family in monetary distress. This impressed upon Titchener the need for a practical education for women, and indeed, close to 40 percent of his 56 Ph.D. students were females, a figure quite remarkable for his day (Evans, 1995). His first doctoral student was a female, Margaret Floy Washburn, who had a difficult time gaining admittance to Columbia University as a full-time student (Washburn, 1932).

Titchener was a good student and was fortunately able to attend Oxford University on scholarship. While there, he concentrated on philosophy and the classics but had a wide range of interests that included Darwinism, ethology, and psychology. Completing his undergraduate degree in 1890 and having a strong interest in psychology, he naturally migrated to Leipzig, Germany, then the mecca of scientific psychology, where Wilhelm Wundt had established the first psychology laboratory 11 years earlier in 1879. Fluent in German, Titchener arrived in Leipzig having translated Wundt's third edition of *Principles of Physiological Psychology* only to find that the professor had recently finished the fifth edition!

---

[1] A great deal of excellent biographic material concerning Titchener is available in Boring's (1927) necrology, upon which this section is based.

In 1892, at the age of 25, Titchener received his doctorate under the aegis of Wundt. He then returned to England and Oxford, where he hoped to teach psychology. However, there was little interest in scientific psychology at Oxford, so he accepted the invitation of Cornell University in Ithaca, New York, to direct their psychological laboratory, a post vacated by one of his classmates in Leipzig, the American Frank Angell.

Titchener arrived at Cornell in 1892 and stayed there until his death in 1927. His effect on psychology in general and Cornell in particular was enormous. Concerning that era, Boring (1927) states: ". . . within psychology Cornell and Titchener have become almost interchangeable words" (p. 493). Although Wundt's personal relationship with Titchener was minimal, his impact was substantial. Titchener was the epitome of the German *Herr Doktor Professor* and even wore his Oxford master's gown to lecture because it gave him the "right to be dogmatic." He had a flair for the dramatic and would enter the lecture hall precisely as the university chimes were tolling (Dallenbach, 1967). His productivity, especially during his early tenure at Cornell, was prodigious; between 1893 and 1900, he published 62 articles. In addition, he published several influential books, helped edit *The American Journal of Psychology*, and was the dissertation advisor to 56 Ph.D. students. Yet, when he died in 1927, his approach to psychology was no longer a significant force.

Washburn (1932), his first Ph.D. student, provides a significant insight into the fate of Titchener. He surrounded himself with subordinates and was spared the healthy criticism that helps one grow intellectually. Boring (1927) suggests that he was not constituted for team work and was, for example, but a nominal member of the American Psychological Association. Since Titchener rejected all but his own psychology, mainstream psychology left him behind. Why then is he important? The structuralistic system and Titchener's dogmatic approach gave other experimental psychologists something against which they could rail and thus was a great heuristic value. (An idea is of heuristic value when it stirs up debate and observation.) In the United States, for many years, Titchener played the role of the loyal opposition to new and developing systems. What was the nature of Titchener's psychology to which so many psychologists objected?

TITCHENER'S STRUCTURALISM

Like his famous mentor, Wundt, Titchener made his business the scientific study of conscious awareness. The term *physiological psychology* then, meant that psychological experience was related to external physical influences that could be isolated, varied, and replicated. In other words, mental experience had an orderly relationship to physical independent variables. Titchener (1909), in his convincingly written *Test-Book of Psychology*, clearly states that the experience in which he was interested was the experience dependent on the experiencing individual. Using the core subjects of physics, space, time, and mass, he clearly illustrates his point. From the viewpoint of the physicist, a centimeter is a centimeter, a second is a second, and a gram is a gram under all instances. This is not so from a psychological standpoint, that is, from the standpoint of the experiencing individual. The two lines in the famous Muller–Lyer illusion, though equal, are experienced as unequal. An hour watching an amusing play is experienced differently from an hour spent in a dreary, out-of-the-way railroad station. Fifty grams in a container of a smaller diameter are perceived as heavier than 50 grams in a container with a larger diameter. From Titchener's standpoint, therefore, space, time, and mass can be viewed from a psychological as well as a physical perspective.

Titchener was also concerned with the chemistry of consciousness. In his (1898) *Outline of Psychology,* an excerpt of which constitutes the first reading, he clearly calls for something akin to a psychological periodic table of elements, indicating that this enterprise is essential before psychologists can undertake more complex problems.[2] Titchener used graduate students trained in a special brand of introspection, *analytic introspection,* a detailed looking within, to arrive at the elements of any conscious experience. He had his doctoral student, Karl Dallenbach (1967), introspect to see what images, sensations, and affections were present while he was playing chess. This was an extremely dull and tedious process that, as Washburn (1933) suggests, turned consciousness into something it never was. Boring (1953) in the second reading states well why this method fell out of favor in psychology, "it could take twenty minutes to describe the conscious content of a second and a half . . . introspection . . . becomes a dull taxonomic account of sensory events which, since they suggest almost no functional value for the organism, are particularly uninteresting to the American scientific temper" (p. 174). In 1927, Titchener died having lived long enough to see what he called his "right little, tight little system" become obsolete.

REFERENCES

Boring, E. G. (1927). Edward Bradford Titchener (1867–1927). *The American Journal of Psychology,* 38, 489–506.

Boring, E. G. (1953). A history of introspection. *Psychological Bulletin,* 50, 169–189.

Dallenbach, K. M. (1967). Karl M. Dallenbach. In E. G. Boring & G. Lindzey (Eds.) *A history of psychology in autobiography* (Vol. 5, pp. 57–93). Engelwood Cliffs, NJ: Prentice-Hall.

Evans, R. V. (1994 April). E. B. Titchener. In T. C. Caldwallader (Chair) *Wundt's and Titchener's relationshop revisited.* Symposium conducted at the annual meeting of the Eastern Psychological Association, Providence, RI.

Leahey, T. H. (1991) *A history of psychology: Main currents in psychological thought* (4th ed.). Engelwood Cliffs, NJ: Prentice-Hall.

Titchener, E. B. (1897). *An outline of psychology* (2nd ed.). New York: Macmillan.

Titchener, E. B. (1909). *Text-book of psychology* (Rev ed.). New York: Macmillan.

Washburn, M. F. (1932). Some Recollections. In C. Murchison (Ed.) *An history of psychology in autobiography.*

---

[2]Leahey (1991) feels that Titchener's emphasis on elementalism, that is, finding the discrete elements of consciousness, represents his unique stamp on structuralism. Leahey points out that his mentor, Wundt, whose psychology was called *ganzheit,* that is, holistic psychology, did not share this elementalism.

The Meaning and Problem of Psychology

Edward Bradford Titchener

Every one knows in a rough way what it is that psychology deals with. It treats of 'mind' and 'consciousness,' and of the laws of mind and consciousness. My 'mind' is that in me which thinks, understands, reasons, chooses, directs my actions. And my 'consciousness' is my inner knowledge of my thought and action: I am 'conscious' of the awkwardness of my movements, or of the correctness of my answer to an examination question. In these senses, the words 'mind' and 'consciousness' are familiar to all of us.

Now it is quite true that psychology deals with mind and consciousness, and with their laws. But it often happens that the scientific use of words is different from their popular or ordinary use. Thus the word 'law' means, in everyday language, an ordinance or regulation imposed by authority; whereas, in the language of natural science, it means simply a regularity or unbroken uniformity of natural events. It should not be surprising, then, that the 'mind' and 'consciousness' of psychological science differ a little in their meanings from the 'mind' and 'consciousness' of our daily conversation. We shall see, later on, that the current usage of the words is metaphysical as well as psychological.

It will, perhaps, be easiest for us to get rid of our preconceived opinions as to the meanings of these familiar terms, if we have before us, from the very outset, a scientific definition of psychology, and postpone for the present our discussion of 'mind' and 'consciousness' in their technical psychological senses. Psychology may be defined as the *science of mental processes*. Each of the three terms included in the definition requires a brief explanation.

A *process* is any object of scientific knowledge which is not a 'thing.' A 'thing' is permanent, relatively unchanging, definitely marked off from other things. A process is, by etymology, a 'moving forward.' It is a *becoming something*,—a continuous operation, a progressive change, which the scientific observer can trace throughout its course. It melts into and blends with operations and changes which follow and precede it. Thus the chemist speaks of the 'process of decomposition.' The changes which constitute decomposition are the 'process'; the final products of decomposition are 'things.' The wearing away of a cliff by the action of water is a process; the rock itself is a thing. The thing 'is,' here or there; the process 'takes place.'—Psychology deals always with *processes,* and never with things.

A *mental* process is any process, falling within the range of our experience, in the origination and continuance of which we are ourselves necessarily concerned. Heat is a process. But heat, regarded simply as a 'mode of motion' is independent of us; the movement continues, whether or not we are present to sense the heat. When, however, heat falls within our sensible experience, we, the experiencing individuals, have something to say to it; it is what it is, in part at any rate, because of *us*. The (physical) movement is translated by us into the (psychological) sensation of heat. More than that: if we are cold, to start with, the same physical heat will seem hotter to us than it would have done, had we been warm. *This* heat process, then, is a mental process. Or again: the space of geometry is independent of us. It has its laws, which hold good whether we know them or not. But space may be a matter of our experience, and may be modified by our experience. "I had such pleasant thoughts," we may say, "that the road seemed much shorter than usual." *This* space is a mental process.—Psychology deals with none but *mental* processes.

A *science* is a sum of knowledge which has been classified and arranged under certain general rules and comprehensive laws; it is coherent and unified knowledge. We may know, from our boyish discoveries, that the eggs of some gulls and some plovers are speckled with green and brown; but this knowledge is not scientific. It becomes scientific when we include it in the knowledge that the speckling is characteristic of the eggs of the Laridae and Charadriidae; and when we use it to link these two groups together, in making out the inter-relations and lines of descent of the different bird forms—Psychology is not a string of unconnected observations, but a *science*. . . .

§ 4. **The Problem of Psychology.**—The aim of the psychologist is threefold. He seeks (1) to analyse concrete (actual) mental experience into its simplest components. (2) to discover how these elements combine, what are the laws which govern their combination, and (3) to bring them into connection with their physiological (bodily conditions).

(1) We saw above that all science begins with analysis. The original material of science is complex; science itself introduces order into chaos by reducing the complex to its elements, by tracing the proportion of identical elements in different complexes, and by determining (where that is possible) the relations of the elements to one another. Psychology is no exception to the rule. Our concrete mental experience, the experience of 'real life,' is always complex. However small a fragment we may seize upon,—a single wish, a single idea, a single resolution,—we find invariably that close inspection of it will reveal its complexity, will show that it is composed of a number of more rudimentary processes. The first object of the psychologist, therefore, is to ascertain the *nature and number of the mental elements*. He takes up mental experience, bit by bit, dividing and subdividing, until the division can go no further. When that point is reached, he has found a conscious element.

The mental or conscious elements are those mental processes which cannot be further analysed, which are absolutely simple in nature, and which consequently cannot be reduced, even in part, to other processes. The special reasons which lead the psychologist to look upon various special processes as elements will be discussed in their places, in following chapters.

We have already seen that an 'idea' is a complex process. We may here illustrate the complexity of concrete mental experiences by examining an experience of a different order,—say, an emotion. The emotion of *anger* seems, at first sight, to be a single experience; it has a single name. Really, it is highly complex. It contains, *e.g.*, the idea of the person with whom one is angry; the idea of the act of his, at which one is displeased; the idea of a retaliatory action on one's own part; a mass of bodily sensations, attending the flushing of one's face, the tendency to clench the fist, the bracing of the whole muscular system,—one 'feels stronger' when angry. It begins with a feeling of displeasure, of pained surprise or wounded pride; but this soon gives way to the pleasantness of anger itself, the delight in the idea of re-taliation and in the fact that one is strong enough to retaliate,—a delight that has come down to civilised man from his primitive ancestors, and that shows itself con-tinually in the actions of the child. These processes—themselves by no means sim-ple—all take part, crossing and recrossing, shifting and recombining, in the emo-tion. They need not all be present together in the angry consciousness of a given moment; but all have their share in the experience of anger.

(2) Analysis needs to be tested in two ways. We must always ask, with regard to it: Has it gone as far as it can go? and: Has it taken account of all the elements which are contained in the experience? To answer the first question, the analysis must be repeated: analysis is its own test. When one psychologist says that a process is elemental, other psychologists repeat his analysis for themselves, trying to carry it further than he could do. If they stop short where he did, he was right; if they find his 'simple' process to be complex, he was wrong. As regards the second ques-tion, on the other hand, the test of analysis is *synthesis*. When we have analysed a complex into the elements *a, b, c,* we test our analysis by trying to put it together again, to get it back from *a, b* and *c.* If the complex can be thus restored, the analy-sis is correct; but if the combination of *a, b* and *c* does not give us back the origi-nal complex, the analyst has failed to discover some one or more of its ingredients. Hence the psychologist, when he has analysed consciousness, must put together the results of his analysis, must synthetise, and compare his reconstruction of mental experience with the experience as originally given. If the two tally, his work on that mental experience is done, and he can pass on to another; if not, he must repeat his analysis, watching constantly for the factors which he had previously missed. If the conscious elements were 'things,' the task of reconstruction of an expe-rience would not be difficult. We should put the simple bits of mind together, as the bits of wood are put together in a child's puzzle-map or kindergarten cube. But the conscious elements are 'processes': they do not fit together, side to side and an-gle to angle; they flow together, mix together, overlapping, reinforcing, modifying or arresting one another, in obedience to certain psychological laws. The psychol-ogist must, therefore, in the second place, seek to ascertain the *laws which govern the connection of the mental elements*. Knowledge of these laws renders the syn-thesis of elements into a concrete experience possible, and is of assistance also in subsequent analysis.

When we try for the first time to analyse anger, we may very easily overlook the fourth factor mentioned above,—the mass of sensations accompanying the flush of anger, the doubling of the fist, etc. We discover that we have omitted something, however, as soon as ever we put together the ingredients which we have noticed, and ask if they actually make up the experience of anger, and if they exhaust all that we 'feel' when we are angry. *Something* is still lacking. This discovery shows us that the processes which are analysis has brought to light must somehow have obscured certain other processes, connected with them in the actual emotion. We have now, therefore, to repeat our analysis, keeping a sharp lookout for the missing processes: we shall do well to try to analyse some other emotions, since the processes which are obscure in anger may, perhaps, come to the front in them. After many trials we find what the lacking something is; and our synthesis is satisfactory. At this stage we note carefully the manner in which the items which we missed at first are connected with the other processes in anger,—we seek to determine how they could have been obscured so completely by the other processes. And having made a large number of similar notes, and compared them methodically, we are finally able to write out a law of mental combination or connection. When we have our law, we can apply it in difficult cases as they occur, and so gain help in our later analyses.

(3) Every mental process is connected with bodily process; we do not know anything of mind apart from body. Mind and body, that is, always go together in our experience. And ordinary observation will convince us that body influences mind in various ways. Consciousness when the eyes are closed is different from consciousness when the eyes are open; if the bodily state varies, the mental state varies also; the dropping of the eyelids prevents the ether waves from gaining access to the sensitive parts of the eyes, and with this physical fact go the mental facts of the sensation of darkness, the 'feeling' of bodily unsteadiness and uncertainty, etc. The mind of a man who has been blind from his birth is essentially different from the mind of one endowed with normal vision. Where the latter sees, the former hears and touches: I *see* my path, but the blind man *hears* and *'feels'* his way. Even the highest and most abstract processes of thought give evidence of the close connection of mind with body. We cannot think, unless we have ideas in which to think: and ideas are built up from impressions received through bodily sense-organs. Thus most of us remember, imagine dream, and think in terms of sight. When we remember an event, we *see* it occurring 'in our mind's eye'; when we 'imagine' an experience, we have a mental 'image' of it, we seem to *see* it take place; when we dream we ordinarily *see* ourselves or our friends engaged in the action or in that; and when we think, we often *see* the words in which we are thinking, as if they were printed or written on an imagined page. Psychology is not complete, then, until we have brought the results of our analysis of mental experience, the mental elements, into connection with the *bodily structures and functions* which condition them.

Put in another way, the problem of psychology may be said to consist in the description and explanation of mental processes. Exact *description* implies analysis and synthesis; you cannot describe accurately unless you have taken the object of your description to pieces, observed it in all its parts, and then replaced the parts and reconstructed the whole. When we have described, we can go on to *explain,* to state the circumstances under which the process takes place. Explanation is always that: the statement of the circumstances or conditions under which the described phenomenon occurs. The conditions of mental processes are partly mental and partly bodily: the laws of mental connection, on the one hand, and the laws (functions) of certain bodily structures on the other.

The psychologist has to pull mental experience to pieces,—to put it together again,—and to note what happens to the particular processes involved, and what goes on in the body while the experience is in progress. This is the 'problem' of psychology.

Classical Introspection

Edward G. Boring

We may regard that introspection as classical which was defined by fairly formal rules and principles and which directly emerged from the early practices in Wundt's laboratory at Leipzig. Of course, there were no immutable rules for introspection. The great men kept disagreeing with one another and changing their minds. Nevertheless, there was a body of opinion which was in general shared by Wundt, by Külpe before he left Leipzig, by G.E. Müller at Göttingen, by Titchener at Cornell and by many other less important "introspectionists" who accepted the leadership of these men. Stumpf at Berlin held to less constrained principles, and Külpe's later doctrine of introspection after he had gone to Würzburg was opposed by Wundt and Titchener.

Classical introspection is the common belief that the description of consciousness reveals complexes that are constituted of patterns of sensory elements. It was against this doctrine that Külpe at Würzburg, the behaviorists under Watson and the Gestalt psychologists at Wertheimer's initiative revolted. Introspection got its *ism* because these protesting new schools needed a clear and stable contrasting background against which to exhibit their novel features. No proponent of introspection as the basic method of psychology ever called himself an *introspectionist*. Usually he called himself a *psychologist*.

Wundt, undertaking to establish the new psychology as a science, turned to chemistry for his model. This choice landed him in elementism, with associationism to provide for synthesis. The psychological atoms were thus sensations and perhaps also feelings and images. The psychological molecules were perceptions and ideas (*Vorstellungen*) and the more complex combinations (*Verbindungen*). Because Wundt changed hs views from time to time about images and feelings, the sensation became the example of the sort of stuff that appears in a good description of consciousness. Thus, half a century later, we find Titchener concluding that *sensory* is the adjective that best indicates the nature of the contents of consciousness. Thus, half a century later, we find Titchener concluding that *sensory* is the adjective that best indicates the nature of the contents of consciousness. In this way Wundt fixed both elementism and sensationism upon introspection, and introspectionism in the proper laboratories always yielded sensory elements because that was "good" observation. It seems reasonable to suppose that laboratory atmosphere and local cultural tradition did more to perpetuate this value than did any published admonitions about observation.

Although Wundt defined the subject matter of psychology as immediate experience, he did distinguish introspection (*Selbstbeobachtung*) from inner perception (*innere Wahrnehmung*) Inner perception might be self-validating, but it was not science. Wundt insisted on the training of observers. Even in the reaction experiment Leipzig observers had to be trained to perform the prescribed acts in perception, apperception, cognition, discrimination, judgment, choice, and the like, and to report when consciousness deviated from what had been called for. Thus it is said that no observer who had performed less than 10,000 of these introspectively controlled reactions was suitable to provide data for published research from Wundt's laboratory. Some Americans, like Cattell, had the idea that the minds of untrained observers might also be of interest to psychology, and later a bitter little quarrel on this matter developed between Baldwin and Titchener. For all that, Wundt's notion of what constitutes proper introspection was much more liberal than is generally supposed, for he left room in formal introspection for introspection and for indirect report. He was much less flexible in respect of the elements and their sensory nature.

What happened next to introspection was the acceptance of the conception that physics and psychology differ from each other in points of view but not in fundamental materials. Mach in 1886 argued that experience ("sensation") is the subject matter of all the sciences, and Avenarius a few years later that psychology views experience as dependent upon the functioning of the nervous system (he called it the "System C") and physics as independent of the action of the nervous system. Presently, after the two men had agreed that they agreed, they had great influence upon Külpe and Titchener who were both then at Leipzig. In his textbook of 1893 Külpe accepted this distinction by point of view, but Titchener is the person who emphasized it most. In 1910, he was saying that the data of introspection are "the sum-total of human experience considered as dependent upon the experiencing person," and later he could write the formula:

$$\text{Introspection} = \text{psychological (clear experience} \rightarrow \text{report),}$$

which means that introspection is the having of clear experience under the psychological point of view and the reporting upon it also under the psychological point of view. Substitute physical for psychological, and you have the formula for physics. The stock example for introspection is the illusion, the case where perception differs from stimulus-object in some respect. For perception experience is regarded just as it comes, dependent upon the perceiving of the perceiving person and thus the action his nervous system. For the physical account of the object, however, the perceiver must be abstracted from and the physicist has resort to measurement and other physical technics. Titchener held to this distinction by point of view all his life.

It was Külpe who split Wundt's psychological atom, analyzing sensation into its four inseparable but in dependently variable attributes: quality, intensity, extensity, and duration. Titchener later held to this view which served to tighten rather than to loosen the constraints of atomism upon introspective psychology.

One of the most thorough discussions of introspection was provided by the erudite G. E. Müller in 1911. Müller was more liberal than Wundt and left room for all the indirect and retrospective forms of introspection. Being primarily interested in the application of introspection to memory, he distinguished, for instance, between the present recall of the past apperception of a past event and the present apperception of the present recall of a past event, an important distinction, since present apperception can be interrogated as to detail whereas past apperception has become fixed and no longer subject to exploration.

It was Titchener who placed the greatest constraints upon introspection by his requirement that the description of consciousness should exclude statements of meaning. At first Titchener had perception in mind and called the report of meanings the *stimulus-error,* insisting that trained observers by taking the psychological point of view would describe consciousness ("dependent experience") and attempt no statements about the stimulus-objects ("independent experience" as given by the point of view of physics). After Külpe had claimed to find imageless (nonsensory) thoughts in the consciousnesses of judgment, action, and other thought processes, Titchener broadened his criticism to an objection against the inclusion of any meanings at all in the data of introspection. He was arguing that straight description (*Beschreibung, cognitiorei*) would yield the kind of sensory contents that had become standard in classical introspection, and that inferences about conscious data (*Kundgabe, cognitio circa rem*) are meanings which do not exist as do the observed sensory processes.

Thus his psychology has even been called *existential psychology,* because he believed that the meanings, occurring as inferences, lack the positive character of sensations and images, the existential data.

It was never wholly true that introspection was photographic and not elaborated by inferences or meanings. Reference to typical introspective researches from Titchener's laboratory establishes this point. There was too much dependence upon retrospection. It could take twenty minutes to describe the conscious content of a second and a half and at the end of that period the observer was cudgeling his brain to recall what had actually happened more than a thousand seconds ago, relying, of course, on inference. At the Yale meeting of the APA in 1913, J. W. Baird with great enthusiasm arranged for a public demonstration of introspection with the trained observers from his laboratory at Clark, but the performance was not impressive. Introspection with inference and meaning left out as much as possible becomes a dull taxonomic account of sensory events which, since they suggest almost no functional value for the organism, are peculiarly uninteresting to the American scientific temper.

Classical introspection, it seems to me, went out of style after Titchener's death (1927) because it had demonstrated no functional use and therefore seemed dull, and also because it was unreliable. Laboratory atmosphere crept into the descriptions, and it was not possible to verify, from one laboratory to another, the introspective accounts of the consciousnesses of action, feeling, choice, and judgment. It is not surprising, therefore, that Külpe, Watson and Wertheimer, all within a decade (1904–1913), reacted vigorously against the constraints of this idealistic but rigid pedantry.

FUNCTIONALISM: ANTECEDENT INFLUENCES

ERASMUS DARWIN (1731–1802)

Erasmus Darwin, a physician, freethinker, poet, and naturalist, was the grandfather of both Charles Darwin and Frances Galton. Although he died well before either of them was born, Erasmus Darwin left an indelible mark on the lifework of both men. Erasmus Darwin was one of the earliest proponents of the idea of transmutation of species (the theory that species change and that the changes are passed on from one generation to the next). However, being more a poet than a scientist, he chose to set his ideas to verse. They did not translate well to rhyme and had little impact on his generation. Nonetheless, he planted the seed of an idea that would revolutionize scientific thinking in the hands of his grandsons.

CHARLES ROBERT DARWIN (1809–1882)

Charles Robert Darwin was born in Shrewsbury, England, on February 12, 1809. Darwin was one of six children born to Robert Waring Darwin (1768–1848) and Susannah Wedgewood (1765–1817). Darwin's mother died when he was only 8 years old. Although he had little memory of her, it is clear that she had some influence over his early interest in nature, as evidenced by an account in which the young Charles brought a flower to school, stating that his mother had taught him how "by looking at the inside of the blossom, the name of the plant could be discovered" (Huxley, *Darwinia,* p. 254, as cited in Huxley, 1888). It appears from this account that Darwin's mother may have been teaching him the rudiments of the Linnean system of classification.

The young Darwin was a bright child with early interests in natural history and in assorted collections (shells, beetles, minerals, coins). His early education came at home, where he was tutored by his sister Caroline and, later, at a boarding school located within a few miles of his home. His father, hoping to interest him in the family tradition of a medical career, sent the 16-year-old Charles to the University of Edinburgh in Scotland. Charles lasted two years at Edinburgh, but was unhappy in medicine. His father eventually sent him to Christ's College in Cambridge to become a clergyman. While at Cambridge, Darwin was fortunate to take botany lectures from John Stevens Henslow (1796–1861), who would later arrange for the 22-year-old Darwin to take his place as the volunteer naturalist on a voyage around the world aboard the *H.M.S. Beagle.* The *Beagle* sailed from England on December 27, 1831, and did not return home for four years, nine months, and two days. During his voyage on the *Beagle,* Darwin meticulously cataloged the flora, fauna, and geology of such distinct regions as Tenerife, the Cape Verde Islands, Brazil, Montevideo, Tierra del Fuego, Buenos Aires, Valparaiso, Chile, the Galapagos, Tahiti, New Zealand, Tasmania, and the Keeling Islands. His discoveries planted the seeds of his theory of evolution, although it would be 6 years before he developed even a tentative outline of his ideas, and another 16 before he would publish it.

Upon Darwin's return to England, he began to pursue his personal and professional lives with renewed purpose. He moved to London, published numerous works on the geological and zoological discoveries of his voyage, and in 1839, married his cousin, Emma Wedgewood (1808–1896). Charles and Emma were to share 43 loving years of marriage and the birth of 10 children, 7 of whom would live to adulthood. In 1842, suffering from ill health and desiring a quieter place to ponder his theories, Darwin moved his family to a country home in Kent. There, he began to write the outlines of what would eventually become the landmark treatise, *Origin of the Species.*

Darwin's reticence to publish his radical ideas was characteristic of his conservative scientific perspective. He simply wanted to present so much compelling data that his theory would be irrefutable. In fact, the *Origin* might never have been published if not for a bright young scientist by the name of Alfred Russel Wallace (1823–1913), who, in 1858, sent Darwin an article he had written while doing research in the Malay Archipelago. Wallace's letter presented a less-documented theory of evolution startlingly similar to Darwin's. Darwin was now forced to either publish his views or risk being superseded by the younger scientist. With an admirable sense of fair play, Darwin presented both Wallace's paper and his own to the Linnean Society on July 1, 1858. Darwin then completed work on *The Origin of the Species by Means of Natural Selection,* which was finally published in 1859. The introduction to this landmark book is the first reading for this chapter.

SIR FRANCIS GALTON (1822–1911)

Francis Galton was born in Warwickshire, near Birmingham, England, the youngest of nine children in a prominent, wealthy family. Galton was a precocious child who learned to read by age 2½, wrote a letter by age 4, and could read virtually any book in the English language by age 5. Despite his precocity, Galton's academic career was unremarkable. He began a study of medicine at his father's insistence, but clearly had no love for the field. He terminated his medical studies at age 22, upon his father's death.

Free of his obligation to study medicine, and the beneficiary of a substantial inheritance, Galton began to explore the world. He traveled extensively, visiting Egypt, the Sudan, and Syria. He explored and mapped more than 1,000 miles of the interior of Southwest Africa, earning a gold medal from the Royal Geographic Society. Galton was reportedly impressed with the indigenous people he encountered in his travels, noting how well they had adapted to their harsh environment. That same harsh environment took a toll on Galton's health, and in 1855, he retired from traveling, devoting himself instead to educating others in the art of traveling. Galton's book, *Art of Travel: Shifts and Contrivances Available in Wild Countries,* was published in eight editions.

Soon after Galton's return to England, his cousin, Charles Darwin, published *Origin of the Species.* Galton's interest in evolution was immediate and intense. The diversity of the people he had encountered in his travels had prompted a fascination with individual differences. Now, Darwin had stimulated in him an interest in how those differences might be inherited to the benefit of the human species. Galton reasoned that if gifted individuals were selected and mated generation after generation, the human race would be strengthened. Galton referred to this science as "eugenics," literally, "good genes." To promote his theory, Galton and his followers collected enormous amounts of data about a variety of human characteristics and pioneered some of psychology's most sophisticated statistical techniques, including correlational coefficients and factor analysis.[1]

Galton began by examining the heritability of genius. He sought to demonstrate that individual greatness ran in families with a frequency that could not be explained through environment alone. Galton reported the results of his study in the influential book *Hereditary Genius,* in which he coined the phrase "nature vs. nurture." Following the publication of the first edition of *Hereditary Genius,* Galton expanded his program of testing to measure the heritability of a wide variety of human characteristics, both physical and mental. He established his best known laboratory for mental and physical testing at the South Kensington Museum in 1888. In the 1880s and 1890s, approximately 17,000 people were tested in Galton's various laboratories. The reading is a report on some of this data and is representative of Galton's

---

[1]Galton was the first to attempt to quantify the concept of "co-relation" among measures. In 1896, Karl Pearson, using Galton's work, as well as that of the French mathematician A. Bravais, gave correlational theory its current mathematical form.

pioneering use of statistical techniques. As reflected in the reading, Galton's measures of mental processes relied heavily on reaction times and other measures of sensory acuity. This program of anthropomorphic testing would be a significant influence on the work of the young American psychologist James McKeen Cattell.

Galton's influence on the field of psychology is difficult to overestimate. He was a man of uncommon intellect, far-reaching interest, and considerable energy. He pioneered the field of mental testing, and even though anthropomorphic testing was eventually discredited (see Chapter 8), he was enormously influential in the course of the testing movement. He was the first researcher to make extensive use of sophisticated correlational techniques. He started the eugenics movement, which for good or ill, remains a central and controversial theme in psychology.

REFERENCES

Boring, E. G. (1950). *A history of experimental psychology* (2nd ed.). New York: Appleton-Century-Crofts.

Hothersall, D. (1995). *History of psychology* (3rd ed.). New York: McGraw-Hill.

Huxley, T. H. (1888). Obituary: Charles Robert Darwin *Obituary Notices of the Proceedings of the Royal Society, 44.* Online available at: http://aleph0.clarku.edu/huxley/CE2/DarwObit.html#cite1

Schultz, D. & Schultz, S. E. (1996). *The history of modern psychology* (6th ed.). Fort Worth: Harcourt Brace College Publishers.

Urbanowicz, C. F. (1995). *Urbanowicz on Darwin.* California State University, Chico. Online available at: http://www.csuchico.edu/~curban/Darwin/DarwinSem-S95.html#anchor604264

Darwin, C. (1936). *The origin of the species.* New York: Modern Library. (Originally published in 1859).

Galton. F. (1888). Co-relations and their measurement, chiefly from anthopometric data. *Proceedings of the Royal Society of London, 15,* 135–145.

An Historical Sketch of the Progress of Opinion on the Origin of Species, Previously to the Publication of the First Edition of This Work

Charles Darwin

I will here give a brief sketch of the progress of opinion on the Origin of Species. Until recently the great majority of naturalists believed that species were immutable productions, and had been separately created. This view has been ably maintained by many authors. Some few naturalists, on the other hand, have believed that species undergo modification, and that the existing forms of life are the descendants by true generation of pre-existing forms. Passing over allusions to the subject in the classical writers,* the first author who in modern times has treated it in a scientific spirit was Buffon. But as his opinions fluctuated greatly at different periods, and as he does not enter on the causes or means of the transformation of species, I need not here enter on details.

Lamarck was the first man whose conclusions on the subject excited much attention. This justly celebrated naturalist first published his views in 1801; he much enlarged them in 1809 in his 'Philosophie Zoologique,' and subsequently, in 1815, in the Introduction to his 'Hist. Nat. des Animaux sans Vertébres.' In these works he upholds the doctrine that all species, including man, are descended from other species. He first did the eminent service of arousing attention to the probability of all change in the organic, as well as in the inorganic world, being the result of law, and not of miraculous interposition. Lamarck seems to have been chiefly led to his conclusion on the gradual change of species, by the difficulty of distinguishing species and varieties, by the almost perfect gradation of forms in certain groups, and by the analogy of domestic productions. With respect to the means of modification, he attributed something to the direct action of the physical conditions of life, something to the crossing of already existing forms, and much to use and disuse, that is, to the effects of habit. To this latter agency he seems to attribute all the beautiful adaptations in nature;—such as the long neck of the giraffe for brows-

---

*Aristotle, in his 'Physicæ Ausultationes' (lib. 2, cap. 8, s. 2), after remarking that rain does not fall in order to make the corn grow, any more than it falls to spoil the farmer's corn when threshed out of doors, applies the same argument to organisation; and adds (as translated by Mr. Clair Grece, who first pointed out the passage to me), "So what hinders the different parts [of the body] from having this merely accidental relation in nature? as the teeth, for example, grow by necessity, the front ones sharp, adapted for dividing, and the grinders flat, and serviceable for masticating the food; since they were not made for the sake of this, but it was the result of accident. And in like manner as to the other parts in which there appears to exist an adaptation to an end. Wheresoever, therefore, all things together (that is all the parts of one whole) happened like as if they were made for the sake of something, these were preserved, having been appropriately constituted by an internal spontaneity; and whatsoever things were not thus constituted, perished, and still perish." We here see the principle of natural selection shadowed forth, but how little Aristotle fully comprehended the principle, is shown by his remarks on the formation of the teeth.

ing on the branches of trees. But he likewise believed in a law of progressive development; and as all the forms of life thus tend to progress, in order to account for the existence at the present day of simple productions, he maintains that such forms are now spontaneously generated.*

Geoffroy Saint-Hilaire, as is stated in his 'Life,' written by his son, suspected, as early as 1795, that what we call species are various degenerations of the same type. It was not until 1828 that he published his conviction that the same forms have not been perpetuated since the origin of all things. Geoffroy seems to have relied chiefly on the conditions of life, or the *'monde ambiant'* as the cause of change. He was cautious in drawing conclusions, and did not believe that existing species are now undergoing modification; and, as his son adds, "C'est donc un problème à réserver entièrement à l'avenir, supposé même que l'avenir doive avoir prise sur lui."

In 1813, Dr. W. C. Wells read before the Royal Society 'An Account of a White female, part of whose skin resembles that of a Negro'; but his paper was not published until his famous 'Two Essays upon Dew and Single Vision' appeared in 1818. In this paper he distinctly recognises the principle of natural selection, and this is the first recognition which has been indicated; but he applies it only to the races of man, and to certain characters alone. After remarking that Negroes and mulattoes enjoy an immunity from certain tropical diseases, he observes, firstly, that all animals tend to vary in some degree, and, secondly, that agriculturists improve their domesticated animals by selection; and then, he adds, but what is done in this latter case "by art, seems to be done with equal efficacy, though more slowly, by nature, in the formation of varieties of mankind, fitted for the country which they inhabit. Of the accidental varieties of man, which would occur among the first few and scattered inhabitants of the middle regions of Africa, some one would be better fitted than the others to bear the diseases of the country. This race would consequently multiply, while the others would decrease; not only from their inability to sustain the attacks of disease, but from their incapacity of contending with their more vigorous neighbors. The colour of this vigorous race I take for granted, from what has been already said, would be dark. But the same disposition to form varieties still existing, a darker and a darker race would in the course of time occur: and as the darkest would be the best fitted for the climate, this would at length become the most prevalent, if not the only race, in the particular country in which it had originated." He then extends these same views to the white inhabitants of colder

---

*I have taken the date of the first publication of Lamarck from Isid. Geoffroy Saint-Hilaire's ('Hist. Nat. Générale,' tom. ii. p. 405, 1859) excellent history of opinion on this subject. In this work a full account is given of Buffon's conclusions on the same subject. It is curious how largely my grandfather, Dr. Erasmus Darwin, anticipated the views and erroneous grounds of opinion of Lamarck in his 'Zoonomia' (vol. i. pp. 500–510), published in 1794. According to Isid. Geofroy there is no doubt that Goethe was an extreme partisan of similar views, as shown in the Introduction to a work written in 1794 and 1795, but not published till long afterwards: he has pointedly remarked ('Goethe als Naturforscher,' von Dr. Karl Meding, s. 34) that the future question for naturalists will be how, for instance, cattle got their horns, and not for what they are used. It is rather a singular instance of the manner in which similar views arise at about the same time, that Goethe in Germany, Dr. Darwin in England, and Geoffroy Saint-Hilaire (as we shall immediately see) in France, came to the same conclusion on the origin of species, in the years 1794–5.

climates. I am indebted to Mr. Rowley, of the United States, for having called my attention, through Mr. Brace, to the above passage in Dr. Wells' work.

The Hon. and Rev. W. Herbert, afterwards Dean of Manchester, in the fourth volume of the 'Horticultural Transactions,' 1822, and in his work on the 'Amaryllidacea' (1837, pp. 19, 339), declares that "horticultural experiments have established, beyond the possibility of refutation, that botanical species are only a higher and more permanent class of varieties." He extends the same view to animals. The Dean believes that single species of each genus were created in an originally highly plastic condition, and that these have produced, chiefly by intercrossing, but likewise by variation, all our existing species.

In 1826 Professor Grant, in the concluding paragraph in his well-known paper ('Edinburgh Philosophical Journal,' vol. xiv. p. 283) on the Spongilla, clearly declares his belief that species are descended from other species, and that they become improved in the course of modification. This same view was given in his 55th Lecture, published in the 'Lancet' in 1834.

In 1831 Mr. Patrick Matthew published his work on 'Naval Timber and Arboriculture,' in which he gives precisely the same view on the origin of species as that (presently to be alluded to) propounded by Mr. Wallace and myself in the 'Linnean Journal,' and as that enlarged in the present volume. Unfortunately the view was given by Mr. Matthew very briefly in scattered passages in an Appendix to a work on a different subject, so that it remained unnoticed until Mr. Matthew himself drew attention to it in the 'Gardener's Chronicle,' on April 7th, 1860. The differences of Mr. Matthew's view from mine are not of much importance: he seems to consider that the world was nearly depopulated at successive periods, and then re-stocked; and he gives as an alternative, that new forms may be generated "without the presence of any mould or germ of former aggregates." I am not sure that I understand some passages; but it seems that he attributes much influence to the direct action of the conditions of life. He clearly saw, however, the full force of the principle of natural selection.

The celebrated geologist and naturalist, Von Buch, in his excellent 'Description Physique des Isles Canaries' (1836, p. 147), clearly expresses his belief that varieties slowly become changed into permanent species, which are no longer capable of intercrossing.

Rafinesque, in his 'New Flora of North America,' published in 1836, wrote (p. 6) as follows:—"All species might have been varieties once, and many varieties are gradually becoming species by assuming constant and peculiar characters;" but farther on (p. 18) he adds, "except the original types or ancestors of the genus."

In 1843-44 Professor Haldemar ('Boston Journal of Nat. Hist. U. States,' vol. iv. p. 468) has ably given the arguments for and against the hypothesis of the development and modification of species: he seems to learn towards the side of change.

The 'Vestiges of Creation' appeared in 1844. In the tenth and much improved edition (1853) the anonymous author says (p. 155):—"The proposition determined on after much consideration is, that the several series of animated beings, from the simplest and oldest up to the highest and most recent, are, under the providence of God, the results, *first*, of an impulse which has been imparted to the forms of life, advancing them, in definite times, by generation, through grades of organisation terminating in the highest dicotyledons and vertebrata, these grades being few in number, and generally marked by intervals of organic character, which we find to be a practical difficulty in ascertaining affinities; *second,* of another impulse connected with the vital forces, tending, in the course of generations, to modify organic structures in accordance with external circumstances, as food, the nature of the habitat, and the meteoric agencies, these being the "adaptations" of the natural theologian." The author apparently believes that organisation progresses by sudden leaps, but that the effects produced by the conditions of life are gradual. He argues with much force on general grounds that species are not immutable productions. But I cannot see how the two supposed 'impulses' account in a scientific sense for the numerous and beautiful coadaptations which we see throughout nature; I cannot see that we thus gain any insight how, for instance, a woodpecker has become adapted to its peculiar habits of life. The work, from its powerful and brilliant style, though displaying in the earlier editions little accurate knowledge and a great want of scientific caution, immediately had a very wide circulation. In my opinion it has done excellent service in this country in calling attention to the subject, in removing prejudice, and in thus preparing the ground for the reception of analogous views.

In 1846 the veteran geologist M. J. d'Omalius d'Halloy published in an excellent through short paper ('Bulletins de l'Acad. Roy. Bruxelles,' tom. xiii. p. 581) his opinion that it is more probable that new species have been produced by descent with modification than that they have been separately created: the author first promulgated this opinion in 1831.

Professor Owen, in 1849 ('Nature of Limbs,' p. 86), wrote as follows:—"The archetypal idea was manifested in the flesh under diverse such modifications, upon this planet, long prior to the existence of those animal species that actually exemplify it. To what natural laws or secondary causes the orderly succession and progression of such organic phenomena may have been committed, we, as yet, are ignorant." In his Address to the British Association, in 1858, he speaks (p. li.) of "the axiom of the continuous operation of creative power, or of the ordained becoming of living things." Farther on (p. xc.), after referring to geographical distribution, he adds, "These phenomena shake our confidence in the conclusion that the Apteryx of New Zealand and the Red Grouse of England were distinct creations in and for those islands respectively. Always, also, it may be well to bear in mind that by the word 'creation' the zoologist means 'a process he knows not what.'" He amplifies this idea by adding that when such cases as that of the Red Grouse are "enumerated by the zoologist as evidence of distinct creation of the bird in and for such islands, he chiefly expresses that he knows not how the Red Grouse came to be there, and there exclusively; signifying also, by this mode of expressing such ignorance, his belief that both the bird and the islands owed their origin to a great first Creative Cause." If we interpret these sentences given in the same Address, one by the other, it appears that this eminent philosopher felt in 1858 his confidence shaken that the Apteryx and the Red Grouse first appeared in their respective homes, "he knew not how," or by some process "he knew not what."

This Address was delivered after the papers by Mr. Wallace and myself on the Origin of Species, presently to be referred to, had been read before the Linnean

Society. When the first edition of this work was published, I was so completely deceived, as were many others, by such expressions as "the continuous operation of creative power," that I included Professor Owen with other paleontologists as being firmly convinced of the immutability of species; but appears ('Anat. of Vertebrates,' vol. iii. p. 796) that this was on my part a preposterous error. In the last edition of this work I inferred, and the inference still seems to me perfectly just, from a passage beginning with the words "no doubt the type-form," &c. (Ibid. vol. i. p. xxxv.), that Professor Owen admitted that natural selection may have done something in the formation of a new species; but this it appears (Ibid. vol. iii. p. 798) is inaccurate and without evidence. I also gave some extracts from a correspondence between Professor Owen and the Editor of the 'London Review,' from which it appeared manifest to the Editor as well as to myself, that Professor Owen claimed to have promulgated the theory of natural selection before I had done so; and I expressed my surprise and satisfaction at this announcement; but as far as it is possible to understand certain recently published passages (Ibid. vol. iii. p. 798) I have either partially or wholly again fallen into error. It is consolatory to me that others find Professor Owen's controversial writings as difficult to understand and to reconcile with each other, as I do. As far as the mere enunciation of the principle of natural selection is concerned, it is quite immaterial whether or not Professor Owen preceded me, for both of us, as shown in this historical sketch, were long ago preceded by Dr. Wells and Mr. Matthew.

Mr. Isidore Geoffroy Saint-Hilaire, in his lectures delivered in 1850 (of which a Résumé appeared in the 'Revue et Mag. de Zoolog.,' Jan. 1851), briefly gives his reason for believing that specific characters "sont fixés pour chaque espèce, tant qu'elle se perpétue au milieu des mêmes circonstances: ils se modifient, si les circonstances ambiantes viennent à changer." "En-résumé, *l'observation* des animaux sauvages démontre déjà la variabilité *limitée* des espèces. Les *expériences* sur les animaux sauvages, devenus domestiques, et sur les animaux domestiques redevenus sauvages, la démontrent plus clairement encore. Ces mêmes expériences prouvent, de plus, que les différences produites peuvent être de *valeur générique.*" In his 'Hist. Nat. Générale' (tom. ii. p. 430, 1859) he amplifies analogous conclusions.

From a circular lately issued it appears that Dr. Freke, in 1851 ('Dublin Medical Press,' p. 322), propounded the doctrine that all organic beings have descended from one primordial form. His grounds of belief and treatment of the subject are wholly different from mine; but as Dr. Freke has now (1861) published his Essay on the 'Origin of Species by means of Organic Affinity,' the difficult attempt to give any idea of his views would be superfluous on my part.

Mr. Herbert Spencer, in an Essay (originally published in the 'Leader,' March, 1852, and republished in his 'Essays,' in 1858), has contrasted the theories of the Creation and the Development of organic beings with remarkable skill and force. He argues from the analogy of domestic productions, from the changes which the embryos of many species undergo, from the difficulty of distinguishing species and varieties, and from the principle of general graduation, that species have been modified; and he attributes the modification to the change of circumstances. The author (1855) has also treated Psychology on the principle of the necessary acquirement of each mental power and capacity by gradation.

In 1852 M. Naudin, a distinguished botanist, expressly stated, in an admirable paper on the Origin of Species ('Revue Horticole,' p. 102; since partly republished in the 'Nouvelles Archives du Muséum,' tom. i. p. 171), his belief that species are formed in an analogous manner as varieties are under cultivation; and the latter process he attributes to man's power of selection. But he does not show how selection acts under nature. He believes, like Dean Herbert, that species, when nascent, were more plastic than at present. He lays weight on what he calls the principle of finality, "puissance mystérieuse, indéterminée; fatalité pour les uns; pour les autres, volonté providentielle, dont l'action incessante sur les êtres vivants détermine, à toutes les époques de l'existence du monde, la forme, le volume, et la durée de chacun d'eux, en raison de sa destinée dans l'ordre de choses dont il fait partie. C'est cette puissance qui harmonise chaque membre à l'ensemble, en l'appropriant à la fonction qu'il doit remplir dans l'organisme général de la nature, fonction qui est pour lui sa raison d'être."*

In 1853 a celebrated geologist, Count Keyserling ('Bulletin de la Soc. Géolog.,' 2nd Ser., tom. x. p. 357), suggested that as new diseases, supposed to have been caused by some miasma, have arisen and spread over the world, so at certain periods the germs of existing species may have been chemically affected by circumambient molecules of a particular nature, and thus have given rise to new forms.

In this same year, 1853, Dr. Schaaffhausen published an excellent pamphlet ('Verhand. des Naturhist. Vereins der Preuss. Rheinlands,' &c.), in which he maintains the development of organic forms on the earth. He infers that many species have kept true for long periods, whereas a few have become modified. The distinction of species he explains by the destruction of intermediate graduated forms. "Thus, living plants and animals are not separated from the extinct by new creations, but are to be regarded as their descendants through continued reproduction."

A well-known French botanist, M. Lecoq, writes in 1854 ('Etudes sur Géograph. Bot.,' tom. i. p. 250), "On voit que nos recherches sur la fixité ou la variation de l'espèce, nous conduisent directement aux idées émises, par deux hommes justement célèbres, Geoffroy Saint-Hilaire et Goethe." Some other passages scattered through M. Lecoq's large work, make it a little doubtful how far he extends his views on the modification of species.

The 'Philosophy of Creation' has been treated in a masterly manner by the Rev. Baden Powell, in his 'Essays on the Unity of Worlds,' 1855. Nothing can be more striking than the manner in which he shows that the introduction of new species is "a regular, not a casual phenomenon," or, as Sir John Herschel expresses it, "a natural in contradistinction to a miraculous process."

---

*From references in Bronn's 'Untersuchungen über die Entwickelungs-Gesetze,' it appears that the celebrated botanist and palæontologist Unger published, in 1852, his belief that species undergo development and modification. Dalton, likewise, in Pander and Dalton's work on Fossil Sloths, expressed, in 1821, a similar belief. Similar views have, as is well known, been maintained by Oken in his mystical 'Natur-Philosophie.' From other references in Godron's work 'Sur l'Espèce,' it seems that Bory St. Vincent, Burdach, Poiret, and Fries, have all admitted that new species are continually being produced.

I may add, that of the thirty-four authors named in this Historical Sketch, who believe in the modification of species, or at least disbelieve in separate acts of creation, twenty-seven have written on special branches of natural history or geology.

The third volume of the 'Journal of the Linnean Society' contains papers, read July 1st, 1858, by Mr. Wallace and myself, in which, as stated in the introductory remarks to this volume, the theory of Natural Selection is promulgated by Mr. Wallace with admirable force and clearness.

Von Baer, towards whom all zoologists feel so profound a respect, expressed about the year 1859 (see Prof. Rudolph Wagner, 'Zoologisch-Anthropologische Untersuchungen,' 1861, s. 51) his conviction, chiefly grounded on the laws of geographical distribution, that forms now perfectly distinct have descended from a single parent-form.

In June, 1859, Professor Huxley gave a lecture before the Royal Institution on the 'Persistent Types of Animal Life.' Referring to such cases, he remarks, "It is difficult to comprehend the meaning of such facts as these, if we suppose that each species of animal and plant, or each great type of organisation, was formed and placed upon the surface of the globe at long intervals by a distinct act of creative power; and it is well to recollect that such an assumption is as unsupported by tradition or revelation as it is opposed to the general analogy of nature. If, on the other hand, we view 'Persistent Types' in relation to that hypothesis, which supposes the species living at any time to be the result of the gradual modification of pre-existing species a hypothesis which, though unproven, and sadly damaged by some of its supporters, is yet the only one to which physiology lends any countenance; their existence would seem to show that the amount of modification which living beings have undergone during geological time is but very small in relation to the whole series of changes which they have suffered."

In December, 1859, Dr. Hooker published his 'Introduction to the Australian Flora.' In the first part of this great work he admits the truth of the descent and modification of species, and supports this doctrine by many original observations.

The first edition of this work was published on November 24th, 1859, and the second edition on January 7th, 1860.

Co-Relations and Their Measurement, Chiefly from Anthropometric Data 1888

Francis Galton

"Co-relation or correlation of structure" is a phrase much used in biology, and not least in that branch of it which refers to heredity, and the idea is even more frequently present than the phrase; but I am not aware of any previous attempt to define it clearly, to trace its mode of action in detail, or to show how to measure its degree.

Two variable organs are said to be co-related when the variation of the one is accompanied on the average by more or less variation of the other, and in the same direction. Thus the length of the arm is said to be co-related with that of the leg, because a person with a long arm has usually a long leg, and conversely. If the co-relation be close, then a person with a very long arm would usually have a very long leg; if it be moderately close, then the length of his leg would be only long, not very long; and if there were no co-relation at all then the length of his leg would on the average be mediocre. It is easy to see that co-relation must be the consequence of the variations of the two organs being partly due to common causes. If they were wholly due to common causes, the co-relation would be perfect, as is approximately the case with the symmetrically disposed parts of the body. If they were in no respect due to common causes, the co-relation would be nil. Between these two extremes are an endless number of intermediate cases, and it will be shown how the closeness of co-relation in any particular case admits of being expressed by a simple number.

To avoid the possibility of misconception, it is well to point out that the subject in hand has nothing whatever to do with the average proportions between the various limbs, in different races, which have been often discussed from early times up to the present day, both by artists and by anthropologists. The fact that the average ratio between the stature and the cubit is as 100 to 37, or thereabouts, does not give the slightest information about the nearness with which they vary together. It would be an altogether erroneous inference to suppose their average proportion to be maintained so that when the cubit was, say, one-twentieth longer than the average cubit, the stature might be expected to be one-twentieth greater than the average stature, and conversely. Such a supposition is easily shown to be contradicted both by fact and theory.

The relation between the cubit and the stature will be shown to be such that for every inch, centimetre, or other unit of absolute length that the cubit deviates from the mean length of cubits, the stature will on the average deviate from the mean length of statures to the amount of 2.5 units, and in the same direction. Conversely, for each unit of deviation of stature, the average deviation of the cubit will be 0.26 unit. These relations are not numerically reciprocal, but the exactness of the corelation becomes established when we have transmuted the inches or other measurement of the cubit and of the stature into units dependent on their respective scales of variability. We thus cause a long cubit and an equally long stature, as compared to the general run of cubits and statures, to be designated by an identical scale-value. The particular unit that I shall employ is the value of the probable error of any single measure in its own group. In that of the cubit, the probable error is 0.56 inch = 1.42 cm.; in the stature it is 1.75 inch = 4.44 cm. Therefore the measured lengths of the cubit in inches will be transmuted into terms of a new scale, in which each unit = 0.56 inch, and the measured lengths of the stature will be transmuted into terms of another new scale in which each unit is 1.75 inch. After this has been done, we shall find the deviation of the cubit as compared to the mean of the corresponding deviations of the stature, to be as 1 to 0.8. Conversely, the deviation of the stature as compared to the mean of the corresponding deviations of the cubit will also be as 1 to 0.8. Thus the existence of the co-relation is established, and its measure is found to be 0.8.

Now as to the evidence of all this. The data were obtained at my anthropometric laboratory at South Kensington. They are of 350 males of 21 years and upwards, but as a large proportion of them were students, and barely 21 years of age, they were not wholly fullgrown; but neither that fact nor the small number of observations is prejudicial to the conclusions that will be reached. They were measured in various ways, partly for the purpose of this inquiry. It will be sufficient to give some of them as examples. The exact number of 350 is not preserved throughout, as injury to some limb or other reduced the available number by 1, 2, or 3 in different cases. After marshalling the measures of each limb in the order of their magnitudes, I noted the measures in each series that occupied respectively the positions of the first, second, and third quarterly divisions. Calling these measures in any one series, Q_1, M, and Q_3, I take M, which is the median or middlemost value, as that whence the deviations are to be measured, and $\frac{1}{2}(Q_3 - Q_1) = Q$, as the probable error of any single measure in the series. This is practically the same as saying that one-half of the deviations fall within the distance to $\pm Q$ from the mean value, because the series run with fair symmetry. In this way I obtained the following value of M and Q, in which the second decimal must be taken as only roughly approximate. The M and Q of any particular series may be identified by a suffix, thus M_c, Q_c might stand for those of the cubit, and M_s, Q_s for those of the stature.

Tables were then constructed, each referring to a different pair of the above elements, like Tables II and III, which will suffice as examples of the whole of them. It will be understood that the Q value is a universal unit applicable to the most varied measurements, such as breathing capacity, strength, memory, keenness of eyesight, and enables them to be compared together on equal terms notwithstanding their intrinsic diversity. It does not only refer to measures of length, though partly for the sake of compactness, it is only those of length that will be here given as examples. It is unnecessary to extend the limits of Table II, as it includes every line and column in my MS. table that contains not less than twenty entries. None of the entries lying within the flanking lines and columns of Table II were used.

TABLE I

	Inch	M. Centim.	Inch	Q. Centim.
Head length	7.62	19.35	0.19	0.48
Head breadth	6.00	15.24	0.18	0.46
Stature	67.20	170.69	1.75	4.44
Left middle finger	4.54	11.53	0.15	0.38
Left cubit	18.05	45.70	0.56	1.42
Height of right knee	20.50	52.00	0.80	2.03

Note.—The head length is its maximum length measured from the notch between and just below the eyebrows. The cubit is measured with the hand prone and without taking off the coat; it is the distance between the elbow of the bent left arm and the tip of the middle finger. The height of the knee is taken sitting when the knee is bent at right angles, less the measured thickness of the heel of the boot.

TABLE II

Stature in inches.	Length of left cubic in inches, 348 adult males.								Total cases
	Under 16.5	*16.5 and under 17.0*	*17.0 and under 17.5*	*17.5 and under 18.0*	*18.0 and under 18.5*	*18.5 and under 19.0*	*19.0 and under 19.5*	*19.5 and above*	
71 and above				1	3	4	15	7	30
70					1	5	13	11	30
69		1	1	2	25	15	6		50
68		1	3	7	14	7	4	2	48
67		1	7	15	28	8	2		61
66		1	7	18	15	6			48
65		4	10	12	8	2			36
64		5	11	2	3				21
Below 64	9	12	10	3	1				34
	9	25	49	61	102	55	38	9	348

The measures were made and recorded to the nearest tenth of an inch. The heading of 70 inches of stature includes all records between 69.5 and 70.4 inches; that of 69 includes all between 68.5 and 69.4, and so on.

The values derived from Table II, and from other similar tables, are entered in Table III, where they occupy all the columns up to the last three, the first of which is headed "smoothered." These smoothed values were obtained by plotting the observed values, after transmuting them as above described into their respective Q units, upon a diagram such as is shown in the figure. The deviations of the "subject" are measured parallel to the axis of y in the figure, and those of the mean of the corresponding values of the "relative" are measured parallel to the axis of x. When the stature is taken as the subject, the median positions of the corresponding cubits, which are given in the successive lines of Table III, are marked with small circles. When the cubit is the subject, the mean positions of the corresponding statures are marked with crosses. The firm line in the figure is drawn to represent the general run of the small circles and crosses. It is here seen to be a straight line, and it was similarly found to be straight in every other figure drawn from the different pairs of co-related variables that I have as yet tried. But the inclination of the line to the vertical differs considerably in different cases. In the present one the inclination is such that a deviation of 1 on the part of the subject, whether it be stature or cubit, is accompanied by a mean deviation on the part of the relative, whether it be cubit or stature, of 0.8. This decimal fraction is consequently transmuted into inches. If the stature be taken as the subject, then Q_s is associated with $Q_c \times 0.8$; that is, a deviation of 1.75 inches in the one with 0.56×0.8 of the other. This is the same as 1 inch of stature being associated with a mean length of cubit equal to 0.26 inch. Conversely, if the cubit be taken as the subject, then Q_c is associated with $Q_x 0.8$; that is, a deviation of 0.56 inch in the one with 1.75×0.8

TABLE III

Stature M_s = 67.2 inches; Q_s = 1.75 inch. Left Cubit M_c = 18.05 inches; Q_c = 0.56 inch.

No. of cases.	Stature.	Deviation from M_s reckoned in		Mean of corresponding left cubits.	Deviation from M_c reckoned in			Smoothed values Multiplied by Q_c	Added to M_c
		Inches	Units of Q_s		Inches	Units of Q_c Observed	Smoothed		
	inches			inches					
30	70.0	+2.8	+1.60	18.8	+0.8	+1.42	+1.30	+0.73	18.8
50	69.0	+1.8	+1.03	18.3	+0.3	+0.53	+0.84	+0.47	18.5
38	68.0	+0.8	+0.46	18.2	+0.2	+0.36	+0.38	+0.21	18.3
61	67.0	−0.2	−0.11	18.1	+0.1	+0.18	−0.08	−0.04	18.0
48	66.0	−1.2	−0.69	17.8	−0.2	−0.36	−0.54	−0.30	17.8
36	65.0	−2.2	−1.25	17.7	−0.3	−0.53	−1.00	−0.56	17.5
21	64.0	−3.2	−1.83	17.2	−0.8	−1.46	−1.46	−0.80	17.2

No. of cases.	Left Cubit	Deviation from M_s reckoned in		Mean of corresponding statures	Deviation from M_c reckoned in			Smoothed values multiplied by Q_s	Added to M_s
		Inches	Units of Q_s		Inches	Units of Q_s Observed	Smoothed		
38	19.25	+1.20	+2.14	70.3	+3.1	+1.8	+1.70	+3.0	70.2
55	18.75	+0.70	+1.25	68.7	+1.5	+0.9	+1.00	+1.8	69.0
102	18.25	+0.20	+0.36	67.4	+0.2	+0.1	+0.28	+0.5	67.7
61	17.75	−0.30	−0.53	66.3	−0.9	−0.5	−0.43	−0.8	66.4
49	17.25	−0.80	−1.42	65.0	−2.2	−1.3	−1.15	−2.0	65.2
25	16.75	−1.30	−2.31	63.7	−3.5	−2.0	−1.85	−3.2	64.0

of the other. This is the same as 1 inch of cubit being associated with a mean length of 2.5 inches of stature. If centimetre be read for inch the same holds true.

Six other tables are now given in a summary form, to show how well calculation on the above principles agrees with observation.

From Table IV the deductions given in Table V can be made; but they may be made directly from tables of the form of Table III, whence Table IV was itself derived.

When the deviations of the subject and those of the mean of the relatives are severally measured in units of their own Q, there is always a regression in the value of the latter. This is precisely analogous to what was observed in kinship, as I showed in my paper read before this Society on "Hereditary Stature" (*Roy. Soc. Proc.*, XL, (1886), 42). The statures of kinsmen are co-related variables; thus, the stature of the father is correlated to that of the adult son, and the stature of the adult son to that of the father; the stature of the uncle to that of the adult nephew, and the stature of the adult nephew to that of the uncle, and so on; but the index of co-

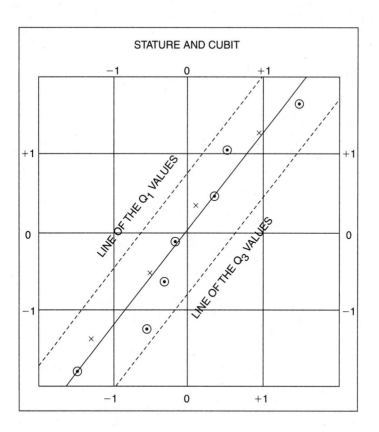

FIGURE 6.1

relation, which is what I there called "regression," is different in the different cases. In dealing with kinships there is usually no need to reduce the measures to units of Q, because the Q values are alike in all the kinsmen, being of the same value as that of the population at large. It however happened that the very first case that I analysed was different in this respect. I was the reciprocal relation between the statures of what I called the "mid-parent" and the son. The mid-parent is an ideal progenitor, whose stature is the average of that of the father on the one hand and of that of the mother on the other, after her stature has been transmuted into its male equivalent by the multiplication of the factor of 1.08. The Q of the mid-parental statures was found to be 1.2, that of the population dealt with was 1.7. Again, the mean deviation measured in inches of the statures of the sons was found to be two-thirds of the deviation of the mid-parents, while the mean deviation in inches of the mid-parent was one-third of the deviation of the sons. Here the re-

gression, when calculated in Q units, is in the first case from $\dfrac{1}{1.2}$ to $\dfrac{2}{3} \times 1.7 = 1$

to 0.47, and in the second case from $\dfrac{1}{1.7}$ to $\dfrac{1}{3} \times \dfrac{1}{1.2} = 1$ to 0.44, which is prac-

tically the same.

TABLE IV

No. of cases	Length of head	Mean of corresponding statures		No. of cases	Height	Mean of corresponding lengths of head	
		Observed	Calculated			Observed	Calculated
32	7.90	68.5	68.1	26	70.5	7.72	7.75
41	7.80	67.2	67.8	30	69.5	7.70	7.72
46	7.70	67.6	67.5	50	68.5	7.65	7.68
52	7.60	66.7	67.2	49	67.5	7.65	7.64
58	7.50	66.8	66.8	56	66.5	7.57	7.60
34	7.40	66.0	66.5	43	65.5	7.57	7.69
26	7.30	66.7	66.2	31	64.5	7.54	7.65

No. of cases	Height	Mean of corresponding length of left middle finger		No. of cases	Length of left middle finger	Mean of corresponding statures	
		Observed	Calculated			Observed	Calculated
30	70.5	4.71	4.74	23	4.80	70.2	69.4
50	69.5	4.55	4.68	49	4.70	68.1	68.5
37	68.5	4.57	4.62	62	4.60	68.0	67.7
62	67.5	4.58	4.56	63	4.50	67.3	66.9
48	66.5	4.50	4.50	57	4.40	66.0	66.1
37	65.5	4.47	4.44	35	4.30	65.7	65.3
20	64.5	4.33	4.38				

No. of cases	Left middle finger	Mean of corresponding lengths of left cubit		No. of cases	Length of left cubit	Mean of corresponding length of left middle finger	
		Observed	Calculated			Observed	Calculated
23	4.80	18.97	18.80	29	19.00	4.76	4.75
50	4.70	18.55	18.49	32	18.70	4.64	4.69
62	4.60	18.24	18.18	48	18.40	4.60	4.62
62	4.50	18.00	17.87	70	18.10	4.56	4.55
57	4.40	17.72	17.55	37	17.80	4.49	4.48
34	4.30	17.27	17.24	31	17.50	4.40	4.41
				28	17.20	4.37	4.34
				24	16.90	4.32	4.28

No. of cases	Length of head	Mean of corresponding breadths of head		No. of cases	Breadth of head	Mean of corresponding lengths of head	
		Observed	Calculated			Observed	Calculated
32	7.90	6.14	6.12	27	6.30	7.72	7.84
41	7.80	6.05	6.08	36	6.20	7.72	7.75
46	7.70	6.14	6.04	53	6.10	7.65	7.65
52	7.60	5.98	6.00	58	6.00	7.68	7.60
58	7.50	5.98	5.96	56	5.90	7.50	7.55
34	7.40	5.96	5.91	37	5.80	7.55	7.50
26	7.30	5.85	5.87	30	5.70	7.45	7.46

TABLE IV (cont.)

No. of cases	Stature	Mean of corresponding heights of knee		No. of cases	Height of knee	Mean of corresponding statures	
		Observed	*Calculated*			*Observed*	*Calculated*
30	70.0	21.7	21.7	23	22.2	70.5	70.6
50	69.0	21.1	21.3	32	21.7	69.8	69.6
38	68.0	20.7	20.9	50	21.2	68.7	68.6
61	67.0	20.5	20.5	68	20.7	67.3	67.7
49	66.0	20.2	20.1	74	20.2	66.2	66.7
36	65.0	19.7	19.7	41	19.7	65.5	65.7
				26	19.2	64.3	64.7

No. of cases	Left cuit	Mean of corresponding heights of knee		No. of cases	Height of knee	Mean of corresponding left cubit	
		Observed	*Calculated*			*Observed*	*Calculated*
29	19.0	21.5	21.6	23	22.25	18.98	18.97
32	18.7	21.4	21.2	30	21.75	18.68	18.70
48	18.4	20.8	20.9	52	21.25	18.38	18.44
70	17.1	20.7	20.6	69	20.75	18.15	18.17
37	17.8	20.4	20.2	70	20.25	17.75	17.90
31	17.5	20.0	19.9	41	19.75	17.55	17.63
28	17.2	19.8	19.6	27	19.25	17.02	17.36
23	16.9	19.3	19.2				

TABLE V

Subject	Relative		r.	$\sqrt{(1-r^2)} = f$	In units of ordinary measure As 1 to	f
Stature	Cubit	} 0.8		0.60	0.26	0.45
Cubit	Stature				2.5	1.4
Stature	Head length	} 0.35		0.93	0.38	1.63
Head length	Stature				3.2	0.17
Stature	Middle finger	} 0.7		0.72	0.06	0.10
Middle finger	Stature				8.2	1.26
Middle finger	Cubit	} 0.85		0.61	3.13	0.34
Cubit	Middle finger				0.21	0.09
Head length	Head breadth	} 0.45		0.89	0.43	0.16
Head breadth	Head length				0.48	0.17
Stature	Height of knee	} 0.9		0.44	0.41	0.35
Height of knee	Stature				1.20	0.77
Cubit	Height of knee	} 0.8		0.60	1.14	0.64
Height of knee	Cubit				0.56	0.45

In the "In units of Q" column group, the heading **In units of Q** spans the **r.** and **√(1 − r²) = f** columns.

The rationale of all this will be found discussed in the paper on "Hereditary Stature," to which reference has already been made, and in the appendix to it by Mr. J. D. Hamilton Dickson. The entries in any table, such as Table II, may be looked upon as the values of the vertical ordinates to a surface of frequency, whose mathematical properties were discussed in the above-mentioned appendix, therefore I need not repeat them here. But there is always room for legitimate doubt whether conclusions based on the strict properties of the ideal law of error would be sufficiently correct to be serviceable in actual cases of co-relation between variables that conform only approximately to that law. It is therefore exceedingly desirable to put the theoretical conclusions to frequent test, as has been done with these anthropometric data. The result is that anthropologists may now have much less hesitation than before, in availing themselves of the properties of the law of frequency of error.

I have given in Table V a column headed $\sqrt{(1 - r^2)} = f$. The meaning off is explained in the paper on "Hereditary Stature." It is the Q value of the distribution of any system of x values, as x_1, x_2, x_3, &c., round the mean of all of them, which we may call X. The knowledge of f enables dotted lines to be drawn, as in the figure above, parallel to the line of M values, between which one half of the x observations, for each value of y, will be included. This value of f has much anthropological interest of its own, especially in connexion with M. Bertillon's system of anthropometric identification, to which I will not call attention now.

It is not necessary to extend the list of examples to show how to measure the degree in which one variable may be co-related with the combined effect on other variables, whether these be themselves co-related or not. To do so, we begin by reducing each measure into others, each having the Q of its own system for a unit. We thus obtain a set of values that can be treated exactly in the same way as the measures of a single variable were treated in Tables II and onwards. Neither is it necessary to give examples of a method by which the degree may be measured, in which the variables in a series each member of which is the summed effect of n variables, may be modified by their partial co-relation. After transmuting the separate measures as above, and then summing them, we should find the probable error of any one of them to be $\sqrt{n}$ if the variables were perfectly independent, and n if they were rigidly and perfectly co-related. The observed value would be always somewhere intermediate between these extremes, and would give the information that is wanted.

To conclude, the prominent characteristics of any two co-related variables, so far at least as I have as yet tested them, are four in number. It is supposed that their respective measures have been first transmuted into others of which the unit is in each case equal to the probable error of a single measure in its own series. Let y = the deviation of the subject, which ever of the two variables may be taken in that capacity; and let x_1, x_2, x_3, &c., be the corresponding deviations of the relative, and let the mean of these be X. Then we find: (1) that y = rX for all values of y; (2) that r is the same, whichever of the two variables is taken for the subject; (3) that r is always less than 1; (4) that r measures the closeness of co-relation.

CHAPTER 7

FUNCTIONALISM: DEVELOPMENT AND FOUNDING

WILLIAM JAMES (1842–1910)

William James was born in the Astor House, in New York City, on January 11, 1842.[1] James came from a wealthy family. His grandfather, an Irish immigrant after whom he was named, was reputedly the second richest person in the state of New York (Ross, 1991). James, the oldest of five children, was not the prototypic oldest child, that is, organized and conservative. Throughout his life, James exhibited a remarkably open-minded nature. His father, Henry, did not have to work and was an avid intellectual and traveler. The young James's education alternated between the United States and Europe. His family, in addition, exposed him to many leading intellectuals of the time. James's grandfather had been a martinet; perhaps in reaction to this, his father was most liberal with his children, allowing them to interact freely with his distinguished guests.

Though widely educated, at 18 James was undecided as to the direction of his career. At this point, he undertook his first occupation, artist and painter, studying under William Morris Hunt in Newport, Rhode Island. Leary (1992) states that the year spent in Rhode Island as an artist may very well have been important in shaping James's subsequent psychological views. Like an artist, James was always sympathetic to the idea that one could "see" the same thing in many different ways.

---

[1]There is an enormous amount of biographic material about William James. The present sketch is an amalgamation of Perry (1948), Allen (1967), and Meyers (1986).

Certainly, as a psychological theorist, he liked to paint with broad strokes. In fact, when his famous textbook, *The Principles of Psychology* (1890), was published, G. Stanley Hall (1890), founder of the American Psychological Association, called it "impressionistic." At the end of a year, James left Newport still uncertain about his career.[2]

Having left the formal study of art in 1861, it was not until 1864 that James entered Medical School at Harvard, a decision that would eventually lead to a professorship and career as a psychologist/philosopher at his alma mater. On the way to his medical degree in 1869, James made two important side trips. In 1865, he went with the famous Harvard paleontologist, Agassiz, as an unpaid assistant to Brazil. While there, James was more interested in drawing his surroundings than research. (This antipathy toward empirical research was present later when he was a psychologist.) After returning to the United States and briefly resuming his medical studies, James traveled to Europe to recuperate from ill health.[3] During this period, 1867–1868, he visited the laboratories of Helmholtz and Wundt and was thus aware that psychology was becoming a science in Germany. In 1869, he received his degree in medicine but never intended to practice. James was still without direction and suffered a panoply of psychosomatic disorders. Moreover, he found that depressive thoughts and suicidal ideation were usurping an undue portion of his time. At this time, two things were crucial in saving his life, the philosophy of Renouvier and a teaching post at Harvard College.

Renouvier's *Second Essay* persuaded him of the freedom of the will. As a result, James decided that he was not obligated to spend so much of his time with melancholy brooding. In 1872, Charles William Eliot, president of Harvard and a family friend, offered James a position of instructor of physiology that he eventually accepted.[4] This was a propitious time for James to arrive at Harvard because Eliot, like many college presidents of that era, was interested in expanding the curriculum. In 1875, James offered a new course on the relation between physiology and psychology.[5] Having never had a formal course in psychology, he heard his first classroom lecture on psychology from himself!

In 1878, James married Alice Gibbons, to whom his family had introduced him, and signed a contract with Henry Holt publishers to write a psychology textbook. His wife added order to his scattered life, and the textbook kept him busy for the next 12 years. The textbook, *The Principles of Psychology,* was a *tour de force,* and along with its abridgment, *The Briefer Course,* was used for many years worldwide. In this book, James displayed his characteristically open-minded attitude. He

---

[2]It is too facile to state that James left Hunt at the end of a year because he lacked talent. In a letter to the editor of *The New York Times,* shortly after James's death in 1910, noted artist, John Le Farge (1910), stated that James, "had the promise of being a remarkable, perhaps a great painter" (p. 8). (James was able enough to have acted as Hunt's assistant on a project in Albany.)

[3]Throughout his life, James sought travel as a cure for his ill health.

[4]The Harvard of that day was quite different from the Harvard of today. There were only 23 faculty members on the arts and science faculty to teach a student body of 539 (Maddocks, 1986).

[5]He established the first psychological laboratory at Harvard the same year for the sum of $300 Watson (1968).

thus gave the psychological scene an approach dramatically different from that of the highly circumscribed structuralists.

Emphasizing *both* behavior and consciousness, James stressed three themes that undergird his and the ensuing functionalistic psychology: (1) the adaptive nature of mental activity, (2) the ongoing nature of mental activity, and (3) the physiological undergirding of all psychological activity. These three themes reflect the influence of Darwinian theory on James and his successors. The evolutionary process, like day-to-day behavior, helps the individual adapt to the environment. Moreover, the evolutionary and psychological processes are never complete and can be understood only in the context of an organism's past, present, and projected future. That is, all psychological processes are part of an ongoing stream.[6] The results of these processes are reflected in one's physiological constitution, and therefore to understand any organism, human or animal, the psychologist must understand their respective physiologies. The emphasis on physiology and adaptation is evident in both selections for this chapter, the first chapter of James's *Principles of Psychology* and an abridgment of Angell's (1907) "The Province of Functional Psychology."

James taught few students and would dislike the thought of founding any school since he found the idea of a school too limiting. Nevertheless, his pupils, all famous psychologists in their own right, Angell, Thorndike, Woodworth, and Calkins,[7] show evidence of James's teaching. The most clear line of influence to the functionalists is via Frank Angell who went west from Harvard to chair the fledgling department of psychology at the University of Chicago, for many years the seat of the functionalistic approach.

James, never interested in laboratory work, hired Hugo Munsterburg in 1892 to take over the laboratory and then turned his mind to religious and philosophical matters (see James, 1902, 1907, 1909). James, however, kept some of his ties with psychology since he served a second term as president of the American Psychological Association in 1904. He died in 1910 at his country home in Mount Chicora, New Hampshire, leaving a triple legacy in psychology, religion, and philosophy. His life reflected a lesson he learned as a painter: the same thing can be seen many different ways.

REFERENCES

Allen, G. W. (1967). *William James: A biography.* New York: Viking.

Angell, J. R. (1907). The province of functional psychology. *Psychological Review,* 14, 61–91.

Furomoto, L. (1979). Mary Whilton Calkins (1863–1930): Fourteenth president of the American Psychological Association. *Journal of the History of the Behavior Sciences,* 15, 346–356.

---

[6]In this context, it is significant that James spoke of a stream of consciousness.

[7]Calkins was the first psychologist to use the paired-associate method of investigating memory (Madigan & O'Hara, 1992). She studied interference effects, a staple interest of the functionalists (Hilgard & Bower, 1975). Calkins participated in James's graduate seminars but was denied her Ph.D. at Harvard because of her gender (Furumoto, 1991). In 1905, she succeeded James and was the first female president of the American Psychological Association.

Hall, G. S. (1890). [Review of the book *Principles of psychology*]. *The American Journal of Psychology, 3*, 578–591.

Hilgard, E. R. & Bower, G. H. *Theories of learning* (4th ed.). Engelwood Cliffs, NJ: Prentice-Hall.

James, W. (1890). *Principles of Psychology*. New York: Holt, pp. 1–11.

James, W. (1902). *The varieties of religious experience*. New York: Longmans, Green.

James, W. (1907). *Pragmatism*. New York: Longmans, Green.

James, W. (1909). *The meaning of truth: A sequel to pragmatism*. New York: Longmans, Green.

Leary, D. E. (1992). William James and the art of human understanding. *American Psychologist, 47*, 152–160.

Le Farge, J. (1910, September 2). A new side of Prof. James. *The New York Times*, p. 8.

Maddocks, M. (1986). Harvard was once unimaginably small and humble. *Smithsonian, 16*, 140–160.

Madigan, S. & O'Hara, R. (1992). Short-term memory at the turn of the century: Mary Whilton Calkins's memory research. *American Psychologist, 47*, 170–174.

Ross, B. (1992). William James: Spoiled child of American psychology. In Kimble, G. A., Wertheimer, M., & White, C. L., *Portraits of pioneers in psychology* (pp. 13–26). Hillsdale, NJ: Earlbaum.

Watson, R. I. *The great psychologist*. (2nd ed). Philadelphia: Lippincott.

Principles of Psychology

William James

CHAPTER I.
THE SCOPE OF PSYCHOLOGY.

Psychology is the Science of Mental Life, both of its phenomena and their conditions. The phenomena are such things as we call feelings, desires, cognitions, reasonings, decisions, and the like; and, superficially considered, their variety and complexity is such as to leave a chaotic impression on the observer. The most natural and consequently the earliest way of unifying the material was, first, to classify it as well as might be, and, secondly, to affiliate the diverse mental modes thus found, upon a simple entity, the personal Soul, of which they are taken to be so many facultative manifestations. Now, for instance, the Soul manifests its faculty of Memory, now of Reasoning, now of Volition, or again its Imagination or its Appetite. This is the orthodox 'spiritualistic' theory of scholasticism and of common-sense. Another and a less obvious way of unifying the chaos is to seek common elements *in* the divers mental facts rather than a common agent behind them, and to explain them constructively by the various forms of arrangement of these elements, as one explains houses by stones and bricks. The 'associationist' schools of Herbart in Germany, and of Hume the Mills and Bain in Britain have thus constructed a *psychology without a soul* by taking discrete 'ideas,' faint or vivid, and showing how, by their cohesions, repulsions, and forms of succession, such things as reminiscences, perceptions, emotions, volitions, passions, theories, and all the other furnishings of an individual's mind may be engendered. The very Self or *ego* of the individual comes in this way to be viewed no longer as the pre-existing source of the representations, but rather as their last and most complicated fruit.

Now, if we strive rigorously to simplify the phenomena in either of these ways, we soon become aware of inadequacies in our method. Any particular cognition, for example, or recollection, is accounted for on the soul-theory by being referred to the spiritual faculties of Cognition or of Memory. These faculties themselves are thought of as absolute properties of the soul; that is, to take the case of memory, no reason is given why we should remember a fact as it happened, except that so to remember it constitutes the essence of our Recollective Power. We may, as spiritualists, try to explain our memory's failures and blunders by secondary causes. But its *successes* can invoke no factors save the existence of certain objective things to be remembered on the one hand, and of our faculty of memory on the other. When, for instance, I recall my graduation-day, and drag all its incidents and emotions up from death's dateless night, no mechanical cause can explain this process, nor can any analysis reduce it to lower terms or make its nature seem other than an ultimate *datum,* which, whether we rebel or not at its mysteriousness, must simply be taken for granted if we are to psychologize at all. However the associationist may represent the present ideas as thronging and arranging themselves, still, the spiritualists insists, he has in the end to admit that *something,* be it brain, be it 'ideas,' be it 'association,' *knows* past time *as* past, and fills it out with this or that event. And when the spiritualist calls memory an 'irreducible faculty,' he says no more than this admission of the associationist already grants.

And yet the admission is far from being a satisfactory simplification of the concrete facts. For why should this absolute god-given Faculty retain so much better the events of yesterday than those of last year, and, best of all, those of an hour ago? Why, again, in old age should its grasp of childhood's events seem firmest? Why should illness and exhaustion enfeeble it? Why should repeating an experience strengthen our recollection of it? Why should drugs, fevers, asphyxia, and excitement resuscitate things long since forgotten? If we content ourselves with merely affirming that the faculty of memory is so peculiarly constituted by nature as to exhibit just these oddities, we seem little the better for having invoked it, for our explanation becomes as complicated as that of the crude facts with which we started. Moreover there is something grotesque and irrational in the supposition that the soul is equipped with elementary powers of such an ingeniously intricate sort. Why *should* our memory cling more easily to the near than the remote? Why should it lose its grasp of proper sooner than of abstract names? Such peculiarities seem quite fantastic; and might, for aught we can see *a priori,* be the precise opposites of what they are. Evidently, then, *the faculty does not exist absolutely, but works under conditions; and the quest of the conditions* becomes the psychologist's most interesting task.

However firmly he may hold to the soul and her remembering faculty, he must acknowledge that she never exerts the latter without a *cue,* and that something must always precede and *remind* us of whatever we are to recollect. "An *idea!*" says the associationist, "an idea associated with the remembered thing; and this explains also why things repeatedly met with are more easily recollected, for their associates on the various occasions furnish so many distinct avenues of recall." But this does not explain the effects of fever, exhaustion, hypnotism, old age, and the like. And in general, the pure associationist's account of our mental life is almost as bewildering as that of the pure spiritualist. This multitude of ideas, existing absolutely, yet clinging together, and weaving an endless carpet of themselves, like dominoes in ceaseless change, or the bits of glass in a kaleidoscope,—whence do they get their fantastic laws of clinging, and why do they cling in just the shapes they do?

For this the associationist must introduce the order of experience in the outer world. The dance of the ideas is a copy, somewhat mutilated and altered, of the order of phenomena. But the slightest reflection shows that phenomena have absolutely no power to influence our ideas until they have first impressed our senses and our brain. The bare existence of a past fact is no ground for our remembering it. Unless we have seen it, or somehow *undergone* it, we shall never know of its having been. The experiences of the body are thus one of the conditions of the faculty of memory being what it is. And a very small amount of reflection on facts shows that one part of the body, namely, the brain, is the part whose experiences are directly concerned. If the nervous communication be cut off between the brain and other parts, the experiences of those other parts are non-existent for the mind. The eye is blind, the ear deaf, the hand insensible and motionless. And conversely, if the brain be injured, consciousness is abolished or altered, even although every other organ in the body be ready to play its normal part. A blow on the head, a sudden subtraction of blood, the pressure of an apoplectic hemorrhage, may have the first effect; whilst a very few ounces of alcohol or grains of opium or hasheesh, or a whiff of chloroform or nitrous oxide gas, are sure to have the second. The delirium of fever, the altered self of insanity, are all due to foreign matters circulating through the brain, or to pathological changes in that organ's substance. The fact that the brain is the one immediate bodily condition of the mental operations is indeed so universally admitted nowadays that I need spend no more time in illustrating it, but will simply postulate it and pass on. The whole remainder of the book will be more or less of a proof that the postulate was correct.

Bodily experiences, therefore, and more particularly brain-experiences, must take a place amongst those conditions of the mentallife of which Psychology need take account. *The spiritualist and the associationist must both be 'cerebralists,'* to the extent at least of admitting that certain peculiarities in the way of working of their own favorite principles are explicable only by the fact that the brain laws are a codeterminant of the result.

Our first conclusion, then, is that a certain amount of brain-physiology must be presupposed or included in Psychology.*

In still another way the psychologist is forced to be something of a nerve-physiologist. Mental phenomena are not only conditioned *a parte ante* by bodily processes; but they lead to them *a parte post*. That they lead to *acts* is of course the most familiar of truths, but I do not merely mean acts in the sense of voluntary and deliberate muscular performances. Mental states occasion also changes in the calibre of blood-vessels, or alteration in the heart-beats, or processes more sub-

---

*Cf. Geo. T. Ladd: Elements of Physiological Psychology (1887), pt. III, chap. III, §§9, 12.

tle still, in glands and viscera. If these are taken into account, as well as acts which follow at some *remote period* because the mental state was once there, it will be safe to lay down the general law that *no mental modification ever occurs which is not accompanied or followed by a bodily change.* The ideas and feelings, *e.g.,* which these present printed characters excite in the reader's mind not only occasion movements of his eyes and nascent movements of articulation in him, but will some day make him speak, or take sides in a discussion, or give advice, or choose a book to read, differently from what would have been the case had they never impressed his retina. Our psychology must therefore take account not only of the conditions antecedent to mental states, but of their resultant consequences as well.

But actions originally prompted by conscious intelligence may grow so automatic by dint of habit as to be apparently unconsciously performed. Standing, walking, buttoning and unbuttoning, piano-playing, talking, even saying one's prayers, may be done when the mind is absorbed in other things. The performances of animal *instinct* seem semi-automatic, and the *reflex acts* of self-preservation certainly are so. Yet they resemble intelligent acts in bringing about the *same ends* at which the animals' consciousness, on other occasions, deliberately aims. Shall the study of such machine-like yet purposive acts as these be included in Psychology?

The boundary line of the mental is certainly vague. It is better not to be pedantic, but to let the science be as vague as its subject, and include such phenomena as these if by so doing we can throw any light on the main business in hand. It will ere long be seen, I trust, that we can; and that we gain much more by a broad than by a narrow conception of our subject. At a certain stage in the development of every science a degree of vagueness is what best consists with fertility. On the whole, few recent formulas have done more real service of a rough sort in psychology than the Spencerian one that the essence of mental life and of bodily life are one, namely. 'the adjustment of inner to outer relations.' Such a formula is vagueness incarnate; but because it takes into account the fact that minds inhabit environments which act on them and on which they in turn react; because, in short, it takes mind in the midst of all its concrete relations, it is immensely more fertile than the old-fashioned 'rational psychology,' which treated the soul as a detached existent, sufficient unto itself, and assumed to consider only its nature and properties. I shall therefore feel free to make any sallies into zoology or into pure nerve-physiology which may seem instructive for our purposes, but otherwise shall leave those sciences to the physiologists.

Can we state more distinctly still the manner in which the mental life seems to intervene between impressions made from without upon the body, and reactions of the body upon the outer world again? Let us look at a few facts.

If some iron filings be sprinkled on a table and a magnet brought near them, they will fly through the air for a certain distance and stick to its surface. A savage seeing the phenomenon explains it as the result of an attraction or love between the magnet and the filings. But let a card cover the poles of the magnet, and the filings will press forever against its surface without its ever occurring to them to pass around its sides and thus come into more direct contact with the object of their love. Blow bubbles through a tube into the bottom of a pail of water, they will rise to the surface and mingle with the air. Their action may again be poetically interpreted as due to a longing to recombine with the mother-atmosphere above the surface. But if you invert a jar full of water over the pail, they will rise and remain lodged beneath its bottom, shut in from the outer air, although a slight deflection from their course at the outset, or a re-descent towards the rim of the jar when found their upward course impeded, would easily have set them free.

If now we pass from such actions as these to those of living things, we notice a striking difference. Romeo wants Juliet as the filings want the magnet; and if no obstacles intervene he moves towards her by as straight a line as they. But Romeo and Juliet, if a wall be built between them, do not remain idiotically pressing their faces against its opposite sides like the magnet and the filings with the card. Romeo soon finds a circuitous way, by scaling the wall or otherwise, of touching Juliet's lips directly. With the filings the path is fixed; whether it reaches the end depends on accidents. With the lover it is the end which is fixed, the path may be modified indefinitely.

Suppose a living frog in the position in which we placed our bubbles of air, namely, at the bottom of a jar of water. The want of breath will soon make him also long to rejoin the mother-atmosphere, and he will take the shortest path to his end by swimming straight upwards. But if a jar full of water be inverted over him, he will not, like the bubbles, perpetually press his nose against its unyielding roof, but will restlessly explore the neighborhood until by re-descending again he has discovered a path round its brim to the goal of his desires. Again the fixed end, the varying means!

Such contrasts between living and inanimate performances end by leading men to deny that in the physical world final purposes exist at all. Loves and desires are to-day no longer imputed to particles of iron or of air. No one supposes now that the end of any activity which they may display is an ideal purpose presiding over the activity from its outset and soliciting or drawing it into being by a sort of *vis a fronte.* The end, on the contrary, is deemed a mere passive result, pushed into being *a tergo,* having had, so to speak, no voice in its own production. Alter the pre-existing conditions, and with inorganic materials you bring forth each time a different apparent end. But with the intelligent agents, altering the conditions changes the activity displayed, but not the end reached; for here the idea of the yet unrealized end co-operates with the conditions to determine what the activities shall be.

The pursuance of future ends and the choice of means for their attainment are thus the mark and criterion of the presence of mentality in a phenomenon. We all use this test to discriminate between an intelligent and a mechanical performance. We impute no mentality to sticks and stones, because they never seem to move for *the sake of* anything, but always when pushed, and then indifferently and with no sign of choice. So we unhesitatingly call them senseless.

Just so we form our decision upon the deepest of all philosophic problems: Is the Kosmos an expression of intelligence rational in its inward nature, or a brute external fact pure and simple? If we find ourselves, in contemplating it, unable to banish the impression that it is a realm of final purposes, that it exists for the sake of something, we place intelligence at the heart of it and have a religion. If, on the contrary, in surveying its irremediable flux, we can think of the present only as so much mere mechanical sprouting from the past, occurring with no reference to the future, we are atheists and materialists.

In the lengthy discussions which psychologists have carried on about the amount of intelligence displayed by lower mammals, or the amount of consciousness involved in the functions of the nerve-centres of reptiles, the same test has always been applied: Is the character of the actions such that we must believe them to be performed *for the sake* of their result? The result in question, as we shall hereafter abundantly see, is as a rule a useful one,—the animal is, on the whole, safer under the circumstances for bringing it forth. So far the action has a teleological character; but such mere outward teleology as this might still be the blind result of *vis a tergo.* The growth and movements of plants, the processes of development, digestion, secretion, etc., in animals, supply innumerable instances of performances useful to the individual which may nevertheless be, and by most of us are supposed to be, produced by automatic mechanism. The physiologist does not confidently assert conscious intelligence in the frog's spinal cord until he has shown that the useful result which the nervous machinery brings forth under a given irritation *remains the same when the machinery is altered.* If, to take the stock instance, the right knee of a headless frog be irritated with acid, the right foot will wipe it off. When, however, this foot is amputated, the animal will often raise the *left* foot to the spot and wipe the offending material away.

Pflüger and Lewes reason from such facts in the following way: If the first reaction were the result of mere machinery, they say; if that irritated portion of the skin discharged the right leg as a trigger discharges its own barrel of a shotgun; then amputating the right foot would indeed frustrate the wiping, but would not make the *left* leg move. It would simply result in the right stump moving through the empty air (which is in fact the phenomenon sometimes observed). The right trigger makes no effort to discharge the left barrel if the right one be unloaded; nor does an electrical machine ever get restless because it can only emit sparks, and not hem pillow-cases like a sewing-machine.

If, on the contrary, the right leg originally moved for the *purpose* of wiping the acid, then nothing is more natural than that, when the easiest means of effecting that purpose prove fruitless, other means should be tried. Every failure must keep the animal in a state of disappointment which will lead to all sorts of new trials and devices; and tranquillity will not ensue till one of these, by a happy stroke, achieves the wished-for end.

In a similar way Goltz ascribes intelligence to the frog's optic lobes and cerebellum. We alluded above to the manner in which a sound frog imprisoned in water will discover an outlet to the atmosphere. Goltz found that frogs deprived of their cerebral hemispheres would often exhibit a like ingenuity. Such a frog, after rising from the bottom and finding his farther upward progress checked by the glass bell which has been inverted over him, will not persist in butting his nose against the obstacle until dead of suffocation, but will often re-descend and emerge from under its rim as if, not a definite mechanical propulsion upwards, but rather a conscious desire to reach the air by hook or crook were the main-spring of his activity. Goltz concluded from this that the hemispheres are the seat of intellectual power in frogs. He made the same inference from observing that a brainless frog will turn over from his back to his belly when one of his legs is sewed up, although the movements required are then very different from those excited under normal circumstances by the same annoying position. They seem determined, consequently, not merely by the antecedent irritant, but by the final end,—though the irritant of course is what makes the end desired.

Another brilliant German author, Liebmann,* argues against the brain's mechanism accounting for mental action, by very similar considerations. A machine as such, he says, will bring forth right results when it is in good order, and wrong results if out of repair. But both kinds of result flow with equally fatal necessity from their conditions. We cannot suppose the clock-work whose structure fatally determines it to a certain rate of speed, noticing that this speed is too slow or too fast and vainly trying to correct it. Its conscience, if it have any, should be as good as that of the best chronometer, for both alike obey equally well the same eternal mechanical laws—laws from behind. But if the *brain* be out of order and the man says "Twice four are two," instead of "Twice four are eight," or else "I must go to the coal to buy the wharf," instead of "I must go to the wharf to buy the coal," instantly there arises a consciousness of error. The wrong performance, though it obey the same mechanical law as the right, is nevertheless condemned,—condemned as contradicting the inner law—the law from in front, the purpose or ideal for which the brain *should* act, whether it do so or not.

We need not discuss here whether these writers in drawing their conclusion have done justice to all the premises involved in the cases they treat of. We quote their arguments only to show how they appeal to the principle that *no actions but such as are done for an end, and show a choice of means, can be called indubitable expressions of Mind.*

I shall then adopt this as the criterion by which to circumscribe the subject-matter of this work so far as action enters into it. Many nervous performances will therefore be unmentioned, as being purely physiological. Nor will the anatomy of the nervous system and organs of sense be described anew. The reader will find in H. N. Martin's 'Human Body,' in G. T. Ladd's 'Physiological Psychology,' and in all the other standard Anatomies and Physiologies, a mass of information which we must regard as preliminary and take for granted in the present work.* Of the functions of the cerebral hemispheres, however, since they directly subserve consciousness, it will be well to give some little account.

---

*Zur Analysis der Wirklichkeit, p. 489.

*Nothing is easier than to familiarize one's self with the mammalian brain. Get a sheep's head, a small saw, chisel, scalpel and forceps (all three can best be had from a surgical-instrument maker), and unravel its parts either by the aid of a human dissecting book, such as Holden's 'Manual of Anatomy,' or by the specific directions *ad hoc* given in such books as Foster and Langley's 'Practical Physiology' (Macmillan) or Morrell's 'Comparative Anatomy and Dissection of Mammalia' (Longmans).

The Province of Functional Psychology*

James Rowland Angell

Functional psychology is at the present moment little more than a point of view, a program, an ambition. It gains its vitality primarily perhaps as a protest against the exclusive excellence of another starting point for the study of the mind, and it enjoys for the time being at least the peculiar vigor which commonly attaches to Protestantism of any sort in its early stages before it has become respectable and orthodox. The time seems ripe to attempt a somewhat more precise characterization of the field of functional psychology than has as yet been offered. What we seek is not the arid and merely verbal definition which to many of us is so justly anathema, but rather an informing appreciation of the motives and ideals which animate the psychologist who pursues this path. His status in the eye of the psychological public is unnecessarily precarious. The conceptions of his purposes prevalent in non-functional circles range from positive and dogmatic misapprehension, through frank mystification and suspicion up to moderate comprehension. Nor is this fact an expression of anything peculiarly abstruse and recondite in his intentions. It is due in part to his own ill-defined plans, in part to his failure to explain lucidly exactly what he is about. Moreover, he is fairly numerous and it is not certain that in all important particulars he and his confreres are at one in their beliefs. The considerations which are herewith offered suffer inevitably from this personal limitation. No psychological council of Trent has as yet pronounced upon the true faith. But in spite of probable failure it seems worth while to hazard an attempt at delineating the scope of functionalist principles. I formally renounce any intention to strike out new plans; I am engaged in what is meant as a dispassionate summary of actual conditions.

Whatever else it may be, functional psychology is nothing wholly new. In certain of its phases it is plainly discernible in the psychology of Artistotle and in its more modern garb it has been increasingly in evidence since Spencer wrote his *Psychology* and Darwin his *Origin of Species*. Indeed, as we shall soon see, its crucial problems are inevitably incidental to any serious attempt at understanding mental life. All that is peculiar to its present circumstances is a higher degree of self-consciousness than it possessed before, a more articulate and persistent purpose to organize its vague intentions into tangible methods and principles.

A survey of contemporary psychological writing indicates as was intimated in the preceding paragraph, that the task of functional psychology is interpreted in several different ways. Moreover, it seems to be possible to advocate one or more

---

*This paper, more than any other, outlines the platform of the functional school of psychology. It is reprinted by permission of the author and of the American Psychological Association, publisher of the *Psychological Review,* where the article appeared (1907), XIV, 61–91.

of these conceptions while cherishing abhorrence for the others. I distinguish three principal forms of the functional problem with sundry subordinate variants. It will contribute to the clarification of the general situation to dwell upon these for a moment, after which I propose to maintain that they are substantially but modifications of a single problem.

I

There is to be mentioned first the notion which derives most immediately from contrast with the ideals and purposes of structural psychology so-called. This involves the identification of functional psychology with the effort to discern and portray the typical operations of consciousness under actual life conditions, as over against the attempt to analyze and describe its elementary and complex contents. The structural psychology of sensation, e.g., undertakes to determine the number and character of the various unanalyzable sensory materials, such as the varieties of color, tone, taste, etc. The functional psychology of sensation would on the other hand find its appropriate sphere of interest in the determination of the character of the various sense activities as differing in their modus operandi from one another and from other mental processes such as judging, conceiving, willing and the like.

In this its older and more pervasive form functional psychology has until very recent times had no independent existence. No more has structural psychology for that matter. It is only lately that any motive for the differentiation of the two has existed and structural psychology—granting its claims and pretensions of which more anon—is the first, be it said, to isolate itself. But in so far as functional psychology is synonymous with descriptions and theories of mental action as distinct from the materials of mental constitution, so far it is everywhere conspicuous in psychological literature from the earliest times down.

Its fundamental intellectual prepossessions are often revealed by the classifications of mental process adopted from time to time. Witness the Aristotelian bipartite division of intellect and will and the modern tripartite division of mental activities. What are cognition, feeling and will but three basally distinct modes of mental action? To be sure this classification has often carried with it the assertion, or at least the implication, that these fundamental attributes of mental life were based upon the presence in the mind of corresponding and ultimately distinct mental elements. But so far as concerns our momentary interest this fact is irrelevant. The impressive consideration is that the notion of definite and distinct forms of mental action is clearly in evidence and even the much-abused faculty psychology is on this point perfectly sane and perfectly lucid. The mention of this classic target for psychological vituperation recalls the fact that when the critics of functionalism wish to be particularly unpleasant, they refer to it as a bastard offspring of the faculty psychology masquerading in biological plumage.

It must be obvious to any one familiar with psychological usage in the present year of grace that in the intent of the distinction herewith described certain of our familiar psychological categories are primarily structural—such for instance as affection and image—whereas others immediately suggest more explicit functional relationships—for example, attention and reasoning. As a matter of fact it seems clear that so long as we adhere to these meanings of the terms structural and functional every mental event can be treated from either point of view, from the standpoint of describing its detectable contents and from the standpoint of characteristic mental activity differentiable from other forms of mental process. In the practice of our familiar psychological writers both undertakings are somewhat indiscriminately combined.

The more extreme and ingenuous conceptions of structural psychology seem to have grown out of an unchastened indulgence in what we may call the "states of consciousness" doctrine. I take it that this is in reality the contemporary version of Locke's "idea." If you adopt as your material for psychological analysis the isolated "moment of consciousness," it is very easy to become so absorbed in determing its constitution as to be rendered somewhat oblivious to its artificial character. The most esential quarrel which the functionalist has with structuralism in its thoroughgoing and consistent form arises from this fact and touches the feasibility and worth of the effort to get at mental process as it is under the conditions of actual experience rather than as it appears to a merely postmortem analysis. It is of course true than for introspective purposes we must in a sense always work with vicarious representatives of the particular mental processes which we set out to observe. But it makes a great difference even on such terms whether one is engaged simply in teasing apart the fibers of its tissues. The latter occupation is useful and for certain purposes essential, but it often stops short of that which is as a life phenomenon the most essential, i.e., the modus operandi of the phenomenon.

As a matter of fact many modern investigations of an experimental kind largely dispense with the usual direct form of introspection and concern themselves in a distinctly functionalistic spirit with a determination of what work is accomplished and what the conditions are under which it is achieved. Many experiments in memory and association, for instance, are avowedly of this character.

The functionalist is committed *vom Grunde auf* to the avoidance of that special form of the psychologist's fallacy which consists in attributing to mental states without due warrant, as part of their overt constitution in the moment of experience, characteristics which subsequent reflective analysis leads us to suppose they must have possessed. When this precaution is not scrupulously observed we obtain a sort of *pate de foie gras* psychology in which the mental conditions portrayed contain more than they every naturally would or could hold.

It should be added that when the distinction is made between psychic structure and psychic function, the anomalous position of structure as a category of mind is often quite forgotten. In mental life the sole appropriateness of the term structure hinges on the fact that any amount of consciousness can be regarded as a complex capable of analysis, and the terms into which our analyses resolve such complexes are the analogues—and obviously very meager and defective ones at that—of the structures of anatomy and morphology.

The fact that mental contents are evanescent and fleeting marks them off in an important way from the relatively permanent elements of anatomy. No matter how much we may talk of the preservation of psychical dispositions, nor how many metaphors we may summon to characterize the storage of ideas in some hypothetical deposit chamber of memory, the obstinate fact remains that when we are not experiencing a sensation or an idea it is, strictly speaking, non-existent. Moreover, when we manage by one or another device to secure that which we designate the same sensation or the same idea, we not only have no guarantee that our second edition is really a replica of the first, we have a good bit of presumptive evidence that from the content point of view the original never is and never can be literally duplicated.

Functions, on the other hand, persist as well in mental as in physical life. We may never have twice exactly the same idea viewed from the side of sensuous structure and composition. But there seems nothing whatever to prevent our having as often as we will contents of consciousness which mean the same thing. They function in one and the same practical way, however discrepant their momentary texture. The situation is rudely analogous to the biological case where very different structures may under different conditions be called on to perform identical functions; and the matter naturally harks back for its earliest analogy to the instance of protoplasm where functions seem very tentatively and imperfectly differentiated. Not only then are general functions like memory persistent, but special functions such as the memory of particular events are persistent and largely independent of the specific conscious contents called upon from time to time to subserve the functions.

When the structural psychologists define their field as that of mental process, they really preempt under a fictitious name the field of function, so that I should be disposed to allege fearlessly and with a clear conscience that a large part of the doctrine of psychologists of nominally structural proclivities is in point of fact precisely what I mean by one essential part of functional psychology, i.e., an account of psychical operations. Certain of the official exponents of structuralism explicitly lay claim to this as their field and do so with a flourish of scientific rectitude. There is therefore after all a small but nutritious core of agreement in the structure-function apple of discord. For this reason, as well as because I consider extremely useful the analysis of mental life into its elementary forms, I regard much of the actual work of my structuralist friends with highest respect and confidence. I feel, however, that when they use the term structural as opposed to the term functional to designate their scientific creed they often come perilously near to using the enemy's colors.

Substantially identical with this first conception of functional psychology, but phrasing itself somewhat differently, is the view which regards the functional problem as concerned with discovering how and why conscious processes are what they are, instead of dwelling as the structuralist is supposed to do upon the problem of determining the irreducible elements of consciousness and their characteristic modes of combination. I have elsewhere defended the view that however it may be in other sciences dealing with life phenomena, in psychology at least the answer to the question "what" implicates the answer to the questions "how" and "why."

Stated briefly the ground on which this position rests is as follows: In so far as you attempt to analyze any particular state of consciousness you find that the mental elements presented to your notice are dependent upon the particular exigencies and conditions which call them forth. Not only does the affective coloring of such a psychical moment depend upon one's temporary condition, mood and aims, but the very sensations themselves are determined in their qualitative texture by the totality of circumstances subjective and objective within which they arise. You cannot get a fixed and definite color sensation, for example, without keeping perfectly constant the external and internal conditions in which it appears. The particular sense quality is in short functionally determined by the necessities of the existing situation which it emerges to meet. If you inquire then deeply enough what particular sensation you have in a given case, you always find it necessary to take account of the manner in which, and the reasons why, it was experienced at all. You may of course, if you will, abstract from these considerations, but in so far as you do so, your analysis and description is manifestly partial and incomplete. Moreover, even when you do so abstract and attempt to describe certain isolable sense qualities, your descriptions are of necessity couched in terms not of the experienced quality itself, but in terms of the conditions which produced it, in terms of some other quality with which it is compared, or in terms of some more overt act to which the sense stimulation led. That is to say, the very description itself is functionalistic and must be so. The truth of this assertion can be illustrated and tested by appeal to any situation in which one is trying to reduce sensory complexes, e.g., colors or sounds, to their rudimentary components. . . .

IV

If we now bring together the several conceptions of which mention has been made it will be easy to show them converging upon a common point. We have to consider (1) functionalism conceived as the psychology of mental operations in contrast to the psychology of mental elements; or, expressed otherwise, the psychology of the how and why of consciousness as distinguished from the psychology of the what of consciousness. We have (2) the functionalism with deals with the problem of mind conceived as primarily engaged in mediating between the environment and the needs of the organism. This is the psychology of the fundamental utilities of consciousness; (3) and lastly we have functionalism described as psychophysical psychology, that is the psychology which constantly recognizes and insists upon the essential significance of the mind-body relationship for any just and comprehensive appreciation of mental life itself.

The second and third delineations of functional psychology are rather obviously correlated with each other. No description of the actual circumstances attending the participation of mind in the accommodatory activities of the organism could be other than a mere empty schematism without making reference to the manner in which mental processes eventuate in motor phenomena of the physiological organism. The overt accommodatory act is, I take it, always sooner or later a muscular movement. But this fact being admitted, there is nothing for it, if one will describe accommodatory processes, but to recognize the mind-body relations and in some way give expression to their practical significance. It is only in this regard, as was indicated a few lines above, that the functionalist departs a trifle in his practice and a trifle more in his theory from the rank and file of his colleagues.

The effort to follow the lead of the natural sciences and delimit somewhat rigorously—albeit artificially—a field of inquiry, in this case consciousness conceived as an independent realm, has led in psychology to a deal of excellent work and to the uncovering of much hidden truth. So far as this procedure has resulted in a focusing of scientific attention and endeavor on a relatively narrow range of problems the result has more than justified the means. And the functionalist by no means holds that the limit of profitable research has been reached along these lines. But he is disposed to urge in season and out that we must not forget the arbitrary and self-imposed nature of the boundaries within which we toil when we try to eschew all explicit reference to the physical and physiological. To overlook this fact is to substitute a psychology under injunction for a psychology under free jurisdiction. He also urges with vigor and enthusiasm that a new illumination of this preempted field can be gained by envisaging it more broadly, looking at it as it appears when taken in perspective with its neighboring territory. And if it be objected that such an inquiry however interesting and advantageous is at least not psychology, he can only reply: psychology is what we make it, and if the correct understanding of mental phenomena involves our delving in regions which are not at first glance properly mental, what recks it, provided only that we are nowhere guilty of untrustworthy and unverifiable procedure, and that we return loaded with the booty for which we set out, and by means of which we can the better solve our problem?

In its more basal philosophy this last conception is of course intimately allied to those appraisals of mind which emphasize its dominantly social characteristics, its rise out of social circumstances and the pervasively social nature of its constitutive principles. In our previous intimations of this standpoint we have not distinguished sharply between the physical and the social aspect of environment. The adaptive activities of mind are very largely of the distinctly social type. But this does not in any way jeopardize the genuineness of the connection upon which we have been insisting between the psychophysical aspects of a functional psychology and its environmental adaptive aspects.

It remains then to point out in what manner the conception of functionalism as concerned with the basal operations of mind is to be correlated with the other two conceptions just under discussion. The simplest view to take of the relations involved would apparently be such as would regard the first as an essential propaedeutic to the other two. Certainly if we are intent upon discerning the exact manner which mental process contributes to accommodatory efficiency, it is natural to begin our undertaking by determining what are the primordial forms of expression peculiar to mind. However plausible in theory this conception of the intrinsic logical relations of these several forms of functional psychology, in practice it is extremely difficult wholly to sever them from one another.

Again like the biological accommodatory view the psychophysical view of functional psychology involves as a rational presupposition some acquaintance with mental processes as these appear to reflective consciousness. The intelligent correlation in a practical way of physiological and mental operations evidently involves a preliminary knowledge of the conspicuous differentiations both on the side of conscious function and on the side of physiological function.

In view of the considerations of the last few paragraphs it does not seem fanciful nor forced to urge that these various theories of the problem of functional psychology really converge upon one another, however divergent may be the introductory investigations peculiar to each of the several ideals. Possibly the conception that the fundamental problem of the functionalist is one of determining just how mind participates in accommodatory reactions, is more nearly inclusive than either of the others, and so may be chosen to stand for the group. But if this vicarious duty is assigned to it, it must be on clear terms of remembrance that the other phases of the problem are equally real and equally necessary. Indeed the three things hand together as integral parts of a common program.

The functionalist's most intimate persuasion leads him to regard consciousness as primarily and intrinsically a control phenomenon. Just as behavior may be regarded as the most distinctly basic category of general biology in its functional phase so control would perhaps serve as the most fundamental category in functional psychology, the special forms and differentiations of consciousness simply constituting particular phases of the general process of control. At this point the omnipresent captious critic will perhaps arise to urge that the knowledge process is no more truly to be explained in terms of control than is control to be explained in terms of knowledge. Unquestionably there is from the point of view of the critic a measure of truth in this contention. The mechanism of control undoubtedly depends if one assumes the vitalistic point of view for one's more final interpretations, if one regards the furtherance of life in breadth and depth and permanence as an end in itself, and if one derives his scale of values from a contemplation of the several contributions toward this end represented by the great types of vital phenomena, with their apex in the moral, scientific and aesthetic realms, one must certainly find control a category more fundamental than the others offered by psychology. Moreover, it may be urged against the critic's attitude that even knowledge itself is built up under the control mechanism represented by selective attention and apperception. The basic character of control seems therefore hardly open to challenge. . . .

A sketch of the kind we have offered is unhappily likely to leave on the mind an impression of functional psychology as a name for a group of genial but vague ambitions and good intentions. This, however, is a fault which must be charged to the artist and to the limitations of time and space under which he is here working. There is nothing vaguer in the program of the functionalist when he goes to his work than there is in the purposes of the psychologist wearing any other livery. He goes to his laboratory, for example, with just the same resolute interest to discover new facts and new relationships, with just the same determination to verify and confirm his previous observations, as does his colleague who calls himself perhaps a structuralist. But he looks out upon the surroundings of his science with a possibly greater sensitiveness to its continuity with other ranges of human interest and with certainly a more articulate purpose to see the mind which he analyzes as it actually is when engaged in the discharge of its vital functions. If his method tempts him now and then to sacrifice something of petty exactitude, he is under no obligation to yield, and in any case he has for his compensation the power which comes from breadth and sweep of outlook.

So far as he may be expected to develop methods peculiar to himself—so far, indeed, as in genetic and comparative psychology, for example, he has already developed such—they will not necessarily be iconoclastic and revolutionary, nor such as flout the methods already devised and established on a slightly different foundation. They will be distinctly complementary to all that is solid in these. Nor is it in any way essential that the term functionalism should cling to this new-old movement. It seems at present a convenient term, but there is nothing sacrosanct about it, and the moment it takes unto itself the pretense of scientific finality its doom will be sealed. It means to-day a broad and flexible and organic point of view in psychology. The moment it becomes dogmatic and narrow its spirit will have passed and undoubtedly some worthier successor will fill its place.

C H A P T E R 8

THE LEGACY OF FUNCTIONALISM: APPLIED PSYCHOLOGY

PSYCHOMETRICS

The late 1880s and early 1890s saw a movement in psychology toward assessment of individual differences in human abilities. Sir Frances Galton, widely accepted as the pioneer in this field (see Chapter 6), established the first laboratory for the testing of mental abilities in the South Kensington Museum in 1882. Following Galton, numerous laboratories in Germany, France, and the United States set forth to develop a variety of tests. Two psychologists rapidly emerged at the forefront of this movement: Alfred Binet and James McKeen Cattell.

ALFRED BINET (1857–1911)

Alfred Binet was born in Nice, France, on July 8, 1857, the only child of a physician father and an artist mother.[1] When Binet was 15, he traveled to Paris with his mother to attend the prestigious *Lycée* Louis-le Grand and prepare himself to study, not psychology, but law. He received his license as an attorney in 1878. Although

---

[1] The material in this biographic sketch of Alfred Binet is drawn from Varon (1935) and Neisser et al. (1996) as well as from Wolf's (1961) fascinating interview with Binet's closest associate, Theodore Simon, who at the time of their conversation, was 87 years old and still actively continuing Binet's legacy as the director of the *Société Alfred Binet*.

his formal education was in law, Binet was widely read (in several languages and disciplines), and his independent reading in psychology soon led to a more structured pursuit of psychological issues.

A significant turning point in Binet's life and approach to psychology came with his marriage and the subsequent birth of his two daughters. These events piqued Binet's interest in the development of children. From 1890 to 1895, Binet published a series of articles, all related to individual differences in children's development. Then, in 1895, Binet published an article with Victor Henri that would chart the course of his research for the next decade and mark the beginning of his contribution as a giant in the field of psychology.

In *La psychologie individuelle* (Binet & Henri, 1895), Binet states clearly that the problem of psychology is to study individual differences, qualitative and quantitative. Futhermore, Binet and Henri suggest that the most significant differences among individuals are arrived at through the study of "higher processes." Their recommended areas of study include memory, nature of mental images, imagination, attention, comprehension, and acuity of observation.

Binet's study of individual differences took a significant and practical turn in 1904 when the minister of public instruction in Paris appointed him to a committee with the charge to find a method of separating the subnormal children in the schools from the normal. It was in response to this call that Binet, later joined by the young Théodore Simon, developed the first objective, empirically tested measure of "higher" mental processes. The product of Binet and Simon's work is described in more detail in the first reading.

In the reading, Binet discusses the problems of labeling children "suspected of retardation" without using some objective criteria for their classification. The reading provides some insight into the haphazard classification systems used to sort children with special needs prior to the development of standardized tests. Also set forth briefly are Binet's views on the development of intelligence in children. Binet did not hold intelligence as a static entity that simply increases in quantity as the child grows older; rather, he states that the "child differs from the adult not only in the degree and quantity of his intelligence, but also in its form." In this respect, Binet anticipates the later writings of Piaget, who would spend his early career working in Binet's laboratory.

JAMES MCKEEN CATTELL (1860–1944)

James McKeen Cattell was born in 1860, in Easton, Pennsylvania.[2] He graduated from Lafayette College in 1880, and immediately went abroad to study. While traveling in Europe, the young Cattell came under the influence of Hermann Lotze. Lotze, a philosopher-physician, was a guiding force behind the empirical theories of Helmholtz and Wundt. It is apparently Lotze who first interested Cattell in the

---

[2]The material in this biographic sketch of James McKeen Cattell is drawn from Boring (1950), Hothersall (1995), and Sokal (1980, 1992).

study of human capacities. It was also during this initial visit to Europe that Cattell first encountered Wilhelm Wundt, in whose laboratory Cattell would later complete his doctoral dissertation as well as much of his seminal work on the study of individual differences. Cattell returned to the United States for a year of study at Johns Hopkins, then returned to Leipzig in 1883 where he spent three years working in Wundt's lab, completing his doctorate under Wundt in 1886. He was Wundt's first American graduate student.

Cattell returned to the United States and to a brief series of lectureships at Bryn Mawr, St. John's College, and Cambridge University. It was during this period that he first came into contact with Sir Frances Galton. Cattell and Galton shared an interest in the measurement of human capacity, and Cattell was much impressed with Galton's work. Much of Cattell's later work reflects Galton's interests in precise mental measurement and in eugenics.[3] Cattell became a professor of psychology at the University of Pennsylvania in 1888. There, he established a laboratory where he used a number of psychophysical measures, such as reaction time tests, to examine mental abilities among students. This work reflected both Galton's influence and Cattell's desire to use the precision of statistical methods to examine individual differences, while retaining the traditional methods of psychophysics. It is during this period that Cattell coined the phrase "mental test" in a paper published in 1890 in *Mind*.

In 1891, Cattell accepted a position at Columbia College, where he continued his program of mental testing. His tests included measures of sensation, perception, strength, rate of movement, attention span, reaction time, time estimation, and memory for letters. These largely anthropomorphic tests contrasted sharply with the tests of higher mental processes being developed by Binet's laboratory. By 1901, one of Cattell's own graduate students, Clark Wissler, had demonstrated that Cattell's measures showed little or no relationship to student academic performance or, for that matter, to any other tests of mental abilities. Tests of higher mental processes, however, were enjoying tremendous success in the laboratories of Binet and others. Cattell was forced to abandon his program.

Though Cattell's tests failed, his influence on the growth of psychology as a science was profound. Cattell was a generous mentor, a prolific writer, an able administrator, an astute businessman, and an outspoken advocate for the field. A list of Cattell's graduate students reads like a Who's Who of American Psychologists. Among their ranks are Edward Lee Thorndike, Robert S. Woodworth (who succeeded Cattell as head of the department at Columbia), Edward K. Strong (best known for the Strong Vocational Interest Test), and Margaret Washburn (the first major American female experimental psychologist).

In all, Cattell edited more than seven journals, including *Science, Scientific Monthly,* and *School and Society.* He co-founded the journal *Psychological Review,* and purchased a failing *Popular Science Monthly* from Alexander Graham Bell,

---

[3]Eugenics, which means literally "good genes," is the science of improving the qualities of a species. Both Galton and Cattell were interested in improving the quality of the human gene pool. Cattell went so far as to offer each of his seven children $1,000 as an incentive to marry the child of a college professor (on the assumption that such a person would have superior intellectual genes).

turning it into one of the nation's leading scientific publications. He co-founded the American Psychological Association and became its fourth president. Cattell also established the Psychological Corporation for the purpose of applying psychology to industry and education. The corporation is still active in marketing psychological tests such as the Wechsler Adult Intelligence Scale (WAIS), the Wechsler Intelligence Scale for Children (WISC), the Thematic Apperception Test (TAT), and the Beck Depression Inventory (BDI). Cattell ensured that much of the profits of the corporation were reinvested in supporting independent psychological research. Cattell's contributions to psychology far outstrip his contributions as an individual researcher. He became an ambassador for the science and remains a major figure in shaping the history of psychology.

The reading, an address given by Cattell at the International Congress of Arts and Science in St. Louis in the fall of 1904, reflects Cattell's vision of psychology as a broad and growing science encompassing a range of methodologies. It also reflects Cattell's firmly held belief that psychology ought to be practical, with its findings used to improve individual lives and the overall social order.

REFERENCES

Binet, A. & Simon, T. (1905). *Sur la necissite a etablis un diagnostic scientific des etate inferieurs de l'intelligence.* *L'Anee Psychologique,* 11, 163–190.

Binet, A. & Simon, T. (1908). *La developpment de l'intelligence chez les infants. L'Anee Psychologique,* 14, 1–94.

Cattell, J. M. (1904). The conceptions and methods of psychology. *Popular Science Monthly,* 66, 176–186.

Boring, E. G. (1950). *A history of experimental psychology* (2nd ed.). New York: Appleton-Century-Crofts.

Hothersall, D. (1995). *History of psychology* (3rd ed.). New York: Mcgraw-Hill.

Neisser, U., Boodoo, G., Bouchard, T. J., Boykin, A. W., Brody, N., Ceci, S. J., Halpern, D. F., Loehlin, J. C.,

Perloff, R., Sternberg, R. J., & Urbina, S. (1996). Intelligence: Knowns and unknowns. *American Psychologist,* 51(2), 77–101.

Sokal, M. M. (1992). Origin and early years of the American Psychological Association. *American Psychologist,* 47, 111–122.

Sokal, M. M. (1980). Science and James McKeen Cattell. *Science,* 209, 43–52.

Varon, E. J. (1935). The development of Alfred Binet's psychology. *Psychological Monographs,* 46(3, whole no. 207).

Wolf, T. H. (1961). An individual who made a difference. *American Psychologist,* 16, 245–248.

The Binet Simon Scale & Its Developments

Binet, A., & Simon, T.

UPON THE NECESSITY OF ESTABLISHING A SCIENTIFIC DIAGNOSIS OF INFERIOR STATES OF INTELLIGENCE

We here present the first rough sketch of a work which was directly inspired by the desire to serve the interesting cause of education of subnormals.

In October, 1904, the Minister of Public Instruction named a commission which was charged with the study of measures to be taken for insuring the benefits of instruction to defective children. After a number of sittings, this commission regulated all that pertained to the type of establishment to be created, the conditions of admission into the school, the teaching force, and the pedagogical methods to be employed. They decided that no child suspected of retardation should be eliminated from the ordinary school and admitted into a special class, without first being subjected to a pedagogical and medical examination from which it could be certified that because of the state of his intelligence, he was unable to profit, in an average measure, form the instruction given in the ordinary schools.

But how the examination of each child should be made, what methods should be followed, what observations taken, what questions asked, what tests devised, how the child should be compared with normal children, the commission felt under no obligation to decide. It was formed to do a work of administration, not a work of science.

It has seemed to us extremely useful to furnish a guide for future Commissions' examination. Such Commissions should understand from the beginning how to get their bearings. It must be made impossible for those who belong to the Commission to fall into the habit of making haphazard decisions according to impressions which are subjective, and consequently uncontrolled. Such impressions are sometimes good, sometimes bad, and have at all times too much the nature of the arbitrary, of caprice, of indifference. Such a condition is quite unfortunate because the interest of the child demand a more careful method. To be a member of a special class can never be a mark of distinction, and such as do not merit it, must be spared the record. Some errors are excusable in the beginning, but if they become too frequent, they may ruin the reputation of these new institutions. Furthermore, in principle, we are convinced, and we shall not cease to repeat, that the precision and exactness of science should be introduced into our practice whenever possible, and in the great majority of cases it is possible.

The problem which we have to solve present many difficulties both theoretical and practical. It is a hackneyed remark that the definitions, thus far proposed, for the different states of subnormal intelligence, lack precision. These inferior states are indefinite in number, being composed of a series of degrees which mount from the lowest depths of idiocy, to a condition easily confounded with normal intelligence. Alienists have frequently come to an agreement concerning the terminology to be employed for designating the difference of these degrees; at least, in spite of certain individual divergence of ideas to be found in all questions, there has been an agreement to accept *idiot* as applied to the lowest state, *imbecile* to the intermediate, and *moron (debile)* to the state nearest normality. Still among the numerous alienists, under this common and apparently precise terminology, different ideas are concealed, variable and at the same time confused. The distinction between idiot, imbecile, and moron is not understood in the same way by all practitioners. We have abundant proof of this in the strikingly divergent medical diagnoses made only a few days apart by different alienists upon the same patient.

Dr. Blin, physician of the Vaucluse Asylum, recently drew the attention of his fellow physicians to these regrettable contradictions. He states that the children who are sent to the colony come provided with several dissimilar certificates. "One child, called imbecile in the first certificate, is marked idiot in the second, feeble-minded *(debile)* in the third, and degenerate in the fourth." M. Damaye, former house surgeon of Dr. Blin, adds this observation: "One would have only to look through several folders of records belonging to children of the colony, in order to collect almost the same number of different diagnoses." Perhaps this last affirmation is a little exaggerated, but a statistical study would show the exact truth on this point.

We cannot sufficiently deplore the consequence of this state of uncertainty recognized today by all alienists. The simple fact, that specialists do not agree in the use of the technical terms of their science, throws suspicion upon their diagnoses, and prevents all work of comparison. We ourselves have made similar observations. In synthesizing the diagnoses made by Mr. Bourneville upon patients leaving the Bicetre, we found that in the space of four years only two feeble-minded individuals have left his institution although during that time the Bureau of Admission has sent him more than thirty. Nothing could show more clearly than this change of label, the confusion of our nomenclature.

What importance can be attached to public statistics of different countries concerning the percentage of backward children if the definition for backward children is not the same in all countries? How will it be possible to keep a record of the intelligence of pupils who are treated and instructed in a school, if the terms applied to them, feeble-minded, retarded, imbecile, idiot, vary in meaning according to the doctor who examines them? The absence of a common measure prevents comparison of statistics, and makes one lose all interest in investigations which may have been very laborious. But a still more serious fact is that, because of lack of methods, it is impossible to solve those essential questions concerning the afflicted, whose solution presents the greatest interest; for example, the real results gained by the treatment of inferior states of intelligence by doctor and educator; the educative value of one pedagogical method compared with another; the degree of curability of incomplete idiocy, etc. It is not by means of a *priori* reasonings, of vague considerations, of oratorical displays, that these questions can be solved; but by minute investigation, entering into the details of fact, and considering the effects of the treatment for each particular child. There is but one means of knowing if a child, who has passed six years in a hospital or in a special class, has profited from that stay, and to what degree he has profited; and that is to compare his certificate of entrance with his certificate of dismissal, and by that means ascertain if he shows a special amelioration of his condition beyond that which might be credited simply to the considerations of growth. But experience has shown how imprudent it would be to place confidence in this comparison, when the two certificates come from different doctors, who do not judge in exactly the same way, or who use different words to characterize the mental status of patients.

It might happen that a child, who had really improved in school, had received in the beginning the diagnosis of moron (*debile*), and on leaving, the prejudicial diagnosis of imbecile, simply because the second doctor spoke a different language from the first. If one took these certificates literally, this case would be considered a failure. On the contrary, the appearance of amelioration would be produced if the physician who delivered the certificate of dismissal had the habit of using higher terms than the one who furnished the certificate of entrance. One can even further. The errors which we note, do not necessarily emanate from the disagreement of different physicians. It would suffice for the same physician to deliver the two certificates, if he did not employ for each one the same criterion, and it would certainly be possible for him to vary unconsciously after an interval of several years if he had nothing to guide him but his own subjective impressions. Might not the same thing also happen if his good faith as a physician happened to be in conflict with the interests of the institution which he directed? Might he not unconsciously as it were, have a tendency to lower the mental status of patients on entering and to raise it on dismissal, in order to emphasize the advantages of the methods which he had applied? We are not incriminating anyone, but simply calling attention to methods actually in use which, by their lack of precision, favor the involuntary illusions of physicians and relatives, in a word, of all those who, having an interest in the amelioration of the condition of the defective child, would have a tendency to confound their desires with the reality.

Perhaps someone will raise an objection and say this uncertainty has no special application to diagnosis of the degrees of mental debility; it is also to be found in mental pathology and, in a general way, in the diagnosis of all maladies; it is the result of the empirical nature which is characteristic of clinical studies. It might be added, that, if anyone took the trouble to make a statistical study of the divergence in the diagnosis of different physicians upon the same patient, it would probably be found that the percentage of disagreement is very great in all branches of medicine.

We believe it worth while to examine their objection because it permits us to enter more deeply into the analysis of the question. The disagreements of practitioners might come from three very different classes of causes:

1. Ignorance, that is, the lack of aptitude of certain physicians. This is an individual failure, for which abstract science is not responsible. It is certain that, even when the symptoms of a disease are absolutely clear, such a physician might fail to recognize them through incapacity. There are many accountants who make mistakes in calculation, but these errors do not discredit mathematics. A physician might not be able to recognize a "p.g." if he is himself a "p.g."

2. The variable meaning of terms. Since the same expression has a different sense according to the person who uses it, it is possible that the disagreement of diagnosis may be simply a disagreement of words, due to the use of different nomenclature.

3. Lack of precision in the description of the symptoms which reveal or which constitute a certain particular malady; different physicians do not examine the same patient in the same manner and do not give the symptoms the same importance; or, it may be they make no effort to find out the precise symptoms, and no effort to analyze carefully in order to distinguish and interpret them.

Of these three kinds of error, which is the one that actually appears in the diagnosis of inferior states of intelligence? Let us set aside the first. There remain the faults of nomenclature, and the insufficiency of methods of examination.

The general belief seems to be that the confusion arises wholly from an absence of a uniform nomenclature. There is some truth in this opinion. It can be proved by a comparison of terms used by authors belonging to the different countries. Even in France the terms differ somewhat according to the physician, the order of the admitted subdivisions not being rigorously followed. The classification of Magnan is not that of Voisin, and his, in turn, differs from that of Bourneville. Undoubtedly it would be a good work to bring about a unification of this nomenclature as has been done for the standard of measurements and for electric units. But this reform in itself is not sufficient and we are very sure that they deceive themselves who think that at bottom this is only a question of terminology. It is very much more serious. We find physicians who, though using the same terminology, constantly disagree in their diagnosis of the same child. The examples cited from M. Blin prove this. There the doctors had recourse to the terminology of Morel, who classifies those of inferior intelligence as idiots, imbeciles and *debiles*. Notwithstanding this use of the same terms, they do not agree in the manner of applying them. Each one according to his own fancy, fixes the boundary line separating these states. It is in regard to the facts that the doctors disagree.

In looking closely one can see that the confusion comes principally from a fault in the method of examination. When an alienist finds himself in the presence of a child of inferior intelligence, he does not examine him by bringing out each one of the symptoms which the child manifests and by interpreting all symptoms and classifying them; he contents himself with taking a subjective impression, an impression as a whole, of his subject, and of making his diagnosis by instinct. We do not think that we are going too far in saying that at the present time very few physicians would be able to cite with absolute precision the objective and invariable sign, or signs, by which they distinguish the degrees of inferior mentality.

THE MEASUREMENT OF DEVELOPMENT OF INTELLIGENCE IN THE CHILD

"The Measurement of Intelligence" is, perhaps, the most oft repeated expression in psychology during these last few years. Some psychologists affirm that intelligence can be measured; others declare that it is impossible to measure intelligence. But there are still others, better informed, who ignore these theoretical discussions and apply themselves to the actual solving of the problem. The readers of *L'Annee* know that for some time we have been trying approximations, but they were not so well thought out as are those which we now present.

We have constantly kept in mind the point of view of pedagogy, normal as well as pathological. For several years we have tried to gather all the data and material capable of shedding light upon the intellectual and moral character of children. This is by no means the minor part of pedagogy, the least important, nor the least difficult. We set for ourselves the following program: first, to determine the law of the intellectual development of children and to devise a method of measuring their intelligence; and, second, to study the diversity of their intellectual aptitudes.

We hope that we shall be able to keep faithfully to this rather extensive program, and especially that we shall have the time and the strength to realize it, but already we see that the subject is far richer than we at first imagined. Our minds always tend to simplify nature. It had seemed to us sufficient to learn how to measure the child's intelligence. This method of measurement we now set forth, which if not complete is at least established upon correct lines, and already usable. But our experience has taught us that there are other problems equally important connected with this. The child differs from the adult not only in the degree and quantity of his intelligence, but also in its form.

This measurement is taken by means of a series of tests, the gradation of which constitutes what we call a "Measuring Scale Intelligence." It is important, above all, to set forth these tests with sufficient precision to enable anyone to repeat them correctly who will take the trouble to assimilate them.

GENERAL CONDITIONS OF THE EXAMINATION

First the testing should take place in a quiet isolated room. The examiner should be alone with the child and when possible he should have a secretary whose duty is to record verbatim the child's answers. This secretary may be a child of thirteen or fourteen years, provided he is very intelligent and one can supervise his work a little. The subject to be examined should be kindly received; if he seems timid he should be reassured at once, not only by a kind tone but also by giving him first the tests which seem most like play, for example—giving change for 20 sous. Constantly encourage him during the tests in a gentle voice; one should show satisfaction with his answers whatever they may be. One should never criticize nor lose time by attempting to teach him the test; there is a time for everything. The child is here that his mental capacity may be judged, not that he may be instructed. Never help him by supplementary explanation which may suggest the answer. Often one is tempted to do so, but it is wrong.

Do not become over anxious nor ask the child if *he* has understood, a useless scruple since the test is such that he ought to understand. Therefore one should adhere rigorously to the formulas of the experiment, without any addition or omission. Encouragement should be in the tone of voice or in meaningless words, which serve only to arouse him. "Come now! Very good! Hurry a little! Good! Very good! Perfect! Splendid! etc. etc." If witnesses are inevitable impose upon them a rigorous silence. How difficult this is to obtain! Every teacher wishes to interfere in the examination, to supplement the explanation of an embarrassed pupil, especially if he belongs to her class. Have the courage to insist that they keep silent.

Always begin the tests that fit the child's age. If one gives him too difficult work at first he is discouraged. If, on the contrary, it is too easy it arouses his contempt, and he asks himself if he is not being made fun of, and so makes no effort. We have seen manifestations of this misplaced self-esteem.

On the part of the experimenter, some conditions are necessary. He must not allow himself to be influenced by information regarding the child obtained from other sources. He must say to himself that nothing which he already knows about the child counts at all. He must consider the child as an X to be solved by this means alone. He must be entirely convinced that by using this method, he will be able by it alone to obtain a thorough knowledge of the child without depending on any outside help. But this self-confidence is liable to many fluctuations. In the beginning everything seems easy; it is the period of illusions. After a few trials, if one has at all the critical spirit, errors are seen everywhere, and this leads to discouragement. But if one keeps at it faithfully, patiently, confidence will return little by little; it is no longer the optimism of the beginner, but a confidence grounded upon deliberate reason and proof; one has a consciousness of his own power as well as of his limitations.

This period of imitation should last through at least 5 or 6 sessions of two hours each, and bear upon a total of twenty children. Every experimenter wishing to commence should submit himself to a similar preparation.

CLASSIFICATION OF THE TESTS ACCORDING TO AGE

We here give the series of tests[1] ranged according to the ages at which the majority of children succeed in them. This constitutes our measuring scale of intelligence. Those who adopt our method will very often need to refer to it.

THREE YEARS

Show eyes, nose, mouth

Name objects in a picture

Repeat 2 figures

Repeat a sentence of 6 syllables

Give last name

---

[1]These tests are not the first ones of which we had thought; if we keep them it is after long trial; they appear to us all good and practical. But we are far from claiming that they are the best. Those who will take up this work after us will find better; they will certainly succeed in eliminating more strictly than we have been able to do, the tests that are influenced by education. In pursuing the experiments we have ourselves succeeded in making some improvements. But we have made no record of them, in order not to change the economy of the work and the value of our figures as to the result. The main point after all is that on the one hand the principle of the measure of intelligence be stated, and on the other that our method be, in spite of its defects, good enough to be put into practice.

We lack time to establish tests corresponding to ages under 3 years. Our experiment in hospitals showed us which are the tests to be used, but we do not yet know to which exact age of normal development they correspond. In any case we give them here for reference.

*Voluntary look (follow a lighted match which the experimenter moves).

*Prehension of an object by contact (put the object in contact with the hand).

*Prehension after visual perception. (One hands the object and the child must try to take it.)

*Knowledge of food. (One presents a piece of wood, then a biscuit. One notices if the child rejects the piece of wood to take the biscuit.)

*Execution of order given by gestures. (For instance, the order to sit down.)

*Imitation of simple gestures. (For instance, clap the hands.)

FOUR YEARS

Give sex

Name key, knife, penny

Repeat 3 figures

Compare 2 lines

FIVE YEARS

Compare 2 boxes of different weights

Copy a square

Repeat a sentence of 10 syllables

Count 4 sous

Put together two pieces in a "game of patience"

SIX YEARS

Repeat a sentence of 16 syllables

Compare two figures from an esthetic point of view

Define by use only, some simple objects

Execute 3 simultaneous commissions

Give one's age

Distinguish morning and evening

SEVEN YEARS

Indicate omissions in drawings

Give the number of fingers

Copy a written sentence

Copy a triangle and a diamond

Repeat 5 figures

Describe a picture

Count 13 single sous

Name 4 pieces of money

EIGHT YEARS

Read selection and retain two memories

Count 9 sous (3 single and 3 double)

Name four colors

Count backward from 20–0

Compare 2 objects from memory

Write from dictation

NINE YEARS

Give the date complete (day, month, day of the month, year)

Name the days of the week

Give definitions superior to use

Retain 6 memories after reading

Make change, 4 sous from 20 sous

Arrange 5 weights in order

TEN YEARS

Name the months

Name 9 pieces of money

Place 3 words in 2 sentences

Answer 3 comprehension questions

Answer 5 comprehension questions

ELEVEN YEARS

Criticize sentences containing absurdities

Place 3 words in 1 sentence

Find more than 60 words in 3 minutes

Give abstract definitions

Place disarranged words in order

TWELVE YEARS

Repeat 7 figures

Find 3 rhymes

Repeat a sentence of 26 syllables

Interpret pictures

Problem of facts

THIRTEEN YEARS

Paper cutting

Reversed triangle

Give differences of meaning

A few words upon the value of this classification. It is not exact for the age of three years, because certain tests placed at the level of that age can be done by much younger children, children of two years for instance. But this does not trouble us, for the measuring scale that we present is designed only for children of school age. Should a child of three years present himself these tests are sufficient to classify him. The only difficulty that could arise would be in classifying a child of two years.

At the other extremity of the scale, there is also a little uncertainty. A pupil who passes all the tests for the thirteenth year may have a mental capacity superior to that age. But how much? Our tests do not show us.

THE USE OF THE MEASURING SCALE OF INTELLIGENCE

Our principal conclusion is that we actually possess an instrument which allows us to measure the intellectual development of young children whose age is included between three and twelve years. This method appears to us practical, convenient and rapid. If one wishes to know summarily whether a child has the intelligence of his age, or if he is advanced or retarded, it suffices to have him take the tests of his age; and the performance of these tests certainly does not require more than thirty minutes which should be interrupted by ten minutes rest if one thinks this necessary for the child.

Furthermore when one wishes to be more precise, or to make a closer approximation, one may make many more tests; if the child is seven years old, he may attempt the tests of eight, nine and ten years for example. One would also be able after an interval of several days to substitute analogous tests.

One question remains to be examined. To what purpose are these studies? In reading the reflections which we have interspersed in the course of our treatise, it will be seen that a profound knowledge of the normal intellectual development of the child would not only be of great interest but useful in formulating a course of instruction really adapted to their aptitudes. We fear that those who have drawn up the programs actually in force, are educated men who in their work have been led more by the fancies of their imagination than by well-grounded principle. The pedagogical principle which ought to inspire the authors of programs seems to us to be the following: the instruction should always be according to the natural evolution of the child, and not precede it by a year or two. In other words the child should be sufficiently mature to understand; all precocious instruction is lost time, for it is not assimilated. We have cited an example of it in regard to the date, which is taught in the Maternal School, but which is not known and assimilated before the age of nine years. This is only one example, but it is eloquent; it shows the error of what has hitherto been done; it suggests a method which will enable us to improve upon the past—a method less literary, less rapid, and even extremely laborious, for it demands that one establish by careful investigations the normal evolution of a child's intelligence, in order to make all our programs and methods of instruction conform to that evolution, when it is once known. If by this labor we have succeeded in showing the necessity for a thorough investigation conducted after this plan, our time has not been lost. But we are far from flattering ourselves that we have inaugurated a reform. Reforms in France do not succeed except through politics, and we cannot readily imagine a secretary of state busying himself with a question of this kind. What is taught to children at school! As though legislators could become interested in that!

It now remains to explain the use of our measuring scale which we consider a standard of the child's intelligence. Of what use is a measure of intelligence? Without doubt one could conceive many possible applications of the process, in dreaming of a future where the social sphere would be better organized than ours; where the social sphere would be better organized than ours; where every one would work according to his known aptitudes in such a way that no particle of psychic force should be lost for society. That would be the ideal city. It is indeed far from us. But we have to remain among the sterner and the matter-of-fact realities of life, since we here deal with practical experiments which are the most commonplace realities.

These examples to which we could add many others[2] show that the methods of measuring the individual intelligence have not a speculative interest alone; by the direction, by the organization of all the investigations, psychology has finished the proof (we do not say for the first time but in a more positive manner than ever before), that it is in a fair way to become a Science of great social utility.

---

[2]Let us point out the very great utility to humanity that would result from giving the intellectual test to young recruits before enlisting them. Many morons, that is to say, young men who on account of their weak minds are unable to learn and understand the theory and drill of arms and to submit to a regular discipline, come to the medical examination, and are pronounced "good for the military service," because one does not know how to examine them from the intellectual point of view. We have learned that in Germany they pay attention to the mental debility of the recruits who are measured before enlistment by means of examination questions, written by Dr. Schultze, professor of psychiatry, on the Faculty of Medicine at Greifewald. These examination questions are made so that a twelve year old child of average intelligence and without any training can answer them. One of us referred these questions to the Minister of War, who answered that he would ask for a report on the matter. We have reason to believe that this answer is not the polite refusal which is customary with the State Administration, when they are importuned with propositions from the outside. And we shall most probably soon have the pleasure of telling the readers of *L'Anne* the result of our experiments on defectiveness among the recruits, and the means of detecting it and avoiding the simulation.

The Conceptions and Methods of Psychology.

By J. McKeen Cattell.

One of the verses in the treasure-house of Greek letters warns us against calling any man happy before he is dead. The greatest living English author lets one of his favorite characters say: 'But does incessant battling keep the intellect clear?' Such reflections may well lead us to distrust any attempt, by one in the ranks, to sum up the fundamental conceptions and methods of a science, especially of a young and growing science. It may be the prerogative of the student of psychology to write the biography of an infant, but he has not hitherto penetrated very far into its real life. I disagree completely with the eminent psychologist to whom the plan of this great congress is chiefly due when he claims that 'the presuppositions with which a science starts decide for all time the possibilities of its outer extension.' Sciences are not immutable species, but developing organisms. Their fundamental conceptions and methods at any period can only be approached by a research into work actually accomplished. Had time and circumstance permitted, I should have attempted to make an inductive study of the contents and methods of psychology rather than to prepare three quarters of an hour of generalities and platitudes. But as even the pedant knows, 'die Kunst ist lang, und kurz ist unser Leben.' The court poet must console himself for the deficiencies of his ceremonial verses by reflecting on the honor of being permitted to write them.

The concept of a science is an abstraction from an abstraction. The concrete fact is the individual experience of each of us. Certain parts of this experience are forcibly and artificially separated from the rest and become my science of psychology, your science of psychology, his science of psychology. From all these individual sciences, shifting not only from person to person but also from day to day, there arises by a kind of natural selection a *quasi* objective science of psychology. In a well-bred science, such as chemistry, the conventions have become standardized; the dogmas impose themselves on the neophyte. But projectiles as small as ions or electrons break up the idols, and the map of science is remodeled more quickly and completely than the map of Asia.

Psychology has never had a well-defined territory. As states of consciousness appear to be less stable and definite than the objects of the material world, so the science of psychology is more shifting in its contents and more uncertain in its methods than any physical science. We are told indeed in our introductory text-books that psychology is the science of mind and that mind and matter are the most diverse things in the world. It is said further that psychology is a positive science and is thus clearly distinguished from the normative disciplines, such as logic and ethics. Words are also used to set psychology off from sociology, history, philology and

---

*An address at the International Congress of Arts and Science, St. Louis, September, 1904.

the rest. But while all these verbal definitions may satisfy the college sophomore, they must be perplexing to the candidate for the doctor's degree.

The distinction between mind and matte is one of the last words of a philosophy which does not yet exist, rather than an axiom of every-day experience on which preliminary definitions may be based. We can not rest satisfied with an empirical psychology in which the distinction is self-evident, an epistemology in which it is explained and a metaphysics in which it disappears. It may be that we follow Descartes rather than Aristotle in our psychology, not so much from the needs of the science itself as from the demands of the church, on the one hand, and of physical science, on the other. The church required souls that might be saved or damned; physics wanted a world independent of individual perception, and as the methods of exact science were extended to the human body it became a part of the physical system.

To us who have been brought up in the orthodox tradition, the views of some of those who have passed from natural science to metaphysics seem decidedly naive. Thus Mach entitles the concluding section of his *Science of Mechanics* "The Relations of Mechanics to Physiology," when he is discussing not the question as to whether vital phenomena may be reduced to the laws of matter in motion, but the relations between sensations and the physical stimulus. Pearson tells us in his *Grammar of Science* that if the cortex of one brain were connected with another by a commissure of nerve substance, there would be "physical verification of other consciousness." Ostwald lets energy do hermaphroditic service in the physical and the extra-physical households.

But it is not certain that such ingenuous commingling of the mental and the physical worlds is more repugnant to common sense or natural science than the logical subtleties of the schools, which undertake to define, relate or obliterate them. It is generally assumed that a psychologist must be either an interactionist or a parallelist. According to the definitions with which our psychologies start, it is indeed true that mind and matter must either interact or in some way correspond without interaction. If the psychologist asserts that each brain is a center for the creation of new energy or for interference with the configuration of a material system, he obviously subverts the principal generalizations of physical science. He doubtless has a right to do so, but in the same sense as the cow has a right to stop the locomotive engine. If, on the other hand, the psychologist modestly admits that mind does not affect the physical order, he runs counter to the principal generalization of biological science. If pleasure and pain, memory and forethought, are of no use in the struggle for organic survival, why should they ever have evolved?

It requires less temerity to question the theories of biology than to deny the laws of physics. The survival of the fit may be regarded as a truism rather than as a discovery, if we call that fit which does survive. But fitness of this kind is so protean in its manifestations in organic nature that the formula becomes somewhat vague. If an animal is inconspicuously colored, it is protective coloration and so useful; if conspicuously colored, it is directive coloration and so useful. It is somewhat difficult to guess the utility of the fantastic shape and color of each deep-sea fish that lives in perpetual darkness. Then there are admittedly correlated variations, by-products of evolution, diseases and the like; it may be that consciousness is that sort of thing. If some kinds of consciousness, as the sense of beauty, are of no use in the struggle for existence, all the rest maybe equally useless—an efflorescence exhibited when there is friction due to lack of adjustment between the organism and its environment. Finally, and most plausibly, it may be argued that minds have evolved in answer to final causes, and that organic evolution must adopt the principles of psychology rather than prescribe to it.

The interactionist seems to be in a worse plight than the parallelist in the conflicts with our sister sciences, but the case is different before the court of common sense. The present writer can not conceive how the parallelist gets outside the limits of consciousness. Why does he want any thing to run parallel with the only thing he knows? He becomes at once a subjective idealist, and there may be no harm in that. But when the subjective idealist wants to live in a world with other men, he reinvents the distinctions that he had verbally obliterated. What he knows about the physical world is what his senses and the physicists ell him; if he likes to call it all consciousness or the unconscious, mind-stuff, will or God's thought, this may be emotionally stimulating, but no fact or law is thereby altered. The world may be God's thought, without in the least preventing the parallelist from thinking illogically.

If clarified experience is subverted by logic, we can of course become skeptics; but it is safer and wiser to wait awhile. Experience may become more clarified, our premises may prove to be at fault, even our syllogisms may be false. When it is said that a psychologist must be either an interactionist or a parallelist, and we find insurmountable difficulties in the way of his being either, the trouble may be with the original assumptions. Matter and consciousness may not be two entities set over against each other. A perception may be both a part of my consciousness and a part of the physical world; an object may be at the same time in a world of matter in motion and in the microcosm of my individual mind. As my colleague, Professor Dewey, starting from an idealistic standpoint, claims, we may simply be giving different names to activity when it is tensional and when it is relatively stable; or as my colleague, Professor Woodbridge, starting from a realistic standpoint, suggests, the relation of consciousness to objects may be analogous to that of space to objects.

As I have said, the relations of mind to body and the distinction between consciousness and matte are the last word of a philosophy that is not yet written, and I have no competence or with to discuss them here. But the task has been assigned to me of considering the scope, conceptions and methods of psychology, and it is my business to define the field of psychology or to acknowledge my inability to do so. I must choose the latter alternative. I can only say that psychology is what the psychologist is interested in *qua* psychologist. If it is said that this is tautological, it may be replied that tautology is characteristic of definitions. If psychology is defined as the "science of mind" or, what in my opinion is better, "the science of minds" the tautology is equal, and it appears to be more possible to determine by an inductive study the professional interests of psychologists than to define the nature of mind or consciousness. Further, I am not convinced that psychology should be limited to the study of consciousness as such, in so far as this can be set off from the physical world. Psychology apart from consciousness is doubtless an absurdity, but so also is mathematics or botany. I admire the products of the Herbartian school and the ever-increasing acuteness of introspective analysis from Locke to Ward. All this forms an important chapter in modern psychology; but the positive scientific results are small in quantity when compared with the objective experimental work accomplished in the past fifty years. There is no conflict between introspective analysis and objective experiment—on the contrary, they should and do continually cooperate. But the rather widespread notion that there is no psychology apart from introspection is refuted by the brute argument of accomplished fact.

It seems to me that most of the research work that has been done by me or in my laboratory is nearly as independent of introspection as work in physics or in zoology. The time of mental processes, the accuracy of perception and movement, the range of consciousness, fatigue and practice, the motor accompaniments of thought, memory, the association of ideas, the perception of space, color-vision, preferences, judgments, individual differences, the behavior of animals and of children, these and other topics I have investigated without requiring the slightest introspection on the part of the subject or undertaking such on my own part during the course of the experiments. It is usually no more necessary for the subject to be a psychologist than it is for the vivisected frog to be a psychologist.

James and Wundt agree in telling us that the experimental method is chiefly of use as a servant of introspection; indeed James says that there is no "new psychology," "nothing but the old psychology which began in Locke's time, plus a little physiology of the brain and senses and theory of evolution, and a few refinements of introspective detail." But our leaders in psychology have become our leaders by belying such partial statements. Although neither Wundt nor James has attempted any considerable experimental research, yet we look up to them as the founders of modern psychology. Wundt's original and laborious *Physiologische Psychologie*, the Leipzig laboratory and the *Philosophische Studien* have been in large measure the foundation stones of experimental psychology. The broad opportunistic treatment of James, instinct with genius and fearless of logical inconsistency, has been of immense service in freeing psychology from traditional fetters. I see no reason why psychology, at least the psychology of twenty years ago, may not be said to be the subjects treated in James's *Principles of Psychology* and Wundt's *Physiologische Psychologie* with such additional subjects as other psychologists have included or might have included in their treatises.

When the introspective purist says that the treatises of Wundt and James are potpouris of sciences, or that the kind of work that some of us have attempted to do belongs to physiology or to anthropometry or nowhere in particular, there is a natural temptation to reply that much of introspective and analytic psychology belongs to art rather than to science. Such things may be ingenious and interesting, like the personae of Bernard Shaw or the mermaids of Burne Jones, but we don't expect to meet them in the street. An attitude of this kind would, however, be as partial as that which it seeks to controvert. Let us take a broad outlook and be liberal in our appreciation; let us welcome variations and sports; if birth is given to monstrosities on occasion, we may be sure that they will not survive.

Any attempt at *a priori* limitation of the field of a science is futile. Even if, for example, consciousness and matter in motion were distinct and distinguishable, this would be no argument against a science of physiological psychology. Cerebral and psychical phenomena form one series, and if we have at present no adequate science which concerns itself with this series, it is owing to ignorance of facts, not at all to logical limitations. Matter, time, space and the differential calculus may be as disparate as possible, but are brought together in the science of physics. If the psychologist can not be shut out of the physical world, still less can he be excluded from the sphere of the so-called normative sciences. If any one takes a modern work on ethics or esthetics and tries to separate the treatment of "what is" from that of "what ought to be," he will find himself engaged in an idle task.

It appears that the limits of science are set largely by a psychological constant. A single science has practically the range that can be covered by a single mind or man. From Aristotle to Hobbes and Descartes there were philosophers who could master nearly the whole range of knowledge and advance it in whatever direction they cared to turn. But even in this period as knowledge accumulated, specialization began, and we find astronomers, anatomists and other students of particular sciences. After Galileo and Newton the physico-mathematical sciences became completely divorced from the descriptive natural sciences, while psychology remained under the shelter of philosophy. It was only in the second half of the nineteenth century that the accumulation of certain facts and theories warranted their becoming the chief interest of a psychologist, and even yet it is more usual for a man to pass through a psychological period than to be a permanent psychologist.

While the first result of increased knowledge has been the establishment of a number of sciences—say a dozen or a score—which have secured proselytes and to a certain extent limited and directed their activities, the further increase of knowledge must break down the artificial limitations. The late emergence of psychology has made easy an elective selection of material. We not only have psychologists who are also philosophers, but psychologists who are also physiologists, anatomists, pathologists, zoologists, anthropologist, philologists, sociologists, physicists or mathematicians. Psychology is and will increasingly become untied with professions and arts, with education, medicine, music, painting and the rest. Even sciences remote from psychology, astronomy, for example, may have sufficient points of contact to occupy the entire time of a specialist. We not only have combinations between the orthodox sciences, but cross-sections through them, which may to advantage occupy the student, and which have full rights to be ranked as sciences. The phenomena of vision, for example, are scattered among the sciences of psychology, physics, physiology, anatomy, anthropology, zoology, embryology, pathology, chemistry, mathematics, etc.; they are important factors in certain fine and industrial arts; they are the basis of one of the most important medical disciplines. Why should not a man be a "visionologist" or "sightonomer"? When President Hall gives us an original and unique book on adolescence, nothing is gained by attempting to assign it to one of the conventional sciences. The work of Dr. Galton appears to me to be particularly unified, but it does not belong to psychology, nor to any other science. Why not call him an opportunist, or a liberal unionist, or a Galtonist, or better still call him no name at all?

In objecting to an artificial limitation of the field of the psychologist, I by no means want to aggrandize his office or to let psychology eat up the other sciences.

The student of psychology is limited by the capacity of the human mind and of his own particular mind; he can, on the average, cover a range about as large as that of the student of any other science. If he would gladly get, he would also gladly give. If he is an imperialist who would set his flag on every corner of the earth, he yet tears down no other flag and welcomes the invasion of his own territory by every science.

As I claim for psychology the freedom of the universe in its subject-matter, so I believe that every method of science can be used by the psychologist. The two great achievements of science have been the elaboration of the quantitative method on the one hand and of the genetic method on the other. The uniformity of nature and the rationality of things are here presented in their most convincing, or at all events most plausible form. It would be an irreparable limitation if either of these methods did not apply in psychology. In my option they not only do obtain but must obtain. The mental and the physical are so inextricably interfused that quantitative and genetic uniformities could not exist in the physical world if absent from consciousness. If our mental processes did not vary in number, if they did not have time, intensity and space relations, we should never have come to apply these categories in physics, chemistry or astronomy. I am not prepared to attempt to clear up the logical questions involved; when water is muddy it is often wise to wait for it to settle rather than to keep stirring it up.

Under the conditions of modern science nearly all observations are experiments and nearly all experiments are measurements. A sharp distinction is usually drawn between an experiment and an observation. Thus Wundt, following Mill and other logicians, defines an experiment as an observation connected with an intentional interference on the part of the observer in the rise and course of the phenomena observed. But it is as properly an experiment to alter the conditions of observation as to alter the course of the phenomena observed. If the astronomer goes to the ends of the earth and photographs a solar eclipse, making all sorts of measurements and calculations, we may say that this is an observation and not an experiment, but we have not made a useful definition; neither do we gain anything by deciding whether it is an experiment when a baby pulls apart a doll to see what is inside. The real distinction is between the casual experimenting and observing of daily life, and the planned and purposive experiment and observation of science. Science is experimental *qua* science.

I consequently object to making experimental psychology a branch of psychology. It is a method in psychology, which is extended just as rapidly as psychology becomes a science. The purely introspective or analytic observer does, according to the current definition, continually made experiments, because his introspection itself alters the process that he is observing, thus sometimes making his observations invalid as a description of natural conditions. On the other hand, the student in the laboratory may measure the process without any introspection or interference with it, and this may not be technically an experiment at all, but it gives a scientific description of the normal course of mental life. We are told that Adam gave a very appropriate name to the hog; science is not always so fortunate in its nomenclature.

Most experiments, letting experiments mean attempts to increase scientific knowledge, are also measurements. Measurement is only a description; but it has proved itself to be the most economical, wide-reaching and useful form of description. What language was for the evolution of primitive man, measurement is for the advance of modern science. As a word selects similarities and ignores differences, so a measurement selects certain similarities from the concrete manifoldness of things. That such a great part of the world can be described in terms of a few units of measurement, and that this description should lead to such useful applications, is truly marvelous and admirable. As I am writing these paragraphs, I have received a manuscript in which the author explains that the fact that the earth rotates on its axis in twenty-four hours, not varying a second from day to day, is a conclusive proof that it was created and set rotating by a benevolent being. If the days were shorter, he says, we could not get our work done, and if the days were longer, we should be too tired by night. It almost seems as though the world were made in such comparatively rational fashion in order that we may measure it.

The physicist counts, and he measures time, space and energy. He has intractable matter with its seven and seventy elements, and he may come across a substance as complex and perplexing as radium. But by and large he can describe his world in certain quantitative formulas. It is true that he accomplishes this in part by unloading on psychology qualitative differences, such as colors and tones. So much the more satisfaction to us if we can reduce them to quantitative order. Perhaps we shall have only partial success; but it may fairly be urged that psychology has done as much in this direction in fifty years as physics accomplished to the time of Galileo or chemistry to the time of Lavoisier.

The psychologist counts and he measures time, space and intensity. Even if it were true—I think it is not true—that mental magnitudes are not measurable, it would none the less be the case that mental processes are described in quantitative terms. This is attempted and accomplished in most of the researches published in our psychological journals. They describe measurements and the correlation of quantities; they show that a mental mechanics is more than a possibility.

The physical sciences have been primarily quantitative and the biological sciences are primarily genetic, but the physical sciences must become genetic and the biological sciences must become quantitative. Psychology is from the start both quantitative and genetic. It may indeed be claimed that it is the science in which the genetic method has the most complete application. Every mental state and every form of activity is the result of development from previous conditions. If explanation, as distinguished from description, is possible anywhere in science it is possible here. It is certainly difficult to penetrate by analogy into the consciousness of the lower animals, of savages and of children, but the study of their behavior has already yielded much and promises much more. Although those who make their psychology coterminous with introspection can not enter far into this field, they still have their own genetic problems. In whatever direction we turn the harvest is waiting; it is only the reapers who are few. Almost every observation, experiment or theory of organic evolution offers parallel problems for the psychologist. The development of the individual opens questions more numerous and more important for psychology than does the development of the body for other sciences.

Senile, degenerative and pathological conditions are all there for psychological investigation. The evolution of society and the inter-relations of individuals are being gradually brought within the range of genetic psychology. It is quite possible that the chief scientific progress of the next fifty years will be in this direction.

The problems of psychology are certainly made endlessly complex by the fact that we have to do not with the development and condition of a single mind or individual, but with innumerable individuals. The traditional psychology has been disposed to ignore individual differences; but in attempting to prescribe conditions for all minds, it becomes schematic and somewhat barren. It is surely wasteful to select those uniformities that are true for all and to throw away those differences which are equally fit material for scientific treatment. Linnaeus instructed his pupils to attend to species and to ignore varieties, and this in the end tended to make systematic botany and zoology unfruitful. If the zoologist had limited his work to the discovery of facts that are true for all animals and had ignored the differences between animals, he would have done something analogous to what the psychologist has actually done.

It may be that individuals can not be grouped into species or even varieties, but animals and plants are separated into species in accordance with the noticeable differences between them, and there are as many degrees of just noticeable difference between men as between related species. We have in any case the different species of the animal series and the different races of men for psychological study; it may be that instincts and mental traits have specific or racial significance for the zoologist or anthropologist. We have the infant, the child, the adolescent and the aged; we have the two sexes; we have the geniuses, the feeble-minded, the criminals and the insane—complex groups to be sure, but open to psychological investigation. It may be that mental imagery or types of character will give workable groups. But even if mental traits and their manifestations are continuous, we can study the continuum. The study of distribution and correlation appears to open up subjects of great interest and having important practical applications.

The question of the practical applications of psychology is the last which I shall touch. There are those who hold that there is something particularly noble in art for art's sake or in science divorced from any possible application. We are told of the mathematician who boasted that his science was a virgin that had never been prostituted by being put to any use. It is doubtless true that science justifies itself if it satisfies mental needs. It may also be true that pure science should precede the applications of science. But of this I am not sure; it appears to me that the conditions are most healthful when science and its applications proceed hand in hand, as is now the case in engineering, electricity, chemistry, medicine, etc. If I did not believe that psychology affected conduct and could be applied in useful ways, I should regard my occupation as nearer to that of the professional chess-player or sword swaller than to that of the engineer or scientific physician.

It seems quite obvious that such knowledge as each of us has of his own perceptions, mental processes and motor responses and of the reactions and activities of others, is being continually used, more continually indeed than any other knowledge whatever. This knowledge is partly organized into reflexes and instincts; it is in part acquired by each individual. Control of the physical world is secondary to the control of ourselves and of our fellow men. The child must observe and experiment to fit itself into the social order, and we are always experimenting on it and trying to make it different from what it is. All our systems of education, our churches, our legal systems, our governments and the rest are applied psychology. It may be at present pseudo-science, in the sense that we have drawn conclusions without adequate knowledge, but it is none the less the best we can do in the way of the application of systematized knowledge to the control of human nature.

It certainly is not essential and perhaps is not desirable for every mother, for every teacher, for every statesman, to study psychology, especially the kind of psychology at present available. It is not necessary for a man to be either a psychologist or a fool at forty; he may, for example, be both. But surely it is possible to discover whether or not it is desirable to feed a baby every time it cries, to whip a boy when he disobeys or to put a man in prison when he breaks a law. If each man were given the work he is most competent to do and were prepared for this work in the best way, the work of the world all the way from the highest manifestations of genius to the humblest daily labor would be more than doubled. I see no reason why the application of systematized knowledge to the control of human nature may not in the course of the present century accomplish results commensurate with the nineteenth century applications of physical science to the material world.

The present function of a physician, a lawyer, a clergyman, a teacher or a man of business is to a considerable extent that of an amateur psychologist. In the inevitable specialization of modern society, there will become increasing need of those who can be paid for expert psychological advice. We may have experts who will be trained in schools as large and well-equipped as our present schools of medicine, and their profession may become as useful and as honorable. Such a profession clearly offers an opportunity to the charlatan, but it is not the only profession open to him. For the present the psychological expert should doubtless be a member of one of the recognized professions who has the natural endowments, special training and definite knowledge of the conditions that will make his advice and assistance of value. But in the end there will be not only a science but also a profession of psychology.

CHAPTER 9

BEHAVIORISM: ANTECEDENT INFLUENCES

IVAN PETROVITCH PAVLOV (1849 – 1936)

Pavlov, the oldest of 4 children and the son of a Russian Orthodox priest, was born on September 14, 1849, in Ryazan, a town 250 miles from Moscow.[1] Besides his father, his maternal grandfather and two paternal uncles were priests. It is not surprising, therefore, that Pavlov initially considered the priesthood as a vocation and entered the seminary. He, however, was led from this career by reading Darwin's (1859) *The Origin of the Species* and Sechenov's (1863) *Reflexes of the Brain*.[2]

Pavlov left the seminary in 1870 and entered the University of St. Petersburg to study natural science, graduating in 1875. An extremely able student, he immediately entered medical school with an eye toward research. Upon graduation from medical school in 1883, he went to Germany to study under the eminent physiologist Karl Ludwig, a radical positivist, that is, one who feels that knowledge comes through observation, not theorization. Pavlov was so influenced by Ludwig that he had carved in stone at the entrance of one of his laboratories, "Observation— Observation."

---

[1] For biographic material concerning Pavlov, see Anokihin (1971), Asratyan (1953), Babkin (1949), Frolov (1938), Gannt (1973, 1979), Giurgiea (1985), Thomas (1994), and Windholz (1984, 1990, 1991).

[2] Pavlov was so influenced by Darwin and Sechenov he kept a bust of them along with that of the eminent geneticist Mendel. Their influence was also evident in his theory of conditioning, in which he maintained that conditioned reflexes were adaptive and physiologically based.

After three years in Germany, Pavlov returned to Russia where he established the Institute for the Experimental Study of Medicine and eventually became a professor of physiology at the University of St. Petersburg. Pavlov's initial research at the institute involved digestion and resulted in a book, *The Work of the Principle Digestive Glands* (1897) plus the Nobel Prize in 1904. Pavlov's absorption in his work made him the archetypical absent-minded professor who cared for little other than his research. On one occasion absorbed in thought, he stepped from a tram breaking his leg, and on another occasion, he yelled at an assistant who was late because of the dangerous conditions caused by the Bolshevik revolution (Gannt, 1979).

As early as 1891, Pavlov and his co-workers noticed that visual or auditory stimuli could initiate digestive activity. The sight of a feeding bowl or the sounds of a caretaker's footsteps, for example, could trigger salivation. From this time until his death, Pavlov and his colleagues studied classical conditioning, the evocation of a reflex by a previously neutral, that is, conditional stimulus. These studies resulted in a book first published in English in 1927, *Conditioned Reflexes*. It is from this book that the first reading for this chapter is taken. Here, Pavlov describes the nature of the conditioned reflex and some of his very first studies of the phenomenon. In studying classical conditioning, Pavlov described many basic principles of learning such as extinction, stimulus generalization, and discrimination. He even developed a classical conditioning paradigm for the development of neurosis.[3]

An ardent worker, Pavlov worked until four days before his death. Even during his final illness, he remained an acute observer, carefully describing the symptoms of the pneumonia that took his life on February 27, 1936. Although critical of psychology, which he doubted ". . . . can be regarded as science at all" (Pavlov, 1927, p. 3), he left behind a legacy upon which many psychologists have built, including the behaviorist John Watson. Pavlov did, however, admire the research of the American psychologist Edward Lee Thorndike.

EDWARD LEE THORNDIKE (1874–1949)

Edward Lee Thorndike, the son of a Methodist minister, was born into an old New England family on August 31, 1874.[4] Because of the policies of the Methodist church, the Thorndike family moved a great deal. The young Thorndike, however, consistently excelled in school, being either number one or number two in his class. Upon graduation from high school, he entered Wesleyan University in Connecticut

---

[3]His colleague Petrova demonstrated an effective psychopharmaceutical intervention for neurosis based on Pavlov's theory (Windholz, 1989).

[4]For biographic details of Thorndike's life see Boakes (1984), Joncich (1968), and Thorndike (1936).

and continued to excel, winning numerous prizes for his academic prowess. During his junior year, he took psychology and found it to be dull. He, nevertheless, read James's *Principles of Psychology,* and it energized him intellectually.[5]

After receiving his undergraduate degree with highest honors, he entered Harvard, intending to study English, philosophy, and psychology. His interest in English and philosophy soon diminished, and he concentrated on psychology working under the direction of William James. Initially wishing to study the behavior of children, Thorndike found subjects difficult to obtain and thus switched to the use of animals, specifically chickens that were housed in his room. His landlady objected, and he turned to James who allowed Thorndike to conduct his experiments in the basement of his home! There, using ramshackle mazes made from piles of books, Thorndike conducted some of the earliest experiment in operant (instrumental) conditioning. He, however, did not take his degree from Harvard. Spurned as suitor, he left New England and went to New York and Columbia where he studied under the aegis of James McKeen Cattell.

At Columbia, Thorndike continued his work in animal psychology, and history repeated itself. His New York landlady also objected to his menagerie, and Thorndike was forced to remove his animals, mostly cats, to laboratory space at the university. There, he continued to study operant conditioning by putting cats in homemade puzzle boxes from which they had to escape by pulling strings, turning buttons, and so on.[6] Breaking away from the older anthropomorphic approaches of investigators like Romanes, Thorndike concluded that animal learning was primarily a trial-and-error process, where chance-correct responses were stamped in because of their satisfying consequences. This stamping in is part of what Thorndike dubbed the law of effect, a precursor to the concept of reinforcement. These experiments were basis of Thorndike's dissertation and were published as monograph (Thorndike, 1898b) and republished in 1911 as a book, *Animal Intelligence.* The second article for this chapter is a short report of his work that preceded the monograph (Thorndike, 1898a).

After obtaining his degree, Thorndike spent one year at Western Reserve University in Ohio before returning to Columbia in 1899 for the rest of his career. Turning to human psychology, he was immensely productive, publishing more than 500 articles and books on a variety of topics such as transfer of training (Thorndike & Woodworth, 1901; Thorndike & Ruger, 1923), educational psychology (Thorndike, 1913),[7] word usage, (Thorndike, 1921, 1932), and the quantification of the quality of city life (Thorndike, 1939).

Immensely successful, he achieved many honors, including the presidencies of the American Psychological Association and the American Association for the Advancement of Science. Thorndike fulfilled his youthful pledge to arrive at the "top

---

[5]He, in fact, criticized his instructor for not using James's book.

[6]Burnham (1972) indicates that these were crudely constructed. Here, Thorndike stands in stark contrast to Pavlov.

[7]This work was dedicated to the memory of William James.

of the psychology heap" (Boakes, 1984, p. 72). Today, Thorndike is remembered mostly for his early work in animal learning. He died in 1949, nine years after retiring from Columbia.

REFERENCES

Anokhin, P. K. (1971, March). Three giants of Soviet psychology. *Psychology Today*, pp. 43–78.

Asratyan, E. A. (1953). *I. P. Pavlov: His life and his work.* Moscow, Foreign Languages Publishing House.

Babkin, B. P. (1949). *Pavlov: A biography.* Chicago: University of Chicago Press.

Boakes, R. (1984). *From Darwin to behaviorism: Psychology and the minds of animals.* Cambridge, England: Cambridge University Press.

Burnham, J. C. (1972). Thorndike's puzzle boxes. *Journal of the History of the Behavioral Sciences*, 8, 159–167.

Darwin, C. (1936). *The origin of the species.* New York: Modern Library. (Originally published in 1859).

Frolov, Y. P. (1938). *Pavlov and his school.* London: Kegan-Paul.

Gannt, W. H. (1973). Reminiscences of Pavlov. *Journal of the Experimental Analysis of Behavior*, 20, 131–136.

Gannt, W. H. (1979, February). Interview with Professor Emeritus. W. Horsley Gannt. *Johns Hopkins Magazine*, pp. 26–32.

Giurgea, C. E. (1985). On the facts and ideologies in the Pavlovian saga. *Pavlovian Journal of Biological Science.* 20, 7–10.

Joncich, G. (1968). *The sane positivist: A biography of Edward L. Thorndike.* Middletown CT: Wesleyan University Press.

Pavlov, I. P. (1960). *Conditioned reflexes.* London: Dover. (Originally published in 1927).

Sechenov, I. M. (1965). *Reflexes of the brain.* Cambridge, MA: MIT Press. (Originally published in 1863).

Thomas, R. K. (1994). Pavlov was "mugged." *History of Psychology Newsletter*, 26, 86–91.

Thorndike, E. L. (1898a). Some experiments on animal intelligence. *Science*, 7, 818–824.

Thorndike, E. L. (1898b). Animal intelligence: An experimental study of the associative processes in animals. [Monograph supplement]. *Psychological Review*, 2, (8).

Thorndike, E. L. (1911). *Animal intelligence.* New York: Macmillan.

Thorndike, E. L. (1913). *Educational Psychology* (3 vols.). New York: Teachers College, Columbia University.

Thorndike, E. L. (1921). *The teachers word book.* New York: Bureau of Publications, Teachers College, Columbia University.

Thorndike, E. L. (1932). (Rev. Ed.) *A teachers word book of the twenty thousand words found most frequently and widely in general reading for children and young people.* New York: Bureau of Publications, Teachers College, Columbia University.

Thorndike, E. L. (1936). Edward Lee Thorndike. In C. Murchison (Ed.) *A history of psychology in autobiography* (Vol. 3, pp. 263–270). Worcester, MA: Clark University Press.

Thorndike, E. L. (1939). *Your city.* New York: Harcourt Brace.

Thorndike, E. L., & Woodworth, R. S. (1901). The influence of improvement in one mental function upon the efficiency of other mental functions, I. *Psychological Review*, 8, 247–261.

Thorndike, E. L. & Ruger, G. J. (1923). The effect of first year Latin upon knowledge of English words of Latin derivation. *School and Society*, 18, 260–270.

Windholz, G. (1984). Pavlov vs. Köhler: Pavlov's little-known primate research. *Pavlovian Journal of Biological Science*, 21, 23–31.

Windholz, G. (1990). Pavlov and the Pavlovians in the laboratory. *Journal of the history of the Behavioral Sciences*, 26, 64–74.

Windholz, G. (1991). I. P. Pavlov as a youth. *Integrative Physiological and Behavioral Science*, 26, 51–67.

Conditioned Reflexes

I. P. Pavlov

LECTURE II

Technical methods employed in the objective investigation of the functions of the cerebral hemispheres.—Response to signals as reflex action.—Unconditioned and conditioned reflexes.—Necessary conditions for the development of conditioned reflexes.

In the previous lecture I gave an account of the reasons which led us to adopt, for the investigation of the functions of the cerebral hemispheres, the purely objective method used for investigating the physiological activity of the lower parts of the nervous system. In this manner the investigation of the cerebral hemispheres is brought into line with the investigations conducted in other branches of natural science, and their activities are studied as purely physiological facts, without any need to resort to fantastic speculations as to the existence of any possible subjective state in the animal which may be conjectured on analogy with ourselves. From this point of view the whole nervous activity of the animal must be regarded as based firstly on inborn reflexes. These are regular causal connections between certain definite external stimuli acting on the organism and its necessary reflex reactions. Such inborn reflexes are comparatively few in number, and the stimuli setting them in action act close up, being as a rule the general physical and chemical properties of the common agencies which affect the organism. The inborn reflexes by themselves are inadequate to ensure the continued existence of the organism, especially of the more highly organized animals, which, when deprived of their highest nervous activity, are permanently disabled, and if left to themselves, although retaining all their inborn reflexes, soon cease to exist. The complex conditions of everyday existence require a much more detailed and specialized correlation between the animal and its environment than is afforded by the inborn reflexes alone. This more precise correlation can be established only through the medium of the cerebral hemispheres; and we have found that a great number of all sorts of stimuli always act through the medium of the hemispheres as temporary and inter-changeable signals for the comparatively small number of agencies of a general character which determine the inborn reflexes, and that this is the only means by which a most delicate adjustment of the organism to the environment can be established. To this function of the hemispheres we gave the name of "signalization."

Before passing on to describe the results of our investigation it is necessary to give some account of the purely technical side of the methods employed, and to describe the general way in which the signalizing activity of the hemispheres can be studied. It is obvious that the reflex activity of any effector organ can be chosen for the purpose of this investigation, since signalling stimuli can get linked up with any of the inborn reflexes. But, as was mentioned in the first lecture, the starting point for the present investigation was determined in particular by the study of two reflexes—the food or "alimentary" reflex, and the "defence" reflex in its mildest form, as observed when a rejectable substance finds its way into the mouth of the animal. As it turned out, these two reflexes proved a fortunate choice in many ways. Indeed, while any strong defence reflex, *e.g.* against such a stimulus as a powerful electric current, makes the animal extremely restless and excited; and while the sexual reflexes require a special environment—to say nothing of their periodic character and their dependence upon age—the alimentary reflex and the mild defence reflex to rejectable substances are normal everyday occurrences.

It is essential to realize that each of these two reflexes—the alimentary reflex and the mild defence reflex to rejectable substances—consists of two distinct components, a motor and a secretory. Firstly the animal exhibits a reflex activity directed towards getting hold of the food and eating it or, in the case of rejectable substances, towards getting rid of them out of the mouth; and secondly, in both cases an immediate secretion of saliva occurs, in the case of food, to start the physical and chemical processes of digestion and, in the case of rejectable substances, to wash them out of the mouth. We confined our experiments almost entirely to the secretory component of the reflex: the allied motor reactions were taken into account only where there were special reasons. The secretory reflex presents many important advantages for our purpose. It allows of an extremely accurate measurement of the intensity of reflex activity, since either the number of drops in a given time may be counted or else the saliva may be caused to displace a coloured fluid in a horizontally placed graduated glass tube. It would be much more difficult to obtain the same accuracy of measurement for any motor reflex, especially for such complex motor reactions as accompany reflexes to food or to rejectable substances. Even by using most delicate instruments we should never be able to reach such precision in measuring the intensity of the motor component of the reflexes as can easily be attained with the secretory component. Again, a very important point in favour of the secretory reflexes is the much smaller tendency to interpret them in an anthropomorphic fashion—*i.e.* in terms of subjective analogy. Although this seems a trivial consideration from our present standpoint, it was of importance in the earlier stages of our investigation and did undoubtedly influence our choice.

For the purpose of registering the intensity of the salivary reflex all the dogs employed in the experiments are subjected to a preliminary minor operation, which consists in the transplantation of the opening of the salivary duct from its natural place on the mucous membrane of the mouth to the outside skin. For this purpose the terminal portion of the salivary duct is dissected and freed from the surrounding tissue, and the duct, together with a small portion of the mucous membrane surrounding its natural opening, is carried through a suitable incision, to the outside of the cheek in the case of the parotid gland, or under the chin in the case of the submaxillary gland. In this new position the duct is fixed by a few stitches which are removed when the wound has healed. As a result of the operation the saliva now flows to the outside, on to the cheek or chin of the animal, instead of into the mouth, so that the measurement of the secretory activity of the gland is greatly facilitated. It is only necessary for this purpose to adjust a small glass funnel over the opening of the duct on to the skin, and for this we find a special cement prepared according to a formula of Mendeléeff[1] most useful. As an alternative, very suitable and accurate as a recording apparatus is a hemispherical bulb which also can be hermetically sealed on to the skin. From the bulb project two tubes, one pointing up and the other pointing down. The latter tube is used for drawing off the saliva which collects during each observation, while the former tube connects by air transmission with a horizontal graduated glass tube filled with coloured fluid. As the saliva flows into the hemispherical bulb the coloured fluid is displaced along the graduated tube, where the amount of secretion can be read off accurately. Further, it is not difficult to fix up an automatic electrically-recording device which will split up the displaced fluid into drops of exactly equal volume and reduce any lag in the movement of the fluid to a minimum.[2] (see figure 1)

To come to the general technique of the experiments, it is important to remember that our research deals with the highly specialized activity of the cerebral cortex, a signalizing apparatus of tremendous complexity and of most exquisite sensitivity, through which the animal is influenced by countless stimuli from the outside world. Every one of these stimuli produces a certain effect upon the animal, and all of them taken together may clash and interfere with, or else reinforce, one another. Unless we are careful to take special precautions the success of the whole investigation may be jeopardized, and we should get hopelessly lost as soon as we began to seek for cause and effect among so many and various influences, so intertwined and entangled as to form a veritable chaos. It was evident that the experimental conditions had to be simplified, and that this simplification must consist in eliminating as far as possible any stimuli outside our control which might fall upon the animal, admitting only such stimuli as could be entirely controlled by the experimenter. It was thought at the beginning of our research that it would be sufficient simply to isolate the experimenter in the research chamber with the dog on its stand, and to refuse admission to anyone else during the course of an experiment. But this precaution was found to be wholly inadequate, since the experimenter, however still he might try to be, was himself a constant source of a large number of stimuli. His slightest movements—blinking of the eyelids or movement of the eyes, posture, respiration and so on—all acted as stimuli which, falling upon the dog, were sufficient to vitiate the experiments by making exact interpretation of the results extremely difficult. In order to exclude this undue influence on the part of the experimenter as far as possible, he had to be stationed outside the room

---

[1]*Mendeléeff's cement:* Colophonium, 50 grammes; ferric oxide, 40 grammes; yellow beeswax, 25 grammes.

[2]In almost all the experiments quoted in these lectures the amount of salivary secretion is, for the sake of uniformity, given in drops. It was, however, only in the very earliest period of the research—before the separation of the experimenter from the animal was made—that the actual number of drops falling from a small funnel fixed over the fistula was counted, and only a few of these experiments are given. In the great majority of the experiments the salivary secretion was measured by the displacement of water in a graduated tube or by the electric recorder, allowing a much greater accuracy of measurement. The readings so obtained have been converted, in the tables, into drops. Thus, in some experiments it will be noticed that the number of drops is given to an accuracy of one-tenth.

The apparatus used for recording the salivary secretion in experiments on conditioned reflexes. A, hemispherical bulb which is fixed over the fistula. aaa, connecting tube leading through the partition separating the animal's room from the experimenter and connecting the bulb A to the registering apparatus, B. bb, tube connecting the bulb with bottle, C.

   After each observation a vacuum is created in the bottle C by depression of the rubber balloon D; the saliva accumulating in A is thus sucked away. During the observation A is automatically disconnected from C and connected with the registering apparatus. During the aspirations of the saliva from bulb A the latter is automatically disconnected from the registering apparatus.

FIGURE 1.

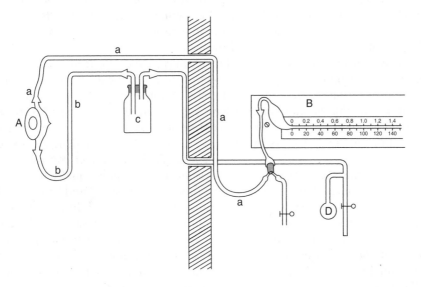

in which the dog was placed, and even this precaution proved unsuccessful in laboratories not specially designed for the study of these particular reflexes. The environment of the animal, even when shut up by itself in a room, is perpetually changing. Footfalls of a passer-by, chance conversations in neighbouring rooms, slamming of a door or vibration from a passing van, street-cries, even shadows cast through the windows into the room, any of these casual uncontrolled stimuli falling upon the receptors of the dog set up a disturbance in the cerebral hemispheres and vitiate the experiments. To get over all these disturbing factors a special laboratory was built at the Institute of Experimental Medicine in Petrograd, the funds being provided by a keen and public-spirited Moscow business man. The primary task was the protection of the dogs from uncontrolled extraneous stimuli, and this was effected by surrounding the building with an isolating trench and employing other special structural devices. Inside the building all the research rooms (four to each floor) were isolated from one another by across-shaped corridor; the top and ground floors, where these rooms were situated, were separated by an intermediate floor. Each research room was carefully partitioned by the use of sound-proof materials into two compartments—one for the animal, the other for the experimenter. For stimulating the animal, and for registering the corresponding reflex response, electrical methods or pneumatic transmission were used. By means of these arrangements it was possible to get something of that stability of environmental conditions so essential to the carrying out of a successful experiment.

Another point should be mentioned—although in this respect the means at our disposal still leave something to be desired. In analysing the exceedingly complex influence of the external environment upon the animal, the experimenter must be able to exercise full control over all the conditions obtaining during the course of any experiment. He should therefore have at his disposal various instruments for affecting the animal by different kinds of stimuli, singly or combined, so as to imitate simple natural conditions. But we were often handicapped by the conditions in which we had to work and by the shortcomings of the instruments at our disposal, for we always found that he cerebral hemispheres were sensitive to far finer gradations of stimulus than we could furnish.

It is possible that the experimental conditions I have described may raise somewhere the objection of being abnormal and artificial. However it is hardly likely, in view of the infinite variety of stimuli met with under natural conditions, that we shall hit on one that is quite unprecedented in the life of the animal. Moreover, in dealing with any phenomenon of vast complexity it is absolutely necessary to isolate the different single factors involved, so as to study them independently, or in arbitrary groups in which we can keep the individual units under control. But as a matter of fact the same objection and the same answer apply equally to the whole of animal physiology. For instance, the methods of vivisection and of the study of isolated organs and tissues, which aim at the same isolation of different individual functions, have been constantly employed, and we may safely say that the greater part of the achievements of physiology are due to the successful application of such methods of control. In our experiments it is the whole animal which is placed under a limited number of rigidly defined conditions, and only by this method is it possible to study the reflexes independently of one another.

The foregoing remarks give an idea of our general aim and of the technical side of our methods. I propose to introduce you to the first and most elementary principles of the subject matter of our research by means of a few demonstrations:

Demonstration.—The dog used in the following experiment has been operated upon as described previously. It can be seen that so long as no special stimulus is applied the salivary gland remain quite inactive. But when the sounds from a beating metronome are allowed to fall upon the ear, a salivary secretion begins after 9 seconds, and in the course of 45 seconds eleven drops have been secreted. The activity of the salivary gland has thus been called into play by impulses of sound—a stimulus quite alien to food. This activity of the salivary gland cannot be regarded as anything else than a component of the alimentary reflex. Besides the secretory, the motor component of the food reflex is also very apparent in experiments of this kind. In this very experiment the dog turns in the direction from which it has been customary to present the food and begins to lick its lips vigorously.

This experiment is an example of a central nervous activity depending on the integrity of the hemispheres. A decerebrate dog would never have responded by salivary secretion to any stimulus of the kind. It is obvious also that the underlying principle of this activity is signalization. The sound of the metronome is the signal for food, and the animal reacts to the signal in the same way as if it were food; no distinction can be observed between the effects produced on the animal by the sounds of the beating metronome and showing it real food.

Demonstration.—Food is shown to the animal. The salivary secretion begins after 5 seconds, and six drops are collected in the course of 15 seconds. The effect is the same as that observed with the sounds of the metronome. It is again a case of signalization, and is due to the activity of the hemispheres.

That the effect of sight and smell of food is not due to an inborn reflex, but to a reflex which has been acquired in the course of the animal's own individual existence, was shown by experiments carried out by Dr. Zitovich in the laboratory of the late Prof. Vartanov. Dr. Zitovich took several young puppies away from their mother and fed them for a considerable time only on milk. When the puppies were a few months old he established fistulae of their salivary ducts, and was thus able to measure accurately the secretory activity of the glands. He now showed these puppies some solid food—bread or meat—but no secretion of saliva was evoked. It is evident, therefore, that the sight of food does not in itself at as a direct stimulus to salivary secretion. Only after the puppies have been allowed to eat bread and meat on several occasions does the sight or smell of these foodstuffs evoke the secretion.

The following experiment serves to illustrate the activity of the salivary gland as an inborn reflex in contrast to signalization:

Demonstration.—Food is suddenly introduced into the dog's mouth; secretion begins in 1 to 2 seconds. The secretion is brought about by the physical and chemical properties of the food itself acting upon receptors in the mucous membrane of the mouth and tongue. It is purely reflex.

This comparatively simple experiment explains how a decerebrate dog can die of starvation in the midst of plenty, for it will only start eating if food chances to come into contact with its mouth or tongue. Moreover, the elementary nature of the inborn reflexes, with their limitations and inadequacy, are clearly brought out in these experiments, and we are now able to appreciate the fundamental importance of those stimuli which have the character of *signals*.

Our next step will be to consider the question of the nature of signalization and of its mechanism from a purely physiological point of view. It has been mentioned already that a reflex is an inevitable reaction of the organism to an external stimulus, brought about along a definite path in the nervous system. Now it is quite evident that in signalization all the properties of a reflex are present. In the first place an external stimulus is required. This was given in our first experiment by the sounds of a metronome. These sounds falling on the auditory receptor of the dog caused the propagation of an impulse along the auditory nerve. In the brain the impulse was transmitted to the secretory nerves of the salivary glands, and passed thence to the glands, exciting them to active secretion. It is true that in the experiment with the metronome an interval of several seconds elapsed between the beginning of the stimulus and the beginning of the salivary secretion, whereas the time interval for the inborn reflex secretion was only 1 to 2 seconds. The longer latent period was, however, due to some special conditions of the experiment, as will come out more clearly as we proceed. But generally speaking the reaction to signals under natural conditions is as speedy as are the inborn reflexes. We shall be considering the latent period of signalization in fuller detail in a further lecture.

In our general survey we characterized a reflex as a necessary reaction following upon a strictly definite stimulus under strictly defined conditions. Such a definition holds perfectly true also for signalization; the only difference is the type of the effective reaction to signals depends upon a greater number of conditions. But this does not make signalization differ fundamentally from the better known reflexes in any respect, since in the latter, variations in character or force, inhibition and absence of reflexes, can also be traced to some definite change in the conditions of the experiment.

Thorough investigation of the subject shows that accident plays no part whatever in the signalizing activity of the hemispheres, and all experiments proceed strictly according to plan. In the special laboratory I have described, the animal can frequently be kept under rigid experimental observation for 1 to 2 hours without a single drop of saliva being secreted independently of stimuli applied by the observer, although in the ordinary type of physiological laboratory experiments are very often distorted by the interference of extraneous and uncontrolled stimuli.

All these conditions leave no grounds for regarding the phenomena which we have termed "signalization" as being anything else than reflex. There is, however, another aspect of the question which at a first glance seems to point to an essential difference between the better known reflexes and signalization. Food, through its chemical and physical properties, evokes the salivary reflex in every dog right from birth, whereas this new type claimed as reflex—"the signal reflex"—is built up gradually in the course of the animal's own individual existence. But can this be considered as a fundamental point of difference, and can it hold as a valid argument against employing the term "reflex" for this new group of phenomena? It is certainly a sufficient argument for making a definite distinction between the two types of reflex and for considering the signal reflex in a group distinct from the inborn reflex. But this does not invalidate in any way our right logically to term both "reflex," since the point of distinction does not concern the character of the response on the part of the organism, but only the mode of formation of the reflex mechanism. We may take the telephonic installation as an illustration. Communication can be effected in two ways. My residence may be connected directly with the laboratory by a private line, and I may call up the laboratory whenever it pleases me to do so; or on the other hand, a connection may have to be made through the central exchange. But the result in both cases is the same. The only point of distinction between the methods is that the private line provides a permanent and readily available cable, while the other line necessitates a preliminary central connection being established. In the one case the communicating wire is always complete, in the other case a small addition must be made to the wire at the central exchange. We have a similar state of affairs in reflex action. The path of the inborn reflex is already completed at birth; but the path of the signalizing reflex has still to be completed in the higher nervous centres. We are thus brought to consider the mode of formation of new reflex mechanisms. A new reflex is formed inevitably under a given set of physiological conditions, and with the greatest ease, so that there is no need to take the subjective states of the dog into consideration. With a complete understanding of all the factors involved, the new signalizing reflexes are under the absolute control of the experimenter; they proceed according to as rigid laws as do any other physiological processes, and must be regarded as being in every sense a part of the physiological activity of living beings. I have termed this new group of reflexes conditioned reflexes to distinguish them from the inborn or unconditioned reflexes. The term "conditioned" is becoming more and more generally employed, and I think its use is fully justified in that, compared with the inborn reflexes, these new reflexes actually do depend on very many conditions, both in their formation and in the maintenance of their physiological activity. Of course the terms "conditioned" and "unconditioned" could be replaced by others of arguably equal merit. Thus, for example, we might retain the term "inborn reflexes," and call the new type "acquired reflexes"; or call the former "species reflexes" since they are characteristic of the species, and the latter "individual reflexes" since they vary from animal to animal in a species, and even in the same animal at different times and under different conditions. Or again we might call the former "conduction reflexes" and the latter "connection reflexes."

There should be no theoretical objection to the hypothesis of the formation of new physiological paths and new connections within the cerebral hemispheres. Since the especial function of the central nervous system is to establish most complicated and delicate correspondences between the organism and its environment we may not unnaturally expect to find there, on the analogy of the methods used by the technician in everyday experience, a highly developed connector system superimposed on a conductor system. The physiologist certainly should not object to this conception seeing that he has been used to employing the German conception of "Bahnung," which means a laying down of fresh physiological paths in the centres. Conditioned reflexes are phenomena of common and widespread occurrence: their establishment is an integral function in everyday life. We recognize them in ourselves and in other people or animals under such names as "education," "habits," and "training;" and all of these are really nothing more than the results of an establishment of new nervous connections during the post-natal existence of the organism. They are, in actual fact, links connecting definite extraneous stimuli with their definite responsive reactions. I believe that the recognition and the study of the conditioned reflex will throw open the door to a true physiological investigation probably of all the highest nervous activities of the cerebral hemispheres, and the purpose of the present lectures is to give some account of what we have already accomplished in this direction.

We come now to consider the precise conditions under which new conditioned reflexes or new connections of nervous paths are established. The fundamental requisite is that any external stimulus which is to become the signal in a conditioned reflex must overlap in point of time with the action of an unconditioned stimulus. In the experiment which I chose as my example the unconditioned stimulus was food. Now if the intake of food by the animal takes place simultaneously with the action of a neutral stimulus which has been hitherto in no way related to food, the neutral stimulus readily acquires the property of electing the same reaction in the animal as would food itself. This was the case with the dog employed in our experiment with the metronome. On several occasions this animal had been stimulated by the sound of the metronome and immediately presented with food—*i.e.* a stimulus which was neutral of itself had been superimposed upon the action of the inborn alimentary reflex. We observed that, after several repetitions of the combined stimulation, the sounds from the metronome had acquired the property of stimulating salivary secretion and of evoking the motor reactions characteristic of the alimentary reflex. The first demonstration was nothing but an example of such a conditioned stimulus in action. Precisely the same occurs with the mild defence reflex to rejectable substances. Introduction into the dog's mouth of a little of an acid solution brings about a quite definite responsive reaction. The animal sets about getting rid of the acid, shaking its head violently, opening its mouth and making movements with its tongue. At the same time it produces a copious salivary secretion. The same reaction will infallibly be obtained from any stimulus which has previously been applied a sufficient number of times while acid was being introduced into the dog's mouth. Hence a first and most essential requisite for the formation of a new conditioned reflex lies in a coincidence in time of the action of any previously neutral stimulus with some definite unconditioned stimulus. Further, it is not enough that there should be overlapping between the two stimuli; it is also and equally necessary that the conditioned stimulus should begin to operate before the unconditioned stimulus comes into action.

If this order is reversed, the unconditioned stimulus being applied first and the neutral stimulus second, the conditioned reflex cannot be established at all. Dr. Krestovnikov performed these experiments with many different modifications and controls, but the effect was always the same. The following are some of his results:

In one case 427 applications were made in succession of the odour of vanillin together with the introduction of acid into the dog's mouth, but the acid was always made to precede the vanillin by some 5 to 10 seconds. Vanillin failed to acquire the properties of a conditioned stimulus. However, in the succeeding experiment, in which the order of stimuli was reversed, the odour, this time of amyl acetate, became an effective conditioned stimulus after only 20 combinations. With another dog the loud buzzing of an electric bell set going 5 to 10 seconds after administration of food failed to establish a conditioned alimentary reflex even after 374 combinations, whereas the regular rotation of an object in front of the eyes of the animal, the rotation beginning before the administration of food, acquired the properties of a conditioned stimulus after only 5 combinations. The electric buzzer set going before the administration of food established a conditioned alimentary reflex after only a single combination.

Dr. Krestovnikov's experiments were carried out on five dogs, and the result was always negative when the neutral stimulus was applied, whether 10 seconds, 5 seconds or only a single second after the beginning of the unconditioned stimulus. During all these experiments not only the secretory reflex but also the motor reaction of the animal was carefully observed, and these observations always corroborated one another. We thus see that the first set of conditions required for the formation of a new conditioned reflex encompasses the time relation between the presentation of the unconditioned stimulus and the presentation of that agent which has to acquire the properties of a conditioned stimulus.

As regards the condition of the hemispheres themselves, an alert state of the nervous system is absolutely essential for the formation of a new conditioned reflex. If the dog is mostly drowsy during the experiments, the establishment of a conditioned reflex becomes a long and tedious process, and in extreme cases is impossible to accomplish. The hemispheres must, however, be free from any other nervous activity, and therefore in building up a new conditioned reflex it is important to avoid foreign stimuli which, falling upon the animal, would cause other reactions of their own. If this is not attended to, the establishment of a conditioned reflex is very difficult, if not impossible. Thus, for example, if the dog has been so fastened up that anything causes severe irritation, it does not matter how many times the combination of stimuli is repeated, we shall not be able to obtain a conditioned reflex. A somewhat similar case was described in the first lecture—that of the dog which exhibited the *freedom reflex* in an exaggerated degree. It can also be stated as a rule that the establishment of the first condition reflex in an animal is usually more difficult than the establishment of succeeding ones. It is obvious that this must be so, when we consider that even in the most favourable circumstances the experimental conditions themselves will be sure to provoke numerous different reflexes—*i.e.* will give rise to one or other disturbing activity of the hemispheres. But this statement must be qualified by remarking that in cases where the cause of these uncontrolled reflexes is not found out, so that we are not able to get rid of them, the hemispheres themselves will help us. For if the environment of the animal during the experiment does not contain any powerful disturbing elements, then practically always the extraneous reflexes will with time gradually and spontaneously weaken in strength.

The third factor determining the facility with which new conditioned reflexes can be established is the health of the animal. A good state of health will ensure the normal functioning of the cerebral hemispheres, and we shall not have to bother with the effects of any internal pathological stimuli.

The fourth, and last, group of conditions has to do with the properties of the stimulus which is to become conditioned, and also with the properties of the unconditioned stimulus which is selected. Conditioned reflexes are quite readily formed to stimuli to which the animal is more or less indifferent at the outset, though strictly speaking no stimulus within the animal's range of perception exists to which it would be absolutely indifferent. In a normal animal the slightest alteration in the environment—even the very slightest sound or faintest odour, or the smallest change in intensity of illumination—immediately evokes the reflex which I referred to in the first lecture as the investigatory reflex—"What is it?"—manifested by a very definite motor reaction. However, if these neutral stimuli keep recurring, they spontaneously and rapidly weaken in their effect upon the hemispheres, thus bringing about bit by bit the removal of this obstacle to the establishment of a conditioned reflex. But if the extraneous stimuli are strong or unusual, the formation of a conditioned reflex will be difficult, and in extreme cases impossible.

It must also be remembered that in most cases we are not acquainted with the history of the dog before it came into the laboratory, and that we do not know what sort of conditioned reflexes have been established to stimuli which appear to be of the simplest character. But in spite of this we have, in a large number of cases, found it possible to take a strong stimulus which evoked some strong unconditioned response of its own, and still succeed in converting it into a conditioned stimulus for another reflex. Let us take for example a nocuous stimulus, such as a strong electric current or wounding or cauterization of the skin. These are obviously stimuli to vigorous unconditioned defence reflexes. The organism responds by a violent motor reaction directed towards removal of the nocuous stimulus or to its own removal from it. But we may, nevertheless, make use even of these stimuli for the establishment of a new conditioned reflex. Thus in one particular experiment a strong nocuous stimulus—an electric current of great strength—was converted into an alimentary conditioned stimulus, so that its application to the skin did not evoke the slightest defence reaction. Instead, the animal exhibited a well-marked alimentary conditioned reflex, turning its head to where it usually received the food and smacking its lips, at the same time producing a profuse secretion of saliva. The following is a record taken from a research by Dr. Eroféeva:

After each stimulation the dog was allowed to eat food for a few seconds.

Time	Distance of Secondary Coil in cms.	Part of Skin Stimulated	Secretion of Saliva in Drops During 30 secs.	Motor Reaction
4.23 p.m.	4	usual place	6	In all cases the motor reaction displayed
4.45 „	4	„ „	5	was that characteristic of an alimen-
5.7 „	2	new place	7	tary reflex; there was no slightest trace
5.17 „	0	„ „	9	of any motor defence
5.45 „	0	„ „	6	reflex.

Similar results were obtained from dogs in which cauterization or pricking of the skin deep enough to draw blood was made to acquire the properties of an alimentary conditioned stimulus. These experiments have been apt to upset very sensitive people; but we have been able to demonstrate, though without any pretension of penetrating into the subjective world of the dog, that they were labouring under a false impression. Subjected to the very closest scrutiny, not even the tinniest and most subtle objective phenomenon usually exhibited by animals under the influence of strong injurious stimuli can be observed in these dogs. No appreciable changes in the pulse or in the respiration occur in these animals, whereas such changes are always most prominent when the nocuous stimulus has not been converted into an alimentary conditioned stimulus. Such a remarkable phenomenon is the result of diverting the nervous impulse from one physiological path to another. This transference is dependent, however, upon a very definite condition—namely, upon the relative strengths of the two unconditioned reflexes.

Successful transformation of the unconditioned stimulus for one reflex into the conditioned stimulus for another reflex can be brought about only when the former reflex is physiologically weaker and biologically of less importance than the latter. We are led to this conclusion from a consideration of Dr. Eroféeva's experiments. A nocuous stimulus applied to the dog's skin was transformed into a conditioned stimulus for the alimentary reflex. This, we consider, was due to the fact that the alimentary reflex is in such cases stronger than the defence reflex. In the same way we all know that when dogs join in a scuffle for food they frequently sustain skin wounds, which however play no dominant part as stimuli to any defence reflex, being entirely subordinated to the reflex for food. Nevertheless there is a certain limit—there are stronger reflexes than the alimentary reflex. One is the reflex of self-preservation, of existence or non-existence, life or death. To give only one example, it was found impossible to transform a defence reaction into an alimentary conditioned reflex when the stimulus to the unconditioned defence reaction was a strong electric current applied to skin overlying bone with no muscular layer intervening. This signifies that the afferent nervous impulses set up by injury to the bone, and signalizing far greater danger than those set up by injury to the skin, cannot acquire even a temporary connection with the part of the brain from which the alimentary reflex is controlled. Nevertheless, on the whole, the foregoing considerations emphasize the advantage of using the alimentary reflex for most of our experiments, since in the hierarchy of reflexes this holds a very high place.

While, as we have seen, very strong and even specialized stimuli can under certain conditions acquire the properties of conditioned stimuli, there is, on the other hand, a minimum strength below which stimuli cannot be given conditioned properties. Thus a thermal stimulus of 45° C. applied to the skin can be made into an alimentary conditioned reflex, whereas at 38° to 39°C. (approximately 2°C. above the skin temperature in the dog) a thermal stimulus is ineffective [experiments of Dr. Solomonov]. Similarly, while with the help of a very strong unconditioned stimulus it is possible to convert a very unsuitable stimulus—for example, one which naturally evokes a different unconditioned reflex—into a conditioned stimulus, it is exceedingly difficult or even impossible with the help of only a weak unconditioned stimulus to transform even a very favourable neutral stimulus into a conditioned stimulus. Even where such a conditioned reflex is successfully established, into occurrence results only in a very small reflex response. Some unconditioned stimuli may be permanently weak, others may display a weakness which is only temporary—varying with the condition of the animal. As an example of the last we may take food. In the hungry animal food naturally brings about a powerful unconditioned reflex, and the conditioned reflex develops quickly. But in a dog which has not long been fed the unconditioned stimulus has only a small effect, and alimentary conditioned reflexes either are not formed at all or are established very slowly.

By complying with all the conditions which I have enumerated—which is not a very difficult task—a new conditioned reflex is infallibly obtained. We apply to the receptors of the animal rigidly defined stimuli; these stimuli necessarily result in the formation of a new connection in the hemispheres with a consequent development of a typical reflex reaction.

To sum up, we may legitimately claim the study of the formation and properties of conditioned reflexes as a special department of physiology. There is no reason for thinking about all these events in any other way, and it is my belief that in these questions prejudices blunt the intellect and that generally speaking the preconceptions of the human mind stand in the way of any admission that the highest physiological activity of the hemispheres is rigidly determined. The difficulty is mainly due to the tremendous complexity of our subjective states; and, of course, these cannot yet be traced to their primary causations.

Some Experiments on Animal Intelligence

Edward Lee Thorndike

The results of a recent investigation on animal intelligence, the details of which are about to be published,[*] seem to be of sufficient general interest to deserve an independent statement here. The experiments were upon the intelligent acts and habits of a considerable number of dogs, cats and chicks. The method was to put the animals when hungry in enclosures from which they could escape (and so obtain food) by operating some simple mechanism, *e.g.*, by turning a wooden button that held the door, pulling a loop attached to the bolt, or pressing down a lever. Thus one readily sees what sort of things the animals can learn to do and just how they learn to do them. Not only were the actions of the animals in effecting escape observed, but also in every case an accurate record was kept of the times taken to escape in the successive trials. The first time that a cat is put into such an enclosure, some minutes generally elapse before its instinctive struggles hit upon the proper movement, while after enough trials it will make the right movement immediately upon being put in the book. The time records show exactly the method and rate of progress from the former to the latter condition of affairs. A graphic representation of the history of six kittens that learned to get out of a box 20 × 15 × 12 inches, the door of which opened when a wooden button 3½ inches long, ⅞ inch wide, was turned, is found in the curves in Figure 1. These curves are formed by joining the tops of perpendiculars erected along the abscissa at intervals of 1 mm. Each perpendicular represents one trial in the box; its height represents the time taken by the animal to escape, every 1 mm. Equaling 10 seconds. A break in the curve means that in the trials it stands for, the animal failed in ten minutes to escape. Short perpendiculars below the abscissa mark intervals of twenty-four hours between trials. Longer intervals are designated by figures for the number of days or hours. The small curves at the right of the main ones are as the figures beneath them show, records of the skill of the animal after a very long interval without practice. This process of associating a certain act with a certain situation is the type of all the intelligent performances of animals, and by thus recording the progress of a lot of animals, each in informing a lot of each kind of association, one gets a quantitative estimate of what animals can learn and how they learn it.

---

[*]Animal Intelligence; An Experimental Study of the Associative Processes in Animals; *Psychological Review,* Supplement No. 8.

The upper tracing is a record of a conditioned salivary reflex to a tone of 637 · 5 d.v. The tone lasted ▶
30 seconds—began at the first and ended at the second downward mark. The third mark shows the beginning of the unconditioned stimulus. Each mark upwards = 1 drop = 0 · 01 c.c. Each bigger mark = to each tenth drop. Reflex = 68 drops.
   The lower tracing is a similar record, but the tone is continued for 60 seconds. Reflex = 128 drops. (Experiments by Dr. Anrep).

FIGURE 1.

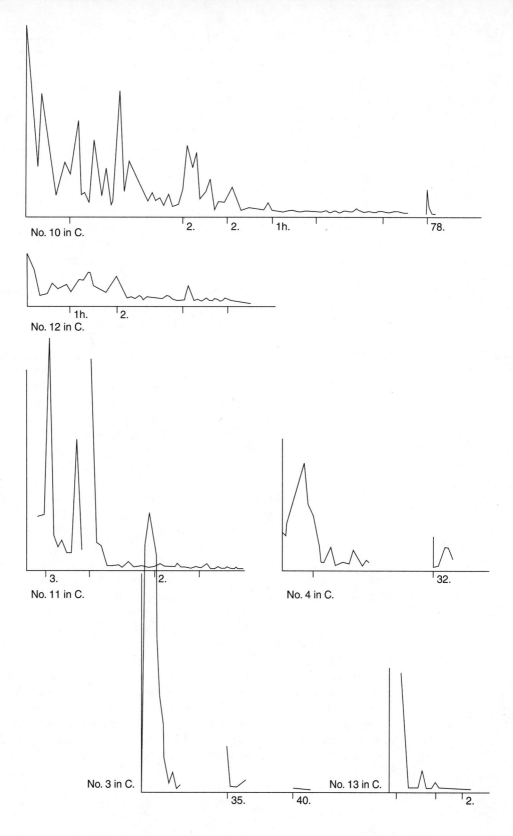

No. 10 in C.

No. 12 in C.

No. 11 in C.

No. 4 in C.

No. 3 in C.

No. 13 in C.

What happens in all these cases is this: The animal on being put into the box, and so confronted with the situation 'confinement with food outside,' bursts forth into the instinctive activities which have in the course of nature been connected with such a situation. It tries to squeeze through any openings, claws and bites at the walls confining it, puts its paws through and claws at things outside trying to pull itself out. It may rush around, doing all this with extraordinary vehemence and persistence. If these impulsive activities fail to include any movement which succeeds in opening the door, the animal finally stops them and remains quietly in the box. If in their course the animal does accidentally work the mechanism (claw the button round, for instance), and thus win freedom and food, the resulting pleasure will stamp in the act, and when again put in the box the animal will be likely to do it sooner. This continues; all the squeezings and bitings and clawings which do not hit the vital point of the mechanism, and so do not result in any pleasure, get stamped out, while the particular impulse, which made the successful clawing or biting, gets stamped in, until finally it alone connected with the sense-impression of the box's interior, and it is done at once when the animal is shut in. The starting point or the formation of any association is the fund of instinctive reactions. Whether or not in any case the necessary act will be learned depends on the possibility that in the course of these reactions the animal will accidentally perform it. The progress from accidental performance to regular, immediate, habitual performance depends on the inhibiting power of effort without pleasure and the strengthening by pleasure of any impulse that leads to it.

Although it was of the utmost importance to them to get out of the various boxes and was, therefore, certain that they would use to the full all their mental powers, none of the animals gave any sign of the possession of powers of inference, comparison or generalization. Moreover, certain of the experiments seem to take the ground from beneath the feet of those who credit reason to animals. For it was found that acts (*e.g.,* opening doors by depressing thumb-latches and turning buttons) which these theorizers have declared incapable of performance by mere accident *certainly can be so done.* It is, therefore, unnecessary to invoke reasoning to account for these and similar success with mechanical contrivances, and the argument based on them falls to the ground. Moreover, besides destroying the value of the evidence which has been offered for the presence of reason in animals, the time-records give us positive evidence that the subjects of these experiments could not reason. For the slopes of the curves are *gradual.* Surely if a cat made the movement from an inference that it would open the door, it ought, when again put in, to make the movement *immediately.* If its first success was due to an inference, all trials after the first should take a minimum time. And if there were any slightest rudiment of a reasoning faculty, even if no real power of inference, the cat ought at least sometime, in the course of ten or twenty successful trials, to realize that turning that button means getting out. And thenceforth make the movement from a decision, not a mere impulse. There ought, that is, to be a sudden change from the long, irregular times of impulsive activity to a regular minimum time. The change is as a fact very gradual.

Finally, experiments made in another connection show that these animals could not learn to perform even the simplest acts by seeing another do them or by being put through them by the experimenter. They were thus unable to infer that since another by pulling a string obtained fish, they might, or that since fish were gained when I pushed round a bar with their paws it would be gained if they pushed it round themselves.

Experiments were made on imitation by giving the animals a chance to see one of their fellows escape by clawing down a string stretched across the box, and then putting them in the same box alone. It was found that, no matter how many times they saw the act done, they could not thereby learn anything which their own impulsive activity had failed to teach them, and did not learn any more quickly what they would have sooner or later learned by themselves. One important consequence of these results is the resulting differentiation of the Primates from the other orders of mammals. If the Primates do imitate and the rest do not, we have located a definite step in the evolution of mind and given a new meaning to the line of human ancestry. I do not, however, hold that these results eliminate the possibility of an incipient faculty of imitation among mammals in general. They do deny the advisability of presupposing it without proof, and emphatically deny its presence in anything equivalent to the human form. Finally many actions which seem due to imitation may be modifications of some single instinct, such as that of following.

Perhaps the most valuable of the experiments were those which differentiate the process of association in animals from the ordinary 'association by contiguity' of human psychology. A man, if in a room from which he wishes to get out, may think of being outside, think of how he once opened the door, and accordingly go turn the knob and pull the door open. The *thought* of opening the door is sufficient to arouse the act of opening the door, and in most human association-series the *thoughts* are the essential and sufficient factors. It has been supposed that the same held true of animals, that if the thought *of doing* a thing were present an impulse *to do* it would be readily supplied from a general stock. Such is not the case. *None of these animals could form an association leading to an act unless there was included in the association an impulse of its own which led to the act.* Thus cats who had been induced to crawl into a box as the first element in a pleasurable association-series soon acquired the habit of crawling in of their own accord, while cats who had been *dropped in* did not. In the second case the *idea of being in* would be present as strongly as in the first, but the particular *impulse to go in* was not. So also cats who failed of themselves to learn certain acts could not be taught to do them by being put through them, while cats who were thus put through acts which accident would of itself alone have taught them, learned them no more quickly and often made the movement in a way quite different from that which they were shown. Their associations are not primarily associations of ideas with ideas, but associations of sense-impressions and ideas *with impulses to acts, muscular innervations.* The impulse, the innervation, is the essential.

This does not mean that the animals can have no representations or images at all. Another set of experiments show that they probably can. It means that they have no stock of free-floating impulses which can be called on at will; that the elements of their associations occur chiefly just in their particular connections; that their ideational life consists not of a multitude of separate ideas, but of a number of specific connections between ideas and impulses.

Having thus denied that animal association is homologous with human association, as the latter is ordinarily conceived, we find the true homologue of animal association in the mental process involved when a man learns to play tennis or billiards or to swim. Both contain sense-impressions, impulses, acts, and possibly representations. Both are learned gradually. Such human associations cannot be formed by imitation or by being put through the movement. Nor do its elements have any independent existence in a life of free ideas apart from their place in the associations. No tennis player's stream of thought is filled with representations of the tens of thousands of sights he has seen or movements he has made on the tennis-court, though his whole attention was on them at the time.

The great step in the evolution of human intellection is then not a jump to reason through language, but a change from a consciousness which equals a lot of specific connections to a consciousness which includes a multitude of free ideas. This is the prerequisite of all the human advance. Once get free ideas in abundance, and comparison, feelings of transition or relation, abstractions and 'meanings' of all sorts may emerge. In this respect, as in imitation, the monkeys bear the marks of their relationship.

Besides the experiments resulting in this new analysis of the mental processes of animals, others were made to discover the delicacy, complexity, number and permanence of their associations. It was found that naturally they discriminate very little, that what they react to is a vague, unanalyzed total situation. Thus, cats that had learned to climb up the front of a cage on hearing the words, 'I must feed those cats,' would climb up just as readily if you said, 'What time is it?' or any short sentence. By associating only the right reaction with pleasure, however, you can render the association delicate to any degree consistent with their sense powers. For instance, a cat was taken that was just beginning to form the association between the words, 'I must feed those cats,' and the act of climbing up the front of the cage (after she climbed up she was given a bit of fish). She was now given a lot of trials, some as just described, some with the signal changed to, 'I will not feed them.' At these trials she got no fish. The purpose was to see how many trials would be required before she would learn always to climb up at the 'I must feed' and always stay down at the 'I will not.' The two sorts of trials were mixed indiscriminately. 60 of the 'I must feed''s were, in addition to its previous training, enough to make the proper reaction to it inevitable. 380 of the 'I will not''s were required before perfect discrimination between it and the former signal was attained.

It was found that complex associations (such, *e.g.,* as the way to escape from a box where the door fell open only after a platform had been pushed down, a string clawed and a bar turned around) were very slowly formed and never really formed at all. That is, the animals did not get so that they went through the several acts in a regular order and without repeating uselessly one element. In respect to delicacy and complexity, then, we see a tremendous difference between association in animals and association in man.

Equally great is the difference in number. A practised billiard player has more associations due to just this one pastime than a dog has for his whole life's activity. The increase in the number of associations is a sign, and very likely a cause, of the advance to a life of free ideas. Yet, small as it is, in comparison with our own, the number of associations which an animal may acquire is probably much larger than previous writers have fancied.

A great many experiments were made on the permanence of associations after from 10 to 70 days. Samples of the results will be found in the figure given. What an animal once acquires is long in being lost, and this power of retention thus renders the power of acquisition a big factor in the struggle for existence. But these experiments give better information than this quantitative estimate of the value of past experience, for they demonstrate conclusively that the animals have no real memory. The cat or dog that is put into a box from which he has escaped thirty or forty times, after an interval of fifty days without any experience with it, will escape quicker than he did in his first experience and will reach a perfect mastery of the association in much fewer trials than he did before, but he will reach it *gradually.* If he had true memory he would, when put in the box after the interval, after a while think, "Oh, yes! Pulling this string let me out," and thenceforth would pull the string *as soon as dropped in the box.* In the case of genuine memory you either know a thing and do it or forget it utterly and fail to do it at all. So with a man recalling the combination to a safe, for instance. But the memory of the animal is only that of a billiard player who hasn't played for a long interval and who gradually recovers his skill. No billiard player keeps thinking, "Two years ago I hit a ball placed like this in such and such a way." And the cat or dog does not think, "When I was in this box before, I got out by pulling that string." Not only the gradual recovery of skill, but also the actions of the animal show this. In case of an association only partially permanent the animal claws around the vital spot, or claws feebly and intermittently, or varies it attacks on the loop or what not, by instinctive bitings and squeezings. Memory in animals is permanence of associations, not conscious realization that a certain event or sequence occurred in the past.

So much for some of the experiments and what theoretical consequences they seem directly to involve. The general view which the entire investigation has forced upon me is that animals do not think *about* things at all, that consciousness is for them always consciousness in its first intention, 'pure experience,' as Lloyd Morgan says. They feel all their sense-impressions as we feel the sky and water and movements of our body when swimming. They see the thumb-latch as the ball-player sees the ball speeding toward him. They depress the thumb-piece, not because they think about the act, but just because they feel like doing so. And so their mental life never gets beyond the limits of the least noticeable sort of human intellection. Conception, inference, judgment, memory, self-consciousness, social consciousness, imagination, association and perception, in the common acceptation of the terms, are all absent from the animal mind. Animal intellection is made up of a lot of specific connections, whose elements are restricted to them, and which subserve practical ends *directly,* and is homologous with the intellection involved in such human associations as regulate the conduct of a man playing tennis. The fundamental phenomenon which I find presented in animal consciousness is one which can harden into inherited connections and reflexes, on the one hand, and thus connect naturally with a host of the phenomena of natural life; on the other hand, it emphasizes the fact that our mental life has grown up as a mediation between stimulus and reaction. The old view of human consciousness is that it is built up out of elementary sensations, that very minute bits of consciousness come first and gradually get built up into the complex web. It looks for the beginnings of consciousness to *little* feelings. This our view abolishes, and declares that the progress is not from little and simple to big and complicated, but from direct connections to indirect connections in which a stock of isolated elements plays a part; is from 'pure experience' or undifferentiated feelings to discrimination, on the one hand, to generalizations, abstractions, on the other. If, as seems probable, the Primates display a vast increase of associations, and a stock of free-swimming ideas, our view gives to the line of descent a meaning which it never could have so long as the question was the vague one of more or less 'intelligence.' It will, I hope, when supported by an investigation of the mental life of the Primates and of the period in child life when these directly practical associations become overgrown by a rapid luxuriance of free ideas, show us the real history of the origin of human faculty.

C H A P T E R 10

BEHAVIORISM: THE BEGINNING

JOHN BROADUS WATSON (1878–1958)

John Broadus Watson was born in 1878 in Travelers Rest, South Carolina, a small village outside Greenville.[1] His mother, Emma, a devout Baptist, gave the young Watson his middle name after a founder of the Southern Seminary in Louisville. She had her son pledge that he would be a Baptist minister when he reached maturity. His father, Pickens, was a devout loafer and hell-raiser. He too appeared to leave his mark on his son since in his autobiography Watson (1936) describes himself as lazy and insubordinate during his grammar and high school years. He even states that, "Twice I was arrested, once for 'nigger fighting' and the second time for shooting off firearms inside the city limits" (p. 271). What a fitting memory for a person who later in life would fight the psychological establishment.

As might be expected, the young Broadus's academic record was undistinguished. Yet, through a personal appeal to the president, he managed to be admitted as a subfreshman to Furman College at the age of 16. There, he was academically successful and especially enjoyed philosophy and psychology. Still, little of his college life was of interest to him and he is self-described as having few close friends. He claims to have stayed on at Furman for a fifth year to gain an M.A. because he failed a course by turning in his exam backwards.[2] This delay, however, released

---

[1]There is a great deal of excellent biographic material about Watson, including his autobiography, Watson (1936). This section is based on his autobiography plus Buckley (1989), Brewer (1991), and Cohen (1979).

[2]Buckley (1989) contends that this may be apocryphyl since there is no record of Watson having failed the course in question.

him from the necessity of studying for the ministry since his mother died when he was 20. Consequently, he chose to study philosophy at the University of Chicago. He chose Chicago because it did not require a reading knowledge of Latin and Greek but did have the famous philosopher John Dewey on its staff.

Watson arrived at Chicago with $50 in his pocket, yet, with his characteristic energy and enterprise, he worked his way through school by working "as a kind of assistant janitor" (Watson, 1936, p. 273). Arriving at Chicago, his primary interest was in philosophy, but he soon found that the "spark was not there" (p. 274). His most telling comment about philosophy concerns John Dewey, "I never knew what he was talking about then, and unfortunately for me, I still don't know" (p. 274). The story was completely different in psychology and physiology. He was impressed by Jacques Loeb, H. H. Donaldson, and the founder of the functionalistic school of psychology, James. R. Angell. In 1903, he completed his Ph.D. summa cum laude under the joint aegis of Donaldson and Angell.[3] After graduation, Watson stayed at Chicago to teach. While there, he taught Jamesian psychology and even used Titchener's laboratory manual. Even then, however, he was not satisfied with a psychology that emphasized or even recognized consciousness. As early as 1904, he felt that he could learn as much if not more by studying the behavior of animals than could psychologists who studied introspecting human subjects.[4]

It was at Chicago that Watson met his first wife, Mary Ickes, a student who wrote him a love note instead of answering an exam question. With a family and growing financial responsibilities, he eventually found a financially rewarding offer from Johns Hopkins University impossible to resist.

The years from 1908 to 1920 spent at Hopkins were years of triumph and disaster. Shortly after his arrival, he was catapulted into the chairmanship of the department and the editorship of the *Psychological Review,* the American Psychological Association's major organ, by the forced resignation of his predecessor, James Mark Baldwin.[5] During this period, Watson was elected to the presidency of the American Psychological Association and published several well-received papers in which he outlined his conception of behavioristic psychology (Watson, 1913, 1916, 1919). One of these articles, Watson's "Psychology from the Standpoint of a Behaviorist" (1913), his earliest publication on behaviorism, is the first article in this chapter. In 1920, Watson was at the height of his fame when his world crashed around him. Watson's romantic involvement with Rosalie Raynor, the co-author of the famous Little Albert study, led to his forced resignation, not unlike that of Baldwin, from the university (see Cohen (1979) and Buckley (1989) for the amazing de-

---

[3]Watson, reportedly, was the youngest person then to have completed a Ph.D. at the University of Chicago.

[4]Considering this, it is interesting that Watson's son, Jim Watson, reported that his father had difficulty expressing his feelings and that he felt more comfortable with animals than with people (Hannush, 1987).

[5]The police caught Baldwin in a brothel, which ultimately resulted in his forced resignation from the university—see Evans and Scott (1978).

tails of this saga). The article concerning Little Albert, the second article in this chapter, however, remained of monumental importance because in it Watson and Raynor (1920) effectively demonstrated that even a subjective topic such as emotion could be studied objectively using the conditioned reflex method.

Watson left the university, married Rayner, and started a career in advertising with the prestigious firms of J. Walter Thompson and William Estey. Watson made no small impact on the advertising industry (Buckley, 1982) and stated, "I began to learn that it can be just as thrilling to watch the growth of a sales curve of a new product as to watch the learning curve of animals or men" (Watson, 1936, p. 280). During this period, Watson also wrote several articles for popular magazines but removed from the laboratory ceased to be a productive psychologist. However, he had started a revolution, and many of his disciples carried on his work. Mary Cover Jones (1974), his last graduate student, underscores this point well:

> As graduate students at Columbia University, my husband, Harold E. Jones, and other members of our student group were among those to whom Watson "sold" Behaviorism. I can still remember the excitement with which we greeted Watson's (1919) *Psychology from the Standpoint of a Behaviorist.* It shook the foundations of traditional European-bred psychology, and we welcomed it. This was in 1919; it pointed the way to action and reform and was therefore hailed as a panacea. (p. 5)

Perhaps Watson became the evangelistic preacher his mother wanted.

REFERENCES

Brewer, C. L. (1991). Perspectives on John B. Watson. In G. A. Kimble, M. Werheimer, & C. L. White (Eds.) *Portraits of pioneers in psychology* (pp. 171–186). Hillsdale, NJ: Earlbaum.

Buckley, K. W. (1989). *Mechanical man: John Broadus Watson and the beginnings of behaviorism.* New York: Guilford.

Cohen, D. (1979). *J. B. Watson: The founder of behaviorism.* London: Routledge & Kegan Paul.

Evans, R. B., & Scott, F. J. D. (1978). The 1913 International Congress of Psychology: The American congress that wasn't. *American Psychologist, 33,* 711–723.

Hannush, M. J. (1987). John B. Watson remembered: An interview with James B. Watson. *Journal of the History of the Behavioral Sciences, 23,* 137–152.

Jones, M. C. (1974). Albert, Peter, and John B. Watson. *American Psychologist, 27,* 581–583.

Pauly, P. J. (1979). Psychology at Hopkins: Its rise and fall and rise and fall and. *Johns Hopkins Magazine,* December, 36–41.

Watson, J. B. (1913). Psychology as the behaviorist views it. *Psychological Review, 20,* 158–177.

Watson, J. B. (1916). The place of the conditioned reflex in psychology. *Psychological Review, 23,* 89–116.

Watson, J. B. (1919). *Psychology from the standpoint of a behaviorist.* Philadelphia: Lippincott.

Watson, J. B. (1936). Autobiography. In C. Murchison (Ed.) *A history of psychology in autobiography* (Vol. 3, pp. 271–281). Worcester, MA: Clark University Press.

Watson, J. B. & Rayner, R. (1920). Conditioned emotional reactions. *Journal of Experimental Psychology, 3,* 1–14.

Psychology as the Behaviorist Views It* 1913

John Broadus Watson

Psychology as the behaviorist views it is a purely objective experimental branch of natural science. Its theoretical goal is the prediction and control of behavior. Introspection forms no essential part of its methods, nor is the scientific value of its data dependent upon the readiness with which they lend themselves to interpretation in terms of consciousness. The behaviorist, in his efforts to get a unitary scheme of animal response, recognizes no dividing line between man and brute. The behavior of man, with all of its refinement and complexity, forms only a part of the behaviorist's total scheme of investigation.

It has been maintained by its followers generally that psychology is a study of the science of the phenomena of consciousness. It has taken as its problems, on the one hand, the analysis of complex mental states (or processes) into simple elementary constituents, and on the other the construction of complex states when the elementary constituents are given. The world of the physical objects (stimuli, including here anything which may excite activity in a receptor), which forms the total phenomena of the natural scientist, is looked upon merely as means to an end. That end is the production of mental states that may be "inspected" or "observed." The psychological object of observation in the case of an emotion, for example, is the mental state itself. The problem in emotion is the determination of the number and kind of elementary constituents present, their loci, intensity, order of appearance, etc. It is agreed that introspection is the method par excellence by means of which mental states may be manipulated for purposes of psychology. On this assumption, behavior data (including under this term everything which goes under the name of comparative psychology) have no value per se. They possess significance only in so far as they may throw light upon conscious states. Such data must have at least an analogical or indirect reference to belong to the realm of psychology.

Indeed, at times, one finds psychologists who are sceptical of even this analogical reference. Such scepticism is often shown by the question which is put to the student of behavior, "What is the bearing of animal work upon human psychology?" I used to have to study over this question. Indeed it always embarrassed me somewhat. I was interested in my own work and felt that it was important, and yet I could not trace any close connection between it and psychology as my questioner understood psychology. I hope that such a confession will clear the atmosphere to such an extent that we will no longer have to work under false pretences. We must frankly admit that the facts so important to us which we have been able to glean from extended work upon the senses of animals by the behavior method have contributed only in a fragmentary way to the general theory of human sense

---

* From the *Psychological Review*, XX (1913), 158–177. This paper is Watson's earliest publication on behaviorism.

organ processes, nor have they suggested new points of experimental attack. The enormous number of experiments which we have carried out upon learning have likewise contributed little to human psychology. It seems reasonably clear that some kind of compromise must be effected: either psychology must change its viewpoint so as to take in facts of behavior, whether or not they have bearings upon the problems of "consciousness"; or else behavior must stand alone as a wholly separate and independent science. Should human psychologists fail to look with favor upon our overtures and refuse to modify their position, the behaviorists will be driven to using human beings as subjects and to employ methods of investigation which are exactly comparable to those now employed in the animal work. Any other hypothesis than that which admits the independent value of behavior material, regardless of any bearing such material may have upon consciousness, will inevitably force us to the absurd position of attempting to construct the conscious content of the animal whose behavior we have been studying. On this view, after having determined our animal's ability to learn, the simplicity or complexity of its methods of learning, the effect of past habit upon present response, the range of stimuli to which it ordinarily responds, the widened range to which it can respond under experimental conditions,—in more general terms, its various problems and its various ways of solving them,—we should still feel that the task is unfinished and that the results are worthless, until we can interpret them by analogy in the light of consciousness. Although we have solved our problem we feel uneasy and unrestful because of our definition of psychology: we feel forced to say something about the possible mental processes of our animal. We say that, having no eyes, its stream of consciousness cannot contain brightness and color sensations as we know them,—having no taste buds this stream can contain no sensations of sweet, sour, salt and bitter. But on the other hand, since it does respond to thermal, tactual and organic stimuli, its conscious content must be made up largely of these sensations; and we usually add, to protect ourselves against the reproach of being anthropomorphic, "if it has any consciousness." Surely this doctrine which calls for an analogical interpretation of all behavior data may be shown to be false: the position that the standing of an observation upon behavior is determined by its fruitfulness in yielding results which are interpretable only in the narrow realm of (really human) consciousness.

This emphasis upon analogy in psychology has led the behaviorist somewhat afield. Not being willing to throw off the yoke of consciousness he feels impelled to make a place in the scheme of behavior where the rise of consciousness can be determined. This point has been a shifting one. A few years ago certain animals were supposed to possess "associative memory," while certain others were supposed to lack it. One meets this search for the origin of consciousness under a good many disguises. Some of our texts state that consciousness arises at the moment when reflex and instinctive activities fail properly to conserve the organism. A perfectly adjusted organism would be lacking in consciousness. On the other hand whenever we find the presence of diffuse activity which results in habit formation, we are justified in assuming consciousness. I must confess that these arguments had weight with me when I began the study of behavior. I fear that a good many of us are still viewing behavior problems with something like this in mind. More than one student in behavior has attempted to frame criteria of the psychic—to devise a set of objective, structural and functional criteria which, when applied in the particular instance, will enable us to decide whether such and such responses are positively conscious, merely indicative of consciousness, or whether they are purely "physiological." Such problems as these can no longer satisfy behavior men. It would be better to give up the province altogether and to admit frankly that the study of the behavior of animals has no justification, than to admit that our search is of such a "will o' the wisp" character. One can assume either the presence or the absence of consciousness anywhere in the phylogenetic scale without affecting the problems of behavior one jot or one tittle; and without influencing in any way the mode of experimental attack upon them. On the other hand, I cannot for one moment assume that the paramecium responds to light; that the rat learns a problem more quickly by working at the task five times a day than once a day, or that the human child exhibits plateaus in his learning curves. These are questions which vitally concern behavior and which must be decided by direct observation under experimental conditions.

This attempt to reason by analogy from human conscious processes to the conscious processes in animals, and vice versa: to make consciousness, as the human being knows it, the center of reference of all behavior, forces us into a situation similar to that which existed in biology in Darwin's time. The whole Darwinian movement was judged by the bearing it had upon the origin and development of the human race. Expeditions were undertaken to collect material which would establish the position that the rise of the human race was a perfectly natural phenomenon and not an act of special creation. Variations were carefully sought along with the evidence for the heaping up effect and the weeding out effect of selection; for in these and the other Darwinian mechanisms were to be found factors sufficiently complex to account for the origin and race differentiation of man. The wealth of material collected at this time was considered valuable largely in so far as it tended to develop the concept of evolution in man. It is strange that this situation should have remained the dominant one in biology for so many years. The moment zoology undertook the experimental study of evolution and descent, the situation immediately changed. Man ceased to be the center of reference. I doubt if any experimental biologist today, unless actually engaged in the problem of race differentiation in man, tries to interpret his findings in terms of human evolution, or ever refers to it in his thinking. He gathers his data from the study of many species of plants and animals and tries to work out the laws of inheritance in the particular type upon which he is conducting experiments. Naturally, he follows the progress of the work upon race differentiation in man and in the descent of man, but he looks upon these as special topics, equal in importance with his own yet ones in which his interests will never be vitally engaged. It is not fair to say that all of his work is directed toward human evolution or that it must be interpreted in terms of human evolution. He does not have to dismiss certain of his facts on the inheritance of coat color in mice because, forsooth, they have little bearing upon the differentiation of the genus homo into separate races, or upon the descent of the genus homo from some more primitive stock.

In psychology we are still in that stage of development where we feel that we must select our material. We have a general place of discard for processes, which we anathematize so far as their value for psychology is concerned by saying, "this is a reflex"; "that is a purely physiological fact which has nothing to do with psychology." We are not interested (as psychologists) in getting all of the processes of adjustment which the animal as a whole employs, and in finding how these various responses are associated, and how they fall apart, thus working out a systematic scheme for the prediction and control of response in general. Unless our observed facts are indicative of consciousness, we have no use for them, and unless our apparatus and method are designed to throw such facts into relief, they are thought of in just as disparaging a way. I shall always remember the remark one distinguished psychologist made as he looked over the color apparatus designed for testing the responses of animals to monochromatic light in the attic at Johns Hopkins. It was this: "And they call this psychology!"

I do not wish unduly to criticize psychology. It has failed signally, I believe, during the fifty-odd years of its existence as an experimental discipline to make its place in the world as an undisputed natural science. Psychology, as it is generally thought of, has something esoteric in its methods. If you fail to reproduce my findings, it is not due to some fault in your apparatus or in the control of your stimulus, but it is due to the fact that your introspection is untrained. The attack is made upon the observer and not upon the experimental setting. In physics and in chemistry the attack is made upon the experimental conditions. The apparatus was not sensitive enough, impure chemicals were used, etc. In these sciences a better technique will give reproducible results. Psychology is other wise. If you can't observe 3–9 states of clearness in attention, your introspection is poor. If, on the other hand, a feeling seems reasonably clear to you, your introspection is again faulty. You are seeing too much. Feelings are never clear.

The time seems to have come when psychology must discard all reference to consciousness; when it need no longer delude itself into thinking that it is making mental states the object of observation. We have become so enmeshed in speculative questions concerning the elements of mind, the nature of conscious content (for example, imageless thought, attitudes, and Bewusseinslage, etc.) that I, as an experimental student, feel that something is wrong with our premises and the types of problems which develop from them. There is no longer any guarantee that we all mean the same thing when we use the terms now current in psychology. Take the case of sensation. A sensation is defined in terms of attributes. One psychologist will state with readiness that the attributes of a visual sensation are *quality, extension, duration,* and *intensity.* Another will add *clearness.* Still another that of *order.* I doubt if any one psychologist can draw up a set of statements describing what he means by sensation which will be agreed to by three other psychologists of different training. Turn for a moment to the question of the number of isolable sensations. Is there an extremely large number of color sensations—or only four, red, green, yellow and blue? Again, yellow, while psychologically simple, can be obtained by superimposing red and green spectral rays upon the same diffusing surface! If, on the other hand, we say that every just noticeable difference in the spectrum is a simple sensation, and that every just noticeable increase in the white value of a given color gives simple sensations, we are forced to admit that the number is so large and the conditions for obtaining them so complex that the concept of sensation is unusable, either for the purpose of analysis or that of synthesis.

Titchener, who has fought the most valiant fight in this country for a psychology based upon introspection, feels that these differences of opinion as to the number of sensations and their attributes; as to whether there are relations (in the sense of elements) and on the many others which seem to be fundamental in every attempt at analysis, are perfectly natural in the present undeveloped state of psychology. While it is admitted that every growing science is full of unanswered questions, surely only those who are wedded to the system as we now have it, who have fought and suffered for it, can confidently believe that there will ever be any greater uniformity than there is now in the answers we have to such questions. I firmly believe that two hundred years from now, unless the introspective method is discarded, psychology will still be divided on the question as to whether auditory sensations have the quality of "extension," whether intensity is an attribute which can be applied to color, whether there is a difference in "texture" between image and sensation and upon many hundreds of others of like character.

The condition in regard to other mental processes is just as chaotic. Can image type be experimentally tested and verified? Are recondite thought processes dependent mechanically upon imagery at all? Are psychologists agreed upon what feeling is? One states that feelings are attitudes. Another finds them to be groups of organic sensations possessing a certain solidarity. Still another and larger group finds them to be new elements correlative with and ranking equally with sensations.

My psychological quarrel is not with the systematic and structural psychologist alone. The last fifteen years have seen the growth of what is called functional psychology. This type of psychology decries the use of elements in the static sense of the structuralists. It throws emphasis upon the biological significance of conscious processes instead of upon the analysis of conscious states into introspectively isolable elements. I have done my best to understand the difference between functional psychology and structural psychology. Instead of clarity, confusion grows upon me. The terms sensation, perception, affection, emotion, volition are used as much by the functionalist as by the structuralist. The addition of the word "process" ("mental act as a whole," and like terms are frequently met) after each serves in some way to remove the corpse of "content" and to leave "function" in its stead. Surely if these concepts are elusive when looked at from a content standpoint, they are still more deceptive when viewed from the angle of function, and especially so when function is obtained by the introspection method. It is rather interesting that no function psychologist has carefully distinguished between "perception" (and this is true of the other psychological terms as well) as employed by the systematist, and "perceptual process" as used in functional psychology. It seems illogical and hardly fair to criticize the psychology which the systematist gives us, and then to utilize his terms without carefully showing the changes in meaning which are to be attached to them. I was greatly surprised some time ago when I opened Pillsbury's book and saw psychology defined as the "science of behavior." A still more recent text states that psychology is the "science of mental behavior." When I saw these promising statements I thought, now surely we will have texts based upon different lines. After a few pages the science of behavior is dropped and one finds the conventional treatment of sensation, perception, imagery, etc., along with certain shifts in emphasis and additional facts which serve to give the author's personal imprint.

One of the difficulties in the way of a consistent functional psychology is the parallelistic hypothesis. If the functionalist attempts to express his formulations in terms which make mental states really appear to function, to play some active role in the world of adjustment, he almost inevitably lapses into terms which are connotative of interaction. When taxed with this he replies that it is more convenient to do so and that he does it to avoid the circumlocution and clumsiness which are inherent in any thoroughgoing parallelism. As a matter of fact I believe the functionalist actually thinks in terms of interaction and resorts to parallelism only when forced to give expression to his views. I feel that *behaviorism* is the only consistent and logical functionalism. In it one avoids both the Scylla of parallelism and the Charybdis of interaction. Those time-honored relics of philosophical speculation need trouble the student of behavior as little as they trouble the student of physics. The consideration of the mind-body problem affects neither the type of problem selected nor the formulation of the solution of that problem. I can state my position here no better than by saying that I should like to bring my students up in the same ignorance of such hypotheses as one finds among the students of other branches of science.

This leads me to the point where I should like to make the argument constructive. I believe we can write a psychology, define it as Pillsbury, and never go back upon our definition: never use the terms consciousness, mental states, mind, content, introspectively verifiable, imagery, and the like. I believe that we can do it in a few years without running into the absurd terminology of Beer, Bethe, Von Uexkull, Nuel, and that of the so-called objective schools generally. It can be done in terms of stimulus and response, in terms of habit formation, habit integrations and the like. Furthermore, I believe that it is really worth while to make this attempt now.

The psychology which I should attempt to build up would take as a starting point, first, the observable fact that organisms, man and animal alike, do adjust themselves to their environment by means of hereditary and habit equipments. These adjustments may be very adequate or they may be so inadequate that the organism barely maintains its existence; secondly, that certain stimuli lead the organisms to make the responses. In a system of psychology completely worked out, given the stimuli the response can be predicted. Such a set of statements is crass and raw in the extreme, as all such generalizations must be. Yet they are hardly more raw and less realizable than the ones which appear in the psychology texts of the day. I possibly might illustrate my point better by choosing an everyday problem which anyone is likely to meet in the course of his work. Some time ago I was called upon to make a study of certain species of birds. Until I went to Tortugas I had never seen these birds alive. When I reached there I found the animals doing certain things: some of the acts seemed to work peculiarly well in such an environment, while others seemed to be unsuited to their type of life. I first studied the responses of the group as a whole and later those of individuals. In order to understand more thoroughly the relation between what was habit and what was hereditary in these responses, I took the young birds and reared them. In this way I was able to study the order of appearance of hereditary adjustments and their complexity, and later the beginnings of habit formation. My efforts in determining the stimuli which called forth such adjustments were crude indeed. Consequently my attempts to control behavior and to produce responses at will did not meet with much success. Their food and water, sex and other social relations, light and temperature conditions were all beyond control in a field study. I did find it possible to control their reactions in a measure by using the nest and egg (or young) as stimuli. It is not necessary in this paper to develop further how such a study should be carried out and how work of this kind must be supplemented by carefully controlled laboratory experiments. Had I been called upon to examine the natives of some of the Australian tribes, I should have gone about my task in the same way. I should have found the problem more difficult: the types of responses called forth by physical stimuli would have been more varied, and the number of effective stimuli larger. I should have had to determine the social setting of their lives in a far more careful way. These savages would be more influenced by the responses of each other than was the case with the birds. Furthermore, habits would have been more complex and the influences of past habits upon the present responses would have appeared more clearly. Finally, if I had been called upon to work out the psychology of the educated European, my problem would have required several lifetimes. But in the one I have at my disposal I should have followed the same general line of attack. In the main, my desire in all such work is to gain an accurate knowledge of adjustments and the stimuli calling them forth. My final reason for this is to learn general and particular methods by which I may control behavior. My goal is not "the description and explanation of states of consciousness as such," nor that of obtaining such proficiency in mental gymnastics that I can immediately lay hold of a state of consciousness and say, "this, as a whole, consists of gray sensation number 350, of such and such extent, occurring in conjunction with the sensation of cold of a certain intensity; one of pressure of a certain intensity and extent," and so on *ad infinitum*. If psychology would follow the plan I suggest, the educator, the physician, the jurist and the business man could utilize our data in a practical way, as soon as we are able, experimentally, to obtain them. Those who have occasion to apply psychological principles practically would find no need to complain as they do at the present time. Ask any physician or jurist today whether scientific psychology plays a practical part in his daily routine and you will hear him deny that the psychology of the laboratories finds a place in his scheme of work. I think the criticism is extremely just. One of the earliest conditions which made me dissatisfied with psychology was the feeling that there was no realm of application for the principles which were being worked out in content terms.

What gives me hope that the behaviorist's position is a defensible one is the fact that those branches of psychology which have already partially withdrawn from the parent, experimental psychology, and which are consequently less dependent upon introspection are today in a most flourishing condition. Experimental pedagogy, the psychology of drugs, the psychology of advertising, legal psychology, the psychology of tests, and psychopathology are all vigorous growths. These are sometimes wrongly called "practical" or "applied" psychology. Surely there was never a worse misnomer. In the future there may grow up vocational bureaus which really apply psychology. At present these fields are truly scientific and are in search of broad generalizations which will lead to the control of human behavior. For example, we find out by experimentation whether a series of stanzas may be acquired more readily if the whole is learned at once, or whether it is more advantageous to learn each stanza separately and then pass to the succeeding. We do not attempt to apply our findings. The application of this principle is purely voluntary on the part of the teacher. In the psychology of drugs we may show the effect upon behavior of certain doses of caffeine. We may reach the conclusion that caffeine has a good effect upon the speed and accuracy of work. But these are general principles. We leave it to the individual as to whether the results of our tests shall be applied or not. Again, in legal testimony, we test the effects of recency upon the reliability of a witness's report. We test the accuracy of the report with respect to moving objects, stationary objects, color, etc. It depends upon the judicial machinery of the country to decide whether these facts are ever to be applied. For a "pure" psychologist to say that he is not interested in the questions raised in these divisions of the science because they relate indirectly to the application of psychology shows, in the first place, that he fails to understand the scientific aim in such problems, and secondly, that he is not interested in a psychology which concerns itself with human life. The only fault I have to find with these disciplines is that much of their material is stated in terms of introspection, whereas a statement in terms of objective results would be far more valuable. There is no reason why appeal should ever be made to consciousness in any of them. Or why introspective data should ever be sought during the experimentation, or published in the results. In experimental pedagogy especially one can see the desirability of keeping all of the results on a purely objective plane. If this is done, work there on the human being will be comparable directly with the work upon animals. For example, at Hopkins, Mr. Ulrich has obtained certain results upon the distribution of effort in learning—using rats as subjects. He is prepared to give comparative results upon the effect of having an animal work at the problem once per day, three times per day, and five times per day. Whether it is advisable to have the animal learn only one problem at a time or to learn three abreast. We need to have similar experiments made upon man, but we care as little about his "conscious processes" during the conduct of the experiment as we care about such processes in the rats.

I am more interested at the present moment in trying to show the necessity for maintaining uniformity in experimental procedure and in the method of stating results in both human and animal work, than in developing any ideas I may have upon the changes which are certain to come in the scope of human psychology. Let us consider for a moment the subject of the range of stimuli to which animals respond. I shall speak first of the work upon vision in animals. We put our animal in a situation where he will respond (or learn to respond) to one of two monochromatic lights. We feed him at the one (positive) and punish him at the other (negative). In a short time the animal learns to go to the light at which he is fed. At this point questions arise which I may phrase in two ways: I may choose the psychological way and say "does the animal see these two lights as I do, i.e., as two distinct colors, or does he see them as two grays differing in brightness, as does one totally color blind?" Phrased by the behaviorist, it would read as follows: "Is my animal responding upon the basis of the difference in intensity between the two stimuli, or upon the difference in wavelengths?" He nowhere thinks of the animal's response in terms of his own experiences of colors and grays. He wishes to establish the fact whether wave-length is a factor in that animal's adjustment. If so, length must be maintained in the different regions to afford bases for differential responses? If wave-length is not a factor in adjustment he wishes to know what difference in intensity will serve as a basis for response, and whether that same difference will suffice throughout the spectrum. Furthermore, he wishes to test whether the animal can respond to wave-lengths which do not affect the human eye. He is as much interested in comparing the rat's spectrum with that of the chick as in comparing it with man's. The point of view when the various sets of comparisons are made does not change in the slightest.

However we phrase the question to ourselves, we take our animal after the association has been formed and then introduce certain control experiments which enable us to return answers to the questions just raised. But there is just as keen a desire on our part to test man under the same conditions, and to state the results in both cases in common terms.

The man and the animal should be placed as nearly as possible under the same experimental conditions. Instead of feeding or punishing the human subject, we should ask him to respond by setting a second apparatus until standard and control offered no basis for a differential response. Do I lay myself open to the charge here that I am using introspection? My reply is not at all; that while I might very well feed my human subject for a right choice and punish him for a wrong one and thus produce the response if the subject could give it, there is no need of going to extremes even on the platform I suggest. But be it understood that I am merely using this second method as an abridged behavior method. We can go just as far and reach just as dependable results by the longer method as by the abridged. In many cases the direct and typically human method cannot be safely used. Suppose, for example, that I doubt the accuracy of the setting of the control instrument, in the above experiment, as I am very likely to do if I suspect a defect in vision? It is hopeless for me to get his introspective report. He will say: "There is no difference in sensation, both are reds, identical in quality." But suppose I confront him with the standard and the control and so arrange conditions that he is punished if he responds to the "control" but not with the standard. I interchange the positions of the standard and the control at will and force him to attempt to differentiate the one from the other. If he can learn to make the adjustment even after a large number of trials it is evident that the two stimuli do afford the basis for a differential response. Such a method may sound nonsensical, but I firmly believe we will have to resort increasingly to just such a method where we have reason to distrust the language method.

There is hardly a problem in human vision which is not also a problem in animal vision: I mention the limits of the spectrum, threshold values, absolute and relative, flicker, Talbot's law, Weber's law, field of vision, the Purkinje phenomenon, etc. Every one is capable of being worked out by behavior methods. Many of them are being worked out at the present time.

I feel that all the work upon the senses can be consistently carried forward along the lines I have suggested here for vision. Our results will, in the end, give an excellent picture of what each organ stands for in the way of function. The anatomist and the physiologist may take our data and show, on the one hand, the structures which are responsible for these responses, and, on the other, the physico-chemical relations which are necessarily involved (physiological chemistry of nerve and muscle) in these and other reactions.

The situation in regard to the study of memory is hardly different. Nearly all of the memory methods in actual use in the laboratory today yield the type of results I am arguing for. A certain series of nonsense syllables or other material is presented to the human subject. What should receive the emphasis are the rapidity of the habit formation, the errors, peculiarities in the form of the curve, the persistence of the habit so formed, the relation of such habits to those formed when more complex material is used, etc. Now such results are taken down with the subject's introspection. The experiments are made for the purpose of discussing the mental machinery involved in learning, in recall, recollection and forgetting, and not for the purpose of seeking the human being's way of shaping his responses to meet the problems in the terribly complex environment into which he is thrown, nor for that of showing the similarities and differences between man's methods and those of other animals.

The situation is somewhat different when we come to a study of the more complex forms of behavior, such as imagination, judgment, reasoning, and conception. At present the only statements we have of them are in content terms. Our minds have been so warped by the fifty-odd years which have been devoted to the study of states of consciousness that we can envisage these problems only in one way. We should meet the situation squarely and say that we are not able to carry forward investigations along all of these lines by the behavior methods which are in use at the present time. In extenuation I should like to call attention to the paragraph above where I made the point that the introspective method itself has reached a *cul-de-sac* with respect to them. The topics have become so threadbare from much handling that they may well be put away for a time. As our methods become better developed it will be possible to undertake investigations of more and more complex forms of behavior. Problems which are now laid aside will again become imperative, but they can be viewed as they arise from a new angle and in more concrete settings.

The hypothesis that all of the so-called "higher thoughts" processes go on in terms of faint reinstatements of the original muscular act (including speech here) and that these are integrated into systems which respond in serial order (associative mechanisms) is, I believe, a tenable one. It makes reflective processes as mechanical as habit. The scheme of habit which James long ago described—where each return or afferent current releases the next appropriate motor discharge—is as true for "thought processes" as for overt muscular acts. Paucity of "imagery" would be the rule. In other words, wherever there are thought processes there are faint contractions of the systems of musculature involved in the overt exercise of the customary act, and especially in the still finer systems of musculature involved in speech. If this is true, and I do not see how it can be gainsaid, imagery becomes a mental luxury (even if it really exists) without any functional significance whatever. If experimental procedure justifies this hypothesis, we shall have at hand tangible phenomena which may be studied as behavior material. I should say that the day when we can study reflective processes by such methods is about as far off as the day when we can tell by physico-chemical methods the difference in the structure and arrangement of molecules between living protoplasm and inorganic substances. The solutions of both problems await the advent of methods and apparatus.

Will there be left over in psychology a world of pure psychics, to use Yerkes' term? I confess I do not know. The plans which I most favor for psychology lead practically to the ignoring of consciousness in the sense that that term is used by psychologists today. I have virtually denied that this realm of psychics is open to experimental investigation. I don't wish to go further into the problem at present because it leads inevitably over into metaphysics. If you will grant the behaviorist the right to use consciousness in the same way that other natural scientists employ it—that is, without making consciousness a special object of observation—you have granted all that my thesis requires.

In concluding, I suppose I must confess to a deep bias on these questions. I have devoted nearly twelve years to experimentation on animals. It is natural that such a one should drift into a theoretical position which is in harmony with his experimental work. Possibly I have put up a straw man and have been fighting that. There may be no absolute lack of harmony between the position outlined here and that of functional psychology. I am inclined to think, however, that the two positions cannot be easily harmonized. Certainly the position I advocate is weak enough at present and can be attacked from many standpoints. Yet when all this is admitted I still feel that the considerations which I have urged should have a wide influence upon the type of psychology which is to be developed in the future. What we need to do is to start work upon psychology, making *behavior,* not *consciousness,* the objective point of our attack. Certainly there are enough problems in the control of behavior to keep us all working many lifetimes without ever allowing us time to think of consciousness *an sich.* Once launched in the undertaking, we will find ourselves in a sort time as far divorced from an introspective psychology as the psychology of the present time is divorced from faculty psychology.

SUMMARY

1. Human psychology has failed to make good its claim as a natural science. Due to a mistaken notion that its fields of fact are conscious phenomena and that introspection is the only direct method of ascertaining these facts, it has enmeshed itself in a series of speculative questions which, while fundamental to its present tenets, are not open to experimental treatment. In the pursuit of answers to these questions, it has become further and further divorced from contact with problems which vitally concern human interest.

2. Psychology, as the behaviorist views it, is a purely objective, experimental branch of natural science which needs introspection as little as do the sciences of chemistry and physics. It is granted that the behavior of animals can be investigated without appeal to consciousness. Heretofore the viewpoint has been that such

data have value only in so far as they can be interpreted by analogy in terms of consciousness. The position is taken here that the behavior of man and the behavior of animals must be considered on the same plane; as being equally essential to a general understanding of behavior. It can dispense with consciousness in a psychological sense. The separate observation of "states of consciousness" is, on this assumption, no more a part of the task of the psychologist than of the physicist. We might call this the return to a non-reflective and naive use of consciousness. In this sense consciousness may be said to be the instrument or tool with which all scientists work. Whether or not the tool is properly used at present by scientists is a problem for philosophy and not for psychology.

3. From the viewpoint here suggested the facts on the behavior of amoebae have value in and for themselves without reference to the behavior of man. In biology studies on race differentiation and inheritance in amoebae from a separate division of study which must be evaluated in terms of the laws found there. The conclusions so reached may not hold in any other form. Regardless of the possible lack of generality, such studies must be made if evolution as a whole is ever to be regulated and controlled. Similarly the laws of behavior in amoebae, the range of responses, and the determination of effective stimuli, of habit formation, persistency of habits, interference and reinforcement of habits, must be determined and evaluated in and for themselves, regardless of their generality, or of their bearing upon such laws in other forms, if the phenomena of behavior are ever to be brought within the sphere of scientific control.

4. This suggested elimination of states of consciousness as proper objects of investigation in themselves will remove the barrier from psychology which exists between it and the other sciences. The findings of psychology become the functional correlates of structure and lend themselves to explanation in physico-chemical terms.

5. Psychology as behavior will, after all, have to neglect but few of the really essential problems with which psychology as an introspective science now concerns itself. In all probability even this residue of problems may be phrased in such a way that refined methods in behavior (which certainly must come) will lead to their solution.

Conditioned Emotional Reactions

By John B. Watson and Rosalie Rayner

In recent literature various speculations have been entered into concerning the possibility of conditioning various types of emotional response, but direct experimental evidence in support of such a view has been lacking. If the theory advanced by

Watson and Morgan[1] to the effect that in infancy the original emotional reaction patterns are few, consisting so far as observed of fear, rage and love, then there must be some simple method by means of which the range of stimuli which can call out these emotions and their compounds is greatly increased. Otherwise, complexity in adult response could not be accounted for. These authors without adequate experimental evidence advanced the view that this range was increased by means of conditioned reflex factors. It was suggested there that the early home life of the child furnishes a laboratory situation for establishing conditioned emotional responses. The present authors have recently put the whole matter to an experimental test.

Experimental work has been done so far on only one child, Albert B. This infant was reared almost from birth in a hospital environment; his mother was a wet nurse in the Harriet Lane Home for Invalid Children. Albert's life was normal: he was healthy from birth and one of the best developed youngsters ever brought to the hospital, weighing twenty-one pounds at nine months of age. He was on the whole stolid and unemotional. His stability was one of the principal reasons for using him as a subject in this test. We felt that we could do him relatively little harm by carrying out such experiments as those outlined below.

At approximately nine months of age we ran him through the emotional tests that have become a part of our regular routine in determining whether fear reactions can be called out by other stimuli than sharp noises and the sudden removal of support. Tests of this type have been described by the senior author in another place.[2] In brief, the infant was confronted suddenly and for the fist time successively with a white rat, a rabbit, a dog, a monkey, with masks with and without hair, cotton wool, burning newspapers, etc. A permanent record of Albert's reactions to these objects and situations has been preserved in a motion picture study. Manipulation was the most usual reaction called out. *At no time did this infant ever show fear in any situation.* These experimental records were confirmed by the casual observations of the mother and hospital attendants. No one had ever seen him in a state of fear and rage. The infant practically never cried.

Up to approximately nine months of age we had not tested him with loud sounds. The test to determine whether a fear reaction could be called out by a loud sound was made when he was eight months, twenty-six days of age. The sound was that made by striking a hammer upon a suspended steel bar four feet in length and three-fourths of an inch in diameter. The laboratory notes are as follows:

> One of the two experimenters caused the child to turn its head and fixate her moving hand; the other, stationed back of the child, struck the steel bar a sharp blow. The child started violently, his breathing was checked and the arms were raised in a characteristic manner. On the second stimulation the same thing occurred, and in addition the lips began to pucker and tremble. On the third stimulation the child broke into a sudden crying fit. This is the first time an emotional situation in the laboratory has produced any fear or even crying in Albert.

---

[1]'Emotional Reactions and Psychological Experimentation,' *American Journal of Psychology,* April, 1917, Vol. 28, pp. 163–174.

[2]'Psychology from the Standpoint of a Behaviorist,' p. 202.

We had expected just these results on account of our work with other infants brought up under similar conditions. It is worth while to call attention to the fact that removal of support (dropping and jerking the blanket upon which the infant was lying) was tried exhaustively upon this infant on the same occasion. It was not effective in producing the fear response. This stimulus is effective in younger children. At what age such stimuli lose their potency in producing fear is not known. Nor is it known whether less placid children ever lose their fear of them. This probably depends upon the training the child gets. It is well known that children eagerly run to be tossed into the air and caught. On the other hand it is equally well known that in the adult fear responses are called out quite clearly by the sudden removal of support, if the individual is walking across a bridge, walking out upon a beam, etc. There is a wide field of study here which is aside from our present point.

The sound stimulus, thus, at nine months of age, gives us the means of testing several important factors. I. Can we condition fear of an animal, *e.g.*, a white rat, by visually presenting it and simultaneously striking a steel bar? II. If such a conditioned emotional response can be established, will there be a transfer to other animals or other objects? III. What is the effect of time upon such conditioned emotional responses? IV. If after a reasonable period such emotional responses have not died out, what laboratory methods can be devised for their removal?

I. The establishment of conditioned emotional responses. At first there was considerable hesitation upon our part in making the attempt to set up fear reactions experimentally. A certain responsibility attaches to such a procedure. We decided finally to make the attempt, comforting ourselves by reflection that such attachments would arise anyway as soon as the child left the sheltered environment of the nursery for the rough and tumble of the home. We did not begin this work until Albert was eleven months, three days of age. Before attempting to set up a conditioned response we, as before, put him through all of the regular emotional tests. *Not the slightest sign of a fear response was obtained in any situation.*

The steps taken to condition emotional responses are shown in our laboratory notes.

11 Months 3 Days

1. White rat suddenly taken from the basket and presented to Albert. He began to reach for rat with left hand. Just as his hand touched the animal the bar was struck immediately behind his head. The infant jumped violently and fell forward, burying his face in the mattress. He did not cry, however.

2. Just as the right hand touched the rat the bar was again struck. Again the infant jumped violently, fell forward and began to whimper.

In order not to disturb the child too seriously no further tests were given for one week.

11 MONTHS 10 DAYS

1. Rat presented suddenly without sound. There was steady fixation but no tendency at first to reach for it. The rat was then placed nearer, whereupon tentative reaching movements began with the right hand. When the rat nosed the infant's left hand, the hand was immediately withdrawn. He started to reach for the head of the animal with the forefinger of the left hand, but withdrew it suddenly before contact. It is thus seen that the two joint stimulations given the previous week were not without effect. He was tested with his blocks immediately afterwards to see if they shared in the process of conditioning. He began immediately to pick them up, dropping them, pounding them, etc. In the remainder of the tests the blocks were given frequently to quiet him and to test his general emotional state. They were always removed from sight when the process of conditioning was under way.

2. Joint stimulation with rat and sound. Started, then fell over immediately to right side. No crying.

3. Joint stimulation. Fell to right side and rested upon hands, with head turned away from rat. No crying.

4. Joint stimulation. Same reaction.

5. Rat suddenly presented alone. Puckered face, whimpered and withdrew body sharply to the left.

6. Joint stimulation. Fell over immediately to right side and began to whimper.

7. Joint stimulation. Started violently and cried, but did not fall over.

8. Rat alone. *The instant the rat was shown the baby began to cry. Almost instantly he turned sharply to the left, fell over on left side, raised himself on all fours and began to crawl away so rapidly that he was caught with difficulty before reaching the edge of the table.*

This was so convincing a case of a completely conditioned fear response as could have been theoretically pictured. In all seven joint stimulations were given to bring about the complete reaction. It is not unlikely had the sound been of greater intensity or of a more complex clang character that the number of joint stimulations might have been materially reduced. Experiments designed to define the nature of the sounds that will serve best as emotional stimuli are under way.

II. When a conditioned emotional response has been established for one object, is there a transfer? Five days later Albert was again brought back into the laboratory and tested as follows:

11 MONTHS 15 DAYS

1. Tested first with blocks. He reached readily for them, playing with them as usual. This shows that there has been no general transfer to the room, table, blocks, etc.

2. Rat alone. Whimpered immediately, withdrew right hand and turned head and trunk away.

3. Blocks again offered. Played readily with them, smiling and gurgling.

4. Rat alone. Leaned over to the left side as far away from the rat as possible, then fell over, getting up on all fours and scurrying away as rapidly as possible.

5. Blocks again offered. Reached immediately for them, smiling and laughing as before.

The above preliminary test shows that the conditioned response to the rat had carried over completely for the five days in which no tests were given. The question as to whether or not there is a transfer was next taken up.

6. Rabbit alone. The rabbit was suddenly placed on the mattress in front of him. The reaction was pronounced. Negative responses began at once. He leaned as far away from the animal as possible, whimpered, then burst into tears. When the rabbit was placed in contact with him he buried his face in the mattress, then got up on all fours and crawled away, crying as he went. This was a most convincing test.

7. The blocks were next given him, after an interval. He played with them as before. It was observed by four people that he played far more energetically with them than ever before. The blocks were raised high over his head and slammed down with a great deal of force.

8. Dog alone. The dog did not produce as violent a reaction as the rabbit. The moment fixation occurred the child shrank back and as the animal came nearer he attempted to get on all fours but did not cry at first. As soon as the dog passed out of his range of vision he became quite. The dog was then made to approach the infant's head (he was lying down at the moment). Albert straightened up immediately, fell over to the opposite side and turned his head away. He then began to cry.

9. The blocks were again presented. He began immediately to play with them.

10. Fur coat (seal). Withdrew immediately to the left side and began to fret. Coat put close to him on the left side, he turned immediately, began to cry and tried to crawl away on all fours.

11. Cotton wool. The wool was presented in a paper package. At the end the cotton was not covered by the paper. It was placed first on his feet. He kicked it away but did not touch it with his hands. When his hand was laid on the wool he immediately withdrew it but did not show the shock that the animals or fur coat produced in him. He then began to play with the paper, avoiding contact with the wool itself. He finally, under the impulse of the manipulative instinct, lost some of his negativism to the wool.

12. Just in play W. put his head down to see if Albert would play with his hair. Albert was completely negative. Two other observers did the same thing. He began immediately to play with their hair. W. then brought the Santa Claus mask and presented it to Albert. He was again pronouncedly negative.

11 MONTHS 20 DAYS

1. Blocks alone. Played with them as usual.

2. Rat alone. Withdrawal of the whole body, bending over to left side, no crying. Fixation and following with eyes. The response was much less marked than on first presentation the previous week. It was thought best to freshen up the reaction by another joint stimulation.

3. Just as the rat was placed on his hand the rod was struck. Reaction violent.

4. Rat alone. Fell over at once to left side. Reaction practically as strong as on former occasion but no crying.

5. Rat alone. Fell over to left side, got up on all fours and started to crawl away. On this occasion there was no crying, but strange to say, as he started away he began to gurgle and coo, even while leaning far over to the left side to avoid the rat.

6. Rabbit alone. Leaned over to left side as far as possible. Did not fall over. Began to whimper but reaction not so violent as on former occasions.

7. Blocks again offered. He reached for them immediately and began to play.

All of the tests so far discussed were carried out upon a table supplied with a mattress, located in a small, well-lighted dark-room. We wished to test next whether conditioned fear responses so set up would appear if the situation were markedly altered. We thought it best before making this test to freshen the reaction both to the rabbit and to the dog by showing them at the moment the steel bar was struck. It will be recalled that this was the first time any effort had been made to directly condition response to the dog and rabbit. The experimental notes are as follows:

8. The rabbit at first was given alone. The reaction was exactly as given in test (6) above. When the rabbit was left on Albert's knees for a long time he began tentatively to reach out and manipulate its fur with forefingers. While doing this the steel rod was struck. A violent fear reaction resulted.

9. Rabbit alone. Reaction wholly similar to that on trial (6) above.

10. Rabbit alone. Started immediately to whimper, holding hands far up, but did not cry. Conflicting tendency to manipulate very evident.

11. Dog alone. Began to whimper, shaking head from side to side, holding hands as far away from the animal as possible.

12. Dog and sound. The rod was struck just as the animal touched him. A violent negative reaction appeared. He began to whimper, turned to one side, fell over and started to get up on all fours.

13. Blocks. Played with them immediately and readily.

On this same day and immediately after the above experiment Albert was taken into the large well-lighted lecture room belonging to the laboratory. He was placed on a table in the center of the room immediately under the skylight. Four people were present. The situation was thus very different from that which obtained in the small dark room.

1. Rat alone. No sudden fear reaction appeared at first. The hands, however, were held up and away from the animal. No positive manipulatory reactions appeared.

2. Rabbit alone. Fear reaction slight. Turned to left and kept face away from the animal but the reaction was never pronounced.

3. Dog alone. Turned away but did not fall over. Cried. Hands moved as far away from the animal as possible. Whimpered as long as the dog was present.

4. Rat alone. Slight negative reaction.

5. Rat and sound. It was thought best to freshen the reaction to the rat. The sound was given just as the rat was presented. Albert jumped violently but did not cry.

6. Rat alone. At first he did not show any negative reaction. When rat was placed nearer he began to show negative reaction by drawing back his body, raising his hands, whimpering, etc.

7. Blocks. Played with them immediately.

8. Rat alone. Pronounced withdrawal of body and whimpering.

9. Blocks. Played with them as before.

10. Rabbit alone. Pronounced reaction. Whimpered with arms held high, fell over backward and had to be caught.

11. Dog alone. At first the dog did not produce the pronounced reaction. The hands were held high over the head, breathing was checked, but there was no crying. Just at this moment the dog, which had not barked before, barked three times loudly when only about six inches from the baby's face. Albert immediately fell over and broke into a wail that continued until the dog was removed. The sudden barking of the hitherto quiet dog produced a marked fear response in the adult observers!

From the above results it would seem that emotional transfers do take place. Furthermore it would seem that the number of transfers resulting from experimentally produced conditioned emotional reaction may be very large. In our observations we had no means of testing the complete number of transfers which may have resulted.

III. The effect of time upon conditioned emotional responses. We have already shown that the conditioned emotional response will continue for a period of one week. It was desired to make the time test longer. In view of the imminence of Albert's departure from the hospital we could not make the interval longer than one month. Accordingly no further emotional experimentation was entered into for thirty-one days after the above test. During the month, however, Albert was brought weekly to the laboratory for tests upon right and left-handedness, imitation, general development, etc. No emotional tests whatever were given and during the whole month his regular nursery routine was maintained in the Harriet Lane Home. The notes on the test given at the end of this period are as follows:

1 Year 21 Days

1. Santa Claus mask. Withdrawal, gurgling, then slapped at it without touching. When his hand was forced to touch it, he whimpered and cried. His hand was forced to touch it two more times. He whimpered and cried on both tests. He finally cried at the mere visual stimulus of the mask.

2. Fur coat. Wrinkled his nose and withdrew both hands, drew back his whole body and began to whimper as the coat was put nearer. Again there was the strife between withdrawal and the tendency to manipulate. Reached tentatively with left hand but drew back before contact had been made. In moving his body to one side his hand accidentally touched the coat. He began to cry at once, nodding his head in a very peculiar manner (this reaction was an entirely new one). Both hands were withdrawn as far as possible from the coat. The coat was then laid on his lap and he continued nodding his head and whimpering, withdrawing his body as far as possible, pushing the while at the coat with his feet but never touching it with his hands.

3. Fur coat. The coat was taken out of his sight and presented again at the end of a minute. He began immediately to fret, withdrawing his body and nodding his head as before.

4. Blocks. He began to play with them as usual.

5. The rat. He allowed the rat to crawl towards him without withdrawing. He sat very still and fixated it intently. Rat then touched his hand. Albert withdrew it immediately, then leaned back as far as possible but did not cry. When the rat was placed on his arm he withdrew his body and began to fret, nodding his head. The rat was then allowed to crawl against his chest. He first began to fret and then covered his eyes with both hands.

6. Blocks. Reaction normal.

7. The rabbit. The animal was placed directly in front of him. It was very quiet. Albert showed no avoiding reactions at first. After a few seconds he puckered up his face, began to nod his head and to look intently at the experimenter. He next began to push the rabbit away with his feet, withdrawing his body at the same time. Then as the rabbit came nearer he began pulling his feet away, nodding his head, and wailing "da da." After about a minute he reached out tentatively and slowly and touched the rabbit's ear with his right hand, finally manipulating it. The rabbit was again placed in his lap. Again he began to fret and withdrew his hands. He reached out tentatively with his left hand and touched the animal, shuddered and withdrew the whole body. The experimenter then took hold of his left hand and laid it on the rabbit's back. Albert immediately withdrew his hand and began to suck his thumb. Again the rabbit was laid in his lap. He began to cry, covering his face with both hands.

8. Dog. The dog was very active. Albert fixated it intensely for a few seconds, sitting very still. He began to cry but did not fall over backwards as on his last contact with the dog. When the dog was pushed closer to him he at first sat motionless, then began to cry, putting both hands over his face.

These experiments would seem to show conclusively that directly conditioned emotional responses as well as those conditioned by transfer persist, although with a certain loss in the intensity of the reaction, for a longer period than one month. Our view is that they persist and modify personality throughout life. It should be recalled again that Albert was of an extremely phlegmatic type. He had been emotionally unstable probably both the directly conditioned response and those transferred would have persisted throughout the month unchanged in form.

IV. "Detachment" or removal of conditioned emotional responses. Unfortunately Albert was taken from the hospital the day the above tests were made. Hence the opportunity of building up an experimental technique by means of which we could remove the conditioned emotional responses was denied us. Our own view, expressed above, which is possibly not very well grounded, is that these responses in the home environment are likely to persist indefinitely, unless an accidental method for removing them is hit upon. The importance of establishing some method must be apparent to all. Had the opportunity been at hand we should have tried out several methods, some of which we may mention. (1) Constantly confronting the child with those stimuli which called out the responses in the hopes that habituation would come in corresponding to "fatigue" of reflex when differential reactions are to be set up. (2) By trying to "recondition" by showing objects calling out fear responses (visual) and simultaneously stimulating the erogenous zones (tactual). We should try first the lips, then the nipples and as a final resort the sex organs. (3) By trying to "recondition" by feeding the subject candy or other food just as the animal is shown. (4) By building up "constructive" activities around the object by imitation and by putting the hand through the motions of manipulation. At this age imitation of overt motor activity is strong, as our present but unpublished experimentation has shown.

INCIDENTAL OBSERVATIONS

(a) Thumb sucking as a compensatory device for blocking fear and noxious stimuli. During the course of these experiments, especially in the final test, it was noticed that whenever Albert was on the verge of tears or emotionally upset generally he would continually thrust his thumb into his mouth. The moment the hand reached the mouth he became impervious to the stimuli producing fear. Again and again while the motion pictures were begin made at the end of the thirty-day rest period, we had to remove the thumb from his mouth before the conditioned response could be obtained. This method of blocking noxious and emotional stimuli (fear and rage) through erogenous stimulation seems to persist from birth onward. Very often in our experiments upon the work adders with infants under ten days of age the same reaction appeared. When at work upon the adders both of the infants arms are under slight restraint. Often rage appears. They begin to cry, thrashing their arms and legs about. If the finger gets into the mouth crying ceases at once. The organism thus apparently from birth, when under the influence of love stimuli is blocked to all others.[1] This resort to sex stimulation when under the influence of noxious and emotional situations, or when the individual is restless and idle, persists throughout adolescent and adult life. Albert, at any rate, did not resort to thumb sucking except in the presence of such stimuli. Thumb sucking could immediately be checked by offering him his blocks. These invariably called out active manipulation instincts. It is worth while here to call attention to the fact that Freud's conception of the stimulation of erogenous zones as being the expression of an original "pleasure" seeking principle may be turned about and possibly better described as a compensatory (and often conditioned) device for the blockage of noxious and fear and rage producing stimuli.

(b) Equal primacy of fear, love and possibly rage. While in general the results of our experiment offer no particular points of conflict with Freudian concepts, one fact out of harmony with them should be emphasized. According to proper Freudians sex (or in our terminology, love) is the principal emotion in which conditioned responses arise which later limit and distort personality. We wish to take sharp issue with this view on the basis of the experimental evidence we have gathered. Fear is as primal a factor as love in influencing personality. Fear does not gather its potency in any derived manner from love. It belongs to the original and inherited nature of man. Probably the same may be true of rage although at present we are not so sure of this.

The Freudians twenty years from now, unless their hypotheses change, when they come to analyze Albert's fear of a seal skin coat—assuming that he comes to analysis at that age—will probably tease from him the recital of a dream which upon their analysis will show that Albert at three years of age attempted to play with the pubic hair of the mother and was scolded violently for it. (We are by no means denying that this might in some other case condition it). If the analyst has sufficiently prepared Albert to accept such a dream when found as an explanation of his avoiding tendencies, and if the analyst has the authority and personality to put it over, Albert may be fully convinced that the dream was a true revealer of the factors which brought about the fear.

It is probable that many of the phobias in psychopathology are true conditioned emotional reactions either of the direct or the transferred type. One may possibly have to believe that such persistence of early conditioned responses will be found only in persons who are constitutionally inferior. Our argument is meant to be constructive. Emotional disturbances in adults cannot be traced back to sex alone. They must be retraced along at least three collateral lines—to conditioned and transferred responses set up in infancy and early youth in all three of the fundamental human emotions.

---

[1]The stimulus to love in infants according to our view is stroking of the skin, lips, nipples and sex organs, patting and rocking, picking up, etc. Patting and rocking (when not conditioned) are probably equivalent to actual stimulation of the sex organs. In adults of course, as every lover knows, vision, audition and olfaction soon become conditioned by joint stimulation with contact and kinaethetic stimuli.

CHAPTER 11

BEHAVIORISM:
AFTER THE FOUNDING

BURRHUS FREDERICK SKINNER (1904–1990)

B. F. Skinner has been described as one of the best known figures in psychology.[1] He published extensive autobiographic material that gives one excellent insight into his life and thinking.[2] He was born in 1904 in Susquehanna, Pennsylvania, the eldest son of strict parents. His father was a lawyer and hoped that his eldest son would follow his profession. He was a talented, introspective individual who was creative in a number of ways, including a penchant for apparatus building. He graduated Phi Beta Kappa with a B.A. in English literature from Hamilton College, a liberal arts school in Clinton, New York. While at college, he disrupted campus life with numerous tricks and wrote critically of the faculty and administration for the campus paper. Carl Frost had favorably reviewed several of his short stories while he was an undergraduate, and he left Hamilton determined to be a writer. Skinner set himself up in what he envisioned to be a "writer's study," first in his parents attic and then in Greenwich Village in New York City.

While in Greenwich Village, he was exposed to the works of Watson and Pavlov, both of which had an immense impact on him. After spending the summer of 1928 in Europe, he gave up all aspirations of becoming a writer[3] and

---

[1]See Bjork (1997), Evans (1997), Hothersall (1995), and Skinner (1967).

[2]He actually wrote three autobiographic volumes, covering various stages in his life, all of which are currently out of print. The Skinner Foundation has plans to republish them.

[3]For a man who "gave up" a career as a writer, he did a prodigious amount of writing, publishing more than 200 works, including more than 20 books.

turned to psychology and the idea of the conditioning of behavior. He enrolled in the graduate program in psychology at Harvard. There he devoted himself to the life of an aesthetic academic, rising early, studying long hours, and avoiding most entertainment. He earned his M.A. in 1930 and his Ph.D. in 1931, and remained at Harvard for the next five years as a postdoctoral fellow. Here he developed his approach as a behaviorist. In 1936, he began his teaching career at the University of Minnesota. In 1945, he moved to Indiana University as chair of the psychology department, and in 1948, he returned to Harvard where he remained until his death in 1990. In 1938, he published *The Behavior of Organisms*. In 1948, he published *Walden Two*, one of his most famous and popular books describing a utopian society based on behavioral principles. Two chapters from this book have been selected for your reading in this section. In 1953, he published *Science and Human Behavior*; in 1957, *Schedules of Reinforcement*; and in 1971, *Beyond Freedom and Dignity*.

Skinner's theory of operant conditioning is that the organism can "operate on" or emit responses to the environment. The idea that the organism can emit responses that are not linked to any known stimulus is an essential part of this theory and differs from respondent theory (Pavlovian theory). The crux of this idea is contained in his statement: "If the occurrence of an operant is followed by presentation of a reinforcing stimulus the strength is increased" (Skinner, 1938, p. 21).

ALBERT BANDURA (1925–   )

Albert Bandura was born on December 4, 1925, in Mundare, Alberta, Canada. He grew up in this small community where his parents were wheat farmers. He attended local schools similar to American one-room schoolhouses. He attended the University of British Columbia where he received a B.A. in 1949. He then went to graduate school at the University of Iowa, where he received an M.A. (1951) and a Ph.D. (1952) in psychology. He specifically chose Iowa for its strong research and experimental program. He took a clinical internship at the Kansas Guidance Center in Wichita, Kansas, before joining the faculty at Stanford University in 1954. He is currently the David Starr Jordan Professor in Psychology at Stanford.

At Stanford, Bandura studied aggression in children with his first graduate student, Richard Walters. He discovered that child behavior was mirrored in parental behavior and attitude. The outgrowth of this work was the concept of modeling and observational learning in social learning theory, a theory synonymous with the names of Bandura and Walters. His first book, with Walters, in 1959 was entitled *Adolescent Aggression*. He has also published *Social Learning and Personality Development* (1963, also with Walters), *Principles of Behavior Modification* (1969), *Social Learning Theory* (1971), *Aggression: A Social Learning Analysis* (1973), and *Social Foundations of Thought and Action* (1986). He has also published extensively in journals and has been the recipient of many awards, including the James McKeen Cattell and Distinguished Scientist Award from the American Psychological Association. He was the president of the American Psychological Association in 1974.

The focus of his work has been on integrating traditional learning theory and cognitive theories of personality. This break with traditional learning theory builds on the behavioral interpretation of modeling theory proposed by Miller and Dollard (1941). Bandura (1977), in an often quoted passage from his second edition of *Social Learning Theory,* states:

> Learning would be exceedingly laborious, not to mention hazardous, if people had to rely solely on the effects of their own actions to inform them what to do. Fortunately, most human behavior is learned observationally through modeling: from observing others one forms an idea of how new behaviors are performed, and on later occasions this coded information serves as a guide for action. (p. 22)

The article often referred to as the "Bobo doll" study (Bandura, Ross, & Ross, 1963) has been selected for your reading of original work following this introduction because it illustrates most of the major principles discussed here.

Recently, Bandura has focused his attention on the concept of self-efficacy. Here he studies aspects of individuals' control over functioning and events that have an impact on their lives. This concept is about confidence and the idea that individuals with self-efficacy have the confidence that they can achieve what they set out to do. His most recent book (his ninth) is *Self-Efficacy: The Exercise of Control.*

REFERENCES

Bandura, A. (1965). Influence of models' reinforcement contingencies on the acquisition of imitative responses. *Journal of Personality and Social Psychology,* 1, 589–595.

Bandura, A. (1969). Principles of behavior modification. New York: Holt, Rinehart, & Winston.

Bandura, A. (1971). *Social learning theory.* New York: General Learning Press.

Bandura, A. (1973). *Aggression: A social-learning analysis.* Englewood Cliffs, NJ: Prentice-Hall.

Bandura, A. (1977). *Social learning theory* (2nd ed.) Englewood Cliffs, NJ: Prentice-Hall.

Bandura, A. (1993). Perceived self-efficacy in cognitive development and functioning. *Educational Psychologist,* 28(2) 117–148.

Bandura, A. (1997). *Self-efficacy: The exercise of control.* New York: W.H. Freeman.

Bandura, A., Ross, D., & Ross, S. A. (1963). Imitation of film mediated aggressive models. *Journal of Abnormal and Social Psychology,* 66, 3–11.

Bandura, A. & Walters, R. H. (1959). *Adolescent aggression.* New York: Ronald Press.

Bandura, A. & Walters, R. H. (1963). *Social learning and personality development.* New York: Holt, Rinehart & Winston.

Bjork, D. W. (1997). *B. F. Skinner, a life.* Washington, DC: American Psychological Association.

Evans, R. (1997). *B. F. Skinner: The man and his ideas.* New York: Dutton.

Hothersall, D. (1995). *History of psychology* (3rd ed.). New York: McGraw-Hill.

Miller, N. E. & Dollard, J. (1941). *Social learning and imitation.* New Haven: Yale University Press.

Skinner, B. F. (1938). *Behavior of organisms: An experimental analysis.* New York: Appleton-Century.

Skinner, B. F. (1948). *Walden two.* New York: Macmillan.

Skinner, B. F. (1953). *Science and human behavior.* New York: Macmillan.

Skinner, B. F. (1957). *Schedules of reinforcement.* New York: Appleton-Century-Crofts.

Skinner, B. F. (1967). An autobiography. In E. G. Boring and G. Lindzey (Eds.) *A history of psychology in autobiography* (Vol. 5, pp. 387–413). New York: Appleton-Century-Crofts.

Skinner, B. F. (1971). *Beyond freedom and dignity.* New York: Knopf.

Walden Two

B. F. Skinner

7

The dining rooms proved to be even smaller than Frazier's remarks had suggested. Each contained perhaps half a dozen tables of different sizes. The rooms were decorated in various styles. It was possible to dine briskly in a white-walled room bustling with speed and efficiency, or at leisure in a pine-paneled early American dining room in beeswax candlelight, or in an English inn whose walls carried racing pictures, or in a colorful Swedish room. Two carefully designed modern rooms, one with booths along one wall, came off well by comparison.

I was rather offended by this architectural hodgepodge. The purpose, Frazier explained, had been to make the children feel at home in some of the interiors they would encounter outside the community. Through some principle of behavior which I did not fully understand, it appeared that the ingestion of food had something to do with the development of aesthetic preferences or tolerances. The same effect could not have been so easily obtained by decorating the lounges in different styles.

The period rooms were grouped about a serving room which was operated like a cafeteria, although there was no calculated display of foods or production-line delivery. I was reminded, rather, of a buffet supper. As we entered, we followed Frazier's example and took trays. They were of the same thin glass we had seen in the tea service. Frazier took a napkin from a compartment bearing his name, which also contained some mail which he ignored. The rest of us took fresh napkins from a drawer.

"We have made out very well in our linen manufactory," Frazier said, waving his napkin at us. "No wonder it has always been a luxury. A very durable cloth, and pleasant to use. I suppose you expected paper," he added suddenly, looking at me.

There were three main dishes on the menu—a sort of goulash, a soufflé, and lamb chops. A small poster described the goulash, gave something of its history, and showed its country of origin on a small map. Frazier called our attention to the poster and explained that new dishes from all parts of the world were constantly being tried out and included in the Walden Two menus according to demand. We all took the goulash and added salad and fruit tarts to our trays. Frazier urged us to take bread and butter also. It was the same bread that we had had at tea, and it had been delicious, but by force of habit we all started to pass it by. Bread was apparently a favorite topic of Frazier's and served as text for another guidebook harangue.

"The commercial baker," he said as he made sure that we all got thick slices, "tries to produce a satisfactory loaf with the fewest and cheapest materials. Here the goal is in the other direction. Our cooks have to prepare the food we produce so that it will be eaten. They want to get as much *into* a loaf of bread as possible.

It would be no achievement whatsoever to make an equally delicious loaf with less butter or cheaper starches. They would only have to prepare what they had saved in some other form."

He looked at us with raised eyebrows, like a magician who has just performed an astonishing feat, and then led the way toward one of the modern rooms, where we found a brightly colored table against which our glass trays glistened. The trays were elliptical, with a large depression at each end. Smaller compartments and a recess for a cup filled the middle section. We all put the trays down parallel to the edge of the table, but Frazier showed us how to arrange them spokewise around the table, so that we could have the main dish conveniently in front of us, with the cup and smaller compartments within easy reach. When we were ready for dessert, the tray could be reversed. A small cabinet built into the table contained silverware and condiments.

In spite of Castle's obvious impatience with the details of a domestic technology, Frazier talked at length about the trays. One of their innumerable advantages was the transparency, which saved two operations in the kitchen because the tray could be seen to be clean on both sides at once. As Frazier made this point, Castle snorted.

"Mr. Castle is amused," said Frazier, bearing down hard. "Or perhaps it isn't amusement. It might be interesting to ask him to perform an experiment. Mr. Castle, would you mind turning one of these trays over from side to side one thousand times? Perhaps you will concede the result. Either you would work quickly and finish with painfully cramped muscles, or else slowly and be bored. Either would be objectionable. Yet some one of us would be compelled to do just that three times a day if our trays were opaque. And it would be *some one of us,* remember, not an 'inferior' person, hired at low wages. Our consciences are clearer than that! Do you see, now why—but you see the point." Frazier fluttered both hands in the air in token of an easy victory.

"The main advantage of the tray," he went on, "is the enormous saving in labor. You will see what I mean when we visit the dishwashery. Commercial restaurants would give anything to follow our lead, but it requires a bit of cultural engineering that's out of their reach."

He apparently expected someone to ask for further details about "cultural engineering," but we were all busy with our dinners and we finished them in silence. We carried our empty trays to a window which opened into a utility room, and Frazier then turned and led the way toward the Walk. Mary whispered something to Barbara, who said to Frazier, "Aren't we going to see the dishwashing?"

"So soon after dinner?" said Frazier, with heavy surprise. He seemed proud of having achieved a degree of delicacy, but he turned immediately toward the utility room.

On the other side of the window through which we had pushed our trays, a very pretty girl, who seemed to be on excellent terms with Frazier, received each tray, removed inedible objects, and flipped it upside down on a chain carrier. It immediately passed out of sight under a hood, where we were told it was sprayed with skim milk, which together with all the edible waste would go to the pigs.

A distinguished man with a full beard, who stopped Frazier to ask if he thought the library should acquire a more up-to-date musical encyclopedia, received the tray from the milk bath and placed it upside down on a set of revolving brushes which fitted the dishlike depressions. At the same time the tray was flooded with hot soapy water. The man then examined it briefly—saving, I suppose, one of the operations which were supposed to exhaust Castle—and placed it in a rack. When a rack was full, it was lowered into a rinsing vat and carried to a sterilizer.

Meanwhile the cups and silverware received similar treatment in separate production lines under the control of the same operators.

"All your dishwashing seems to be done by two people," I said.

Frazier nodded violently. "And with four or five shifts a day you can say eight or ten people at most," he said. "Compare that with two hundred and fifty housewives washing two hundred and fifty sets of miscellaneous dishes three times a day and you will see what we gain by industrializing housewifery." He pronounced it "huzzifry" and I missed the reference.

"But don't give us too much credit," he went on. "We're less mechanized in our dishwashing than many large hotels and restaurants. We simply make mass production available to everyone as a consequence of cooperative living. We can beat the hotels by introducing labor-saving practices which require a bit of cultural engineering." He paused a moment, but again no one asked the question he was waiting for. "The glass tray, for example," he said almost petulantly. "A very important advance, but impossible for the restaurant which must cater to people of established tastes, you see."

We made a brief inspection of the kitchen and bakery, which were apparently not distinguished by any contribution from cultural engineering, and then returned to the Walk.

8

We found space near the windows of a small lounge and drew up chairs so that we could look out over the slowly darkening landscape. Frazier seemed to have no particular discussion prepared and he had begun to look a little tired. Castle must have been full of things to say, but he apparently felt that I should open the conversation.

"We are grateful for your kindness," I said to Frazier, "not only in asking us to visit Walden Two but in giving us so much of your time. I'm afraid it's something of an imposition."

"On the contrary," said Frazier. "I'm fully paid for talking with you. Two labor-credits are allowed each day for taking charge of guests of Walden Two. I can use only one of them, but it's a bargain even so, because I'm more than fairly paid by your company."

"Labor-credits?" I said.

"I'm sorry. I had forgotten. Labor-credits are a sort of money. But they're not coins or bills—just entries in a ledger. All goods and services are free, as you saw in the dining room this evening. Each of us pays for what he uses with twelve hundred labor-credits each year—say, four credits for each workday. We change the value according to the needs of the community. At two hours of work per credit—an eight-hour day—we could operate at a handsome profit. We're satisfied to keep just a shade beyond breaking even. The profit system is bad even when the worker gets the profits, because the strain of overwork isn't relieved by even a large reward. All we ask is to make expenses, with a slight margin of safety; we adjust the value of the labor-credit accordingly. At present it's about one hour of work per credit."

"Your members work only four hours a day?" I said. There was an overtone of outraged virtue in my voice, as if I had asked if they were all adulterous.

"On the average," Frazier replied casually. In spite of our obvious interest he went on at once to another point. "A credit system also makes it possible to evaluate a job in terms of the willingness of the members to undertake it. After all, a man isn't doing more or less than his share because of the time he puts in; it's what he's doing that counts. So we simply assign different credit values to different kinds of work, and adjust them from time to time on the basis of demand. Bellamy suggested the principle in *Looking Backward*."

"An unpleasant job like cleaning sewers has a high value, I suppose," I said.

"Exactly. Somewhere around one and a half credits per hour. The sewer man works a little over two hours a day. Pleasanter jobs have lower values—say point seven or point eight. That means five hours a day, or even more. Working in the flower gardens has a very low value—point one. No one makes a living at it, but many people like to spend a little time that way, and we give them credit. In the long run, when the values have been adjusted, all kinds of work are equally desirable. If they weren't, there would be a demand for the more desirable, and the credit value would be changed. Once in a while we manipulate a preference, if some job seems to be avoided without cause."

"I suppose you put phonographs in your dormitories which repeat 'I like to work in sewers. Sewers are lots of fun,'" said Castle.

"No, Walden Two isn't that kind of brave new world," said Frazier. "We don't *propagandize*. That's a basic principle. I don't deny that it would be possible. We could make the heaviest work appear most honorable and desirable. Something of the sort has always been done by well-organized governments—to facilitate the recruiting of armies, for example. But not here. You may say that we propagandize *all* labor, if you like, but I see no objection to that. If we can make work pleasanter by proper training, why shouldn't we? But I digress."

"What about the knowledge and skill required in many jobs?" said Castle. "Doesn't that interfere with free bidding? Certainly you can't allow just anyone to work as a doctor."

"No, of course not. The principle has to be modified where long training is needed. Still, the preferences of the community as a whole determine the final value. If our doctors were conspicuously overworked *according to our standards*, it would be hard to get young people to choose that profession. We must see to it that there are enough doctors to bring the average schedule within range of the Walden Two standard."

"What if nobody wanted to be a doctor?" I said.

"Our trouble is the other way round."

"I thought as much," said Castle. "Too many of your young members will want to go into interesting lines in spite of the work load. What do you do, then?"

"Let them know how many places will be available, and let them decide. We're glad to have more than enough doctors, of course, and could always find some sort of work for them, but we can't offer more of a strictly medical practice than our disgustingly good health affords."

"Then you don't offer complete personal freedom, do you?" said Castle, with ill-concealed excitement. "You haven't really resolved the conflict between a *laissez-faire* and a planned society."

"I think we have. Yes. But you must know more about our educational system before I can show you how. The fact is, it's very unlikely that anyone at Walden Two will set his heart on a course of action so firmly that he'll be unhappy if it isn't open to him. That's as true of the choice of a girl as of a profession. Personal jealousy is almost unknown among us, and for a simple reason: we provide a broad experience and many attractive alternatives. The tender sentiment of the 'one and only' has less to do with constancy of heart than with singleness of opportunity. The chances are that our superfluous young premedic will find other courses open to him which will very soon prove equally attractive."

"There's another case, too," I said. "You must have some sort of government. I don't see how you can permit a free choice of jobs there."

"Our only government is a Board of Planners," said Frazier, with a change of tone which suggested that I had set off another standard harangue. "The name goes back to the days when Walden Two existed only on paper. There are six Planners, usually three men and three women. The sexes are on such equal terms here that no one guards equality very jealously. They may serve for ten years, but no longer. Three of us who've been on the Board since the beginning retire this year.

"The Planners are charged with the success of the community. They make policies, review the work of the Managers, keep an eye on the state of the nation in general. They also have certain judicial functions. They're allowed six hundred credits a year for their services, which leaves two credits still due each day. At least one must be worked out in straight physical labor. That's why I can claim only one credit for acting as your Virgil through *il paradiso.*"

"It was Beatrice," I corrected.

"How do you choose your Planners?" said Rodge.

"The Board selects a replacement from a pair of names supplied by the Managers."

"The members don't vote for them?" said Castle.

"*No,*" said Frazier emphatically.

"What are Managers?" I said hastily.

"What the name implies: specialists in charge of the divisions and services of Walden Two. There are Managers of Food, Health, Play, Arts, Dentistry, Dairy, various industries, Supply, Labor, Nursery School, Advanced Education, and dozens of others. They requisition labor according to their needs, and their job is the managerial function which survives after they've assigned as much as possible to others. They're the hardest working among us. It's an exceptional person who seeks and finds a place as Manager. He must have ability and a real concern for the welfare of the community."

"*They* are elected by the members, I suppose?" said Castle, but it was obvious that he hoped for nothing of the sort.

"The Managers aren't honorific personages, but carefully trained and tested specialists. How could the members gauge their ability? No, these are very much like Civil Service jobs. You work up to be a Manager—through intermediate positions which carry a good deal of responsibility and provide the necessary apprenticeship."

"Then the members have no voice whatsoever," said Castle in a carefully controlled voice, as if he were filing the point away for future use.

"Nor do they wish to have," said Frazier flatly.

"Do you count your professional people as Managers?" I said, again hastily.

"Some of them. The Manager of Health is one of our doctors—Mr. Meyerson. But the word 'profession' has little meaning here. All professional training is paid for by the community and is looked upon as part of our common capital, exactly like any other tool."

"*Mr.* Meyerson?" I said. "Your doctor is not an M.D.? Not a real physician?"

"As real as they come, with a degree from a top-ranking medical school. But we don't use honorific titles. Why call him *Doctor* Meyerson? We don't call our Dairy Manager *Dairyman* Larson. The medical profession has been slow to give up the chicanery of prescientific medicine. It's abandoning the hocus-pocus of the ciphered prescription, but the honorific title is still too dear. In Walden Two—"

"Then you distinguish only Planners, Managers, and Workers," I said to prevent what threatened to be a major distraction.

"And Scientists. The community supports a certain amount of research. Experiments are in progress in plant and animal breeding, the control of infant behavior, educational processes of several sorts, and the use of some of our raw materials. Scientists receive the same labor-credits as Managers—two or three per day depending upon the work."

"No pure science?" exclaimed Castle with mock surprise.

"Only in our spare time," said Frazier. "And I shan't be much disturbed by your elevated eyebrows until you show me where any other condition prevails. Our policy is better than that of your educational institutions, where the would-be scientist pays his way by teaching."

"Have you forgotten our centers of pure research?" I said.

"Pure? If you mean completely unshackled with respect to means and ends, I challenge you to name five. It's otherwise pay-as-you-go. Do you know of any 'pure' scientist in our universities who wouldn't settle for two hours of physical labor each day instead of the soul-searing work he's now compelled to do in the name of education?"

I had no ready answer, for I had to consider the cultural engineering needed to equate the two possibilities. My silence began to seem significant, and I cast about for a question along a different line.

"Why should everyone engage in menial work?" I asked. "Isn't that really a misuse of manpower if a man has special talents or abilities?"

"There's no misuse. Some of us would be smart enough to get along without doing physical work, but we're also smart enough to know that in the long run it would mean trouble. A leisure class would grow like a cancer until the strain upon the rest of the community became intolerable. We might escape the consequences in our own lifetime, but we couldn't visualize a permanent society on such a plan. The really intelligent man doesn't want to feel that his work is being done by anyone else. He's sensitive enough to be disturbed by slight resentments which, multiplied a millionfold, mean his downfall. Perhaps he remembers his own reactions when others have imposed on him; perhaps he has had a more severe ethical training. Call it conscience, if you like." He threw his head back and studied the ceiling. When he resumed, his tone was dramatically far-away.

"That's the virtue of Walden Two which pleases me most. I was never happy in being waited on. I could never enjoy the fleshpots for thinking of what might be going on below stairs." It was obviously a borrowed expression, for Frazier's early life had not been affluent. But he suddenly continued in a loud, clear voice which could leave no doubt of his sincerity, "Here a man can hold up his head and say, 'I've done my share!'"

He seemed ashamed of his excitement, of his show of sentiment, and I felt a strange affection for him. Castle missed the overtones and broke in abruptly.

"But can't superior ability be held in check so it won't lead to tyranny? And isn't it possible to convince the menial laborer that he's only doing the kind of work for which he's best suited and that the smart fellow is really working, too?"

"Provided the smart fellow is really working," Frazier answered, rallying himself with an effort. "Nobody resents the fact that our Planners and Managers could wear white collars if they wished. But you're quite right: with adequate cultural design a society might run smoothly, even though the physical work were not evenly distributed. It might even be possible, through such engineering, to sustain a small leisure class without serious danger. A well-organized society is so efficient and productive that a small area of waste is unimportant. A caste system of brains and brawn could be made to work because it's in the interest of brains to make it fair to brawn."

"Then why insist upon universal brawn?" said Castle impatiently.

"Simply because brains and brawn are never exclusive. No one of us is all brains or all brawn, and our lives must be adjusted accordingly. It's fatal to forget the minority element—fatal to treat brawn as if there were no brains, and perhaps more speedily fatal to treat brains as if there were no brawn. One or two hours of physical work each day is a health measure. Men have always lived by their muscles—you can tell that from their physiques. We mustn't let our big muscles atrophy just because we've devised superior ways of using the little ones. We haven't yet evolved a pure Man Thinking. Ask any doctor about the occupational diseases of the unoccupied. Because of certain cultural prejudices which Veblen might have noted, the doctor can prescribe nothing more than golf, or a mechanical horse, or chopping wood, provided the patient has on real need for wood. But what the doctor would like to say is 'Go to work!'

"But there's a better reason why brains must not neglect brawn," Frazier continued. "Nowadays it's the smart fellow, the small-muscle user, who finds himself in the position of governor. In Walden Two he makes plans, obtains materials, devises codes, evaluates trends, conducts experiments. In work of this sort the manager must keep an eye on the managed, must understand his needs, must experience his lot. That's why our Planners, Managers, and Scientists are required to work out some of their labor-credits in menial tasks. It's our constitutional guarantee that the problems of the big-muscle user won't be forgotten."

We fell silent. Our reflections in the windows mingled confusingly with the last traces of daylight in the southern sky. Finally Castle roused himself.

"But four hours a day!" he said. "I can't take that seriously. Think of the struggle to get a forty-hour week! What would our industrialists not give for your secret. Or our politicians! Mr. Frazier, we're all compelled to admire the life you are showing us, but I feel somehow as if you were exhibiting a lovely lady floating in mid-air. You've even passed a hoop about her to emphasize your wizardry. Now, when you pretend to tell us how the trick is done, we're told that the lady is supported by a slender thread. The explanation is as hard to accept as the illusion. Where's your proof?"

"The proof of an accomplished fact? Don't be absurd! But perhaps I can satisfy you by telling you how we knew it could be done before we tried."

"That would be something," said Castle dryly.

"Very well, then," said Frazier. "Let's take a standard seven-day week of eight hours a day. (The forty-hour week hasn't reached into every walk of life. Many a farmer would call it a vacation.) That's nearly 3000 hours per year. Our plan was to reduce it to 1500. Actually we did better than that, but how were we sure we could cut it in half? Will an answer to that satisfy you?"

"It will astonish me," said Castle.

"Very well, then," said Frazier quickly, as if he had actually been spurred on by Castle's remark. "First of all we have the obvious fact that four is more than half of eight. We work more skillfully and faster during the first four hours of the day. The eventual effect of a four-hour day is enormous, provided the rest of a man's time isn't spent too strenuously. Let's take a conservative estimate, to allow for tasks which can't be speeded up, and say that our four hours are the equivalent of five out of the usual eight. Do you agree?"

"I should be contentious if I didn't," said Castle. "But you're a long way from eight."

"Secondly," said Frazier, with a satisfied smile which promised that eight would be reached in due time, "we have the extra motivation that comes when a man is working for himself instead of for a profit-taking boss. That's a true 'incentive wage' and the effect is prodigious. Waste is avoided, workmanship is better, deliberate slowdowns unheard of. Shall we say that four hours for oneself are worth six out of eight for the other fellow?"

"And I hope you will point out," I said, "that the four are no harder than the six. Loafing doesn't really make a job easier. Boredom's more exhausting than heavy work. But what about the other two?"

"Let me remind you that not all Americans capable of working are now employed," said Frazier. "We're really comparing eight hours a day on the part of *some* with four hours on the part of practically *all*. In Walden Two we have no leisure class, no prematurely aged or occupationally disabled, no drunkenness, no criminals, far fewer sick. We have no unemployment due to bad planning. No one is paid to sit idle for the sake of maintaining labor standards. Our children work at an early age—moderately, but happily. What will you settle for, Mr. Castle? May I add another hour to my six?"

"I'm afraid I should let you add more than that," said Castle, laughing with surprising good nature.

"But let's be conservative," said Frazier, obviously pleased, "and say that when every potential worker puts in four hours for himself we have the equivalent of perhaps two-thirds of all available workers putting in seven out of eight hours for somebody else. Now, what about those who are actually at work? Are they working to the best advantage? Have they been carefully selected for the work they are doing? Are they making the best use of labor-saving machines and methods? What percentage of the farms in America are mechanized as we are here? Do the workers welcome and improve upon labor-saving devices and methods? How many good workers are free to move on to more productive levels? How much education do workers receive to make them as efficient as possible?"

"I can't let you claim much credit for a better use of manpower," said Castle, "if you give your members a free choice of jobs."

"It's an extravagance, you're right," said Frazier. "In another generation we shall do better; our educational system will see to that. I agree. Add nothing for the waste due to misplaced talents." He was silent a moment, as if calculating whether he could afford to make this concession.

"You still have an hour to account for," I reminded him.

"I know, I know," he said. "Well, how much of the machinery of distribution have we eliminated—with the release of how many men? How many jobs have we simply eliminated? Walk down any city street. How often will you find people really usefully engaged? There's a bank. And beyond it a loan company. And an advertising agency. And over there an insurance office. And another." It was not effective showmanship, but Frazier seemed content to make his point at the cost of some personal dignity. "We have a hard time explaining insurance to our children. Insurance against what? And there's a funeral home—a crematory disposes of our ashes as it sees fit." He three off this subject with a shake of the head. "And there and there the ubiquitous bars and taverns, equally useless. Drinking isn't prohibited in Walden Two, but we all give it up as soon as we gratify the needs which are responsible for the habit in the world at large."

"If I may be permitted to interrupt this little tour," I said, "What are those needs?"

"Well, why do you drink?" said Frazier.

"I don't—a great deal. But I like a cocktail before dinner. In fact, my company isn't worth much until I've had one."

"On the contrary, I find it delightful," said Frazier.

"It's different here," I said, falling into his trap. Frazier and Castle laughed raucously.

"Of course it's different here!" Frazier shouted. "You need your cocktail to counteract the fatigue and boredom of a mismanaged society. Here we need no antidotes. No opiates. But why else do you drink? Or why does anyone?—since I can see you're not a typical case."

"Why—to forget one's troubles—" I stammered. "Of course, I see what you will say to that. But to get away, let's say, or to get a change—to lower one's inhibitions. You do have inhibitions, don't you? Perhaps someone else can help me out." I turned tactlessly to Barbara, who looked away.

Frazier chuckled quietly for a moment, and struck out again.

"Let me point out a few businesses which we haven't eliminated, but certainly streamlined with respect to manpower," he said. "The big department stores, the meat markets, the corner drugstores, the groceries, the automobile display rooms, the furniture stores, the shoe stores, the candy stores, all staffed with unnecessary people doing unnecessary things. Half the restaurants can be closed for good. And there's a beauty parlor and there a movie palace. And over there a dance hall, and there a bowling alley. And all the time busses and streetcars are whizzing by, carrying people to and fro from one useless spot to another."

It was a bad show but a devastating argument.

"Take your last hour and welcome," said Castle when he saw that Frazier was resting from his labors. "I should have taken your word for it. After all, as you say, it's an accomplished fact."

"Would you like to see me make it *ten* hours?" said Frazier. He smiled boyishly and we all laughed. "I haven't mentioned our most dramatic saving in manpower."

"Then you still have a chance to get away from the book," I said. "I must confess that I'm not quite so impressed as Mr. Castle. Most of what you have said so far is fairly standard criticism of our economic system. You've been pretty close to the professors."

"Of course I have. Even the professors know all this. The economics of a community are child's play."

"What about those two extra hours?" I said, deciding to let the insinuation pass.

Frazier waited a moment, looking from one of us to another.

"*Cherchez la femme!*" he said at last. He stopped to enjoy our puzzlement. "The women! The women! What do you suppose they've been doing all this time? There's our greatest achievement! We have industrialized housewifery!" He pronounced it "huzzifry" again, and this time I got the reference. "Some of our women are still engaged in activities which would have been part of their jobs as housewives, but they work more efficiently and happily. And at least half of them are available for other work."

Frazier sat back with evident satisfaction. Castle roused himself.

"I'm worried," he said bluntly. "You've made a four-hour day seem convincing by pointing to a large part of the population not gainfully employed. But many of those people don't live as well as you. Our present average production may need only four hours per day per man—but that won't do. It must be something more than the average. You'd better leave the unproductive sharecropper out of it. He neither produces *nor consumes*—poor devil."

"It's true, we enjoy a high standard of living," said Frazier. "But our personal wealth is actually very small. The goods we consume don't come to much in dollars and cents. We practice the Thoreauvian principle of avoiding unnecessary possessions. Thoreau pointed out that the average Concord laborer worked ten or fifteen years of his life just to have a roof over his head. We could say ten weeks and be on the safe side. Our food is plentiful and healthful, but not expensive. There's little or no spoilage or waste in distribution or storage, and none due to miscalcu-lated needs. The same is true of other staples. We don't feel the pressure of pro-motional devices which stimulate unnecessary consumption. We have some auto-mobiles and trucks, but far fewer than the hundred family cars and the many business vehicles we should own if we weren't living in a community. Our radio installation is far less expensive than the three or four hundred sets we should oth-erwise be operating—even if some of us were radioless sharecroppers.

"No, Mr. Castle, we strike for economic freedom at this very point—by de-vising a very high standard of living with a low consumption of goods. We con-sume *less* than the average American."

It was not quite dark outside, and very still. Only the faint rhythmic song of frogs and peepers could be heard through the ventilating louvers. The building itself had grown quiet. No one else had been in the lounge for some time, and several of the lights had been frugally turned off. A pleasant drowsiness was creeping over me.

"You know, of course," Frazier said with a frown, "that this is by far the least interesting side of Walden Two." He seemed to have been seized with a sudden fear that we were bored. "And the least important, too—absolutely the least important. How'd we get started on it, anyway?"

"You confessed that you would be paid for talking to us," I said. "And very much underpaid, I may add. I don't know what the dollars-and-cents value of one labor-credit may be, but it's a most inadequate measure of an enjoyable evening."

The others murmured assent, and Frazier smiled with obvious delight.

"While you're in that mood," he said, "I should tell you that you'll be per-mitted to contribute labor-credits while you're here, too. We ask only two per day, since you're not acquiring a legal interest in the community or clothing yourselves at our expense."

"Fair enough," I said, but rather taken aback.

"We don't begrudge you the food you consume or the space you occupy, nor are we afraid of the effect of idleness upon the morale of our members. We ask you to work because we should feel inhospitable if you didn't. Be frank, now. No mat-ter how warmly we welcomed you, wouldn't you soon feel that you ought to leave? But a couple of hours a day will fully pay for the services the community renders and incidentally do you a lot of good. And you may stay as long as you like with no fear of sponging. And because I receive a credit each day for acting as your guide, you needn't feel that you're imposing on me."

"What's to prevent some visitor—say, a writer—from putting in his two hours and staying on for good?" I asked. "He would find ample time for his trade and could buy his own clothes and secure his own future without being a member."

"We've no objection, but we should ask that one half of any money made dur-ing his stay be turned over to Walden Two."

"Oh ho!" cried Castle. "Then it would be possible for a member to accumu-late a private fortune—by writing books, say, in his spare time."

"Whatever for?" Frazier said. It seemed like genuine surprise, but his tone changed immediately. "As it happens, it isn't possible. *All* money earned by mem-bers belongs to the community. Part of our foreign exchange comes from private enterprises of that sort."

"Rather unfair to the member as compared with the guest, isn't it?" said Castle.

"What's unfair about it? What does the member want money for? Remember, the guest doesn't receive medical services, clothing, or security against old age or ill-health."

Frazier had risen as he was speaking, and we all followed his example promptly. It was clear that we had had enough for one day.

"I shouldn't be acting in the interests of the community," said Frazier, "if I kept you from your beds any longer. We expect a full day's work from you tomorrow morning. Can you find your way to your rooms?"

We made arrangements to meet at ten the next day and parted. Castle and I led the way down the silent, dimly lighted Walk. Presently we found that we were alone. Our companions, for reasons best known to themselves, had turned off and gone outside.

"I wonder what their two hours will be worth tomorrow?" said Castle. "Enemies of the people, I suppose you'd call them."

Imitation of Film-Mediated Aggressive Models[1]

Albert Bandura, Dorothea Ross,[2] and Sheila A. Ross
Stanford University

In a test of the hypothesis that exposure of children to film-mediated aggressive models would increase the probability of Ss' aggression to subsequent frustration, 1 group of experimental Ss observed real-life aggressive models, a 2nd observed these same models portraying aggression on film, while a 3rd group viewed a film depicting an aggressive cartoon character. Following the exposure treatment, Ss were mildly frustrated and tested for the amount of imitative and non-imitative aggression in a different experimental setting. The overall results provide evidence for both the facilitating and the modeling influence of film-mediated aggressive stimulation. In addition, the findings reveal that the effects of such exposure are to some extent a function of the sex of the model, sex of the child, and the reality cues of the model.

[1]This investigation was supported in part by Research Grants M-4398 and M-5162 from the National Institute of Health, United States Public Health Service, and the Lewis S. Haas Child Development Research Fund, Stanford University.

The authors are indebted to David J. Hicks for his generous assistance with the photography and to John Steinbruner who assisted with various phases of this study.

[2]This research was carried out while the junior author was the recipient of an American Association of University Women International Fellowship for postdoctoral research.

Most of the research on the possible effects of film-mediated stimulation upon subsequent aggressive behavior has focused primarily on the drive reducing function of fantasy. While the experimental evidence for the catharsis or drive reduction theory is equivocal (Albert, 1957; Berkowitz, 1962; Emery, 1959; Feshbach, 1955, 1958; Kenny, 1952; Lövaas, 1961; Siegel, 1956), the modeling influence of pictorial stimuli has received little research attention.

A recent incident (San Francisco Chronicle, 1961) in which a boy was seriously knifed during a re-enactment of a switchblade knife fight the boys had seen the previous evening on a televised rerun of the James Dean movie, *Rebel Without a Cause*, is a dramatic illustration of the possible imitative influence of film stimulation. Indeed, anecdotal data suggest that portrayal of aggression through pictorial media may be more influential in shaping the form aggression will taken when a person is instigated on later occasions, than in altering the level of instigation to aggression.

In an earlier experiment (Bandura & Huston, 1961), it was shown that children readily imitated aggressive behavior exhibited by a model in the presence of the model. A succeeding investigation (Bandura, Ross, & Ross, 1961), demonstrated that children exposed to aggressive models generalized aggressive responses to a new setting in which the model was absent. The present study sought to determine the extent to which film-mediated aggressive models may serve as an important source of imitative behavior.

Aggressive models can be ordered on a reality-fictional stimulus dimension with real-life models located at the reality end of the continuum, nonhuman cartoon characters at the fictional end, and films portraying human models occupying an intermediate position. It was predicted, on the basis of saliency and similarity of cues, that the more remote the model was from reality, the weaker would be the tendency for subjects to imitate the behavior of the model.

Of the various interpretations of imitative learning, the sensory feedback theory of imitation recently proposed by Mowrer (1960) is elaborated in greatest detail. According to this theory, if certain responses have been repeated positively reinforced, proprioceptive stimuli associated with these responses acquire secondary reinforcing properties and thus the individual is predisposed to perform the behavior for the positive feedback. Similarly, if responses have been negatively reinforced, response correlated stimuli acquire the capacity to arouse anxiety which, in turn, inhibit the occurrence of the negatively valenced behavior. On the basis of these considerations, it was predicted subjects who manifest high aggression anxiety would perform significantly less imitative and nonimitative aggression than subjects who display little anxiety over aggression. Since aggression is generally considered female inappropriate behavior, and therefore likely to be negatively reinforced in girls (Sears, Maccoby, & Levin, 1957), it was also predicted that male subjects would be more imitative of aggression than females.

To the extent that observation of adults displaying aggression conveys a certain degree of permissiveness for aggressive behavior, it may be assumed that such exposure not only facilitates the learning of new aggressive responses but also weakens competing inhibitory responses in subjects and thereby increases the probability of occurrence of previously learned patterns of aggression. It was predicted, therefore, that subjects who observed aggressive models would display significantly more aggression when subsequently frustrated than subjects who were equally frustrated but who had no prior exposure to models exhibiting aggression.

METHOD

Subjects

The subjects were 48 boys and 48 girls enrolled in the Stanford University Nursery School. They ranged in age from 35 to 69 months, with a mean age of 52 months.

Two adults, a male and a female, served in the role of models both in the real-life and the human film-aggression condition, and one female experimenter conducted the study for all 96 children.

General Procedure

Subjects were divided into three experimental groups and one control group of 24 subjects each. One group of experimental subjects observed real-life aggressive models, a second group observed these same models portraying aggression on film, while a third group viewed a film depicting an aggressive cartoon character. The experimental groups were further subdivided into male and female subjects so that half the subjects in the two conditions involving human models were exposed to same-sex models, while the remaining subjects viewed models of the opposite sex.

Following the exposure experience, subjects were tested for the amount of imitative and nonimitative aggression in a different experimental setting in the absence of the models.

The control group subjects had no exposure to the aggressive models and were tested only in the generalization situation.

Subjects in the experimental and control groups were matched individually on the basis of ratings of their aggressive behavior in social interactions in the nursery school. The experimenter and a nursery school teacher rated the subjects on four five-point rating scales which measured the extent to which subjects displayed physical aggression, verbal aggression, aggression toward inanimate objects, and aggression inhibition. The latter scale, which dealt with the subjects' tendency to inhibit aggressive reactions in the face of high instigation, provided the measure of aggression anxiety. Seventy-one percent of the subjects were rated independently by both judges so as to permit an assessment of interrater agreement. The reliability of the composite aggression score, estimated by means of the Pearson product-moment correlation, was .80.

Data for subjects in the real-life aggression condition and in the control group were collected as part of a previous experiment (Bandura et al., 1961). Since the procedure is described in detail in the earlier report, only a brief description of it will be presented here.

Experimental Conditions

Subjects in the Real-Life Aggressive condition were brought individually by the experimenter to the experimental room and the model, who was in the hallway outside the room, was invited by the experimenter to come and join in the game. The subject was then escorted to one corner of the room and seated at a small table which contained potato prints, multicolor picture stickers, and colored paper. After demonstrating how the subject could design pictures with the materials provided, the experimenter escorted the model to the opposite corner of the room which contained a small table and chair, a tinker toy set, a mallet, and a 5-foot inflated Bobo doll. The experimenter explained that this was the model's play area and after the model was seated the experimenter left the experimental room.

The model began the session by assembling the tinker toys but after approximately a minute had elapsed, the model turned to the Bobo doll and spent the remainder of the period aggressing toward it with highly novel responses which are unlikely to be performed by children independently of the observation of the model's behavior. Thus, in addition to punching the Bobo doll, the model exhibited the following distinctive aggressive acts which were to be scored as imitative responses:

The model sat on the Bobo doll and punched it repeatedly in the nose.

The model then raised the Bobo doll and pommeled it on the head with a mallet.

Following the mallet aggression, the model tossed the doll up in the air aggressively and kicked it about the room. This sequence of physically aggressive acts was repeated approximately three times, interspersed with verbally aggressive responses such as "Sock him in the nose . . . ," "Hit him down . . . ," "Throw him in the air . . . ," "Kick him . . . ," and "Pow."

Subjects in the Human Film-Aggression condition were brought by the experimenter to the semi-darkened experimental room, introduced to the picture materials, and informed that while the subjects worked on potato prints, a movie would be shown on a screen, positioned approximately 6 feet from the subject's table. The movie projector was located in a distant corner of the room and was screened from the subject's view by large wooden panels.

The color movie and a tape recording of the sound track was begun by a male projectionist as soon as the experimenter left the experimental room and was shown for a duration of 10 minutes. The models in the film presentations were the same adult males and females who participated in the Real-Life condition of the experiment. Similarly, the aggressive behavior they portrayed in the film was identical with their real-life performances.

For subjects in the Cartoon Film-Aggression condition, after seating the subject at the table with the picture construction material, the experimenter walked over to a television console approximately 3 feet in front of the subject's table, remarked, "I guess I'll turn on the color TV," and ostensibly tuned in a cartoon program. The experimenter then left the experimental room. The cartoon was shown on a glass lens screen in the television set by means of a rear projection arrangement screened from the subject's view by large panels.

The sequence of aggressive acts in the cartoon was performed by the female model costumed as a black cat similar to the many cartoon cats. In order to heighten the level of irreality of the cartoon, the floor area was covered with artificial grass and the walls forming the backdrop were adorned with brightly colored trees, birds, and butterflies creating a fantasyland setting. The cartoon began with a close-up of a stage on which the curtains were slowly drawn revealing a picture of a cartoon cat along with the title, *Herman the Cat*. The remainder of the film showed the cat pommeling the Bobo doll on the head with a mallet, sitting on the doll and punching it in the nose, tossing the doll in the air, and kicking it about the room in a manner identical with the performance in the other experimental conditions except that the cat's movements were characteristically feline. To induce further a cartoon set, the program was introduced and concluded with appropriate cartoon music, and the cat's verbal aggression was repeated in a high-pitched, animated voice.

In both film conditions, at the conclusion of the movie the experimenter entered the room and then escorted the subject to the test room.

Aggression Instigation

In order to differentiate clearly the exposure and test situations subjects were tested for the amount of imitative learning in a different experimental room which was set off from the main nursery school building.

The degree to which a child has learned aggressive patterns of behavior through imitation becomes most evident when the child is instigated to aggression on later occasions. Thus, for example, the effects of viewing the movie, *Rebel Without a Cause,* were not evident until the boys were instigated to aggression the following day, at which time they re-enacted the televised switchblade knife fight in considerable detail. For this reason, the children in the experiment, both those in the control group, and those who were exposed to the aggressive models, were mildly frustrated before they were brought to the test room.

Following the exposure experience, the experimenter brought the subject to an anteroom which contained a varied array of highly attractive toys. The experimenter explained that the toys were for the subject to play with, but, as soon as the subject became sufficiently involved with the play material, the experimenter remarked that these were her very best toys, that she did not let just anyone play with them, and that she had decided to reserve these toys for some other children. However, the subject could play with any of the toys in the next room. The experimenter and the subject then entered the adjoining experimental room.

It was necessary for the experimenter to remain in the room during the experimental session; otherwise, a number of the children would either refuse to remain alone or would leave before the termination of the session. In order to minimize any influence her presence might have on the subject's behavior, the experimenter remained as inconspicuous as possible by busying herself with paper work at a desk in the far corner of the room and avoiding any interaction with the child.

Test for Delayed Imitation

The experimental room contained a variety of toys, some of which could be used in imitative or nonimitative aggression, and others which tended to elicit predominantly nonaggressive forms of behavior. The aggressive toys included a 3-foot Bobo doll, a mallet and peg board, two dart guns, and a tether ball with a face painted on it which hung from the ceiling. The nonaggressive toys, on the other hand, included a tea set, crayons and coloring paper, a ball, two dolls, three bears, cars and trucks, and plastic farm animals.

In order to eliminate any variation in behavior due to mere placement of the toys in the room, the play material was arranged in a fixed order for each of the sessions.

The subject spent 20 minutes in the experimental room during which time his behavior was rated in terms of predetermined response categories by judges who observed the session through a one-way mirror in an adjoining observation room. The 20-minute session was divided in 5-second intervals by means of an electric interval timer, thus yielding a total number of 240 response units for each subject.

The male model scored the experimental sessions for all subjects. In order to provide an estimate of interjudge agreement, the performances of 40% of the subjects were scored independently by a second observer. The responses scored involved highly specific concrete classes of behavior, and yielded high interscorer reliabilities, the product-moment coefficients being in the .90s.

Response Measures

The following response measures were obtained:

Imitative aggression. This category included acts of striking the Bobo doll with the mallet, sitting on the doll and punching it in the nose, kicking the doll, tossing it in the air, and the verbally aggressive responses, "Sock him," "Hit him down," "Kick him," "Throw him in the air," and "Pow."

Partially imitative responses. A number of subjects imitated the essential components of the model's behavior but did not perform the complete act, or they directed the imitative aggressive response to some object other than the Bobo doll. Two responses of this type were scored and were interpreted as primarily imitative behavior:

Mallet aggression. The subject strikes objects other than the Bobo doll aggressively with the mallet.

Sits on Bobo doll. The subject lays the Bobo doll on its side and sits on it, but does not aggress toward it.

Nonimitative aggression. This category included acts of punching, slapping, or pushing the doll, physically aggressive acts directed toward objects other than the

Bobo doll, and any hostile remarks except for those in the verbal imitation category; for example, "Shoot the Bobo," "Cut him," "Stupid ball," "Knock over people," "Horses fighting, biting."

Aggressive gun play. The subject shoots darts or aims the guns and fires imaginary shots at objects in the room.

Ratings were also made of the number of behavior units in which subjects play nonaggressively or sat quietly and did not play with any of the material at all.

RESULTS

The mean imitative and nonimitative aggression scores for subjects in the various experimental and control groups are presented in Table 1.

Since the distributions of scores departed from normality and the assumption of homogeneity of variance could not be made for most of the measures, the Friedman two-way analysis of variance by ranks was employed for testing the significance of the obtained differences.

TABLE 1

Mean Aggression Scores for Subgroups of Experimental and Control Subjects

| Response category | Experimental groups | | | | | |
| | Real-life aggressive | | Human film-aggressive | | | |
	F Model	M Model	F Model	M Model	Cartoon film-aggressive	Control group
Total aggression						
Girls	65.8	57.3	87.0	79.5	80.9	36.4
Boys	76.8	131.8	114.5	85.0	117.2	72.2
Imitative aggression						
Girls	19.2	9.2	10.0	8.0	7.8	1.8
Boys	18.4	38.4	34.3	13.3	16.2	3.9
Mallet aggression						
Girls	17.2	18.7	49.2	19.5	36.8	13.1
Boys	15.5	28.8	20.5	16.3	12.5	13.5
Sits on Bobo doll[a]						
Girls	10.4	5.6	10.3	4.5	15.3	3.3
Boys	1.3	0.7	7.7	0.0	5.6	0.6
Nonimitative aggression						
Girls	27.6	24.9	24.0	34.3	27.5	17.8
Boys	35.5	48.6	46.8	31.8	71.8	40.4
Aggressive gun play						
Girls	1.8	4.5	3.8	17.6	8.8	3.7
Boys	7.3	15.9	12.8	23.7	16.6	14.3

[a]This response category was not included in the total aggression score.

Total Aggression

The mean total aggression scores for subjects in the real-life, human film, cartoon film, and the control groups are 83, 92, 99, and 54, respectively. The results of the analysis of variance performed on these scores reveal that the main effect of treatment conditions is significant ($\chi_r^2 = 9.06$, $p < .05$), confirming the prediction that exposure of subjects to aggressive models increases the probability that subjects will respond aggressively when instigated on later occasions. Further analysis of pairs of scores by means of the Wilcoxon matched-pairs signed-ranks test show that subjects who viewed the real-life models and the film-mediated models do not differ from each other in total aggressiveness but all three experimental groups expressed significantly more aggressive behavior than the control subjects (Table 2).

Imitative Aggressive Responses

The Friedman analysis reveals that exposure of subjects to aggressive models is also a highly effective method for shaping subjects' aggressive responses ($\chi_r^2 = 23.88$, $p < .001$). Comparisons of treatment conditions by the Wilcoxon test reveal that subjects who observed the real-life models and the film-mediated models, relative to subjects in the control group, performed considerably more imitative physical and verbal aggression (Table 2).

Illustrations of the extent to which some of the subjects became virtually "carbon copies" of their models in aggressive behavior [Figure 1 not shown in the reproduction of this article. It consists of 12 frames from the film, Social Learning of Agression through Imitation of Agressive Models.]. The top frame shows the female model performing the four novel aggressive responses; the lower frames de-

TABLE 2

Significance of the Differences Between Experimental and Control Groups in the Expression of Aggression

Response category	χ_r^2	p	Comparison of treatment conditions[a]					
			Live vs. Film p	Live vs. Cartoon p	Film vs. Cartoon p	Live vs. Control p	Film vs. Control p	Cartoon vs. Control p
Total aggression	9.06	<.05	ns	ns	ns	<.01	<.01	<.005
Imitative aggression	23.88	<.001	ns	<.05	ns	<.001	<.001	<.005
Partial imitation								
Mallet aggression	7.36	.10 > p > .05						
Sits on Bobo doll	8.05	<.05	ns	ns	ns	ns	<.05	<.005
Nonimitative aggression	7.28	.10 > p > .05						
Aggressive gun play	8.06	<.05	<.01[b]	ns	ns	ns	<.05	ns

[a]The probability values are based on the Wilcoxon test.

[b]This probability value is based on a two-tailed test of significance.

pict a male and a female subject reproducing the behavior of the female model they had observed earlier on film.

The prediction that imitation is positively related to the reality cues of the model was only partially supported. While subjects who observed the real-life aggressive models exhibited significantly more imitative aggression than subjects who viewed the cartoon model, no significant differences were found between the live and film, and the film and cartoon conditions, nor did the three experimental groups differ significantly in total aggression or in the performances of partially imitative behavior (Table 2). Indeed, the available data suggest that, of the three experimental conditions, exposure to humans on film portraying aggression was the most influential in eliciting and shaping aggressive behavior. Subjects in this condition, in relation to the control subjects, exhibited more total aggression, more imitative aggression, more partially imitative behavior, such as sitting on the Bobo doll and mallet aggression, and they engaged in significantly more aggressive gun play. In addition, they performed significantly more aggressive gun play than did subjects who were exposed to the real-life aggressive models (Table 2).

Influence of Sex of Model and Sex of Child

In order to determine the influence of sex of model and sex of child on the expression of imitative and nonimitative aggression, the data from the experimental groups were combined and the significance of the differences between groups was assessed by t tests for uncorrelated means. In statistical comparisons involving relatively skewed distributions of scores the Mann-Whitney U test was employed.

Sex of subjects had a highly significant effect on both the learning and the performance of aggression. Boys, in relation to girls, exhibited significantly more total aggression ($t = 2.69$, $p < .01$), more imitative aggression ($t = 2.82$, $p < .005$), more aggressive gun play ($z = 3.38$, $p < .001$), and more nonimitative aggressive behavior ($t = 2.98$, $p < .005$). Girls, on the other hand, were more inclined than boys to sit on the Bobo doll but refrained from punching it ($z = 3.47$, $p < .001$).

The analyses also disclosed some influences of the sex of the model. Subjects exposed to the male model, as compared to the female model, expressed significantly more aggressive gun play ($z = 2.83$, $p < .005$). The most marked differences in aggressive gun play ($U = 9.5$, $p < .001$), however, were found between girls exposed to the female model ($M = 2.9$) and males who observed the male model ($M = 19.8$). Although the overall model difference in partially imitative behavior, Sits on Bobo, was not significant, Sex $\times$ Model subgroup comparisons yielded some interesting results. Boys who observed the aggressive female model, for example, were more likely to sit on the Bobo doll without punching it than boys who viewed the male model ($U = 33$, $p < .05$). Girls reproduced the nonaggressive component of the male model's aggressive pattern of behavior (i.e., sat on the doll without punching it) with considerably higher frequency than did boys who observed the same model ($U = 21.5$, $p < .02$). The highest incidence of partially imitative responses was yielded by the group of girls who viewed the aggressive female model ($M = 10.4$), and the lowest values by the boys who were exposed to the male model ($M = 0.3$). This difference was significant beyond the .05 significance level. These findings, along with the sex of child and sex of model differences reported in the preceding sections, provide further support for the view that the influence of models in promoting social learning is determined in part, by the sex appropriateness of the model's behavior (Bandura et al., 1961).

Aggressive Predisposition and Imitation

Since the correlations between ratings of aggression and the measures of imitative and total aggressive behavior, calculated separately for boys and girls in each of the experimental conditions, did not differ significantly, the data were combined. The correlational analyses performed on these pooled data failed to yield any significant relationships between ratings of aggression anxiety, frequency of aggressive behavior, and the experimental aggression measures. In fact, the array means suggested nonlinear regressions although the departures from linearity were not of sufficient magnitude to be statistically significant.

DISCUSSION

The results of the present study provide strong evidence that exposure to filmed aggression heightens aggressive reactions in children. Subjects who viewed the aggressive human and cartoon models on film exhibited nearly twice as much aggression than did subjects in the control group who were not exposed to the aggressive film content.

In the experimental design typically employed for testing the possible cathartic function of vicarious aggression, subjects are first frustrated, then provided with an opportunity to view an aggressive film following which their overt or fantasy aggression is measured. While this procedure yields some information on the immediate influence of film-mediated aggression, the full effects of such exposure may not be revealed until subjects are instigated to aggression on a later occasion. Thus, the present study, and one recently reported by Lövaas (1961), both utilizing a design in which subjects first observed filmed aggression and then were frustrated, clearly reveal that observation of models portraying aggression on film substantially increases rather than decreases the probability of aggressive reactions to subsequent frustrations.

Filmed aggression, not only facilitated the expression of aggression, but also effectively shaped the form of the subjects' aggressive behavior. The finding that children modeled their behavior to some extent after the film characters suggests that pictorial mass media, particularly television, may serve as an important source of social behavior. In fact, a possible generalization of responses originally learned in the television situation to the experimental film may account for the significantly greater amount of aggressive gun play displayed by subjects in the film condition as compared to subjects in the real-life and control groups. It is unfortunate that the qualitative features of the gun behavior were not scored since subjects in the film condition, unlike those in the other two groups, developed interesting elaborations in gun play (for example, stalking the imaginary opponent, quick drawing, and rapid firing), characteristic of the Western gun fighter.

The view that the social learning of aggression through exposure to aggressive film content is confined to deviant children (Schramm, Lyle, & Parker, 1961), finds little support in our data. The children who participated in the experiment are by no means a deviant sample, nevertheless, 88% of the subjects in the Real-Life and in the Human Film condition, and 79% of the subjects in the Cartoon Film condition, exhibited varying degrees of imitative aggression. In assessing the possible influence of televised stimulation on viewers' behavior, however, it is important to distinguish between learning and overt performance. Although the results of the present experiment demonstrate that the vast majority of children *learn* patterns of social behavior through pictorial stimulation, nevertheless, informal observation suggests that children do not, as a rule, *perform* indiscriminately the behavior of televised characters, even those they regard as highly attractive models. The replies of parents whose children participated in the present study to an open-end questionnaire item concerning their handling of imitative behavior suggest that this may be in part a function of negative reinforcement, as most parents were quick to discourage their children's overt imitation of television characters by prohibiting certain programs or by labeling the imitative behavior in a disapproving manner. From our knowledge of the effects of punishment on behavior, the responses in question would be expected to retain their original strength and could reappear on later occasions in the presence of appropriate eliciting stimuli, particularly if instigation is high, the instruments for aggression are available, and the threat of noxious consequences is reduced.

The absence of any relationships between ratings of the children's predisposition to aggression and their aggressive behavior in the experimental setting may simply reflect the inadequacy of the predictor measures. It may be pointed out, however, that the reliability of the ratings was relatively high. While this does not assure validity of the measures, it does at least indicate there was consistency in the raters' estimates of the children's aggressive tendencies.

A second, and perhaps more probable, explanation is that proprioceptive feedback alone is not sufficient to account for response inhibition or facilitation. For example, the proprioceptive cues arising from hitting response directed toward parents and toward peers may differ little, if any; nevertheless, tendencies to aggress toward parents are apt to be strongly inhibited while peer aggression may be readily expressed (Bandura, 1960; Bandura & Walters, 1959). In most social interaction sequences, proprioceptive cues make up only a small part of the total stimulus complex and, therefore, it is necessary to take into consideration additional stimulus components, for the most part external, which probably serve as important discriminative cues for the expression of aggression. Consequently, prediction of the occurrence or inhibition of specific classes of responses would be expected to depend upon the presence of a certain pattern of proprioceptive or introceptive stimulation together with relevant discriminative external stimuli.

According to this line of reasoning, failure to obtain the expected positive relationships between the measures of aggression may be due primarily to the fact that permissiveness for aggression, conveyed by situational cues in the form of aggressive film content and play material, was sufficient to override the influence of internal stimuli generated by the commission of aggressive responses. If, in fact, the behavior of young children, as compared to that of adults, is less likely to be under internal stimulus control, one might expect environmental cues to play a relatively important role in eliciting or inhibiting aggressive behavior.

A question may be raised as to whether the aggressive acts studied in the present experiment constitute "genuine" aggressive responses. Aggression is typically defined as behavior, the goal or intent of which is injury to a person, or destruction of an object (Bandura & Walters, 1959; Dollard, Doob, Miller, Mowrer, & Sears, 1939; Sears, Maccoby, & Levin, 1957). Since intentionality is not a property of behavior but primarily an inference concerning antecedent events, the categorization of an act as "aggressive" involves a consideration of both stimulus and mediating or terminal response events.

According to a social learning theory of aggression recently proposed by Bandura and Walters (in press), most of the responses utilized to hurt or to injure others (for example, striking, kicking, and other responses of high magnitude), are probably learned for prosocial purposes under nonfrustration conditions. Since frustration generally elicits responses of high magnitude, the latter classes of responses, once acquired, may be called out in social interactions for the purpose of injuring others. On the basis of this theory it would be predicted that the aggressive responses acquired imitatively, while not necessarily mediating aggressive goals in the experimental situation, would be utilized to serve such purposes in other social settings with higher frequency by children in the experimental conditions than by children in the control group.

The present study involved primarily vicarious or empathic learning (Mowrer, 1960) in that subjects acquired a relatively complex repertoire of aggressive responses by the mere sight of a model's behavior. It has been generally assumed that the necessary conditions for the occurrence of such learning is that the model perform certain responses followed by positive reinforcement to the model (Hill, 1960; Mowrer, 1960). According to this theory, to the extent that the observer experiences the model's reinforcement vicariously, the observer will be prone to reproduce the model's behavior. While there is some evidence from experiments involving both human (Lewis & Duncan, 1958; McBrearty, Marston, & Kanfer, 1961; Sechrest, 1961) and animal subjects (Darby & Riopelle, 1959; Warden, Fjeld, & Koch, 1940), that vicarious reinforcement may in fact increase the probability of the behavior in question, it is apparent from the results of the experiment reported in this paper that a good deal of human imitative learning can occur without any reinforcers delivered either to the model or to the observer. In order to test systematically the influence of vicarious reinforcement on imitation, however, a study is planned in which the degree of imitative learning will be compared in situations in which the model's behavior is paired with reinforcement with those in which the model's response go unrewarded.

REFERENCES

Albert, R. S. The role of mass media and the effect of aggressive film content upon children's aggressive responses and identification choices. *Genet. psychol. Monogr.,* 1957, 55, 221–285.

Bandura, A. Relationship of family patterns to child behavior disorders. Progress Report, 1960, Stanford University, Project No. M-1734, United States Public Health Service.

Bandura, A., & Huston, Aletha C. Identification as a process of incidental learning. *J. abnorm. soc. Psychol.,* 1961, 63, 311–318.

Bandura, A., Ross, Dorothea, & Ross, Sheila A. Transmission of aggression through imitation of aggressive models. *J. abnorm. soc. Psychol.,* 1961, 63, 575–582.

Bandura, A., & Walters, R. H. *Adolescent aggression.* New York: Ronald, 1959.

Bandura, A., & Walters, R. H. *The social learning of deviant behavior: A behavioristic approach to socialization.* New York: Holt, Rinehart, & Winston, in press.

Berkowitz, L. *Aggression: A social psychological analysis.* New York: McGraw-Hill, 1962.

Darby, C. L., & Riopelle, A. J. Observational learning in the Rhesus monkey. *J. comp. physiol. Psychol.,* 1959, 52, 94–98.

Dollard, J., Doob, L. W., Miller, N. E., Mowrer, O. H., & Sears, R. R. *Frustration and aggression.* New Haven: Yale Univer. Press, 1939.

Emery, F. E. Psychological effects of the Western film: A study in television viewing: II. The experimental study. *Hum. Relat.,* 1959, 12, 215–232.

Feshbach, S. The drive-reducing function of fantasy behavior. *J. abnorm. soc. Psychol.,* 1955, 50, 3–11.

Feshbach, S. The stimulating versus cathartic effects of a vicarious aggressive activity. Paper read at the Eastern Psychological Association, 1958.

Hill, W. F. Learning theory and the acquisition of values. *Psychol. Rev.,* 1960, 67, 317–331.

Kenny, D. T. An experimental test of the catharsis theory of aggression. Unpublished doctoral dissertation, University of Washington, 1952.

Lewis, D. J., & Duncan, C. P. Vicarious experience and partial reinforcement. *J. abnorm. soc. Psychol.,* 1958, 57, 321–326.

Lövaas, O. J. Effect of exposure to symbolic aggression on aggressive behavior. *Child Develpm.,* 1961, 32, 37–44.

McBrearty, J. F., Marston, A. R., & Kanfer, F. H. Conditioning a verbal operant in a group setting: Direct vs. vicarious reinforcement. *Amer. Psychologist,* 1961, 16, 425. (Abstract)

Mowrer, O. H. *Learning theory and the symbolic processes.* New York: Wiley, 1960.

San Francisco Chronicle. "James Dean" knifing in South City. *San Francisco Chron.,* March 1, 1961, 6.

Schramm, W., Lyle, J., & Parker, E. B. *Television in the lives of our children.* Stanford: Stanford Univer. Press, 1961.

Sears, R. R., Maccoby, Eleanor, E., & Levin, H. *Patterns of child rearing.* Evanston: Row, Peterson, 1957.

Sechrest, L. Vicarious reinforcement of responses. *Amer. Psychologist,* 1961, 16, 356. (Abstract)

Siegel, Alberta E. Film-mediated fantasy aggression and strength of aggressive drive. *Child Develpm.,* 1956, 27, 365–378.

Warden, C. J., Fjeld, H. A., & Koch, A. M. Imitative behavior in cebus and Rhesus monkeys. *J. genet. Psychol.,* 1940, 56, 311–322.

CHAPTER 12

GESTALT PSYCHOLOGY

MAX WERTHEIMER (1880–1943)

Max Wertheimer, the son of a school teacher, was born in Prague, where he attended gymnasium and studied law for two and one half years at the university.[1] In Prague, Wertheimer attended lectures by von Ehrenfels and was exposed to the thought of Mach, both of whom insisted that forms took on qualities unique to their constituent parts. This idea became a cornerstone of Gestalt theory. From there, Wertheimer traveled to Berlin and studied under Stumpf, the chair of philosophy, at the prestigious Friedrich-Wihelm University in Berlin. Stumpf was a phenomenologist; that is, he felt that perceptual experience should be studied as given, not analyzed into parts. Stumpf, thus, provided another influence that helped direct Wertheimer to a holistic way of thinking. Stumpf, like von Ehrenfels, was extremely interested in music. In this context, it is significant that Wertheimer always had a piano in his classroom to demonstrate that a melody depends not on the specific notes of a piece but the relation among them. In other words, a piece could be transposed, that is, played in another key and the melody would not be lost.

From Berlin, Wertheimer traveled to the University of Wurzburg, where he received his Ph.D., summa cum laude, under the direction of one of Wundt's former pupils, Oswald Külpe.[2] While in Wurzburg, Wertheimer undoubtedly was intimately aware of the implications of the famous imageless thought controversy. Külpe and his associates conducted a series of experiments that suggested that an unconscious

---

[1]Details of Wertheimer's life can be found in Newman's (1943) necrology.

[2]Wertheimer's dissertation focused on the application of the word association technique to legal issues. Some scholars believe that he anticipated Jung in the use of this method (Wertheimer, Michael, King, D. B., Peckler, M. A., Raney, S., & Schaef, R. W., 1992).

aufgabe (task set) and *einstellung* (mental tuning) influenced how one might see the various parts of a problem. In contemporary terms, one might not see a rip in a pair of pants as potentially life threatening, but if one thinks of the same rip in the context of space travel, the tear takes on an ominous note. Wertheimer was thus exposed to yet another significant intellectual position that maintained that the way parts are psychologically organized, besides the parts themselves, is of crucial significance.

On a train ride in 1910, Wertheimer had a pivotal experience. While looking at the apparent movement of the scenery, Wertheimer became aware of a principle that would shake the foundations of the prevalent elementalistic psychology. This experience so moved him that he got off the train at the next stop, Frankfurt, to buy a child's toy, a carousel-like device that presented successive images. When spun at the correct speed, the device gave the illusion of movement, of a galloping horse, for example, much like a modern movie film. In Frankfurt, with the help of Professor Schuman, the developer of the tachistoscope (an instrument that projects visual images for extremely short periods of time), Wertheimer (1912) studied apparent movement in the laboratory. Wertheimer varied the interval between exposing the subject to two lines, one standing up and one on its side. When the temporal interval was correct, it appeared to the subject as if the line had moved from horizontal to vertical. Here, said Wertheimer, was a phenomenon, apparent movement (he called this the phi phenomenon), that when analyzed, disappeared. The whole was indeed different from the parts and could never be understood by analysis. This theme is evident in the first reading, *Über Gestalttheorie* (1924), in which Wertheimer states, "The fundamental formula of Gestalt theory might be expressed in this way: There are wholes, the behavior of which is not determined by that of their individual elements, but where the part processes are themselves determined by the intrinsic nature of the whole."[3]

His subjects for the phi phenomenon experiment in Frankfurt were Wolfgang Köhler (pronounced "curler") (1887–1967) and Kurt Koffka (1886–1941), psychologists who would go on to become famous contributors to Gestalt theory. Köhler (1925) studied the problem-solving behavior of apes at Tenerife in the Canary Islands during World War I and subsequently went to the University of Berlin, establishing it as a center for Gestalt psychology.[4] The second reading is an excerpt from Köhler's experiments with apes. In this reading, it is clear that Köhler thought that apes were intelligent animals capable of solving problems through insight, that is, seeing the correct relationship among the parts appropriate to the problem.

Koffka went to the relatively provincial university in Giesen. He did, however, attract many able researchers to Geisen, where they studied developmental psychology from a Gestalt perspective.

During the early 1920s, Wertheimer was also in Berlin, and all three, Wertheimer, Köhler, and Koffka, were in constant contact. American students such

---

[3]Köhler's (1944) necrology also provides an excellent reprise of Wertheimer's approach.

[4]Köhler had not intended to stay on the island for such a long duration but was marooned because of the war. Ley (1990) contends he was a German spy, but the truth of this allegation remains unsubstantiated.

as Gordon Allport ventured to Germany and brought the new psychology back home (Allport, 1967). In addition, Köhler and Koffka lectured in the United States during this period (Sokal, 1984). The soil in America was thus prepared for the emigration of Wertheimer, Köhler, and Koffka to the United States as the political situation in Germany grew intolerable (see Henle (1978) for a fascinating account of this period). Wertheimer came to The New School for Social Research in 1934.[5] In the United States, his writing was not as prolific as it had been in Germany. This is understandable given that he was laboring with a new language in a new country. However, he did complete his work, *Productive Thinking*, which was published posthumously in 1945, the year following his death.

REFERENCES

Allport, G. W. (1967). Gordon W. Allport. In E. G. Boring & G. Lindzey (Eds.) *A history of psychology in autobiography* (Vol. 5, pp. 3–25). Engelwood Cliffs, NJ: Prentice-Hall.

Henle, M. E. (1978). One man against the Nazis—Wolfgang Köhler. *American Psychologist, 33,* 939–944.

Köhler, W. (1925). *The mentality of apes.* E. Winter (Trans.). New York: Harcourt Brace.

Köhler, W. (1944). Max Wertheimer: 1880–1943. *The Psychological Review, 51,* 143–146.

Ley, R. (1990). *A whisper of espionage.* Garden City, NY: Aveny.

Newman, E. B. (1944). Max Wertheimer: 1880–1943. *American Journal of Psychology, 57,* 428–435.

Sokal, M. M. (1987). The Gestalt psychologists in behaviorist America. *American Historical Review, 89,* 1240–1263.

Wertheimer, M. (1912). Experimentelle Studien uber das Sehen von Bewegung. *Zeitschrift der Psychologie, 61,* 161–265.

Wertheimer, M. (1938). Gestalt theory. In W. D. Ellis (Ed.) *A source book of Gestalt psychology* (pp. 1–11). New York: Harcourt Brace. (Talk originally given in 1924/1925).

Wertheimer, Michael, King, D. B., Peckler, M. A., Raney, S., & Schaef, R. W. (1992). Carl Jung and Max Wertheimer on a priority issue. *The Journal of the History of the Behavioral Sciences, 28,* 45–56.

1. General Problems
Selection 1
Gestalt Theory

By Max Wertheimer

Über Gestalttheorie [an address before the Kant Society, Berlin, 17th December, 1924], Erlangen, 1925.

What is Gestalt theory and what does it intend? Gestalt theory was the outcome of concrete investigations in psychology, logic, and epistemology. The prevailing situation at the time of its origin may be briefly sketched as follows. We go from the

---

[5]His colleagues Köhler and Koffka relocated to Swarthmore and Smith, respectively

world of everyday events to that of science, and not unnaturally assume that in making this transition we shall gain a deeper and more precise understanding of essentials. The transition *should* mark an advance. And yet, though one may have learned a great deal, one is poorer than before. It is the same in psychology. Here too we find science intent upon a systematic collection of data, yet often excluding through that very activity precisely *that* which is most vivid and real in the living phenomena it studies. Somehow the thing that matters has eluded us.

What happens when a problem is solved, when one suddenly "sees the point"? Common as this experience is, we seek in vain for it in the textbooks of psychology. Of things arid, poor, and inessential there is an abundance, but that which really matters is missing. Instead we are told of formation of concepts, of abstraction and generalization, of class concepts and judgments, perhaps of associations, creative phantasy, intuitions, talents—anything but an answer to our original problem. And what are these last words but *names* for the problem? Where are the penetrating answers? Psychology is replete with terms of great potentiality—personality, essence, intuition, and the rest. But when one seeks to grasp their concrete content, such terms fail.

This is the situation and it is characteristic of modern science that the same problem should appear everywhere. Several attempts have been made to remedy the matter. One was a frank defeatism preaching the severance of science and life: there are regions which are inaccessible to science. Other theories established a sharp distinction between the natural and moral sciences: the exactitude and precision of chemistry and physics are characteristic of natural science, but "scientific" accuracy has no place in a study of the mind and its ways. This must be renounced in favour of *other* categories.

Without pausing for further examples, let us consider rather a question naturally underlying the whole discussion: Is "*science*" really the kind of things we have implied? The word science has often suggested a certain outlook, certain fundamental assumptions, certain procedures and attitudes—but do these imply that this is the only possibility of scientific method? Perhaps science already embodies methods leading in an entirely different direction, methods which have been continually stifled by the seemingly necessary, dominant ones. It is conceivable, for instance, that a host of facts and problems have been concealed rather than illuminated by the prevailing scientific tradition. Even though the traditional methods of science are undoubtedly adequate in many case, there may be others where they lead us astray. Perhaps something in the very nature of the traditional outlook may have led its exponents at times to ignore precisely that which is truly essential.

Gestalt theory will not be satisfied with sham solutions suggested by a simple dichotomy of science and life. Instead, Gestalt theory is resolved to penetrate the *problem* itself by examining the fundamental assumptions of science. It has long seemed obvious—and is, in fact, the characteristic tone of European science—that "science" means breaking up complexes into their component elements. Isolate the elements, discover their laws, then reassemble them, and the problem is solved. All wholes are reduced to pieces and piecewise relations between prices.

The fundamental "formula" of Gestalt theory might be expressed in this way [1]: There are wholes, the behaviour of which is not determined by that of their individual elements, but where the part-processes are themselves determined by the intrinsic nature of the whole. It is the hope of Gestalt theory to determine the nature of such wholes.

With a formula such as this, one might close, for Gestalt theory is neither more nor less than this. It is not interested in puzzling out philosophic questions which such a formula might suggest. Gestalt theory has to do with concrete research; it is not only an *outcome* but a *device:* not only a theory *about* results but a means toward further discoveries. This is not merely the proposal of one or more problems but an attempt to *see* what is really taking place in science. This problem cannot be solved by listing possibilities for systematization, classification, and arrangement. If it is to be attacked at all, we must be guided by the spirit of the new method and by the concrete nature of the things themselves which we are studying, and set ourselves to penetrate to that which is really given by nature.

There is another difficulty that may be illustrated by the following example. Suppose a mathematician shows you a proposition and you begin to "classify" it. This proposition, you say, is of such a such type, belongs in this or that historical category, and so on. Is that how the mathematician works?

"Why, you haven't grasped the thing at all," the mathematician will exclaim. "See here, this formula is not an independent, closed fact that can be dealt with for itself alone. You must see its dynamic *functional* relationship to the whole from which it was lifted or you will never understand it."

What holds for the mathematical formula applies also to the "formula" of Gestalt theory. The attempt of Gestalt theory to disclose the functional meaning of its own formula is no less strict than is the mathematician's. The attempt to explain Gestalt theory in short essay is the more difficult because of the terms which are used: part, whole, intrinsic determination. All of them have in the past been the topic of endless discussions where each disputant has understood them differently. And even worse has been the cataloguing attitude adopted toward them. What they *lacked* has been actual research. Like many another "philosophic" problem they have been withheld from contact with reality and scientific work.

About all I can hope for in so short a discussion is to suggest a few of the problems which at present occupy the attention of Gestalt theory and something of the way they are being attacked.

To repeat: the *problem* has not merely to do with scientific work—it is a fundamental problem of our times. Gestalt theory is not something suddenly and unexpectedly dropped upon us from above; it is, rather, a palpable convergence of problems ranging throughout the sciences and the various philosophic standpoints of modern times.

---

[1] "Man könnte das Grundproblem der Gestalttheorie etwa so zu formulieren suchen: Es gibt Zusammenhänge, bei denen nicht, was im Ganzen geschieht, sich daraus herleitet, wie die einzelne Stücke sind und sich zusammensetzen, sondern umgekehrt, wo—im prägnante Fall—sich *das, was an einem Teil dieses Ganzen geschieht, bestimmt von inneren Strukturgesetzen dieses seines Ganzen.*"

Let us take, for example, and event in the history of psychology. One turned from a living experience to science and asked what it had to say about this experience, and one found an assortment of elements, sensations, images, feelings, acts of will and laws governing these elements—and was told, "Take your choice, reconstruct from them the experience you had." Such procedure led to difficulties in concrete psychological research and to the emergence of problems which defied solution by the traditional analytic methods. Historically the most important impulse came from v. Ehrenfels who raised the following problem. Psychology had said that experience is a compound of elements: we hear a melody and then, upon hearing it again, memory enables us to recognize it. But what is it that enables us to recognize the melody when it is played in a new key? The sum of the elements is different, yet the melody is the same; indeed, one is often not even aware that a transposition has been made.

When in retrospect we consider the prevailing situation we are struck by two aspects of v. Ehrenfels's thesis; on the one hand one is surprised at the essentially summative character of his theory, on the other one admires his courage in propounding and defending his proposition. Strictly interpreted, v. Ehrenfels's position was this: I play a familiar melody of six tones and employ six *new* tones, yet you recognize the melody despite the change. There must be a something *more* than the sum of six tones, viz. a seventh something, which is the form-quality, the *Gestaltqualität,* of the original six. It is this *seventh* factor or element which enabled you to recognize the melody despite its transposition.

However strange this view may seem, it shares with many another subsequently abandoned hypothesis the honour of having clearly seen and emphasized a fundamental problem.

But other explanations were also proposed. One maintained that in addition to the six tones there were intervals—relations—and that *these* were what remained constant. In other words we are asked to assume not only elements but "relations-between-elements" as additional components of the total complex. But this view failed to account for the phenomenon because in some cases the relations *too* may be altered without destroying the original melody.

Another type of explanation, also designed to bolster the elementaristic hypothesis, was that *to* this total of six or more tones there come certain "higher processes" which operate upon the given material to "*produce*" unity.

This was the situation until Gestalt theory raised the radical question: Is it really true that when I hear a melody I have a *sum* of individual tones (pieces) which constitute the primary foundation of my experience? Is not perhaps the reverse of this true? What I really have, what I hear of each individual note, what I experience at each place in the melody is a *part* which is itself determined by the character of the whole. What is given me by the melody does not arise (through the agency of any auxiliary factor) as a *secondary* process from the sum of the pieces as such. Instead, what takes place in each single part already depends upon what the whole is. The flesh and blood of a tone depends from the start upon its role in the melody: a *b* as leading tone to *c* is something radically different from the *b* as tonic. It belongs to the flesh and blood of the things given in experience [*Gegebenheiten*], how, in what role, in what function they are in their whole.

Let us leave the melody example and turn to another field. Take the case of threshold phenomena. It has long been held that a certain stimulus necessarily produces a certain sensation. Thus, when two stimuli are sufficiently different, the sensations also will be different. Psychology is filled with careful inquiries regarding threshold phenomena. To account for the difficulties constantly being encountered it was assumed that these phenomena must be influenced by higher mental functions, judgments, illusions, attention, etc. And this continued until the radical question was raised: Is it really true that a specific stimulus *always* gives rise to the same sensation? Perhaps the prevailing whole-conditions will themselves determine the effect of stimulation? This kind of formulation leads to experimentation, and experiments show, for example, that when I see two colours the sensations I have are determined by the whole-conditions of the entire stimulus situation. Thus, also, the same local *physical* stimulus pattern can give rise to either a unitary and homogeneous figure, or to an articulated figure with different parts, all depending upon the whole-conditions which may favour either unity or articulation. Obviously the task, then, is to investigate these "whole-conditions" and discover what influences they exert upon experience.

Advancing another step we come to the question whether perhaps any part depends upon the particular whole in which it occurs. Experiments, largely on vision, have answered this question in the affirmative. Among other things they demand that the traditional theory of visual contrast be replaced by a theory which takes account of whole-part conditions.

Our next point is that my field comprises also my Ego. There is not from the beginning an Ego over-against others, but the genesis of an Ego offers one of the most fascinating problems, the solution of which seems to lie in Gestalt principles. However, once constituted, the Ego is a functional part of the total field. Proceeding as before we may therefore ask: What happens to the Ego as a part of the field? Is the resulting behaviour the piecewise sort of thing associationism, experience theory, and the like, would have us believe? Experimental results contradict this interpretation and again we often find that the laws of whole-processes operative in such a field tend toward a meaningful behaviour of its parts.

This field is not a summation of sense data and no description of it which considers such separate pieces to be *primary* will be correct. If it were, then for children, primitive peoples and animals experience would be nothing but piece-sensations. The next most developed creatures would have, in addition to independent sensations, something higher, and so on. But this whole picture is the opposite of what actual inquiry has disclosed. We have learned to recognize the "sensations" of our textbooks as products of a late culture utterly different from the experiences of more primitive stages. Who experiences the sensation of a specific red in that sense? What the man of the streets, children, or primitive men normally react to is something coloured but at the same time exciting, gay, strong, or affecting—*not* "sensations".

The programme to treat the organism as a part in a larger field necessitates the reformulation of the problem as to the relation between organism and environment. The stimulus-sensation connection must be replaced by a connection between alteration in the field conditions, the vital situation, and the total reaction of the organism by a change in its attitude, striving, and feeling.

There is, however, another step to be considered. A man is not only a part of his field, he is also one among other men. When a group of people work together it rarely occurs, and then only under very special conditions, that they constitute a mere sum of independent Egos. Instead the common enterprise often becomes their mutual concern and each works *as* a meaningfully functioning part of the whole. Consider a group of South Sea Islanders engaged in some community occupation, or a group of children playing together. Only under very special circumstances does an "I" stand out alone. Then the balance which obtained during harmonious and systematic occupation may be upset and give way to a surrogate (under certain conditions, pathological) *new* balance.

Further discussion of this point would carry us into the work of social and cultural science which cannot be followed here. Instead let us consider certain other illustrations. What was said above of stimulus and sensation is applicable to physiology and the biological sciences no less than to psychology. It has been tried, for example, by postulating sums of more and more special apparatus, to account for meaningful or, as it is often called, purposive behaviour. Once more we find meaninglessly combined reflexes taken for granted although it is probable that even with minute organisms it is not true that a piece-stimulus automatically bring about its corresponding piece-effect.

Opposing this view is *vitalism* which, however, as it appears to Gestalt theory, also errs in its efforts to solve the problem, for it, too, begins with the assumption that natural occurrences are themselves essentially blind and haphazard—and *adds* a mystical something over and above them which imposes order. Vitalism fails to inquire of physical events whether a genuine order might not already prevail amongst them. And yet nature *does* exhibit numerous instances of physical wholes in which part events are determined by the inner structure of the whole.

These brief references to biology will suffice to remind us that whole-phenomena are not "merely" psychological, but appear in other sciences as well. Obviously, therefore, the problem is not solved by separating off various provinces of science and classifying whole-phenomena as something peculiar to psychology.

The fundamental question can be very simply stated: Are the parts of a given whole determined by the inner structure of that whole, or are the events such that, as independent, piecemeal, fortuitous and blind the total activity is a sum of the part-activities? Human beings can, of course, *devise* a kind of physics of their own— e.g. a sequence of machines—exemplifying the latter half of our question, but this does not signify that *all natural* phenomena are of this type. Here is a place where Gestalt theory is least easily understood and this because of the great number of prejudices about nature which have accumulated during the centuries. Nature is thought of as something essentially blind in its laws, where whatever takes place in the whole is purely a sum of individual occurrences. This view was the natural result of the struggle which physics has always had to purge itself of teleology. Today it can be seen that we are obliged to traverse other routes than those suggested by this kind of purposivism.

Let us proceed another step and ask: How does all this stand with regard to the problem of body and mind? What does my knowledge of another's mental experiences amount to and how do I obtain it? There are, of course, old and established dogmas on these points: The mental and physical are wholly heterogeneous:

there obtains between them an absolute dichotomy. (From this point of departure philosophers have drawn an array of metaphysical deductions so as to attribute all the good qualities to mind while reserving for nature the odious.) As regards the second question, my discerning mental phenomena in others is traditionally explained as inference by analogy. Strictly interpreted the principle here is that something mental is meaninglessly coupled with something physical. I observe the physical and infer the mental from it more or less according to the following scheme: I see someone press a button on the wall and infer that he wants the light to go on. There *may be* couplings of this sort. However, many scientists have been disturbed by this dualism and have tried to save themselves by recourse to very curious hypotheses. Indeed, the ordinary person would violently refuse to believe that when he sees his companion startled, frightened, or angry he is seeing only certain physical occurrences which themselves have nothing to do (in their inner nature) with the mental, being only superficially coupled with it: you have frequently seen this and this combined . . . etc. There have been many attempts to surmount this problem. One speaks, for example, of *intuition* and says there can be no other possibility, for I *see* my companion's fear. It is not true, argue the intuitionists, that I see only the bare bodily activities meaninglessly coupled with other and invisible activities. However inadmissible it may otherwise be, an intuition theory does have at least this in its favour, it shows a suspicion that the traditional procedure might be successfully reversed. But the word intuition is at best only a *naming* of that which we must strive to lay hold of.

This and other hypotheses, apprehended as they now are, will not advance scientific pursuit, for science demands fruitful penetration, not mere cataloguing and systematization. But the question is, How does the matter really stand? Looking more closely we find a third assumption, namely that a process such as fear is a matter of consciousness. Is this true? Suppose you see a person who is kindly or benevolent. Does anyone suppose that this person is feeling mawkish? No one could possibly believe that. The characteristic feature of such behaviour has very little to do with consciousness. It has been one of the easiest contrivances of philosophy to identify a man's real behaviour and the direction of his mind with his consciousness. Parenthetically, in the opinion of many people the distinction between idealism and materialism implies that between the noble and ignoble. Yet does one really mean by this to contrast consciousness with the blithesome budding of trees? Indeed, what is there so repugnant about the materialistic and mechanical? What is so attractive about idealistic? Does it come from the *material* qualities of the connected pieces? Broadly speaking most psychological theories and textbooks, despite their continued emphasis upon consciousness, are far more "materialistic", arid, and spiritless than a living tree—which probably has no consciousness at all. The point is not what the material pieces are, but what *kind* of whole it is. Proceeding in terms of specific problems one soon realizes how many bodily activities there are which give no hint of a separation between body and mind. Imagine a dance, a dance full of grace an joy. What is the situation in such a dance? Do we have a summation of *physical* limb movements and a *psychical* consciousness? No. Obviously this answer does not solve the problem; we have to start anew—and it seems to me that a proper and fruitful point of attack has been discovered. One finds many processes which, in their dynamical form, are identical regardless of variations in the material character of their elements. When a man is timid, afraid or energetic, happy or sad, it can often be shown that the course of his physical processes is Gestalt-identical with the course pursued by the mental processes.

Again I can only indicate the direction of thought. I have touched on the question of body and mind merely to show that the problem we are discussing also has its philosophic aspects. To strengthen the import of the foregoing suggestions let us consider the fields of epistemology and logic. For centuries the assumption has prevailed that our world is essentially a summation of elements. For Hume and largely also for Kant the world is like a bundle of fragments, and the dogma of meaningless summations continues to play its part. As for logic, it supplies: *concepts,* which when rigorously viewed are but sums of properties; *classes,* which upon closer inspection prove to be mere catchalls; *syllogisms,* devised by arbitrarily lumping together any two propositions having the character that . . . etc. When one considers what a concept *is* in living thought, what it really means to grasp a conclusion; when one considers what the crucial thing *is* about a mathematical proof and the concrete interrelationships it involves, one sees that the categories of traditional logic have accomplished nothing in this direction.

It is our task to inquire whether a logic is possible which is *not* piecemeal. Indeed the same question arises in mathematics also. Is it *necessary* that all mathematics be established upon a piecewise basis? What sort of mathematical system would it be in which this were *not* the case? There have been attempts to answer the latter question but almost always they have fallen back in the end upon the old procedures. This fate has overtaken many, for the result of training in piecewise thinking is extraordinarily tenacious. It is not enough and certainly does not constitute a solution of the principal problem if one shows that the axioms of mathematics are both piecemeal and that the same time evince something of the opposite character. The problem has been scientifically grasped only when an attack specifically designed to yield positive results have been launched. Just how this attack is to be made seems to many mathematicians a colossal problem, but perhaps the quantum theory will force the mathematicians to attack it.

This brings us to the close of an attempt to present a view of the problem as illustrated by its specific appearances in various fields. In concluding I may suggest a certain unification of these illustrations somewhat as follows. I consider the situation from the point of view of a theory of aggregates and say: How should a world be where science, concepts, inquire, investigation, and comprehension of inner unities were impossible? The answer is obvious. This world would be a manifold of disparate pieces. Secondly, what kind of world would there have to be in which a piecewise science would apply? The answer is again quite simple, for here one needs only a system of recurrent couplings that are blind and piecewise in character, whereupon everything is available for a pursuit of the traditional piecewise methods of logic, mathematics, and science generally in so far as these presuppose this kind of world. But there is a third kind of aggregate which has been but cursorily investigated. These are the aggregates in which a manifold is not compounded from adjacently situated pieces but rather such that a term at its place in that aggregate is determined by the whole-laws of the aggregate itself.

Pictorially: suppose the world were a vast plateau upon which were many musicians. I walk about listening and watching the players. First suppose that the world is a meaningless plurality. Everyone does as he will, each for himself. What happens together when I hear ten players, might be the basis for my guessing as to what they all are doing, but this is merely a matter of chance and probability much as in the kinetics of gas molecules.—A second possibility would be that each time one musician player *c*, another played *f* so and so many seconds later. I work out a theory of blind couplings but the playing as a whole remains meaningless. This is what many people think physics does, but the real work of physics belies this.— The third possibility is, say, a Beethoven symphony where it would be possible for one to select one part of the whole and work from that towards an idea of the structural principle motivating and determining the whole. Here the fundamental laws are not those of fortuitous pieces, but concern the very character of the event.

The Mentality of Apes

Wolfgang Köhler

INTRODUCTION

1. Two sets of interests lead us to test the intelligence of the higher apes. We are aware that it is a question of beings which in many ways are nearer to man than to the other ape species; in particular it has been shown that the chemistry of their bodies, in so far as this may be perceived in the quality of the blood, and the structure of their most highly developed organ, the brain, are more closely related to the chemistry of the human body and human brain-structure than to the chemical nature of the lower apes and *their* brain development. These beings show so many human traits in their "everyday" behaviour that the question was quite automatically suggested whether the animals do not behave with intelligence and insight under conditions which require such behaviour. This question expresses the first, one may say, naïve, interest in the intellectual capacity of animals. We wished to ascertain the degree of relationship between anthropoid ape and man in a field which seems to us particularly important, but on which we have as yet little information.

The second aim is theoretical. Even assuming that the anthropoid ape behaves intelligently in the sense in which the word is applied to man, there is yet from the very start no doubt that he remains in this respect far behind man, becoming perplexed and making mistakes in relatively simple situations; but it is precisely for this reason that we may, under the simplest conditions, gain knowledge of the nature of acts of intelligence; the human adult hardly ever performs for the *first* time in his life tasks involving intelligence, so simple that they can be easily investigated;

and when adult men are the subject of experiment in more complicated tasks, they can only with difficulty observe results. So one may be allowed the expectation that in the intelligent performances of anthropoid apes we may see in their plastic state once more processes with which we have become so familiar that we can no longer immediately recognize their original form: but which because of their very simplicity, we should treat as the logical starting-point of theoretical speculation.

As all the emphasis in the following investigations is laid on the first question, the doubt may be expressed whether it does not rather take for granted a particular solution of the problems treated under the second. One might say that whether intelligent behaviour exists among anthropoid apes can be discussed only after the theoretical necessity of distinguishing between intelligent behaviour and behaviour of any other kind has been realized; and that, as association psychology, in particular, claims to derive from one single principle all behaviour which would come under consideration here, up to the highest level, even that attained by human beings, a theoretical point of view is already assumed by the formulation of problem 1; and one which is antagonistic to association psychology.

This is a misconception. There is probably no association psychologist who does not, in his won unprejudiced observations, distinguish, and, to a certain extent, contrast unintelligent behaviour and intelligent. For what is association psychology other than the theory that one can trace back to the phenomena of a generally-known simple association type even occurrences which, according to unbiassed observation, do not at first make the impression of being identical, above all so-called intelligence performances? In short, it is just these differences which are the starting-point of a strict association psychology; it is they which need to be theoretically accounted for; they are well known to the association psychologist. Thus for instance, we find a radical representative of this school (Thorndike) stating the conclusion, drawn from experiments on dogs and cats: "I failed to find any act that even *seemed* due to reasoning." To anyone who can formulate his results thus, other behaviour must already have seemed to be intelligent; he is already acquainted with the contrast in his observations, perhaps of human beings, even if he discards it afterwards in theory.

Accordingly, if we are to inquire whether the anthropoid ape behaves intelligently, this problem can for the present be treated quite independently of theoretical assumptions, particularly those for or against the association theory. It is true that it then becomes somewhat indefinite; we are not to inquire whether anthropoid apes show something well defined, but whether their behaviour approximates to a type rather superficially known by experience, and which we call "intelligence"[1] in contrast to other behaviour—especially in animals. But in proceeding thus, we are only dealing according to the nature of the subject; for clear definitions have no place at the beginning of experiential sciences; it is only as we advance towards results that we can mark our progress by the formulation of definitions.

Moreover, the type of human and, perhaps, animal behaviour to which the first question animadverts is not so indefinite, even without a theory. As experience

---

[1]See foot-note, p. 228

shows, we do not speak of behaviour as being intelligent, when human beings or animals attain their objective by a direct unquestionable route which without doubt arises naturally out of their organization. But what seems to us "intelligence" tends to be called into play when circumstances block a course which seems obvious to us, leaving open a roundabout path which the human being or animal takes, so meeting the situation. In unexpressed agreement with this, nearly all those observers who heretofore have sought to solve the problem of animal intelligence, have done so by watching animals in just such predicaments. As in cases below the stage of development of anthropoid apes results are, in general, negative, there arose out of those experiments the view widely held at present, i.e. that there is very little intelligent behaviour in animals; only a small number of such experiments have been carried out on anthropoid apes, and they have not yet led to any very definite results. All the experiments described in the following pages are of one and the same kind: the experimenter sets up a situation in which the direct path to the objective is blocked, but a roundabout way left open. The animal is introduced into this situation, which can, potentially, be wholly surveyed, and so who shall be able to see up to which level of behaviour its capabilities take it, and, particularly, whether it can solve the problem in the possible "roundabout" way.

2. The experiments were at first applied to chimpanzees only, with the exception of a few cases taken for comparison, in which human beings, a dog, and hens were observed.

Seven of the animals belonged to the old branch of the anthropoid station which the Prussian Academy of Science maintained in Tenerife from 1912 to 1920. Of these seven the oldest, an adult female, was named Tschego, because of several characteristics which made us, perhaps wrongly, consider her a member of the Tschego species. (We are yet far from possessing a clear and systematized classification of the varieties of the chimpanzee.) The oldest of the smaller animals, called Grande, also differs considerably in several respects from its comrades. But as the differences concern its general character rather than the behaviour investigated in the intelligence tests, a detailed description of them would be out of place here. The other five, two males (Sultan and Konsul), three females (Tercera, Rana, and Chica), are of the usual chimpanzee type.

To the seven animals mentioned, two others were added later, both of which led to valuable observations, but both of which, to our regret, soon died.

Practically all the observations were made in the first six months of 1914.[1] They were often repeated later, but only a few additional experiments and repetitions (dating from the spring of 1916) are incorporated in this report, as, in general, the behaviour observed the first time was repeated; in any case, no important corrections had to be made in the earlier results.

3. Experiments of the kind described may make very different calls upon the animals to be tested, according to the situation in which they are put. In order to discover, even roughly, the zone of difficulty within which the testing of chimpanzees will be of any use, Mr. E. Teuber and I gave them a problem which seemed to us

---

[1]That is, they were made *before* the chimpanzees underwent optical examination. (Cf. These in the *Abh. D. Kgl. Preuss. Akd. d. Wiss*, 1915, Phys.-Math. Section No. 3.)

difficult, but not impossible, of solution for a chimpanzee. How Sultan behaved in this test should be sketched here as a preliminary example.

A long thin string is tied to the handle of a little open basket containing fruit; an iron ring is hung in the wire-roof of the animals' playground, through which the string is pulled till the basket hangs about two metres above the ground; the free end of the string, tied into a wide open loop, is laid over the stump of a tree-branch about three metres away from the basket, and about the same height from the ground; the string forms an acute angle—the bend being at the iron ring. Sultan, who had not seen the preparations, but who knows the basket well from his feeding-times, is let into the playground while the observer takes his place outside the bars. The animal first looks at the hanging basket, but soon shows signs of lively agitation (on account of his unwonted isolation), thunders, in true chimpanzee style, with his feet against a wooden wall, and tries to get into touch with the other animals at the windows of the ape-house and anywhere else where there is a view out, and also with the observer at the bars; but the animals are out of sight, ant the observer remains indifferent. After a time, Sultan suddenly makes for the tree, climbs quickly up to the loop, stops a moment, then, watching the basket, pulls the string till the basket bumps against the ring (at the roof), lets it go again, pulls a second time more vigorously so that the basket turns over, and a banana falls out. He comes down, takes the fruit, gets up again, and now pulls so violently that the string breaks, and the whole basket falls. He clambers down, takes the basket, and goes off to eat the fruit.

Three days later, the same experiment is repeated, except that the loop is replaced by an iron ring at the end of the rope, and the ring hung on a nail instead of put over the branch, the nail driven into a scaffolding (used for the animals' gymnastics). Sultan now shows himself free from all doubt, looks up at the basket an instant, goes straight up to the scaffolding, climbs it, pulls once at the cord, and lets it slip back, pulls again with all his might so that the cord breaks, then he clambers down, and fetches his fruit.

The best solution of the problem which could be expected would be that the animal should take the loop or iron ring off the branch or nail and simply let the basket drop, etc. The actual behaviour of the animal shows plainly that the nub of the situation, i.e. the rope connexion, is grasped as a matter of course, but the further course of action for the experiment is not very clear. The best solution is not even indicated. One cannot tell just why. Did Sultan perhaps not see the loose fixing of the loop to the branch or ring to the nail? If he and noticed it, would he have been able to solve it? Would he in any case expect the basket to fall to the ground if this fastening were loosened? Or does the difficulty lie in the fact that the basket would fall to the ground, and not straight into Sultan's hands? For we cannot even know whether Sultan really pulled at the cord to break it, and thus bring the basket to earth. So we have performed one experiment which, for a beginning, contains conditions too complicated to teach us much, and, therefore, we see the necessity of beginning the next examinations with elementary problems in which, if possible, the animals' conduct could have one meaning only.

Editors' note—The following represents one example where "the animals' conduct could have one meaning only."

THE MAKING OF IMPLEMENTS

Building

When a chimpanzee cannot reach an objective hung high up with *one* box, there is a possibility that he will pile two or more boxes on top of one another and reach it in that way. Whether he *actually* does this seems a simple question that can soon be decided. But if experiments are made, it is quickly seen that the problem for the chimpanzee falls into two very distinct parts: one of which he can settle with ease, whilst the other presents considerable difficulties. We think the first is the *whole* problem; where the animal's difficulties begin, we do not, at first, see any problem at all. If in the description this curious fact is to be emphasized as much as it impressed itself on the observer, the report of the experiment should be divided into two parts in accordance with this fact. I shall begin with the answer to the question that seems to be the only one.

In one of the experiments described previously (p. 47), Sultan came very near putting one box on top of another, when he found the one insufficient; but instead of placing the second box, which he had already lifted, upon the first, he made uncertain movements with in the air around and above the other; then other methods replaced these confused movements. The test is repeated (8.2); the objective is placed very high up, the two boxes are not very far away from each other and about four metres away from the objective; all other means of reaching it have been taken away. Sultan drags the bigger of the two boxes towards the objective, puts it just underneath, gets up on it, and looking upwards, makes ready to jump, but does not jump; gets down, seizes the other box, and, pulling it behind him, gallops about the room, making his usual noise, kicking against the walls and showing his uneasiness in every other possible way.[1] He certainly did not seize the second box to put it on the first; it merely helps him to give vent to his temper. But all of a sudden his behaviour changes completely; he stops making a noise, pulls his box from quite a distance right up to the other one, and stands it upright on it. He mounts the somewhat shaky construction, several times gets ready to jump, but again does not jump; the objective is still too high for this bad jumper. But he has achieved his task.

Now I mentioned, from the very beginning, how in the case of a roundabout-way experiment the single and separate fractions, which, when put together by chance, led to a practical result, are sharply distinguishable from "genuine solutions". In these, the smooth, continuous course, sharply divided by an abrupt beginning from the preceding behaviour, is usually extremely characteristic. At the same time this process as a whole corresponds to the construction of the situation, to the relation of the parts to one another. Thus, for example: one may have the

---

[1] All the animals showed a strong aversion to the room in which these experiments were carried out, not because of the experiments—those they did not mind—but because of the unbearable dry heat that existed there most of the time. In those days, for outside reasons, I could not make my experiments anywhere else, but later I avoided the room whenever possible. Some stupidities that were observed here were, very likely, partly symptoms of fatigue.

objective constructed thus, on free ground then the sudden establishing of the smooth and unchecked movement along the curve, to the achievement of the task. We are forced to the impression that this curve appears requisite to the situation as a whole from the beginning, the product of a complete survey of the whole situation. (Chimpanzees, whose behaviour is incomparably more intelligent than that of hens, show by their very looks that they really begin with something very like an inventory of the situation. And this survey then gives rise to the behaviour required for the solution.)

We can, from our own experience, distinguish sharply between the kind of conduct which from the very beginning arises out of a consideration of the characteristics of a situation, and one that does not. Only in the former case do we speak of insight, and only that behaviour of animals definitely appears to us intelligent which takes account from the beginning of the lie of the land, and proceeds to deal with it in a smooth, continuous course. Hence follows this characteristic: *to set up as the criterion of insight, the appearance of a complete solution with reference to the whole lay-out of the field.*

CONCLUSION

The chimpanzees manifest intelligent behaviour of the general kind familiar in human beings. Not all their intelligent acts are externally similar to human acts, but under well-chosen experimental conditions, the type of intelligent conduct can always be traced. This applies, in spite of very important differences between one animal and another, even to the least gifted specimens of the species that have been observed here, and, therefore, must hold good of every member of the species, as long as it is not mentally deficient, in the pathological sense of the word. With this exception, which is presumably rare, the success of the intelligence tests in general will be more likely endangered by the person making the experiment than by the animal. One must know and, if necessary, establish by preliminary observation, within which limits of difficulty and in which functions the chimpanzee *can possibly* show insight; negative or confused results from complicated and accidentally-chosen test-material, have obviously no bearing upon the fundamental question, and, in general, the experimenter should recognize that every intelligence test is a test, not only of the creature examined, but also of the experimenter himself. I have said that to myself quite often, and yet I have remained uncertain whether the experiments I performed may be considered "satisfactory" in this respect; without theoretical foundations, and in unknown territory, methodological mistakes may quite well have occurred; anyone who continues this work will be able to prevent them more easily.

At any rate, this remains true: Chimpanzees not only stand out against the rest of the animal world by several morphological and, in its narrower sense, physiological, characteristics, but they also behave in a way which counts as specifically human. As yet we know little of their neighbours on the other side, but according to the little we do know, with the results of this report, it is not impossible that, in this region of experimental research, the anthropoid is nearer to man *in intelligence too,* than to many of the lower ape-species. So far, observations agree well with the theories of evolution; in particular, the correlation between intelligence, and the development of the brain, is confirmed.

In the field of the experiments carried out here the insight of the chimpanzee shows itself to be principally determined by his optical apprehension of the situation; at times he even starts solving problems from a too visual point of view, and in many cases in which the chimpanzee *stops* acting with insight, it may have been simply that the lie of the land was too much for his visual grasp (relative "weakness of shape perception"). It is therefore difficult to give a satisfactory explanation of all his performances, so long as no detailed theory of shape (*Gestalt*) has been laid as a foundation. The need for such a theory will be felt the more, when one remembers that *solutions* showing insight in this field of intelligence necessarily take part in the nature of the structure of the situations, in so far as they arise in dynamic processes *co-ordinated with* the situation.

It would be less a boundary-line than a standard for the achievements of intelligence described here that would be arrived at by comparing with our experiments the performances of human beings (sick and well) and, above all, human children of different ages. As the results in this book have special reference to a particular method of testing and the special test-material of optically-given situations, it would be those psychological facts established in human begins (especially children), under the same conditions, which would have to be used. But such comparisons cannot be instituted, as, very much to the disadvantage of psychology, not even the most necessary of such facts have been ascertained. Preliminary experiments—some have been mentioned—have given me the impression that we are inclined to over-estimate the capabilities of children of all ages up to maturity, and even adults, who have had no special technical training in this type of performance. We are in a region of *terra incognita.* Educational psychology, engaged on the well-known quantitative tests for some time, has not yet been able to test how far normal, and how far mentally-deficient, children can go in certain situations. As experiments of this kind can be performed at the very tenderest age, and are certainly as scientifically valuable as the intelligence tests usually employed, it can be forgiven if they do not become immediately practicable for school and other uses. M. Wertheimer has been expressing this view for some years in his lectures; in this place, where the lack of them makes itself so much felt, I should like to emphasize particularly the importance and—if the anthropoids do not deceive us—the fruitfulness of further work in this direction.

Postscript.—At the conclusion of this book I received from Mr R. M. Yerkes (of Harvard University) his work entitled *The Mental Life of Monkeys and Apes: a Study in Ideational Behavior* (*Behavior Monographs,* III, i, 1916). In this book some experiments of the type I have described are recorded. The anthropoid tested is an orang-utan, not a chimpanzee, but, as far as one can judge from the material given, the results agree with mine. Mr Yerkes himself also thinks that intelligence must be attributed to the animal he tested.

C H A P T E R 13

PSYCHOANALYSIS: THE BEGINNINGS

SIGMUND FREUD (1856–1939)

Sigmund Freud was born May 6, 1856, in Freiburg, Moravia, in what was then part of the Austrian Empire (now part of the Czech Republic).[1] At the age of 4, the family moved to Vienna, where Freud lived until 1938, one year before his death. He was the first of six children born to Jacob Freud and his third wife, Amelia Nathanson. She was 20 years younger than Jacob, and by all reports, the young Amelia was beautiful, seductive, and doted on her firstborn son. His father was a marginally successful wool merchant and a stern taskmaster in the home. One can easily see how this family situation was consonant with Freud's later formulation of the Oedipal complex, that is, the belief that a young boy, between 3 and 5, wishes to kill his father and become his mother's lover.

Freud was of Jewish heritage and was well aware of the persecution of the Jews. His family was originally from Cologne but had moved because Jews were not welcome there. In Vienna, his family lived in the ghetto, where conditions were less than favorable. Considering this, it is not surprising that Freud felt society often thwarted the individual.

The young Freud, encouraged by his mother, was an outstanding scholar and graduated from the gymnasium summa cum laude. Besides German, Freud was proficient in French, English, Italian, Spanish, Hebrew, Latin, and Greek. Few occupations were open to young Jewish men during Freud's time. Disliking law, he felt that he entered medicine by default. He entered the University of Vienna in 1873

---

[1]There is a great deal of biographic material concerning Freud. The present material comes from Freud (1935), Jones (1953, 1955, 1957), and Ellenberger, (1970).

and graduated with his medical degree in 1881. While at the university, he was profoundly influenced by his professor of physiology, Ernst Brücke, and even worked in his laboratory.[2] Brücke believed that natural causes could explain all things and had his students sign a pact against vitalism, the belief that organic and inorganic matter are fundamentally different. Brücke's influence is evident in Freud's early theories, which are founded on basic principles of physics.

Freud wished to be a research neurologist and never intended to practice. Economic necessity, however, required him to open a practice in neurology in 1882. Fliess, his intimate friend and fellow physician, chastised Freud for entering clinical practice and leaving research. Freud replied that his patients would now be the source of his data (Rychlack, 1968). He had met the eminent neurologist Josef Breuer in Brücke's lab. Breuer took the beginning physician under his wing, and they consulted about many cases, especially those concerning conversion hysteria (disorder), a physiological manifestation, for instance, paralysis or blindness, with a psychogenic base.

A particularly famous case of conversion disorder was that of Bertha Papenheim, known as Anna O. As Hollender (1980) suggests, it was through the work with Anna O. that the idea of a talking cure was born. In essence, the idea is that through talking about repressed memories, often of traumatic events, the patient achieves catharsis and relief from his or her symptoms.[3] While working with another patient with conversion disorder, Fraulein Elizabeth, Freud made another of what is regarded as his great discoveries, free association. It had been his custom to ask many questions rapidly, but she assured him that if he would just listen, she would say what he wanted to hear. In 1895, Freud published with Breuer *Studies in Hysteria,* in which they chronicled the cases of Anna O and Fraulein Elizabeth among others; this is generally regarded as the beginning of psychoanalysis. In 1885, Freud traveled briefly to Paris and studied under the famous neurologist Charcot. Freud watched Charcot treat patients with conversion disorder and heard him exclaim that sexuality was often at the root of the problem. The first reading, two lectures delivered by Freud at Clark University, outlines the development of the fundamental tenets of psychoanalysis when he was in contact with Breuer and subsequently Charcot (Freud, 1910).

It was also during this period that Freud experimented with the analgesic properties of cocaine. His actual drug addiction, however, was with tobacco; he smoked an endless series of cigars, as many as 20 a day, despite the presence of tobacco angina and cancerous lesions of the palate due to smoking (Rodale, 1970).

The early part of the century was a time of significant productivity for Freud. In 1900, he published what many have regarded as his most significant book, *The Interpretation of Dreams.* In 1901, *The Psychopathology of Everyday Life* ap-

---

[2]While in medical school, he somewhat prophetically conducted research on the gonadal structure of eels.

[3]Although there is debate about the efficacy of the talking cure with Anna O (Freeman, 1972), the story has been repeated as gospel and thus has affected countless numbers of clinicians. However, as Hollender (1980) states, "Before the invention of the talking cure, Hypnosis was used mainly for suggestion and the physician was a doer. With the shift to catharsis, the physician became a listener. This step may seem trivial today, but in its time it was monumental."

peared, in which he described the famous "Freudian slips." The second reading is taken from this book and presents a case in which Freud helps a colleague through free association understand why he "forgot" a Latin word with disturbing implications. In 1905, he described the well-known psychosexual stages of development in *Three Essays on Sexuality*. In 1909, he traveled to Clark University in the United States and thus increased his international stature. Freud continued to study, write, and develop his theory for the rest of his life. His theory, therefore, was dynamic and changed as his thinking developed. In 1920, for example, affected by World War I, he wrote *Beyond the Pleasure Principle* and stated that a death wish was a fundamental human drive (Hall & Lindzey, 1998).[4] A mature expression of Freud's theory can be found in his (1933) *New Introductory Lectures on Psychoanalysis*.

Freud did not appreciate the threat that Hitler's Nazi regime posed to his life (Roazen, 1991). He stayed on at 19 Bergasse, where he had lived for 47 years, even though the Nazis banned his works and burned his books in public. Finally, in 1938, with the aid of several influential politicians, including President Roosevelt, he relocated to London at 20 Maresfield Gardens in the Hampstead Health quarter of London (Hoffman, 1988).[5] He died on September 23, 1939, at the age of 83.

REFERENCES

Ellenberger, H. F. (1970). *The discovery of the unconscious*. New York: Basic Books.

Breuer, J. & Freud, S. (1955). Studies in hysteria. In *Standard edition* (Vol. 2). London: Hogarth. (First German edition, 1895).

Freeman, L. (1972). *The story of Anna O*. New York: Walker.

Freud, S. (1953–1974). *The standard edition of the complete psychological works*. J. Strachey (Ed.) London: Hogarth.

Freud, S. (1953). The interpretation of dreams. In *Standard edition* (Vols. 4 and 5). London: Hogarth. (First German edition, 1900).

Freud, S. (1960). The psychopathology of everyday life. In *Standard edition* (Vol. 6). London: Hogarth. (First German edition, 1901).

Freud, S. (1953). Three essays on sexuality. In *Standard edition* (Vol. 7). London: Hogarth. (First German edition, 1905).

Freud, S. (1955). Beyond the pleasure principle. In *Standard edition* (Vol. 18). London: Hogarth. (First German edition, 1920).

Freud, S. (1964). New introductory lectures on psycho-

analysis. In *Standard Edition* (Vol. 22). London: Hogarth. (First German edition, 1933).

Freud, S. (1910). The origin and development of psychoanalysis. *The American Journal of Psychology, 21,* 181–218.

Freud, S. (1952). *Sigmund Freud: An autobiographical study*. New York: Norton (Originally published in 1935).

Hall, C. S., Lindzey, G., & Campbell (1998). *Theories of personality* (4th ed.). New York: Wiley.

Hoffmann, P. (1988, March 27). Freud's Vienna begins at Bergasse 19. *The New York Times*.

Hollender, M. H. (1980). The case of Anna O: A reformulation. *The American Journal of Psychiatry, 137,* 797–800.

Jones, E. (1953, 1955, 1957). *The life and work of Sigmund Freud* (3 vols.). New York: Basic Books.

Roazen, (P.) Psychoanalytic ethics: Edoardo Weiss, Freud, and Mussolini. *Journal of the History of the Behavioral Sciences, 27,* 366–374.

Rodale, J.I. (1970). *If you must smoke*. Emmaus, PA: Rodale Books.

Rychlack, J. F. (1968) *A philosophy of science for personality theory*. Boston: Houghton Mifflin.

---

[4]Freud has often been called an instinct theorist, and people have referred to a death instinct. This is due to a mistranslation of the German word *trieb*, which means "drive."

[5]This location houses an excellent museum, which includes his famous couch. There is also a museum at 19 Bergasse of Freud's belongings in Vienna.

The Origin and Development of Psychoanalysis[1]

By Prof. Sigmund Freud (Vienna)

FIRST LECTURE

Ladies and Gentlemen: It is a new and somewhat embarrassing experience for me to appear as lecturer before students of the New World. I assume that I owe this honor to the association of my name with the theme of psychoanalysis, and consequently it is of psychoanalysis that I shall aim to speak. I shall attempt to give you in very brief form an historical survey of the origin and further development of this new method of research and cure.

Granted that it is a merit to have created psychoanalysis, it is not my merit. I was a student, busy with the passing of my last examinations, when another physician of Vienna, Dr. Joseph Breuer,[2] made the first application of this method to the case of an hysterical girl (1880-82). We must now examine the history of this case and its treatment, which can be found in detail in "Studien über Hysterie," later published by Dr. Breuer and myself.[3]

But first one word. I have noticed, with considerable satisfaction, that the majority of my bearers do not belong to the medical profession. Now do not fear that a medical education is necessary to follow what I shall have to say. We shall now accompany the doctors a little way, but soon we shall take leave of them and follow Dr. Breuer on a way which is quite his own.

Dr. Breuer's patient was a girl of twenty-one, of a high degree of intelligence. She had developed in the course of her two years' illness a series of physical and mental disturbances which well deserved to be taken seriously. She had a severe paralysis of both right extremities, with anasthesia, and at times the same affection of the members of the left side of the body; disturbance of eye-movements, and much impairment of vision; difficulty in maintaining the position of the head, an intense *Tussis nervosa*, nausea when she attempted to take nourishment, and at one time for several weeks a loss of the power to drink, in spite of tormenting thirst. Her power of speech was also diminished, and this progressed so far that she could neither speak nor understand her mother tongue; and, finally, she was subject to states of "absence," of confusion, delirium, alteration of her whole personality. These states will later claim our attention.

---

[1]Lectures delivered at the Celebration of the Twentieth Anniversary of the opening of Clark University, Sept., 1909; translated from the German by Harry W. Chase, Fellow in Psychology, Clark University, and revised by Prof. Freud.

[2]Dr. Joseph Breuer, born 1842, corresponding member of the "Kaiserliche Akademie der Wissenschaften," is known by works on respiration and the physiology of the sense of equilibrium.

[3]"Studien über Hysterie," 1895, Deuticke, Vienus. Second edition, 1909. Parts of my contributions to this book have been translated into English by Dr. A. A. Brill, of New York. ("Selected Papers on Hysteria and other Psychoneuroses, by S. Freud.")

When one hears of such a case, one does not need to be a physician to incline to the opinion that we are concerned here with a serious injury, probably of the brain, for which there is little hope of cure and which will probably lead to the early death of the patient. The doctors will tell us, however, that in one type of cases with just as unfavorable symptoms, another, far more favorable, opinion is justified. When one finds such a series of symptoms in the case of a young girl, whose vital organs (heart, kidneys), are shown by objective tests to be normal, but who has suffered from strong emotional disturbances, and when the symptoms differ in certain finer characteristics from what one might locally expect, in a case like this the doctors are not too much disturbed. They consider that there is present no organic lesion of the brain, but that enigmatical state, known since the time of the Greek physicians as hysteria, which can simulate a whole series of symptoms of various diseases. They consider in such a case that the life of the patient is not in danger and that a restoration to health will probably come about of itself. The differentiation of such an hysteria from a severe organic lesion is not always very easy. But we do not need to know how a differential diagnosis of this kind is made; you may be sure that the case of Breuer's patient was such that no skillful physician could fail to diagnose au hysteria. We may also add a word here from the history of the case. The illness first appeared while the patient was caring for her father, whom she tenderly loved, during the severe illness which led to his death, a task which she was compelled to abandon because she herself fell ill.

So far it has seemed best to go with the doctors, but we shall soon part company with them. You must not think that the outlook of a patient with regard to medical aid is essentially bettered when the diagnosis points to hysteria rather than to organic disease of the brain. Against the serious brain diseases medical skill is in most cases powerless, but also in the case of hysterical affections the doctor can do nothing. He must leave it to benign nature, when and how this hopeful prognosis will be realized.[1] Accordingly, with the recognition of the disease as hysteria, little is changed in the situation of the patient, but there is a great change in the attitude of the doctor. We can observe that he acts quite differently toward hystericals than toward patients suffering from organic diseases. He will not bring the same interest to the former as to the latter, since their suffering is much less serious and yet seems to set up the claim to be valued just as seriously.

But there is another motive in this action. The physician, who through his studies has learned so much that is hidden from the laity, can realize in his thought the causes and alterations of the brain disorders in patients suffering from apoplexy or deimentia, a representation which must be right up to a certain point, for by it he is enabled to understand the nature of each symptom. But before the details of hysterical symptoms, all his knowledge, his anatomical-physiological and pathological education, desert him. He cannot understand hysteria. He is in the same position before it as the layman. And that is not agreeable to any one, who is in the habit

---

[1] I know that this view no longer holds to-day, but in the lecture I take myself and my hearers back to the time before 1880. If things have become different since that time it has been largely due to the work the history of which I am sketching.

of setting such a high valuation upon his knowledge. Hystericals, accordingly, tend to lose his sympathy; he considers them persons who overstep the laws of his science, as the orthodox regard heretics; he ascribes to them all possible evils, blames them for exaggeration and intentional deceit, "simulation," and he punishes them by withdrawing his interest.

Now Dr. Breuer did not deserve this reproach in this case; he gave his patient sympathy and interest, although at first he did not understand how to help her. Probably this was easier for him on account of those superior qualities of the patient's mind and character, to which he bears witness in his account of the case.

His sympathetic observation soon found the means which made the first help possible. It had been noticed that the patient, in her states of "absence," of psychic alteration, usually mumbled over several words to herself. These seemed to spring from associations with which her thoughts were busy. The doctor, who was able to get these words, put her in a sort of hypnosis and repeated them to her over and over, in order to bring up any associations that they might have. The patient yielded to his suggestion and reproduced for him those psychic creations which controlled her thoughts during her "absences," and which betrayed themselves in these single spoken words. These were fancies, deeply sad, often poetically beautiful, day dreams, we might call them, which commonly took as their starting point the situation of a girl beside the sick-bed of her father. Whenever she had related a number of such fancies, she was, as it were, freed and restored to her normal mental life. This state of health would last for several hours, and then give place on the next day to a new "absence," which was removed in the same way by relating the newly-created fancies. It was impossible not to get the impression that the psychic alteration which was expressed in the "absence" was a consequence of the excitations originating from these intensely emotional fancy-images. The patient herself, who at this time of her illness strangely enough understood and spoke only English, gave this new kind of treatment the name "talking cure," or jokingly designated it as "chimney sweeping."

The doctor soon hit upon the fact that through such cleansing of the soul more could be accomplished than a temporary removal of the constantly recurring mental "clouds." Symptoms of the disease would disappear when in hypnosis the patient could be made to remember the situation and the associative connections under which they first appeared, provided free vent was given to the emotions which they aroused. "There was in the summer a time of intense heat, and the patient had suffered very much from thirst; for, without any apparent reason, she had suddenly become unable to drink. She would take a glass of water in her hand, but as soon as it touched her lips she would push it away as though suffering from hydrophobia. Obviously for these few seconds she was in her absent state. She ate only fruit, melons and the like, in order to relieve this tormenting thirst. When this had been going on about six weeks, she was talking one day in hypnosis about her English governess, whom she disliked, and finally told, with every sign of disgust, how she had come into the room of the governess, and how that lady's little dog, that she abhorred, had drunk out of a glass. Out of respect for the conventions the patient had remained silent. Now, after she had given energetic expression to her restrained anger, she asked for a drink, drank a large quantity of water without trouble, and woke from hypnosis with the glass at her lips. The symptom thereupon vanished permanently."[1]

Permit me to dwell for a moment on this experience. No one had ever cured an hysterical symptom by such means before, or had come so near understanding its cause. This would be a pregnant discovery if the expectation could be confirmed that still other, perhaps the majority of symptoms, originated in this way and could be removed by the same method. Breuer spared no pains to convince himself of this and investigated the pathogenesis of the other more serious symptoms in a more orderly way. Such was indeed the case; almost all the symptoms originated in exactly this way, as remnants, as precipitates, if you like, of affectively-toned experiences, which for that reason we later called "psychic traumata." The nature of the symptoms became clear through their relation to the scene which caused them. They were, to use the technical term, "determined" (*determiniert*) by the scene whose memory traces they embodied, and so could no longer be described as arbitrary or enigmatical functions of the neurosis.

Only one variation from what might be expected must be mentioned. It was not always a single experience which occasioned the symptom, but usually several, perhaps many similar, repeated traumata co-operated in this effect. It was necessary to repeat the whole series of pathogenic memories in chronological sequence, and of course in reverse order, the last first and the first last. It was quite impossible to reach the first and often most essential trauma directly, without first clearing away those coming later.

You will of course want to hear me speak of other examples of the causation of hysterical symptoms beside this of inability to drink on account of the disgust caused by the dog drinking from the glass. I must, however, if I hold to my programme, limit myself to very few examples. Breuer relates, for instance, that his patient's visual disturbances could be traced back to external causes, in the following way. "The patient, with tears in her eyes, was sitting by the sick-bed when her father suddenly asked her what time it was. She could not see distinctly, strained her eyes to see, brought the watch near her eyes so that the dial seemed very large (macropia and strabismus conv.), or else she tried hard to suppress her tears, so that the sick man might not see them."[2]

All the pathogenic impressions sprang from the time when she shared in the care of her sick father. "Once she was watching at night in the greatest anxiety for the patient, who was in a high fever, and in suspense, for a surgeon was expected from Vienna, to operate on the patient. Her mother had gone out for a little while, and Anna sat by the sick-bed, her right arm hanging over the back of her chair. She fell into a revery and saw a black snake emerge, as it were, from the wall and approach the sick man as though to bite him. (It is very probable that several snakes had actually been seen in the meadow behind the house, that she had already been frightened by them, and that these former experiences furnished the material for the hallucination.) She tried to drive off the creature, but was as though paralyzed.

---

[1]"Studien über Hysterie," 2d edition, p. 26.

[2]"Studien über Hysterie," 2d edition, p. 31.

Her right arm which was hanging over the back of the chair, had "gone to sleep," become anasthetic and paretic, and as she was looking at it, the fingers changed into little snakes with deaths-heads. (The nails.) Probably she attempted to drive away the snake with her paralyzed right hand, and so the anasthesia and paralysis of this member formed associations with the snake hallucination. When this had vanished, she tried in her anguish to speak, but could not. She could not express herself in any language, until finally she thought of the words of an English nursery song, and thereafter she could think and speak only in this language."[1] When the memory of this scene was revived in hypnosis the paralysis of the right arm, which had existed since the beginning of the illness, was cured and the treatment ended.

When, a number of years later, I began to use Breuer's researches and treatment on my own patients, may experiences completely coincided with his. In the case of a woman of about forty, there was a tic, a peculiar smacking noise which manifested itself whenever she was laboring under any excitement, without any obvious cause. It had its origin in two experiences which had this common element, that she attempted to make no noise, but that by a sort of counter-will this noise broke the stillness. On the first occasion, she had finally after much trouble put her sick child to sleep, and she tried to be very quiet so as not to awaken it. On the second occasion, during a ride with both her children in a thunderstorm the horses took fright, and she carefully avoided any noise for fear of frightening them still more.[2] I give this example instead of many others which are cited in the "Studien über Hysterie."

Ladies and gentlemen, if you will permit me to generalize, as is indispensable in so brief a presentation, we may express our results up to this point in the formula: *Our hysterical patients suffer from reminiscences.* Their symptoms are the remnants and the memory symbols of certain (traumatic) experiences.

A comparison with other memory symbols from other sources will perhaps enable us better to understand this symbolism. The memorials and monuments with which we adorn our great cities, are also such memory symbols. If you walk through London you will find before one of the greatest railway stations of the city a richly decorated Gothic pillar—"Charing Cross." One of the old Plantagenet kings, in the thirteenth century, caused the body of his beloved queen Eleanor to be borne to Westminster, and had Gothic crosses erected at each of the stations where the coffin was set down. Charing Cross is the last of these monuments, which preserve the memory of this sad journey.[3] In another part of the city, you will see a high pillar of more modern construction, which is merely called "the monument." This is in memory of the great fire which broke out in the neighborhood in the year 1666,

---

[1] "Studien über Hysterie," 2d edition, p. 30.

[2] *Loc cited* ed. pp. 43-46. A selection from this book, augmented by several later treatises on hysteria, lies before me, in an English translation by Dr. A. A. Brill, of New York. It bears the title "Selected Papers on Hysteria and other Psychoneuroses," 1909. [No. 4 of the Nervous and Mental Disease Monograph Series, New York.]

[3] Or rather the later copy of such a monument. The name "Charing" is itself, as Dr. E. Jones tells me, derived from the words *chére reine."*

and destroyed a great part of the city. These monuments are memory symbols like the hysterical symptoms; so far the comparison seems justified. But what would you say to a Londoner who to-day stood sadly before the monument to the funeral of Queen Eleanor, instead of going about his business with the haste engendered by modern industrial conditions, or rejoicing with the young queen of his own heart? Or to another, who before the "Monument" bemoaned the burning of his loved native city, which long since has arisen again so much more splendid than before?

Now hystericals and all neurotics behave like these two unpractical Londoners, not only in that they remember the painful experiences of the distant past, but because they are still strongly affected by them. They cannot escape from the past and neglect present reality in its favor. This fixation of the mental life on the pathogenic traumata is an essential, and practically a most significant characteristic of the neurosis. I will willingly concede the objection which you are probably formulating, as you think over the history of Breuer's patient. All her traumata originated at the time when she was caring for her sick father, and her symptoms could only be regarded as memory symbols of his sickness and death. They corresponded to mourning, and a fixation on thoughts of the dead so short a time after death is certainly not pathological, but rather corresponds to normal emotional behavior. I concede this: there is nothing abnormal in the fixation of feeling on the trauma shown by Breuer's patient. But in other cases, like that of the tic that I have mentioned, the occasions for which lay ten and fifteen years back, the characteristic of this abnormal clinging to the past is very clear, and Breuer's patient would probably have developed it, if she had not come under the "cathartic treatment" such a short time after the traumatic experiences and the beginning of the disease.

We have so far only explained the relation of the hysterical symptoms to the life history of the patient; now by considering two further moments which Breuer observed, we may get a hint as to the processes of the beginning of the illness and those of the cure. With regard to the first, it is especially to be noted that Breuer's patient in almost all pathogenic situations had to suppress a strong excitement, instead of giving vent to it by appropriate words and deeds. In the little experience with her governess' dog, she suppressed, through regard for the conventions, all manifestations of her very intense disgust. While she was seated by her father's sick bed, she was careful to betray nothing of her anxiety and her painful depression to the patient. When, later, she reproduced the same scene before the physician, the emotion which she had suppressed on the occurrence of the scene burst out with especial strength, as though it had been pent up all along. The symptom which had been caused by that scene reached its greatest intensity while the doctor was striving to revive the memory of the scene, and vanished after it had been fully laid bare. On the other hand, experience shows that if the patient is reproducing the traumatic scene to the physician, the process has no curative effect if, by some peculiar chance, there is no development of emotion. It is apparently these emotional processes upon which the illness of the patient and the restoration to health are dependent. We feel justified in regarding "emotion" as a quantity which may become increased, derived and displaced. So we are forced to the conclusion that the patient fell ill because the emotion developed in the pathogenic situation was prevented from escaping normally, and that the essence of the sickness lies in the fact that these "imprisoned" (*eingeklemmt*) emotions undergo a series of abnormal changes. In part they are preserved as a lasting charge and as a source of constant disturbance in psychical life; in part they undergo a change into unusual bodily innervations and inhibitions, which present themselves as the physical symptoms of the case. We have coined the name "hysterical conversion" for the latter process. Part of our mental energy is, under normal conditions, conducted off by way of physical innervation and gives what we call "the expression of emotions." Hysterical conversion exaggerates this part of the course of a mental process which is emotionally colored; it corresponds to a far more intense emotional expression, which finds outlet by new paths. If a stream flows in two channels, an overflow of one will take place as soon as the current in the other meets with an obstacle.

You see that we are in a fair way to arrive at a purely psychological theory of hysteria, in which we assign the first rank to the affective processes. A second observation of Breuer compels us to ascribe to the altered condition of consciousness a great part in determining the characteristics of the disease. His patient showed many sorts of mental states, conditions of "absence," confusion and alteration of character, besides her normal state. In her normal state she was entirely ignorant of the pathogenic scenes and of their connection with her symptoms. She had forgotten those scenes, or at any rate had dissociated them from their pathogenic connection. When the patient was hypnotized, it was possible, after considerable difficulty, to recall those scenes to her memory, and by this means of recall the symptoms were removed. It would have been extremely perplexing to know how to interpret this fact, if hypnotic practice and experiments had not pointed out the way. Through the study of hypnotic phenomena, the conception, strange though it was at first, has become familiar, that in one and the same individual several mental groupings are possible, which may remain relatively independent of each other, "know nothing" of each other, and which may cause a splitting of consciousness along lines which they lay down. Cases of such a sort, known as "double personality" ("*double conscience*"), occasionally appear spontaneously. If in such a division of personality consciousness remains constantly bound up with one of the two states, this is called the *conscious* mental state, and the other the *unconscious*. In the well-known phenomena of so-called post hypnotic suggestion, in which a command given in hypnosis is later executed in the normal state as though by an imperative suggestion, we have an excellent basis for understanding how the unconscious state can influence the conscious, although the latter is ignorant of the existence of the former. In the same way it is quite possible to explain the facts in hysterical cases. Breuer came to the conclusion that the hysterical symptoms originated in such peculiar mental states, which he called "hypnoidal states." (*hypnoide Zustände.*) Experiences of an emotional nature, which occur during such hypnoidal states easily become pathogenic, since such states do not present the conditions for a normal draining off of the emotion of the exciting processes. And as a result there arises a peculiar product of this exciting process, that is, the symptom, and this is projected like a foreign body into the normal state. The latter has, then, no conception of the significance of the hypnoidal pathogenic situation. Where a symptom arises, we also find an amnesia, a memory gap, and the filling of this gap includes the removal of the conditions under which the symptom originated.

I am afraid that this portion of my treatment will not seem very clear, but you must remember that we are dealing here with new and difficult views, which perhaps could not be made much clearer. This all goes to show that our knowledge in this field is not yet very far advanced. Breuer's idea of the hypnoidal states has, moreover, been shown to be superfluous and a hindrance to further investigation, and has been dropped from present conceptions of psychoanalysis. Later I shall at least suggest what other influences and processes have been disclosed besides that of the hypnoidal states, to which Breuer limited the causal moment.

You have probably also felt, and rightly, that Breuer's investigations gave you only a very incomplete theory and insufficient explanation of the phenomena which we have observed. But complete theories do not fall from Heaven, and you would have had still greater reason to be distrustful, had any one offered you at the beginning of his observations a well-rounded theory, without any gaps; such a theory could only be the child of his speculations and not the fruit of an unprejudiced investigation of the facts.

SECOND LECTURE

Ladies and Gentlemen: At about the same time that Breuer was using the "talking-cure" with his patient, M. Charcot began in Paris, with the hystericals of the Salpetrière, those researches which were to lead to a new understanding of the disease. These results were, however, not yet known in Vienna. But when about ten years later Breuer and I published our preliminary communication on the psychic mechanism of hysterical phenomena, which grew out of the cathartic treatment of Breuer's first patient, we were both of us under the spell of Charcot's investigations. We made the pathogenic experiences of our patients, which acted as psychic traumata, equivalent to those physical traumata whose influence on hysterical paralyses Charcot had determined; and Breuer's hypothesis of hypnoidal states is itself only an echo of the fact that Charcot had artificially reproduced those traumatic paralyses in hypnosis.

The great French observer, whose student I was during the years 1885-86, had not natural bent for creating psychological theories. His student, P. Janet, was the first to attempt to penetrate more deeply into the psychic processes of hysteria, and we followed his example, when we made the mental splitting and the dissociation of personality the central points of our theory. Janet propounds a theory of hysteria which draws upon the principal theories of heredity and degeneration which are current in France. According to his view hysteria is a form of degenerative alteration of the nervous system, manifesting itself in a congenital "weakness" of the function of psychic synthesis. The hysterical patient is from the start incapable of correlating and unifying the manifold of his mental processes, and so there arises the tendency to mental dissociation. If you will permit me to use a banal but clear illustration, Janet's hysterical reminds one of a weak woman who has been shopping, and is now on her way home, laden with packages and bundles of every description. She cannot manage the whole lot with her two arms and her ten fingers, and soon she drops one. When she stoops to pick this up, another breaks loose, and so it goes on.

Now it does not agree very well with this assumed mental weakness of hystericals, that there can be observed in hysterical cases, besides the phenomena of lessened functioning, examples of a partial increase of functional capacity, as a sort of compensation. At the time when Breuer's patient had forgotten her mother-tongue and all other languages save English, her control of English attained such a level that if a German book was put before her she could give a fluent, perfect translation of its contents at sight. When later I undertook to continue on my own account the investigations begun by Breuer, I soon came to another view of the origin of hysterical dissociation (or splitting of consciousness). It was inevitable that my views should diverge widely and radically, for my point of departure was not, like that of Janet, laboratory researches, but attempts at therapy. Above everything else, it was practical needs that urged me on. The cathartic treatment, as Breuer had made use of it, presupposed that the patient should be put in deep hypnosis, for only in hypnosis was available the knowledge of his pathogenic associations, which were unknown to him in his normal state. Now hypnosis, as a fanciful, and so to speak, mystical, aid, I soon came to dislike; and when I discovered that, in spite of all my efforts, I could not hypnotize by any means all of my patients, I resolved to give up hypnotism and to make the cathartic method independent of it.

Since I could not alter the psychic state of most of my patients at my wish, I directed my efforts to working with them in their normal state. This seems at first sight to be a particularly senseless and aimless undertaking. The problem was this: to find out something from the patient that the doctor did not know and the patient himself did not know. How could one hope to make such a method succeed? The memory of a very noteworthy and instructive proceeding came to my aid, which I had seen in Bernheim's clinic at Nancy. Bernheim showed us that persons put in a condition of hypnotic somnambulism, and subjected to all sorts of experiences, had only apparently lost the memory of those somnambulic experiences, and that their memory of them could be awakened even in the normal state. If he asked them about their experiences during somnambulism, they said at first that they did not remember, but if he persisted, urged, assured them that they did know, then every time the forgotten memory came back.

Accordingly I did this with my patients. When I had reached in my procedure with them a point at which they declared that they knew nothing more, I would assure them that they did know, that they must just tell it out, and I would venture the assertion that the memory which would emerge at the moment that I laid my hand on the patient's forehead would be the right one. In this way I succeeded, without hypnosis, in learning from the patient all that was necessary for a construction of the connection between the forgotten pathogenic scenes and the symptoms which they had left behind. This was a troublesome and in its length an exhausting proceeding, and did not lend itself to a finished technique. But I did not give it up without drawing definite conclusions from the data which I had gained.

I had substantiated the fact that the forgotten memories were not lost. They were in the possession of the patient, ready to emerge and form associations with his other mental content, but hindered from becoming conscious, and forced to remain in the unconscious by some sort of a force. The existence of this force could be assumed with certainty, for in attempting to drag up the unconscious memories into the consciousness of the patient, in opposition to this force, one got the sensation of his own personal effort striving to overcome it. One could get an idea of this force, which maintained the pathological situation, from the resistance of the patient.

It is an idea of *resistance* that I based my theory of the psychic processes of hystericals. It had been found that in order to cure the patient it was necessary that this force should be overcome. Now with the mechanism of the cure as a starting point, quite a definite theory could be constructed. These same forces, which in the present situation as resistances opposed the emergence of the forgotten ideas into consciousness, must themselves have caused the forgetting, and repressed from consciousness the pathogenic experiences. I called this hypothetical process "repression" (*Verdrängung*), and considered that it was proved by the undeniable existence of resistance.

But now the question arose: what were those forces, and what were the conditions of this repression, in which we were now able to recognize the pathogenic mechanism of hysteria? A comparative study of the pathogenic situations, which the cathartic treatment has made possible, allows us to answer this question. In all those experiences, it had happened that a wish had been aroused, which was in sharp opposition to the other desires of the individual, and was not capable of being reconciled with the ethical, aesthetic and personal pretensions of the patient's personality. There had been a short conflict, and the end of this inner struggle was the repression of the idea which presented itself to consciousness as the bearer of this irreconcilable wish. This was, then, repressed from consciousness and forgotten. The incompatibility of the idea in question with the "ego" of the patient was the motive of the repression, the ethical and other pretensions of the individual were the repressing forces. The presence of the incompatible wish, or the duration of the conflict, had given rise to a high degree of mental pain; this pain; was avoided by the repression. This latter process is evidently in such a case a device for the protection of the personality.

I will not multiply examples, but will give you the history of a single one of my cases, in which the conditions and the utility of the repression process stand out clearly enough. Of course for my purpose I must abridge the history of the case and omit many valuable theoretical considerations. It is that of a young girl, who was deeply attached to her father, who had died a short time before, and in whose care she had shared—a situation analogous to that of Breuer's patient. When her older sister married, the girl grew to feel a peculiar sympathy for her new brother-in-law, which easily passed with her for family tenderness. This sister soon fell ill and died, while the patient and her mother were away. The absent ones were hastily recalled, without being told fully of the painful situation. As the girl stood by the bedside of her dead sister, for one short moment there surged up in her mind an idea, which might be framed in these words: "Now he is free and can marry me."

We may be sure that this idea, which betrayed to her consciousness her intense love for her brother-in-law, of which she had not been conscious, was the next moment consigned to repression by her revolted feelings. The girl fell ill with severe hysterical symptoms, and, when I came to treat the case, it appeared that she had entirely forgotten that scene at her sister's bedside and the unnatural, egoistic desire which had arisen in her. She remembered it during the treatment, reproduced the pathogenic moment with every sign of intense emotional excitement, and was cured by this treatment.[1]

Perhaps I can make the process of repression and its necessary relation to the resistance of the patient, more concrete by a rough illustration, which I will derive from our present situation.

Suppose that here in this hall and in this audience, whose examplary stillness and attention I cannot sufficiently commend, there is an individual who is creating a disturbance, and, by his ill-bred laughing, talking, by scraping his feet, distracts my attention from my task. I explain that I cannot go on with my lecture under these conditions, and thereupon several strong men among you get up, and, after a short struggle, eject the disturber of the peace from the hall. He is now "repressed," and I can continue my lecture. But in order that the disturbance may not be repeated, in case the man who has just been thrown out attempts to force his way back into the room, the gentlemen who have executed my suggestion take their chairs to the door and establish themselves there as a "resistance," to keep up the repression. Now, if you transfer both locations to the psyche, calling this "consciousness," and the outside the "unconscious," you have a tolerably good illustration of the process of repression.

We can see now the difference between our theory and that of Janet. We do not derive the psychic fission from a congenital lack of capacity on the part of the mental apparatus to synthesize its experiences, but we explain it dynamically by the conflict of opposing mental forces, we recognize in it the result of an active striving of each mental complex against the other.

New questions at once arise in great number from our theory. The situation of psychic conflict is a very frequent one; an attempt of the ego to defend itself from painful memories can be observed everywhere, and yet the result is not a mental fission. We cannot avoid the assumption that still other conditions are necessary, if the conflict is to result in dissociation. I willingly concerned that with the assumption of "repression" we stand, not at the end, but at the very beginning of a psychological theory. But we can advance only one step at a time, and the completion of our knowledge must await further and more thorough work.

Now do not attempt to bring the case of Breuer's patient under the point of view of repression. This history cannot be subjected to such an attempt, for it was gained with the help of hypnotic influence. Only when hypnosis is excluded can you see the resistances and repressions and get a correct idea of the pathogenic process. Hypnosis conceals the resistances and so makes a certain part of the mental field freely accessible. By this same process the resistances on the borders of this field are heaped up into a rampart, which makes all beyond inaccessible.

---

[1]This case has been translated by Dr. Brill in "Selected papers on hysteria," etc., p. 31-F4.

The most valuable things that we have learned from Breuer's observations were his conclusions as to the connection of the symptoms with the pathogenic experiences or psychic traumata, and we must not neglect to evaluate this result properly from the standpoint of the repression-theory. It is not at first evident how we can get from the repression to the creation of the symptoms. Instead of giving a complicated theoretical derivation, I will return at this point to the illustration which I used to typify repression.

Remember that with the ejection of the rowdy and the establishment of the watchers before the door, the affair is not necessarily ended. It may very well happen that the ejected man, now embittered and quite careless of consequences, gives us more to do. He is no longer among us, we are free from his presence, his scornful laugh, his half-audible remarks, but in a certain sense the repression has miscarried, for he makes a terrible uproar outside, and by his outcries and by hammering on the door with his fists interferes with my lecture more than before. Under these circumstances it would be hailed with delight if possibly our honored president, Dr. Stanley Hall, should take upon himself the role of peacemaker and mediator. He would speak with the rowdy on the outside, and then turn to us with the recommendation that we let him in again, provided he would guarantee to behave himself better. On Dr. Hall's authority we decide to stop the repression, and now quiet and peace reign again. This is in fact a fairly good presentation of the task devolving upon the physician in the psychoanalytic therapy of neuroses. To say the same thing more directly: we come to the conclusion, from working with hysterical patients and other neurotics, that they have not fully succeeded in repressing the idea to which the incompatible wish is attached. They have, indeed, driven it out of consciousness and out of memory, and apparently saved themselves a great amount of psychic pain, *but in the unconscious the suppressed wish still exists,* only waiting for its chance to become active, and finally succeeds in sending into consciousness, instead of the repressed idea, a disguised and unrecognizable surrogate-creation (*Ersatzbildung*), to which the same painful sensations associate themselves that the patient thought he was rid of through his repression. This surrogate of the suppressed idea—the symptom—is secure against further attacks from the defences of the ego, and instead of a short conflict there originates now a permanent suffering. We can observe in the symptom, besides the tokens of its disguise, a remnant of traceable similarity with the originally repressed idea; the way in which the surrogate is built up can be discovered during the psychoanalytic treatment of the patient, and for his cure the symptom must be traced back over the same route to the repressed idea. If this repressed material is once more made part of the conscious mental functions—a process which supposes the overcoming of considerable resistance—the psychic conflict which then arises, the same which the patient wished to avoid, is made capable of a happier termination, under the guidance of the physician, than is offered by repression. There are several possible suitable decisions which can bring conflict and neurosis to a happy end; in particular cases the attempt may be made to combine several of these. Either the personality of the patient may be convinced that he has been wrong in rejecting the pathogenic wish, and he may be made to accept it either wholly or in part; or this wish may itself by directed to a higher goal which is free from objection, by what is called sublimation (*Sublimierung*); or the rejection may be recognized as rightly motivated, and the automatic and therefore insufficient mechanism of repression by reinforced by the higher, more characteristically human mental faculties: one succeeds in mastering his wishes be conscious thought.

Forgive me if I have not been able to present more clearly these main points of the treatment which is to-day known as "psychoanalysis." The difficulties do not lie merely in the newness of the subject.

Regarding the nature of the unacceptable wishes, which succeed in making their influence felt out of the unconscious, in spite of repression; and regarding the question of what subjective and constitutional factors must be present for such a failure of repression and such a surrogate or symptom creation to take place, we will speak in later remarks.

2. Forgetting of Foreign Words

Sigmund Freud

The ordinary vocabulary of our own language seems to be protected against forgetting within the limits of normal function, but it is quite different with words from a foreign language. The tendency to forget such words extends to all parts of speech. In fact, depending on our own general state and the degree of fatigue, the first manifestation of functional disturbance evinces itself in the irregularity of our control over foreign vocabulary. In a series of cases, this forgetting follows the same mechanism as the one revealed in the example *Signorelli*. As a demonstration of this I shall report a single analysis, characterized, however, by valuable features, concerning the forgetting of a word, not a noun, from a Latin quotation. Before proceeding, allow me to give a full and clear account of this little episode.

Last summer, while journeying on my vacation, I renewed the acquaintance of a young man of academic education, who, as I soon noticed, was conversant with some of my works. In our conversation we drifted—I no longer remember how—to the social position of the race to which we both belonged. He, being ambitious, bemoaned the fact that his generation, as he expressed it, was destined to grow crippled, that it was prevented from developing its talents and from gratifying its desires. He concluded his passionately felt speech with the familiar verse from Virgil: *Exoriare . . .* in which the unhappy *Dido* leaves her vengeance upon *Aeneas* to posterity. Instead of "concluded," I should have said "wished to conclude," for he could not bring the quotation to an end, and attempted to conceal the open gap in his memory by transposing the words:

"*Exoriar(e) ex nostris ossibus ultor!*"

He finally became piqued and said: "Please don't make such a mocking face, as if you were gloating over my embarrassment, but help me. There is something missing in this verse. How does it read in its complete form?"

"With pleasure," I answered, and cited it correctly:

"Exoriare(e) aliquis nostris ex ossibus ultor!"

"It was too stupid to forget such a word," he said. "By the way, I understand you claim that forgetting is not without its reasons; I should be very curious to find out how I came to forget this indefinite pronoun *'aliquis.'*"

I gladly accepted the challenge, as I hoped to get an addition to my collection, and said, "We can easily do this, but I must ask you to tell me frankly and without any criticism everything that occurs to your mind after you focus your attention, without any particular intention, on the forgotten word."[1]

"Very well, the ridiculous idea comes to me to divide the word in the following way: *a* and *liquis.*"

"What does that mean?"

"I don't know."

"What else does that recall to you?"

"The thought goes on the *reliques—liquidation—liquidity—fluid.*"

"Does that mean anything to you now?"

"No, not by a long shot."

"Just go ahead."

"I now think," he said, laughing sarcastically, "of Simon of Trent, whose relics I saw two years ago in a church in Trent. I think of the old accusation which has been brought against the Jews again, and of the work of *Kleinpaul,* who sees in these supposed sacrifices reincarnations or revivals, so to speak, of the Saviour."

"This stream of thoughts has some connection with the theme which we discussed before the Latin word escaped you."

"You are right. I now think of an article in an Italian journal which I have recently read. I believe it was entitled: 'What St. Augustine said Concerning Women.' What can you do with this?"

I waited.

"Now I think of something which surely has no connection with the theme."

"Oh, please abstain from all criticism, and—"

"Oh, I know! I recall a handsome old gentlemen whom I met on my journey last week. He was really an *original* type. He looked like a big bird of prey. His name, if you care to know, is Benedict."

"Well, at least you give a grouping of saints and Church fathers: *St. Simon, St. Augustine,* and *St. Benedict.* I believe that there was a Church father named *Origines.* Three of these, moreover, are Christian names, like *Paul* in the name *Kleinpaul.*"

"Now I think of *St. Januarius* and his blood miracle—I find that the thoughts are running mechanically."

"Just stop a moment; both *St. Januarius* and *St. Augustine* have something to do with the calendar. Will you recall to me the blood miracle?"

---

[1] This is the usual way of bringing to consciousness hidden ideas. Cf. *The Interpretation of Dreams,* pp. 83-4, translated by A. A. Brill, the Macmillan Company, New York, and Allen & Unwin, London.

"Don't you know about it? The blood of St. Januarius is preserved in a phial in a church in Naples, and on a certain holiday a miracle takes place causing it to liquefy. The people think a great deal of this miracle, and become very excited if the liquifying process is retarded, as happened once during the French occupation. The General in command—or Garibaldi, if I am not mistaken—then took the priest aside, and with a very significant gesture pointed out to him the soldiers arrayed without, and expressed his hope that the miracle would soon take place. And it actually took place."

"Well, what else comes to your mind? Why do you hesitate?"

"Something really occurred to me . . . but it is too intimate a matter to impart . . . besides, I see no connection and no necessity for telling it."

"I will take care of the connection. Of course, I cannot compel you to reveal what is disagreeable to you, but then you should not have demanded that I tell you why you forgot the word *'aliquis.'*"

"Really? Do you think so? Well, I suddenly thought of a woman from whom I could easily get a message that would be very annoying to us both."

"That she missed her courses?"

"How could you guess such a thing?"

"That was not very difficult. You prepared me for it long enough. Just think of the *saints of the calendar, the liquefying of the blood on a certain day, the excitement if the event does not take place, and the distinct threat that the miracle must take place* . . . Indeed, you have elaborated the miracle of St. Januarius into a clever allusion to the courses of the woman."

"It was surely without my knowledge. And do you really believe that my inability to reproduce the word *'aliquis'* was due to this anxious expectation?"

"That appears to me absolutely certain. Don't you recall dividing it into *a-liquis* and the association: *reliques, liquidation, fluid?* Shall I also add to this connection the fact that St. Simon, to whom you got by way of the *reliques,* was sacrificed as a child?"

"Please stop, I hope you do not take these thoughts—if I really entertained them—seriously. I will, however, confess to you that the lady is Italian, and that I visited Naples in her company. But may not all this be coincidental?"

"I must leave to your own judgment whether you can explain all these connections through the assumption of coincidence. I will tell you, however, that every similar case that you analyze will lead you to just such remarkable 'coincidences.'"

I have more than one reason for valuing this little analysis, for which I am indebted to my traveling companion. First, because in this case I was able to make use of a source which is otherwise inaccesible to me. Most of the examples of psychic disturbances of daily life that have here complied I was obliged to take from observation of myself. I endeavored to evade the far richer material furnished me by my neurotic patients, because I had to preclude the objection that the phenomena in question were only the result and manifestation of the neurosis. It was therefore of special value for my purpose to have a stranger free from a neurosis offer himself as a subject for such examination. This analysis is also important in to her respects, inasmuch as it elucidates a case of word-forgetting *without* substitutive recollection, and thus confirms the principle formulated above, namely, that the appearance or nonappearance of incorrect substitutive recollections does not constitute an essential distinction.[1]

But the principal value of the example *aliquis* lies in another of its distinctions from the case *Signorelli*. In the latter example the reproduction of the name becomes disturbed through the after-effects of a stream of thought which began shortly before and was interrupted, but whose content had no distinct relation to the new theme which contained the name *Signorelli*. Between the repression and the theme of the forgotten name there existed only the relation of temporal contiguity, which reached the other in order that the two should be able to form a connection through an outer association.[2] On the other hand, in the example *aliquis* one can note no trace of such an independent repressed theme which could occupy conscious thought immediately before and then re-echo as a disturbance. The disturbance of the reproduction proceeded here from the inner part of the theme touched upon, and was brought about by the fact that unconsciously a contradiction arose against the wish-idea represented in the quotation.

The origin must be construed in the following manner: The speaker deplored the fact that the present generation of his people was being deprived of its rights, and like Dido he preseaged that a new generation would take upon itself vengeance against the oppressors. He therefore expressed the wish for posterity. In this moment he was interrupted by the contradictory thought: "Do you really wish so much for posterity? That is not true. Just think in what a predicament you would be if you should now receive the information that you must expect posterity from the quarter you have in mind. No, you want no posterity—as much as you need it for your vengeance." This contradiction asserts itself, just as in the example *Signorelli*, by forming an outer association between one of his ideation elements and an element of the repressed wish, but here it is brought about in a most strained

---

[1]Finer observations reduces somewhat the contrast between the analyses of *Signorelli* and *aliquis* as far as the substitutive recollections are concerned. Here, too, the forgetting seems to be accompanied by substitutive formations. When I later asked my companion whether in his effort to recall the forgotten word he did not think of some substitution, he informed me that he was at first tempted to put an *ab* into the verse: *nostris ab ossibus* (perhaps the disjointed part of *a-liquis*) and that later the word *exoriare* obstruded itself with particular distinctness and persistency. Being skeptical, he added that it was apparently due to the fact that it was the first word of the verse. But when I asked him to focus his attention on the association to *exoriare* he gave me the word *exorcism*. This makes me think that the reinforcement of *exoriare* in the reproduction has really the value of such substitution. It probably came through the association *exorcism* from the names of the saints. However, those are refinements upon which no value need be laid. It seems now quite possible that the appearance of any kind of substitutive recollection is a constant sign—perhaps only characteristic and misleading—of the purposive forgetting motivated by repression. This substitution might also exist in the reinforcement of an element akin to the thing forgotten, even where incorrect substitutive names fail to appear. Thus, in the example *Signorelli*, as long as that name of the painter remained inaccessible to me, I had more than a clear visual memory of the cycle of his frescoes, and of the picture of himself in the corner; at least it was more intensive than any of my other visual memory traces. In another case, also reported in my essay of 1898, I had hopelessly forgotten the street name and address connected with a disagreeable visit in a strange city, but—as if to mock me—the house number appeared especially vivid, whereas the memory of numbers usually causes me the greatest difficulty.

[2]I am not fully convinced of the lack of an inner connection between the two streams of thought in the case of *Signorelli*. In carefully following the repressed thought concerning the theme of death and sexual life, one does strike an idea which shows a near relation to the theme of the frescoes of *Orvieto*.

manner through what seems an artificial detour of associations. Another important agreement with the example *Signorelli* results from the fact that the contradiction originates from repressed sources of emanates from thoughts which would cause a deviation of attention.

So much for the diversity and the inner relationship of both paradigms of the forgetting of names. We have learned to know a second mechanism of forgetting, namely, the disturbance of thought through an inner contradiction emanating from the repression. In the course of this discussion we shall repeatedly meet with this process, which seems to me to be the more easily understood.

CHAPTER 14

PSYCHOANALYSIS: DISSENTERS AND DESCENDANTS

CARL JUNG (1875–1961)

Carl Jung was born in the Kesswill, a small Swiss village near the *Bodensee* (Lake Constance) in the canton of Thurgovia, on July 26, 1875.[1] He was born into a line of scholars; his maternal grandfather was a linguist while his paternal grandfather and namesake was a renowned physician and the rumored illegitimate son of the celebrated writer and intellectual Goethe.

Jung's father, a pastor, was also a scholar; yet, he was an unassuming kindly man who knew how to reach peasant parishioners in his sermons. In contrast, Jung and others described his mother as fat, ugly, and with an almost demonic personality. Jung, clearly, did not have the family background that would predispose him to accept Freud's Oedipal theory that every boy wished to kill his father and sexually possess his mother.

Jung's father fostered his intellectual development, teaching him Latin by the age of 6. This differentiated Jung from others since his schoolmates were mostly of the peasant class. This psychological isolation, plus the contemplative nature of the parsonage may have fueled Jung's lifelong interest in self-reflection.

The youthful Jung was a good student, excelling in language but struggling in mathematics. After passing the examination to graduate from the gymnasium, he

---

[1]This section is based on Brome (1978), Cohen (1975), Ellenberger (1970), Jung (1961), Watson and Evans (1991), and Wehr (1987).

entered the University of Basel and began the study of medicine. He had, initially, wished to study archeology, but they did not offer this at the university.[2] He saw medicine as a way of combining his scientific and humanistic interests. At this point, Jung had already begun to study spiritualism, thus showing an interest in the mystical, a concern that would characterize his brand of psychology. Toward the end of medical school, he became interested in psychiatry, a specialty that allowed him to more deeply pursue his interest in the union of the scientific and spiritual.

Upon graduation from medical school, Jung went to the Burghölzli, where he would stay for the next nine years, except for a one-year hiatus in 1902–1903, to study under Janet in Paris.[3] The Burghölzli was under the direction of Eugene Blueler, an eminent specialist in schizophrenia. There, Jung (1906) empirically studied word association and psychological diagnosis, and wrote a book about schizophrenia (1907).

Blueler had alerted Freud to Jung and his work, so when, in 1906, Jung sent Freud his results on free association, Freud was predisposed to receive it well. This started an intense but brief correspondence and friendship. Freud and Jung exchanged more than 350 known letters and their first fact-to-face meeting lasted 13 hours! Initially, Freud held Jung in high esteem and regarded him as the heir apparent to the psychoanalytic throne. However, Jung's independence and Freud's insistence on orthodoxy foreordained that the relationship would be short-lived. In a book, *On the Psychology of the Unconscious*, (1912a), and in a series of lectures at Fordham University, Jung (1912b) stated that the libido was life energy, not just sexual energy.[4] This and other events led to the demise of their friendship and ultimately to the end of their professional association. In his last letter, dated January 6, 1913, Jung simply stated, "I accede to your wish that we abandon, personal relations, for I never thrust my friendship on anyone" (McGuire, 1974, p. 540).

After this, Jung entered a phase known as his creative illness that lasted from 1913 to 1919. Having left the Burghölzli in 1909, Jung worked primarily out of his home near Zurich in the village of Kusnacht. He spent a great deal of time by himself looking within and found what he had observed in his schizophrenic patients, memories of a mythical and universal nature. An idea such as God or the Devil, he said, was part of the common stock of the collective human experience. After emerging from this experience, he supported his idea by traveling to developing lands and studying their myths, legends, and art. Wherever he traveled, he found common threads, and he concluded that all humans share a collective unconscious. In short, he felt that, "Our mind has its history just as our body has its history" (Jung, 1935, p. 41). These ideas appeared in perhaps his most famous work, *Psychological Types* (1921). In this book, he describes a myriad of archetypical (universal) memories as well as the extroverted and introverted attitude. In this rich volume, he also outlines the functions upon which the Myers–Briggs Type

---

[2]His interest in archeology presaged his later psychology, in which he stated that the human mind carried buried archaic treasure, that is, the archetypes.

[3]Ellenberger (1970) says that he studied more of Paris than of the psychology of Janet.

[4]Freud, eventually embraced this idea.

Inventory is based. The first selection for this chapter is taken from the most concise explication of Jungian theory, *The Tavistock Lectures,* in which he describes the functions of consciousness and the idea of archetypical memories.

Already famous, from this time on, Jung's fame grew almost exponentially, and he was consistently honored with university titles and state honors. Becoming increasingly mystical, he worked and wrote consistently until his death in 1961. He was known as "the wise old man from Kusnacht." He had become a balanced version of the learned Dr. Faustus, the literary creation of his alleged great-grandfather, Goethe.

ALFRED ADLER (1870–1937)

Alfred Adler was born February 7, 1870, in Rudolfsheim, a small village near Vienna and the Hungarian border.[5] When he was 7 his family moved to Vienna, where he spent most of his adult life.

Adler, the second born of seven children, felt that he was his father's favorite. His mother was nervous and gloomy by nature and he considered her an opponent. As with Jung, Adler's rejection of Freud's Oedipal theory in later life was congruent with his family situation. Adler felt competitive toward his older brother, and felt that he was in a contest with him that he could not win.[6] In later life as a professional psychologist, Adler emphasized the importance of birth order and the struggle for power within the family.

Adler was an average student in school, and some even despaired of his eventual success, recommending to his father that he might be a successful shoemaker's assistant. He did well enough, nevertheless, to be admitted to medical school, a field of study he claimed to have entered because of a near brush with death and the death of a younger brother when he was a child. Graduating from medical school in 1885, the place he chose to perfect his medical skills foreshadowed the nature of Adler's practice and theory, the Vienna *Poliklinik,* a benevolent institution that provided medical care to the indigent—a fitting choice for a psychiatrist who would eventually say that community feeling is the essence of mental health.

In 1897, he married Raissa Epstein, a Russian Communist and feminist. Although he was sympathetic to both causes, he disavowed the violent nature of the Bolshevik revolution and found "fighting for the emancipation of women and living with a woman who has emancipated herself are two wholly different things" (Bottome, 1957, p. 34). Yet, it is strife with his liberated wife that helped him develop the concept of masculine protest, the mistaken belief that masculinity and superiority are synonymous. This he said was due to cultural bias.[7]

---

[5]This section is based on Bottome (1957), Ellenberger (1970), and Hoffman (1994).

[6]Ironically, Adler's older brother was named Sigmund!

[7]An extensive compilation of Adler's views on this and related issues is available in *Cooperation Between the Sexes,* edited by the Ansbachers in 1978.

In 1902, at Freud's request, Adler became a member of his inner circle and eventually the president of the Vienna Psychoanalytic Society. Recently, Ansbacher (1997) has suggested that Adler learned the fundamentals of psychotherapy from Freud. There were, however, many theoretical differences between the men; eventually, the strain became too intense, and Adler left Freud's circle with a coterie of followers to pursue his ideas. They dubbed his approach individual psychology since it emphasized the uniqueness and unity of each person.

Adler, as did many physicians of his day, served in World War I. Impressed by the tremendous devastation of the war, Adler was even more convinced that the world needed his message of social interest, and postwar Vienna gave him the opportunity to promulgate his ideas. For example, with the encouragement of the minister of education, Adler volunteered to help teachers with problem children and thus was an early practitioner of primary prevention. He also encouraged the democratization of the educational process and developed the idea of a school council.

Adler brought his message to the new world in 1926. Charming and at ease in a crowd, his lectures were well received. Hoffman (1994) reports that *The New York Herald* stated Adler was "the most accurate and original foreign psychologist now in America." The question naturally arises as to why Adler's work rests in relative obscurity today. Simply put, Adler did not leave behind a viable written heritage since he relied on hastily ghostwritten transformations of his public lectures. Heinz and Rowena Ansbacher, former pupils of Adler, however have edited and systematized his widely spread writings. It is from their work, Adler (1956), that the second selection for this chapter is drawn. In this selection, Adler emphasizes three points that have become touchstones of humanistic psychology: (1) the prime human motive is a striving for completion or actualization; (2) individuals act in the world from unique cognitive schemas; and (3) healthy individuals behave with a positive, empathic regard for others, that is, social interest.[8]

Adler returned to Austria in 1927, but the worsening political climate was not receptive to either Adler, a Jew by birth, or his message.[9] So, in 1930, Adler established permanent residence in New York and took a position as an adjunct professor at Columbia University. He continued to spread the message of individual psychology on lecture tours; it was on such a tour that he died of heart failure in Aberdeen, Scotland, on May 28, 1937.

REFERENCES

Adler, A. (1978). *Cooperation between the sexes*. H. L. & R. R. Ansbacher (Eds.) Garden City, NY: Anchor.

Adler, A. (1956). *The individual psychology of Alfred*

Adler. H. L. & R. R. Ansbacher (Eds.). New York: Basic Books.

Ansbacher, H. L. (1997, May). Concerning the relationship

---

[8]Maslow (1970) adopted Adler's term *gemeinschaftsgefühl*, for describing one of the characteristics of a self-actualized individual.

[9]The Nazi party eventually dismantled the experimental schools he had established in Vienna.

between Freud and Adler. Paper presented at the North American Society for Adlerian Psychology, Vancouver, BC.

Bottome, P. (1957). *Alfred Adler: A portrait from life* (Rev. ed.). New York: Vanguard.

Brome, V. (1978). *Jung.* New York: Atheneum.

Cohen, E. D. (1975). *C. G. Jung and the scientific attitude.* New York: Philosophical Library.

Ellenberger, H. F. (1970). *The discovery of the unconscious.* New York: Basic Books.

Hoffman, E. (1994). *The drive for self.* Reading, MA: Addison Wesley.

Jung, C. G. (1973). Studies in word association. In *Collected works* (Vol. 2). Princeton: Princeton University Press. (Originally published in 1906).

Jung, C. G. (1960). The psychology of dementia praecox. In *Collected works* (Vol. 3). Princeton: Princeton University Press. (Originally published in 1907).

Jung, C. G. (1953). On the psychology of the unconscious. In *Collected works* (Vol. 7). Princeton: Princeton University Press. (Originally published as an article in 1912a).

Jung, C. G. (1961). The theory of psychoanalysis. In *Collected works* (Vol. 4). Princeton: Princeton University Press. (Originally published in 1912b).

Jung, C. G. (1971). Psychological types. In *Collected works* (Vol. 6). Princeton: Princeton University Press. (Originally published 1921).

Jung, C. G. (1950). The Tavistock lectures. In *Collected works* (Vol. 20). Princeton: Princeton University Press. (Originally published in 1935).

Jung, C. G. (1961). *Memories dreams and reflections.* New York: Random House.

McGuire, W. (Ed.) (1974). *The Freud Jung letters.* Princeton: Princeton University Press.

Watson, R. I. & Evans. R. B. (1991). *The great psychologists* (5th ed). New York: Harper Collins.

Wehr, G. (1987). *Jung: A biography.* Boston: Shambhala.

The Tavistock Lectures

C. G. Jung

LECTURE ONE: THE OUTSIDE WORLD AND FOUR WAYS OF KNOWING IT

Psychology is a science of consciousness, in the very first place. In the second place, it is the science of the products of what we call the unconscious psyche. We cannot directly explore the unconscious psyche because the unconscious is just unconscious, and we have therefore no relation to it. We can only deal with the conscious products which we suppose have originated in the field called the unconscious, that field of 'dim representations' which the philosopher Kant in his *Anthropology*[1] speaks of as being half a world. Whatever we have to say about the unconscious is what the conscious mind says about it. Always the unconscious psyche, which is entirely of an unknown nature, is expressed by consciousness and in terms of consciousness, and that is the only thing we can do. We cannot go beyond that, and we should always keep it in mind as an ultimate critique of our judgment.

Consciousness is a peculiar thing. It is an intermittent phenomenon. One-fifth, or one-third, or perhaps even one-half of our human life is spent in an unconscious condition. Our early childhood is unconscious. Every night we sink into the un-

---

[1] [*Anthropologie in pragmatischer Hinsicht* (1798), Pt. I, Bk. I, sec. 5.]

conscious, and only in phases between waking and sleeping have we a more or less clear consciousness. To a certain extent it is even questionable how clear that consciousness is. For instance, we assume that a boy or girl ten years of age would be conscious, but one could easily prove that it is a very peculiar kind of consciousness, for it might be a consciousness without any consciousness of the *ego*. I know a number of cases of children eleven, twelve, and fourteen years of age, or even older, suddenly realizing 'I am'. For the first time in their lives they know that they themselves are experiencing, that they are looking back over a past in which they can remember things happening but cannot remember that they were in them.

We must admit that when we say 'I' we have no absolute criterion whether we have a full experience of 'I' or not. It might be that our realization of the ego is still fragmentary and that in some future time people will know very much more about what the ego means to man than we do. As a matter of fact, we cannot see where the process might ultimately end.

Consciousness is like a surface or a skin upon a vast unconscious area of unknown extent. We do not know how far the unconscious rules because we simply know nothing of it. You cannot say anything about a thing of which you know nothing. When we say 'the unconscious' we often mean to convey something by the term, but as a matter of fact we simply convey that we do not know what the unconscious is. We have only indirect proofs that there is a mental sphere which is subliminal. We have some scientific justification for our conclusion that it exists. From the products which that unconscious mind produces we can draw certain conclusions as to its possible nature. But we must be careful not to be too anthropomorphic in our conclusions, because things might in reality be very different from what our consciousness makes them.

If, for instance, you look at our physical world and if you compare what our consciousness makes of this same world, you find all sorts of mental pictures which do not exist as objective facts. For instance, we see colour and hear sound, but in reality they are oscillations. As a matter of fact, we need a laboratory with very complicated apparatus in order to establish a picture of that world apart from our senses and apart from our psyche; and I suppose it is very much the same with our unconscious—we ought to have a laboratory in which we could establish by objective methods how things really are when in an unconscious condition. So any conclusion or any statement I make in the course of my lectures about the unconscious should be taken with that critique in mind. It is always *as if*, and you should never forget that restriction.

The conscious mind moreover is characterized by a certain narrowness. It can hold only a few simultaneous contents at a given moment. All the rest is unconscious at the time, and we only get a sort of continuation or a general understanding or awareness of a conscious world through the *succession* of conscious moments. We can never hold an image of totality because our consciousness is too narrow; we can only see flashes of existence. It is always as if we were observing through a slit so that we only see a particular moment; all the rest is dark and we are not aware of it at that moment. The area of the unconscious is enormous and always continuous, while the area of consciousness is a restricted field of momentary vision.

You can distinguish a number of functions in consciousness. They enable consciousness to become oriented in the field of ectopsychic facts and endopsychic facts.

What I understand by the *ectopsyche* is a system of relationship between the contents of consciousness and facts and data coming in from the environment. It is a system of orientation which concerns my dealing with the external facts given to me by the function of my senses. The *endopsyche,* on the other hand, is a system of relationship between the contents of consciousness and postulated processes in the unconscious.

In the first place we will speak of the ectopsychic functions. First of all we have *sensation,*[1] our sense function. By sensation I understand what the French psychologists call 'la fonction du réel', which is the sum-total of my awareness of external facts given to me through the function of my senses. So I think that the French term 'la fonction du réel' explains it in the most comprehensive way. Sensation tells me that something *is:* it does not tell me *what* it is and it does not tell me other things about that something; it only tells me that something is.

The next function that is distinguishable is *thinking.*[2] Thinking, if you ask a philosopher, is something very difficult, so never ask a philosopher about it because he is the only man who does not know what thinking is. Everybody else knows what thinking is. When you say to a man, 'Now think properly', he knows exactly what you mean, but a philosopher never knows. Thinking in its simplest form tells you *what* a thing is. It gives a name to the thing. It adds a concept because thinking is perception and judgment. (German psychology calls it apperception.)[3]

The third function you can distinguish and for which ordinary language has a term is *feeling.*[4] Here minds become very confused and people get angry when I speak about feeling, because according to their view I say something very dreadful about it. Feeling informs you through its feeling-tones of the *values* of things. Feeling tells you for instance whether a thing is acceptable or agreeable or not. It tells you what a thing is *worth* to you. On account of that phenomenon, you cannot perceive and you cannot apperceive without having a certain feeling reaction. You always have a certain feeling-tone, which you can even demonstrate by experiment. We will talk of these things later on. Now the 'dreadful' thing about feeling is that it is, like thinking, a *rational*[5] function. All men who think are absolutely convinced that feeling is never a rational function but, on the contrary, most irrational. Now I say: Just be patient for a while and realize that man cannot be perfect in every respect. If a man is perfect in his thinking he is surely never perfect in his feeling, because you cannot do the two things at the same time; they hinder each other. Therefore when you want to think in a dispassionate way, really scientifically or philosophically, you must get away from all feeling-values. You cannot be bothered with feeling-values at the same time, otherwise you begin to feel that it is far more important to think about the freedom of the will than, for instance, about the classification of lice. And certainly if you approach from the point of view of feeling the two objects are not only different as to *facts* but also as to *value.*

---

[1] [*Psychological Types* (C. W., vol. 6), Definition 47.]

[2] [Ibid., Def. 53.]

[3] [Ibid., Def. 5.]

[4] [Ibid., Def. 21 (1923 edn., Def. 20).]

[5] [Ibid., Def. 44.]

Values are no anchors for the intellect, but they exist and giving value is an important psychological function. If you want to have a complete picture of the world you must necessarily consider values. If you do not, you will get into trouble. To many people feeling appears to be most irrational, because you feel all sorts of things in foolish moods: therefore everybody is convinced, in this country particularly, that you should control your feelings. I quite admit that this is a good habit and wholly admire the English for that faculty. Yet there are such things as feelings, and I have seen people who control their feelings marvellously well and yet are terribly bothered by them.

Now the fourth function. Sensation tells us that a thing *is*. Thinking tells us *what* that thing is, feeling tells us what it is *worth* to us. Now what else could there be? One would assume one has a complete picture of the world when one knows there *is* something, *what* it is, and what it is *worth*. But there is another category, and that is time. Things have a past and they have a future. They come from somewhere, they go to somewhere, and you cannot see where they came from and you cannot know where they go to, but you get what the Americans call a hunch. For instance, if you are a dealer in art or in old furniture you get a hunch that a certain object is by a very good master of 1720, you get a hunch that it is good work. Or you do not know what shares will do after a while, but you get the hunch that they will rise. That is what is called *intuition*,[1] a sort of divination, a sort of miraculous faculty. For instance, you do not know that your patient has something on his mind of a very painful kind, but you 'get an idea', you 'have a certain feeling', as we say, because ordinary language is not yet developed enough for one to have suitably defined terms. But the word intuition becomes more and more a part of the English language, and you are very fortunate because in other languages that word does not exist. The Germans cannot even make a linguistic distinction between sensation and feeling. It is different in French; if you speak French you cannot possibly say that you have a certain 'sentiment dans l'estomac', you will say 'sensation'; in English you also have your distinctive words for sensation and feeling. But you can mix up *feeling* and *intuition* easily. Therefore it is an almost artificial distinction I make here, though for practical reasons it is most important that we make such a differentiation in scientific language. We must define what we mean when we use certain terms, otherwise we talk an unintelligible language, and in psychology this is always a misfortune. In ordinary conversation, when a man says feeling, he means possibly something entirely different from another fellow who also talks about feeling. There are any number of psychologists who use the word *feeling,* and they define it as a sort of crippled thought. 'Feeling is nothing but an unfinished thought'—that is the definition of a well-known psychologist. But feeling is something genuine, it is something real, it is a function, and therefore we have a word for it. The instinctive natural mind always finds the words that designate things which really have existence. Only psychologists invent words for things that do not exist.

The last-defined function, intuition, seems to be very mysterious, and you know I am 'very mystical,' as people say. This then is one of my pieces of mysticism! In-

---

[1][Ibid., Def. 35.]

tuition is a function by which you see round corners, which you really cannot do; yet the fellow will do it for you and you trust him. It is a function which normally you do not use if you live a regular life within four walls and do regular routine work. But if you are on the Stock Exchange or in Central Africa, you will use you hunches like anything. You cannot, for instance, calculate whether when you turn round a corner in the bush you will meet a rhinoceros or a tiger—but you get a hunch, and it will perhaps save your life. So you see that people who live exposed to natural conditions use intuition a great deal, and people who risk something in an unknown field, who are pioneers of some sort, will use intuition. Inventors will use it and judges will use it. Whenever you have to deal with strange conditions where you have no established values or established concepts, you will depend upon that faculty of intuition.

I have tried to describe that function as well as I can, but perhaps it is not very good. I say that intuition is a sort of perception which does not go exactly by the senses, but it goes via the unconscious, and at that I leave it and say 'I don't know how it works'. I do not know what is happening when a man knows something he definitely should not know. I do not know how he has come by it, but he has it all right and he can act on it. For instance, anticipatory dreams, telepathic phenomena, and all that kind of thing are intuitions. I have seen plenty of them, and I am convinced that they do exist. You can see these things also with primitives. You can see them everywhere if you pay attention to these perceptions that somehow work through the subliminal data, such as sense-perceptions so feeble that our consciousness simply cannot take them in. Sometimes, for instance, in cryptomnesia, something creeps up into consciousness; you catch a word which gives you a suggestion, but it is always something that is unconscious until the moment it appears, and so presents itself as if it had fallen from heaven. The Germans call the an *Einfall*, which means a thing which falls into your head from nowhere. Sometimes it is like a revelation. Actually, intuition is a very natural function, a perfectly normal thing, and it is necessary, too, because it makes up for what you cannot perceive or think or feel because it lacks reality. You see, the past is not real any more and the future is not as real as we think. Therefore we must be very grateful to haven that we have such a function which gives us a certain light on those things which are round the corners. Doctors, of course, being often presented with the most unheard-of situations, need intuition a great deal. Many a good diagnosis comes from this 'very mysterious' function.

LECTURE TWO
ARCHETYPES

Ladies and Gentlemen, yesterday we dealt with the functions of consciousness. Today I want to finish the problem of the structure of the mind. A discussion of the human mind would not be complete if we did not include the existence of unconscious processes. Let me repeat shortly the reflections which I made last night.

We cannot deal with unconscious processes directly because they are not reachable. They are not directly apprehended; they appear only in their products, and we postulate from the peculiar quality of those products that there must be something behind them from which they originate. We call that dark sphere the unconscious psyche.

The ectopsychic contents of consciousness derive in the first place from the environment, through the data of the senses. Then the contents also come from other sources, such as memory and processes of judgment. These belong to the endopsychic sphere. A third source for conscious contents is the dark sphere of the mind, the unconscious. We approach it through the peculiarities of the endopsychic functions, those functions which are not under the control of the will. They are the vehicle by which unconscious contents reach the surface of consciousness.

The unconscious processes, then, are not directly observable, but those of its products that cross the threshold of consciousness can be divided into two classes. The first class contains recognizable material of a definitely personal origin; these contents are individual acquisitions or products of instinctive processes that make up the personality as a whole. Futhermore, there are forgotten or repressed contents, and creative contents. There is nothing specially peculiar about them. In other people such things may be conscious. Some people are conscious of things of which other people are not. I call that class of contents the subconscious mind or the *personal unconscious,* because, as far as we can judge, it is entirely made up of personal elements, elements that constitute the human personality as a whole.

Then there is another class of contents of definitely unknown origin, or at all events of an origin which cannot be ascribed to individual acquisition. These contents have one outstanding peculiarity, and that is their mythological character. It is as if they belong to a pattern not peculiar to any particular mind or person, but rather to a pattern peculiar to *mankind in general.* When I first came across such contents I wondered very much whether they might not be due to heredity, and I thought they might be explained by racial inheritance. In order to settle that question I went to the United States and studied the dreams of pure-blooded Negroes, and I was able to satisfy myself that these images have nothing to do with so-called blood or racial inheritance, nor are they personally acquired by the individual. They belong to mankind in general, and therefore they are of a *collective* nature.

These collective patterns I have called *archetypes,* using an expression of St Augustine's.[1] An archetype means a *typos* [imprint], a definite grouping of archaic character containing, in form as well as in meaning, *mythological motifs.* Mythological motifs appear in pure form in fairytales, myths, legends, and folklore. Some of the well-known motifs are: the figures of the Hero, the Redeemer, the Dragon (always connected with the Hero, who has to overcome him), the Whale or the Monster who swallows the Hero.[2] Another variation of the motif of the Hero and the Dragon is the Katabasis, the Descent into the Cave, the Nekyia. You remember in the Odyssey where Ulysses descends *ad inferos* to consult Tiresias, the seer.

---

[1][Cf. *The Archetypes and the Collective Unconscious* (C. W., vol. 9, i), par. 5.]

[2]See *Psychology of the Unconscious* [or *Symbols of Transformation* (C. W., vol. 5), index, s.v.].

This motif of the Nekyia is found everywhere in antiquity and practically all over the world. It expresses the psychological mechanism of introversion of the conscious mind into the deeper layers of the unconscious psyche. From these layers derive the contents of an impersonal, mythological character, in other words, the archetypes, and I call them therefore the impersonal or *collective unconscious*.

I am perfectly well aware that I can give you only the barest outline of this particular question of the collective unconscious. But I will give you an example of its symbolism and of how I proceed in order to discriminate it from the personal unconscious. When I went to America to investigate the unconscious of Negroes I had in mind this particular problem: are these collective patterns racially inherited, or are they 'a priori categories of imagination', as two Frenchmen, Hubert and Mauss,[1] quite independently of my own work, have called them. A Negro told me a dream in which occurred the figure of a man crucified on a wheel.[2] I will not mention the whole dream because it does not matter. It contained of course its personal meaning as well as allusions to impersonal ideas, but I picked out only that one motif. He was a very uneducated Negro from the South and not particularly intelligent. It would have been most probable, given the well-known religious character of the Negroes, that he should dream of a man crucified on a *cross*. The cross would have been a personal acquisition. But it is rather improbable that he should dream of the man crucified on a *wheel*. That is a very uncommon image. Of course I cannot prove to you that by some curious chance the Negro had not seen a picture or heard something of the sort and then dreamt about it; but if he had not had any model for this idea it would be an *archetypal image,* because the crucifixion on the wheel is a *mythological motif.* It is the ancient sun-wheel, and the crucifixion is the sacrifice to the sun-god in order to propitiate him, just as human and animal sacrifices formerly were offered for the fertility of the earth. The sun-wheel is an exceedingly archaic idea, perhaps the oldest religious idea there is. We can trace it to the Mesolithic and Paleolithic ages, as the sculptures of Rhodesia prove. Now there were real wheels only in the Bronze Age; in the Paleolithic Age the wheel was not yet invented. The Rhodesian sun-wheel seems to be contemporary with very naturalistic animal pictures, like the famous rhino with the tick-birds, a masterpiece of observation. The Rhodesian sun-wheel is therefore an original vision, presumably an archetypal sun-image.[3] But this image is not naturalistic one, for it is always divided into four or eight partitions (Figure 1). This image, a sort of divided circle, is a symbol which you find throughout the whole history of mankind as well as in the dreams of modern individuals. We might assume that the invention of the actual wheel started from this vision. Many of our inventions came from mythological anticipations and primordial images. For instance, the art of alchemy is the mother of modern chemistry. Our conscious scientific mind started in the matrix of the unconscious mind.

---

[1][Henri Hubert and Marcel Mauss, *Mélanges d'histoire des religions*, p. xxix.]

[2][Cf. *Symbols of Transformation*, par. 154.]

[3][Cf. 'Psychology and Literature' (C. W., vol. 15), par. 150; 'Psychology and Religion' (C. W., vol. 11), par. 100, and 'Brother Klaus' (ibid.), par. 484.

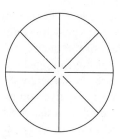

FIGURE 1.   *Sun-wheel*

In the dream of the Negro, the man on the wheel is a repetition of the Greek mythological motif of Ixion, who, on account of his offence against men and gods, was fastened by Zeus upon an incessantly turning wheel. I give you this example of a mythological motif in a dream merely in order to convey to you an idea of the collective unconscious. One single example is of course no conclusive proof. But one cannot very well assume that this Negro had studied Greek mythology, and it is improbable that he had seen any representation of Greek mythological figures. Furthermore, figures of Ixion are pretty rare.

I could give you conclusive proof of a very elaborate kind of the existence of these mythological patterns in the unconscious mind. But in order to present my material I should need to lecture for a fortnight. I would have first to explain to you the meaning of dreams and dream-series and then give you all the historical parallels and explain fully their importance, because the symbolism of these images and ideas is not taught in public schools or universities, and even specialists very rarely know of it. I had to study it for years and to find the material myself, and I cannot expect even a highly educated audience to be *au courant* with such abstruse matters. When we come to the technique of dream-analysis I shall be forced to enter into some of the mythological material and you will get a glimpse of what this work of finding parallels to unconscious products is really like. For the moment I have to content myself with the mere statement that there are mythological patterns in that layer of the unconscious, that it produces contents which cannot be ascribed to the individual and which may even be in strict contradiction to the personal psychology of the dreamer. For instance, you are simply astounded when you observe a completely uneducated person producing a dream which really should not occur with such a person because it contains the most amazing things. And children's dreams often make you think to such a degree that you must take a holiday afterwards in order to recover from the shock, because these symbols are so tremendously profound, and you think: How on earth is it possible that a child should have such a dream?

Documentation of the Rhodesian 'sun-wheels' has not been possible, though such rock-carved forms are noted in Angola and South Africa: cf. Willcox, *The Rock Art of South Africa,* fig. 23 and pls. xvii-xx. Their dating is in doubt. The 'rhino with tick-birds' is from the Transvaal and is in a museum in Pretoria. It was discovered in 1928 and widely publicized.]

It is really quite simple to explain. Our mind has its history, just as our body has its history. You might be just as astonished that man has an appendix, for instance. Does he know he ought to have an appendix? He is just born with it. Millions of people do not know they have a thymus, but they have it. They do not know that in certain parts of their anatomy they belong to the species of the fishes, and yet it is so. Our unconscious mind, like our body, is a storehouse of relics and memories of the past. A study of the structure of the unconscious collective mind would reveal the same discoveries as you make in comparative anatomy. We do not need to think that there is anything mystical about it. But because I speak of a collective unconscious, I have been accused of obscurantism. There is nothing mystical about the collective unconscious. It is just a new branch of science, and it is really common sense to admit the existence of unconscious collective processes. For, though a child is not born conscious, his mind is not a *tabula rasa*. The child is born with a definite brain, and the brain of an English child will work not like that of an Australian blackfellow but in the way of a modern English person. The brain is born with a finished structure, it will work in a modern way, but this brain has its history. It has been built up in the course of millions of years and represents a history of which it is the result. Naturally it carries with it the traces of that history, exactly like the body, and if you grope down into the basic structure of the mind you naturally find traces of the archaic mind.

The Individual Psychology of Alfred Adler

Alfred Adler

A. THE STRIVING FOR PERFECTION

1. The Ceaselessness of Striving

I began to see clearly in every psychological phenomenon the striving for superiority. It runs parallel to physical growth and is an intrinsic necessity of life itself. It lies at the root of all solutions of life's problems and is manifested in the way in which we meet these problems. All our functions follow its direction. They strive for conquest, security, increase, either in the right or in the wrong direction. The impetus from minus to plus never ends. The urge from below to above never ceases. Whatever premises all our philosophers and psychologists dream of—self-preservation, pleasure principle, equalization—all these are but vague representations, attempts to express the great upward drive.

The history of the human race points in the same direction. Willing, thinking, talking, seeking after rest and pleasure, learning, understanding, working and loving, all betoken the essence of this eternal melody. From this network, which in the last analysis is simply given with the man-cosmos relationship, no one may hope to escape. Even if anyone wanted to escape, even if he could escape, he would still find himself in the general system, striving upward from below. This not only states a fundamental category of thought, a thought construct, but, what is more, represents the fundamental fact of our life.

The origin of humanity and the ever-repeated beginning of infant life impresses with every psychological act: "Achieve! Arise! Conquer!" This feeling, this longing for the abrogation's of every imperfection, is never absent. In the search for relief, in Faustian wrestling against the forces of nature, rings always the basic chord: "I relinquish thee not, thou bless me withal." The unreluctant search for truth, the ever-unsatisfied seeking for solution of the problems of life, belongs to this longing for perfection of some sort.

2. The Universality of Striving

We all wish to overcome difficulties. We all strive to reach a goal by the attainment of which we shall feel strong, superior, and complete. John Dewey refers, very rightly, to this tendency as the striving for security. Others call it the striving for self-preservation. But whatever name we give it, we shall always find in human beings this great line of activity—this struggle to rise from an inferior to a superior position, from defeat to victory, from below to above. It begins in earliest childhood and continues to the end of our lives.

As for the striving for perfection, for superiority, or for power, some have always known about it, but not thoroughly enough to spread this knowledge to a larger mass or to illuminate the fundamental significance of this striving for the structure of the entire personality. Only Individual Psychology has pointed out that this striving for perfection is found in every individual and fills every individual [the prepotent dynamic principle]. It is not necessary to inoculate man with the desire to develop into superman, as the daring attempt of Nietzsche has shown.

I should like to emphasize first of all that striving for perfection is innate. This is not meant in a concrete way, as if there were a drive which would later in life be capable of bringing everything to completion and which only needed to develop itself. The striving for perfection is innate in the sense that it is a part of life, a striving, an urge, a something without which life would be unthinkable.

3. Striving As Ultimate Adaptation

Individual Psychology stands firmly on the ground of evolution and, in the light of it, regards all human striving as a striving for perfection. Bodily and psychologically, the urge to life is tied unalterably to this striving.

We must connect our thought with a continuous active adaptation to the demands of the outer world if we are to understand the direction and movement of life. We must think that this is a question of something primordial, of something that was inherent in primeval life. It has always been a matter of overcoming, of the existence of the individual and the human race, always a matter of establishing a favorable relationship between the individual and the outer world. This coercion to carry out a better adaptation can never end. In speaking of active adaptation I am referring to adaptation *sub specie aeternitatis* [under the aspect of eternity, Spinoza], for only that bodily and psychological development is "right" which can be deemed right for the future. Furthermore, the concept of active adaptation implies that body and mind and the whole organization of living must strive toward this ultimate adaptation, toward the conquest of all the advantages and disadvantages set by the cosmos.

An adaptation to immediate reality would be nothing other than an exploitation of the accomplishments of the striving of others, as the picture of the world of the pampered child demands. The continuous striving for security urges toward the overcoming of the present reality in favor of a better one. This goal of perfection must bear within it the goal of an ideal community, because all that we value in life, all that endures and continues to endure, is eternally the product of social interest.

No one knows which is the only correct way. Mankind has frequently made attempts to imagine this final goal of human development. The best conception which one has gained so far of this ideal elevation of mankind is the concept of God. There is no question that the concept of God actually includes this movement as a goal and that it best serves the purpose of a concrete goal of perfection for the obscure desire of man to reach perfection.

Man as an everstriving being cannot be like God. God who is eternally complete, who directs the stars, who is the master of fates, who elevates man from his lowliness to Himself, who speaks from the cosmos to every single human soul, is the most brilliant manifestation of the goal of perfection to date. In God's nature, religious mankind perceives the way to height. In His call it hears again the innate voice of life which must have its direction towards the goal of perfection, towards overcoming the feeling of lowliness and transitoriness of the existence here below. The human soul, as a part of the movement of life, is endowed with the ability to participate in the uplift, elevation, perfection, and completion.

4. Perfection In The Abnormal

Whether one thinks or acts more wisely or less, one always moves along the lines of the upward tendency. In our right and wrong conceptions of life and its problems, in the successful or the unsuccessful solution of any question, this striving for perfection is uninterruptedly at work. And even where foolishness, imbecility, and inexperience seem to belie the striving to conquer some defect or tend to depreciate it, the will to conquer is nevertheless operative.

Of course there are countless attempts to envisage this goal of perfection. Individual Psychologists, especially those of us who are physicians and have to deal with failures, with persons who suffer from a neurosis or psychosis, with delinquents, and alcoholics, see this goal of superiority in them also, but it tends in a direction which is opposed to reason to the extent that we cannot recognize in it a proper goal of perfection. When, for example, a person seeks to concretize his goal by wanting to domineer over others, such a goal of perfection seems unfitted to guide the individual or the mass of men. No one could posit such a goal for himself without being forced to come into conflict with the coercion of evolution, to violate reality, and to protect himself fearfully against the truth and those who stand up to it. A goal of perfection of leaning on others also appears to contradict reason. A goal which leaves the tasks of life unsolved, in order not to suffer sure defeats, also appears altogether unsuited, although many find it acceptable.

By having established that the norm for perfection is social interest, we are in a position to understand approximately the direction towards ideal perfection.

B. STRIVING FOR SELF-ENHANCEMENT

1. Enhancement of the Self-Esteem

The neurotic purpose is the enhancement of the self-esteem, for which the simplest formula can be recognized in the exaggerated "masculine protest." This formula, "I want to be a real man," is the guiding fiction, the "fundamental apperception" (Jerusalem) in every neurosis, where it demands realization to a higher degree than in the normal psyche. The libido, the sex drive, and the inclination toward perversion, irrespective of their origins, become subordinated to this guiding thought.

Form and content of the neurotic guiding line originate from the impressions of the child who feels humiliated. These impressions, which emerge by necessity from an original feeling of inferiority, evoke an attitude of aggression, the purpose of which is the overcoming of a great insecurity.

C. UNIQUENESS AND SUBJECTIVITY

1. The Individual as the Variant

The now antiquated, older natural science with its rigid systems has been generally replaced today by views which attempt biologically, philosophically, and psychologically to comprehend life and its variants in their context (*Zusammenhang*). This is also true of that trend in psychology which I have called Comparative Individual Psychology. It attempts to gain, from the separate life manifestations and forms of expression the picture of the self-consistent personality as a variant, by presupposing the unity and self-consistency [both *Einheit*] of the individuality. The separate traits are then compared with one another, are reduced to their common denominator, and are combined in an individualizing manner into a total portrait. William Stern, in a different way, has arrived at results similar to mine.

The goal of superiority with each individual is personal and unique. It depends upon the meaning he gives to life. This meaning is not a matter of words. It is built up in his style of life and runs through it like a strange melody of his own creation. In his style of life, he does not express his goal so that we can formulate it for all times. He expresses it vaguely, so that we must guess at it from the indications he gives.

Even where the goal has been made concrete, there can be a thousand varieties of striving towards this goal. One man, for example, will want to be a physician, but to be a physician may mean many different things. He may not only wish to be a specialist in internal medicine or a specialist in pathology, but he will show in his activities his own peculiar degree of interest in himself and interest in others. We shall see how far he trains himself to be of help to his fellows and how far he limits his helpfulness. He has made this his aim as a compensation for a specific feeling of inferiority. We must be able to guess, from his expressions in his profession and elsewhere, the specific feeling for which he is compensating. We very frequently find, for example, that physicians in their childhood made early acquaintance with the fact of death, and death was the aspect of human insecurity which made the greatest impression on them. Perhaps a brother or a parent died, and their later training developed with the aim of finding a way, for themselves and others, to be more secure against death. Another man may make it his concrete goal to be a teacher, but we know very well how different teachers may be. If a teacher has a low degree of social feeling, his goal of superiority in being a teacher may be to rule among his inferiors. He may feel secure only with who are weaker and less experienced than himself. A teacher with a high degree of social feeling will treat his pupils as his equals. We need not do more than mention here how different the capacities and interests of teachers may be and how significant of their goal all these expressions will be found.

2. The Schema of Apperception

a. *Opinion of Oneself and the World.* The first four to five years are enough for the child to complete his specific and arbitrary training in the face of impressions from his body and the environment. From then on the creative activity of the style of life begins its work. Experiences become assimilated and utilized according to the style of life, by the structure of which the individual is determined. To facilitate this activity personal rules and principles, character traits, and a conception of the world become elaborated. A well-determined schema of apperception (*Apperzeptionsschema*) is established, and the child's conclusions and actions are directed in full accord with the final ideal end-form to which he aspires.

The apperception connected with the law of movement [see below] is the way in which man looks at himself and the external world. In other words, it is the opinion which the child, and later, in the same direction, the adult has gained of himself and the world. Further, this opinion cannot be gathered from the words and thoughts of the person under examination. These are all far too strongly under the spell of the law of movement which aims at overcoming and therefore, even in the case of self-condemnation, still casts longing glances towards the heights.

For me there can be no doubt that everyone conducts himself in life from the very beginning of his action as if he had a definite opinion of his strength and his abilities and a clear conception of the difficulty or ease of a problem at hand. In a word, I am convinced that a person's behavior springs from his opinion. We should not be surprised at this, because our senses do not receive actual facts, but merely a subjective image of them, a reflection of the external world. *Omnia ad opinionem suspensa sunt.* This saying of Seneca's should not be forgotten in psychological investigations. It has the same effect on me whether a poisonous snake is actually approaching my foot or whether I merely believe that it is a poisonous snake. The pampered child behaves quite the same in his anxiety whether he is afraid of burglars as soon as his mother leaves him, or whether there are really burglars in the house.

A classic example of this play of subjective ideas in human action is furnished by Caesar's landing in Egypt. As he jumped ashore he stumbled and fell on the ground, and the Roman soldiers took this as an unfavorable omen. Brave as they were, they would nonetheless have turned around and gone back, had not Caesar thrown out his arms and cried out, "I embrace you, Africa!" We can see from this how little the structure of reality is causal, and how its effects can be molded and determined by the self-consistent personality.

An interesting fact in connection with the private schema of apperception, which characterizes all individuals, is that children with organic defects tend to connect all their experiences with the function of the defective organ. For instance, a child having stomach trouble is likely to show an abnormal interest in eating, while one with defective eyesight is more apt to be preoccupied with things visible. It might be suggested, therefore, that in order to find out where a child's interest lies, we need only to ascertain which organ is defective. But things do not work out quite so simply. The child does not experience the fact of organ inferiority in the way that an external observer sees it, but as modified by his own schema of apperception. Hence while the fact of organ inferiority counts as an element in the child's schema of apperception, the external observation of the inferiority does not necessarily give the cue to the child's schema of apperception.

In considering the structure of a personality, the chief difficulty is that its unity, its particular style of life and goal, is not built upon objective reality, but upon the subjective view the individual takes of the facts of life. A conception, a view of a fact, is never the fact itself, and it is for this reason that human beings, all of whom live in the same world of facts, mold themselves differently. Each one organizes himself according to his personal view of things, and some views are more sound, some less sound. We must always reckon with these individual mistakes and failures in the development of a human being. Especially must we reckon with the misinterpretations made in early childhood, for these dominate the subsequent course of our existence.

The child always behaves in the circle of his personal mistakes whenever he approaches a new and difficult situation. We know that the depth or character of the impression which the situation makes upon the child does not depend upon the objective fact or circumstance (as for example the birth of a second child), but depends rather on how this child regards the fact. This is sufficient ground for refuting the theory of causality. A necessary connection exists between objective facts and their absolute meaning, but not between mistaken views of facts.

If we wish to understand the essential difference between Freud and myself, we must ask the question, is an impression at all possible and could it have the ascribed effect without a pre-existing schema of apperception? Denying the connection between the experience and the schema of apperception is like taking single notes out of a melody to examine them for their value and meaning.

SOCIAL EMBEDDEDNESS

1. Communal Life as the Absolute Truth

In addition to regarding an individual's life as a unity, we must also take it together with its context of social relations. Thus children when first born are weak, and their weakness makes it necessary for other persons to care for them. The style or the pattern of a child's life cannot be understood without reference to the persons who look after him and who make up for his inferiority. The child has interlocking relations with the mother and family which could never be understood if we confined our analysis to the periphery of the child's physical being in space. The individuality of the child cuts across his physical individuality, it involves a whole context of social relations.

In order to understand what goes on in an individual, it is necessary to consider his attitude toward his fellow men. The relationships of people to one another in part exist naturally and as such are subject to change. In part they take the form of institutionalized relationships which arise from the natural ones. These institutionalized relationships can be observed especially in the political life of nations, in the formation of states, and in community affairs. Human psychological life cannot be understood without the simultaneous consideration of these coherences.

Human psychological life is not capable of doing just as it likes but is constantly confronted with tasks which have arrived from somewhere. All these tasks are inseparably tied up with the logic of man's communal life. This is one of those main conditions which continuously act upon the individual and which yield to his influence only up to a certain degree. When we consider that not even the conditions of human relations can be fully comprehended because they are too numerous and further that these demands are subject to change, then it becomes clear that we are scarcely in a position to gain complete insight into the darknesses of a given psychological life. This difficulty of understanding others becomes all the greater the further we depart from our own circumstances.

One of the basic facts for the advancement of our understanding of human nature is that we must regard the inherent rules of the game of a group as these emerge within the limited organization of the human body and its achievements, as if they were an absolute truth. We are able to approach this truth only slowly and usually only after mistakes and errors have been overcome.

The demands made on man by communal life are really just as self-evident as the demands of climate, the demands of protection against cold, and of building houses. We recognize religion as an expression of this coercion toward communal life, although not yet in a form understood as such. In religion, the sanctification of social forms takes the place of insight into their true significance and serves as a bond between members of the community. If the conditions of life are determined in the first instance by cosmic influences, they are in the second instance determined socially. They are determined by the fact that men live together and by the rules and regularities which spontaneously arise in consequence of this. The demands of society have regulated human relations which had already existed from the beginning as self-understood, as an absolute truth. For before the individual life of man there was the community. In the history of human culture, there is not a singe form of life which was not conducted as social. Never has man appeared otherwise than in society.

2. The Necessity for Communal Life

Darwin already pointed out that one never finds weak animals living alone. Man must be included among these, particularly because he is not strong enough to live alone. He has only little resistance against nature, he needs a larger amount of aids to live and preserve himself. Consider the situation of a man in a jungle, alone and without aids provided by culture. He would appear incomparably more threatened than any other creature. He has not the teeth of the carnivore, the sense of hearing, nor the sharp eyes to prevail in such a struggle.

Now we can understand that man could maintain himself only when he placed himself under particularly favorable conditions. These, however, were afforded to him only by group life. Group life proved to be a necessity because it alone enabled man, through a division of labor, to solve problems in which the individual as such would have been condemned to failure. Division of labor alone was capable of providing man with weapons of offense and defense, as well as with all goods which he needed to maintain himself and which we today include under the concept of culture.

From the point of view of nature, man is an inferior being. But this inferiority with which he is afflicted, and of which he becomes aware through a feeling of deprivation and insecurity, acts as a continuous stimulus to find a way of adjusting, of providing, of creating situations in which the disadvantages of his position seem compensated. Since society played an essential part in this striving for adaptation, the psychological organ had from the beginning to reckon with the conditions of society. All its abilities are developed on a basis which embodies the component of a social life. Every human thought had to be so constituted that it could do justice to a community.

3. Language, Logic, and Rules of the Game

If one considers how progress continued, one arrives at the origins of logic which embodies the demand for general validity. Only that is logical which is generally valid. Language is a further clear result of social life, a miracle which distinguishes man from all other creatures. A phenomenon such as language cannot be thought of without the concept of general validity, which fact indicates that language has its origin in the social life of man. Language is quite unnecessary for a creature living by itself. Language reckons with the social life of man, is its product and, at the same time, its cement. A strong proof for this connection is that individuals who grow up under conditions under which contact with others is made difficult or is prevented, or who themselves refuse such contact, almost always suffer a deficiency in language and language ability. It is as if this bond could be formed and preserved only when the contact with mankind is secure.

Language has an extremely deep significance for the development of the human psychological life. Logical thought is possible only under the supposition of language. By making concept-formation possible, language enables us to make distinctions and to create concepts which are not private but common property. Our thinking and feeling are also understandable only when one presupposes general validity. Our enjoyment of beauty is founded on the understanding that appreciation and recognition of the beautiful and the good must be common property. Thus we arrive at the conclusion that the concepts of reason, logic, ethics, and aesthetics can have taken their origin only in the communal life of man and that they are at the same time the cement which protects culture from disintegration.

We understand now that all the rules of the game—such as education, superstition, totem and tabu, and law—which were necessary to secure the existence of the human race, had first of all to do justice to the idea of a community. What we call justice, considering it the bright side of the human character, is essentially nothing other than the fulfillment of demands which have arisen from man's communal life. It is these demands which have shaped the psychological organ. Dependability, loyalty, frankness, and truthfulness are actually demands posited and maintained by a generally valid principle of the community. What we call a good or a bad character can be judged only from the viewpoint of the community. Character, like any scientific, political, or artistic achievement, will prove it greatness and value only by being valuable to men in general.

An ideal image by which we appraise the individual is created only by considering its value and its usefulness for man in general. We compare the individual with the ideal image of a fellow man who meets his problems in a fashion which has general validity, whose social interest is developed to such an extent that "he follows the rules of the game of human society," as Furtmüller expressed it.

4. The Three General Social Ties

At this point Individual Psychology comes into contact with sociology. For a long time now I have been convinced that all the questions of life can be subordinated to the three major problems—the problems of communal life, of work, and of love. These arise from the inseparable bond that of necessity links men together for association, for the provision of livelihood, and for the care of offspring.

The three ties in which human beings are bound set the three problems of life, but none of these problems can be solved separately. Each of them demands a successful approach to the other two.

a. *Occupation.* The first tie sets the problem of occupation. We are living on the surface of this planet, with only the resources of this planet, with the fertility of its soil, with its mineral wealth, and with its climate and atmosphere. It has always been the task of mankind to find the right answer to the problem these conditions set us, and even today we cannot think that we have found a sufficient answer. In every age, mankind has arrived at a certain level of solution, but it has always been necessary to strive for improvement and further accomplishments.

When somebody makes shoes, he makes himself useful to someone else, and he has the right to a sufficient livelihood, to all the advantages of hygiene, and to a good education of his children. The fact that he receives payment for this is the recognition of his usefulness in an age of developed trade. In this way, he arrives at a feeling of his worth to society, the only possible means of mitigating the universal human feeling of inferiority. The person who performs useful work lives in the midst of the developing human society and helps to advance it.

b. *Society.* The second tie by which men are bound is their membership in the human race and their association with others of their kind. The attitude and behavior of a human being would be altogether different if he were the only one of his kind alive on earth. We have always to reckon with others, to adapt ourselves to others, and to interest ourselves in them. This problem is best solved by friendship, social feeling, and cooperation. With the solution of this problem, we have made an incalculable advance towards the solution of the first. It was only because men learned to cooperate that the great discovery of the division of labor was made, a discovery which is the chief security for the welfare of mankind. Through the division of labor we can use the results of many different kinds of training and organize many different abilities, so that all of them contribute to the common welfare and guarantee relief from insecurity and increased opportunity for all the members of society.

Some people attempt to evade the problem of occupation, to do no work, or to occupy themselves outside of common human interests. We shall always find, however, that if they dodge this problem, they will in fact be claiming support from their fellows. In one way or another, they will be living on the labor of others without making a contribution of their own.

c. *Love.* The third tie of a human being is that he is a member of one of the two sexes and not of the other. On his approach to the other sex and on the fulfillment of his sexual role depends his part in the continuance of mankind. This relationship between the two sexes also sets a problem. It, too, is a problem which cannot be solved apart from the other two problems. For a successful solution of the problem of love and marriage, an occupation contributing to the division of labor is necessary, as well as a good and friendly contact with other human beings. In our own day, the highest solution for this problem, the solution most coherent with the demands of society and of the division of labor, is monogamy. In the way in which an individual answers this problem the degree of his cooperation can always be seen.

These three problems are never found apart, for they all throw crosslights on one another. A solution of one helps towards the solution of the others, and indeed we can say that they are all aspects of the same situation and the same problem— the necessity for a human being to preserve life and to further life in the environment in which he finds himself.

SOCIAL INTEREST

1. Innate Potentiality

The high degree of cooperation and social culture which man needs for his very existence demands spontaneous social effort, and the dominant purpose of education is to evoke it. Social interest is not inborn [as a full-fledged entity], but it is an innate potentiality which has to be consciously developed. We are unable to trust any so-called social instinct, for its expression depends upon the child's conception or vision of the environment.

Social interest is innate, just as the striving for overcoming is innate, with the important difference, however, that social interest must be developed, and that it can be developed only when the child is already in the midst of life. At the present stage of man's psychological and possibly also physical development, we must consider the innate substratum of the social interest as too small, as not strong enough, to become effective or to develop without the benefit of social understanding. This is in contrast to abilities and functions which succeed almost all on their own, such as breathing.

Like the character traits which depend on it, social interest can come to life only in the social context. By social context, of course, is meant the child's subjective understanding of the same. The decision [as to how he will interpret the essentially ambiguous social context] rests in the creative power of the child, guided by the environment, and educational measures, influenced by the experience of his body, and his evaluation of it.

The development of the innate potentiality for cooperation occurs first in the relationship of the child and mother. The mother is the first other person whom the child experiences. Here is the first opportunity for the cultivation of the innate social potentiality. But even here, at the very beginning, many mistakes can be made. For instance, the mother is often satisfied with a restricted social development for the child, and does not concern herself with the fact that he must go from her care into a much wider circle of human contacts. In such a case the mother concentrates the child's social potentialities upon herself. She does not help the child to extend his interest to others besides herself. Even the father may be excluded if he does not make a special effort to enter this "closed circle." Other children and strangers are, of course, excluded also.

2. A Value Expressed Through Empathy

By social interest or social feeling, we understand something different from that which other authors understand. When we say it is a feeling, we are certainly justified in doing so. But it is more than a feeling; it is an evaluative attitude toward life. (*Lebensform*). It is an attitude quite different from what we find in a person whom we call anti-social. This evaluative attitude must not be understood as an external form only, as if it were the expression only of an acquired way of life. It is much more than that. We are not in a position to define it quite unequivocally, but we have found in an English author a phrase which clearly expresses what we could contribute to an explanation: "To see with the eyes of another, to hear with the ears of another, to feel with the heart of another." For the time being, this seems to me an admissible definition of what we call social feeling.

We see immediately that this ability coincides in part with what we call identification or empathy. Herder, Novalis, and Jean Paul were acquainted with the process of empathy, described it, and considered it important. Later Wundt, Volkelt, and especially Lipps stressed empathy as a fundamental fact of our experience. The latter, Dilthey, Müller-Freienfels, and others described the relationship of empathy and understanding. Individual Psychology may claim as its contribution to have pointed out that empathy and understanding are facts of social feeling, of harmony with the universe. This kind of identification or empathy always depends on the degree of our social interest; it is one aspect of social interest and is absolutely essential to the achievement of social living (*Gemeinschaftsleben*). Sympathy is a partial expression of identification.

The ability to identify must be trained, and it can be trained only if one grows up in relation to others and feels a part of the whole. One must sense that not only the comforts of life belong to one, but also the discomforts. One must feel at home on this earth with all its advantages and disadvantages.

Life presents only such problems as require ability to cooperate for their solution. To hear, see, or speak "correctly," means to lose one's self completely in another or in a situation, to become identified with him or with it. The capacity for identification, which alone makes us capable of friendship, love of mankind, sympathy, occupation, and love, is the basis of social interest and can be practiced and exercised only in conjunction with others. In this intended assimilation to another person or to a situation lies the whole meaning of comprehension.

The concept of identification has different usages. We speak of identification if a child aims to become like his father, to see with the eyes of the father, to "understand" him, and so has a useful goal before himself. Freud, unawares, takes identification as meaning to seize the role of another in order to gain a personal advantage. Identification in our sense would be illustrated by the following examples. We identify with a picture by regarding it. But we also identify with other inanimate objects. For example, in playing billiards or in bowling the player follows the ball with his eyes and makes the very movement which he hopes that the ball will make. At a play everyone participates in the feeling and the acting. Such identification does not mean to usurp the role of the father, to become the billiard ball, or to act. In dreams and in group psychology empathy also plays an enormous part.

3. Other-Directedness

The child and mother are dependent on each other; this relationship not only arises out of nature, but is favored by it. When other schools of psychology maintain the child comes into the world a complete egoist with a "drive for destruction" and no other intention than to foster himself cannibalistically on his mother, this is an erroneous inference based on incomplete observation. These schools overlook in the relationship the role of the mother who requires the cooperation of the child. The mother with her milk-filled breasts and all the other altered functions of her body (not to mention the new emotional development of the love for her child) needs the child just as the child needs her. They are dependent on each other by nature. The possibilities for social interest first take on life and become tangible in the relationship between mother and child.

The development of the child is increasingly permeated by the relationships of society to him. In time, the first signs of the innate social interest appear, the organically determined impulses of affection blossom forth, and lead the child to seek the proximity of adults. One can always observe that the child directs impulses of affection towards others and not towards himself, as Freud believes. These impulses vary in degree and differ with respect to different persons. In children over two years once can also see these differences in their verbal expressions. The feeling of belongingness, the social interest, takes root in the psyche of the child and leaves the individual only under the severest pathological changes of his mental life.

Social interest remains throughout life. It becomes differentiated, limited, or expanded and, in favorable cases, extends not only to family members but to the larger group, to the nation, to all of mankind. It can even go further, extending itself to animals, plants, and inanimate objects and finally even to the cosmos.

The educability of the child derives from the breadth of his innate, differentiated, and growing social interest. Through it he gains the connection with the common ideal. In this way the demands of the community become personal demands, and the immanent logic of human society, with its matters of course and necessities, becomes the individual task for the child.

The indomitable progress of social interest, growing through evolution, justifies the assumption that the very existence of mankind is inseparably tied up with being good. Whatever seems to speak against this assumption is to be regarded as a mistake of [societal] evolution and can be traced to errors.

Self-boundedness is an artifact thrust upon the child during his education and by the present state of our social structure. The creative power of the child is misled towards self-boundedness. Teachers, ministers, and physicians must be freed from their own self-boundedness and, together with all those who want to work honestly for the common welfare, must prevent these seductions of the child. Until that time it will always be the single case only which will find its way to the physician, and not before the error of the child has led to considerable damage to all.

A man is called good when he relates himself to other humans in a generally useful way, bad when he acts contrary to social interest. When the educator and especially the psychotherapist frequently come to the erroneous conclusion that man is evil by nature, this is because it is more common for them to observe bad drives and destruction drives than to take note of man's other side.

4 Universality

[While social interest must be developed in the child] there is [on the other hand] no human being who is capable of seriously denying for himself all social interest. There are no words by which one could free oneself from the obligations to our fellow men. Social interest constantly brings itself to mind with its warning voice. This does not mean that we always proceed in accordance with social interest. We do maintain, however, that a certain effort is required to throttle it or to push it aside. We can never find anyone who could say truly, "I am not interested in others." He may act this way—he may act as if he were not interested in the world—but he cannot justify himself. Rather does he claim to be interested in others, in order to hide his lack of social adjustment. This is mute testimony to the universality of social feeling.

5 The Broader Sense

We have already spoken of the great distance to the problems of life, of coming to a halt, and of detachment [in the neurotic]. There can be no question, however, that occasionally such a procedure is correct and in accordance with social interest. Individual Psychology is particularly concerned with cases where this position is justified. This is because we always feel obliged to attribute conditional applicability only to rules and formulas and always to supply new proofs for their confirmation. In the present connection, the exceptions are cases where an individual foregoes the solution of certain aspects of life for the purpose of making a greater contribution to the advancement of society, as the artist and genius do.

A philosopher must from time to tome exile himself from society to think and write his books. But the mistake involved will never be great if a high degree of social interest is bound up with the goal of superiority. Our cooperation has need for many different excellences.

Solitary occupation in children as well as adults need not come off badly. Indeed it should even be encouraged, provided it permits a prospect of later enrichment of society. It is merely due to the technique of certain accomplishments that they can be practiced and carried out only at a distance from other persons. This in no way prevents them from actually being social in character.

C H A P T E R 15

THE CURRENT SCIENCE

ULRIC NEISSER (1928–   )

Ulric Neisser was born in Kiel, Germany, on December 8, 1928. He immigrated to the United States at the age of 4, and grew up in the suburbs of Philadelphia and New York with his parents and older sister.[1] Both of Neisser's parents were intellectuals—his father was a professor of economics at the University of Pennsylvania, and his mother held an advanced degree in sociology.

Neisser completed his undergraduate work at Harvard University, where he went with the intent of studying physics. However, during his junior year, he took an introductory psychology course with E. G. Boring, which created in him such fervor for the field that he published his first article, an exploration of extrasensory perception, in the *Journal of Parapsychology,* within the year. After Harvard, Neisser earned his masters from Swarthmore College, where he studied Gestalt psychology with Kohler. Neisser then went to MIT to study with George Miller (best known for his classic work on the capacity of short-term memory). Neisser quickly developed a distaste for the "machine-oriented atmosphere" at MIT (a dislike that would heavily influence his later perspective on human cognition). He returned for a year to Swarthmore to enable his wife to finish her degree, subsequently returning to Harvard for his Ph.D.

Neisser's first academic position was at Brandeis University, where Abraham Maslow was chair. At a time when behaviorism was the mainstream influence in

---

[1] The material in this sketch is drawn primarily from personal communication (U. Neisser, September 23, 1997). Additional information was gleaned from Baars (1986), Goleman (1983), and Neisser (1997).

psychology, Maslow's leadership gave Neisser the freedom to pursue his interest in cognition. Neisser stayed at Brandeis for several years before retreating to Martin Orne's Laboratory for Experimental Psychology, where he wrote his landmark book, *Cognitive Psychology*.

The publication of *Cognitive Psychology* marked the synthesis of many of the theories, ideas, and issues that had been circulating in scientific circles for more than two decades. Its publication, followed in 1970 by the maiden publication of the academic journal *Cognitive Psychology*, marked the reestablishment of the study of cognition as a valid and central issue in mainstream American psychology. Although cognitive research had been prolific at the time of this publication, there was no single source to which a student or professional could turn for a succinct survey of the "state of the art" of the field. Neisser provided this survey, and in doing so, brought definition to the reborn field of cognitive psychology. Easily the most cited base reading in the field, Neisser's introduction begins with a definition of psychology that is still quoted in nearly every introductory psychology text. The introductory chapter, which is the reading for this section, provides a solid foundation from which to build a preliminary understanding of the broad field of cognitive psychology.

After the completion of the book, Neisser accepted a position at Cornell, where he stayed until 1983. From 1983 to 1996, Neisser served on the faculty of Emory University, only recently returning to Cornell. Over the past 20 years, Neisser has continued to write influential books, including *Cognition and Reality* (1976), *Memory Observed* (1982), *The School Achievement of Minority Children* (1986), and *The Perceived Self* (1993). He has remained an active researcher, focusing on memory in natural settings and, more recently, issues in intelligence testing. In 1995, Neisser headed an American Psychological Association task force that reviewed controversial issues in the study of intelligence (Neisser, et al., 1996). In April 1996, he chaired a conference at Emory that focused on secular changes in intelligence-test scores. A book based on the Emory conference, *The Rising Curve,* is currently in preparation.

ABRAHAM MASLOW (1908–1970)

Abraham Harold Maslow was born in Manhattan on April 1, 1908. The firstborn child of Russian Jewish immigrants, he grew up in a home that today would be described as dysfunctional. As the only Jewish boy in his neighborhood, he found himself without friends. Like many isolated children, he sought comfort in books. He started college by studying law at the insistence of his father, but did not finish the first term since he found the content confining and lacking in moral considerations.[1]

---

[1] For biographic material, see Hoffman (1988) and Goble (1970).

Maslow transferred to Cornell University in 1927. He was there for only one semester and during this time took an elementary psychology course with Edward B. Titchener. Maslow found the course far removed from his moral and social interests. He returned home, and in 1928, married his cousin Bertha Goodman, with whom he had been infatuated since 1922. He transferred at this time to the University of Wisconsin, where he received his B.A. in 1930, his M.A. in 1931, and his Ph.D. in 1934. Shortly before Maslow left for Wisconsin, he discovered the works of J. B. Watson, a discovery he regarded as a turning point in his life and to which he credited his choice of a career in psychology. At Wisconsin, he became Harry Harlow's first graduate student. It may seem strange to those who think of Maslow synonymously with the Third Force in Psychology [Humanism] that his early career was spent as an animal behaviorist.

In 1935, Edward Thorndike offered Maslow a postdoctoral fellowship at Columbia University. New York was a hotbed of new ideas, and here Maslow met or studied with Alfred Adler,[2] Eric Fromm, and Karen Horney, all Freudian dissidants; Kurt Goldstein the famous neuropsychiatrist; and Max Wertheimer and Kurt Koffka who, along with Wolfgang Köhler, are credited with the founding of Gestalt psychology. At this time, he also met Ruth Benedict, the famous anthropologist. His association with Benedict and Wertheimer, along with the birth of his first child, moved him irrevocably away from both Watson and Freud, and toward an understanding of the interaction of the individual and his or her society or culture. While at Columbia, and later Brooklyn College, the influence of these great thinkers shaped the direction of all of his future work. The study of self-actualization presented in this chapter with the edited selection from his book *Motivation and Emotion* (1970) began as:

> the effort of a young intellectual to try to understand two of his teachers [Benedict and Wertheimer] whom he loved, adored, and admired, and who were very, very wonderful people. It was a kind of high-IQ devotion. I could not be content simply to adore, but sought to understand why these two people were so different from the run-of-the-mill people in the world. (Maslow, 1971, p. 41)

Maslow moved to Brandis University in 1951, where he continued his work with dominant and self-actualizing individuals. Maslow was elected president of the American Psychological Association in 1966. In 1969, he became resident fellow at the Laughlin Charitable Foundation in California and later became one of the founders of the Esalen Institute. In this later period, he became strongly associated as one of the main spokespersons for humanistic psychology. He continued working on research about peak experiences, the hierarchy of needs and self-actualization, being motivation (B-values), and the idea of a utopian society, which he called Eupsychia. He died of a heart attack on June 8, 1970.

---

[2]Maslow's doctoral dissertation (1935) was published in the first volume of Adler's *International Journal of Individual Psychology*, 1, 47–59.

REFERENCES

Baars, B. J. (1986). *The cognitive revolution in psychology.* New York: Guilford Press.

Goble, F. G. (1970). *The third force.* New York: Grossman Publishers.

Goleman, D. (1983). A conversation with Ulric Neisser. *Psychology Today,* May, 5–62.

Hoffman, E. (1988). *The right to be human.* Los Angeles: Jeremy P. Tarcher (Distributed by St. Martin's Press, New York).

Lowry, R. J. (Ed.). (1979). *The journals of A. H. Maslow* (Vols. 1–2). Monterey, CA: Brooks/Cole Publishing Company.

Maslow, A. H. (1935). Individual psychology and the social behavior of monkeys and apes. *International Journal of Individual Psychology,* 1, 47–59.

Maslow, A. H. (1965). *Eupsychian management: A journal.* Homewood, IL: Irwin-Dorsey.

Maslow, A. H. (1966). *The psychology of science: A reconnaissance.* New York: Harper and Row.

Maslow, A. H. (1968). *Toward a psychology of being* (2nd ed.). New York: D. Van Nostrand Co.

Maslow, A. H. (1970). *Motivation and personality* (2nd ed.). New York: Harper & Row.

Maslow, A. H. (1971). *The farther reaches of human nature.* New York: Viking.

Neisser, U. (1967). *Cognitive psychology.* New York: Appleton-Century-Crofts.

Neisser, U. (1997). Never a dull moment. *American Psychologist,* 1(1), 79–81.

Chapter 1
The Cognitive Approach

Ulric Neisser (1923–)

It has been said that beauty is in the eye of the beholder. As a hypothesis about localization of function, the statement is not quite right—the brain and not the eye is surely the most important organ involved. Nevertheless it points clearly enough toward the central problem of cognition. Whether beautiful or ugly or just conveniently at hand, the world of experience is produced by the man who experiences it.

This is not the attitude of a skeptic, only of a psychologist. There certainly is a real world of trees and people and cars and even books, and it has a great deal to do with our experiences of these objects. However, we have no direct, *imm*ediate access to the world, nor to any of its properties. The ancient theory of *eidola,* which supposed that faint copies of objects can enter the mind directly, must be rejected. Whatever we know about reality has been *mediated,* not only by the organs of sense but by complex systems which interpret and reinterpret sensory information. The activity of the cognitive systems results in—and is integrated with—the activity of muscles and glands that we call "behavior." It is also partially—very partially—reflected in those private experiences of seeing, hearing, imagining, and thinking to which verbal descriptions never do full justice.

Physically, this page is an array of small mounds of ink, lying in certain positions on the more highly reflective surface of the paper. It is this physical page which Koffka (1935) and others would have called the "distal stimulus," and from which the reader is hopefully acquiring some information. But the sensory input is not the page itself; it is a pattern of light rays, originating in the sun or in some artificial source, that are reflected from the page and happen to reach the eye. Suitably focused by the lens and other ocular apparatus, the rays fall on the sensitive retina, where they can initiate the neural processes that eventually lead to seeing and reading and remembering. These patterns of light at the retina are the so-called "proximal stimuli." They are not the least bit like *eidola*. One-sided in their perspective, shifting radically several times each second, unique and novel at every moment, the proximal stimuli bear little resemblance to either the real object that gave rise to them or to the object of experience that the perceiver will construct as a result.

Visual cognition, then, deals with the processes by which a perceived, remembered, and thought-about world is brought into being from as unpromising a beginning as the retinal patterns. Similarly, auditory cognition is concerned with transformation of the fluctuating pressure pattern at the ear into the sounds and the speech and music that we hear. The problem of understanding these transformations may usefully be compared to a very different question, that arises in another psychological context. One of Freud's papers on human motivation is entitled "Instincts and their Vicissitudes" (1915). The title reflects a basic axiom of psychoanalysis: that man's fundamental motives suffer an intricate series of transformations, reformulations, and changes before they appear in either consciousness or action. Borrowing Freud's phrase—without intending any commitment to his theory of motivation—a book like this one might be called "Stimulus Information and its Vicissitudes." As used here, the term "cognition" refers to all the processes by which the sensory input is transformed, reduced, elaborated, stored, recovered, and used. It is concerned with these processes even when they operate in the absence of relevant stimulation, as in images and hallucinations. Such terms as *sensation, perception, imagery, retention, recall, problem-solving,* and *thinking,* among many others, refer to hypothetical stages or aspects of cognition.

Given such a sweeping definition, it is apparent that cognition is involved in everything a human being might possibly do; that every psychological phenomenon is a cognitive phenomenon. But although cognitive psychology is concerned with all human activity rather than some fraction of it, the concern is from a particular point of view. Other viewpoints are equally legitimate and necessary. Dynamic psychology, which begins with motives rather than with sensory input, is a case in point. Instead of asking how a man's actions and experiences result from what he saw, remembered, or believed, the dynamic psychologist asks how they follow from the subject's goals, needs, or instincts. Both questions can be asked about any activity, whether it be normal or abnormal, spontaneous or induced, overt or covert, waking or dreaming. Asked why I did a certain thing, I may answer in dynamic terms, "Because I wanted . . . ," or, from the cognitive point of view, "Because it seemed to me . . ."

In attempting to trace the fate of the input, our task is both easier and harder than that of dynamic psychology. It is easier because we have a tangible starting point. The pattern of stimulation that reaches the eye or the ear can be directly observed; the beginning of the cognitive transformations is open to inspection. The student of motivation does not have this advantage, except when he deals with the physical-deprivation motives like hunger and thirst. This forces him to rely rather more on speculation and less on observation than the cognitive theorist. But by the same token, the latter has an additional set of responsibilities. He cannot make assumptions casually, for they must conform to the results of 100 years of experimentation.

Recognition of the difference between cognitive and dynamic theory does not mean that we can afford to ignore motivation in a book like this one. Many cognitive phenomena are incomprehensible unless one takes some account of what the subject is trying to do. However, his purposes are treated here primarily as independent variables: we will note that they can affect one or another cognitive mechanism without inquiring closely into their origin. This strategy will break down in the final chapter; remembering and thinking are too "inner-directed" to be treated in such a fashion. As a consequence, the last chapter has a different format, and even a different purpose, from the others.

The cognitive and the dynamic viewpoints are by no means the only possible approaches to psychology. Behaviorism, for example, represents a very different tradition, which is essentially incompatible with both. From Watson (1913) to Skinner (1963), radical behaviorists have maintained that man's actions should be explained only in terms of observable variables, without any inner vicissitudes at all. The appeal to hypothetical mechanisms is said to be speculative at best, and deceptive at worst. For them, it is legitimate to speak of stimuli, responses, reinforcements, and hours of deprivation, but not of categories or images or ideas. A generation ago, a book like this one would have needed at least a chapter of self-defense against the behaviorist position. Today, happily, the climate of opinion has changed, and little or no defense is necessary. Indeed, stimulus-response theorists themselves are inventing hypothetical mechanisms with vigor and enthusiasm and only faint twinges of conscience. The basic reason for studying cognitive processes has become as clear as the reason for studying anything else: because they are there. Our knowledge of the world *must* be somehow developed from the stimulus input; the theory of *eidola* is false. Cognitive processes surely exist, so it can hardly be unscientific to study them.

Another approach to psychological questions, a world apart from behaviorism, is that of the physiologist. Cognition, like other psychological processes, can validly be studied in terms of the underlying neural events. For my part, I do not doubt that human behavior and consciousness depend entirely on the activity of the brain, in interaction with other physical systems. Most readers of this book will probably have the same prejudice. Nevertheless, there is very little of physiology or biochemistry in the chapters ahead. At a time when these fields are making impressive advances, such an omission may seem strange. An example may help to justify it. For this purpose, let us consider recent work on the physical basis of memory.

No one would dispute that human beings store a great deal of information about their past experiences, and it seems obvious that this information must be physically embodied somewhere in the brain. Recent discoveries in biochemistry have opened up a promising possibility. Some experimental findings have hinted that the complex molecules of DNA and RNA, known to be involved in the transmission of inherited traits, may be the substrate of memory as well. Although the supporting evidence so far is shaky, this hypothesis has already gained many adherents. But psychology is not just something "to do until the biochemist comes" (as I have recently heard psychiatry described); the truth or falsity of this new hypothesis is only marginally relevant to psychological questions. A pair of analogies will show why this is so.

First, let us consider the familiar parallel between man and computer. Although it is an inadequate analogy in many ways, it may suffice for this purpose. The task of a psychologist trying to understand human cognition is analogous to that of a man trying to discover how a computer has been programmed. In particular, if the program seems to store and reuse information, he would like to know by what "routines" or "procedures" this is done. Given this purpose, he will not care much whether his particular computer stores information in magnetic cores or in thin films; he wants to understand the program, not the "hardware." By the same token, it would not help the psychologist to know that memory is carried by RNA as opposed to some other medium. He wants to understand its utilization, not its incarnation.

Perhaps this overstates the case a little. The hardware of a computer may have some indirect effects on programming, and likewise the physical substrate may impose some limitations on the organization of mental events. This is particularly likely where peripheral (sensory and motor) processes are concerned, just as the input-output routines of a program will be most affected by the specific properties of the computer being used. Indeed, a few fragments of peripheral physiology will be considered in later chapters. Nevertheless they remain, in the familiar phrase, of only "peripheral interest."

The same point can be illustrated with quite a different analogy, that between psychology and economics. The economist wishes to understand, say, the flow of capital. The object of his study must have some tangible representation, in the form of checks, gold, paper money, and so on, but these objects are not what he really cares about. The physical properties of money, its location in banks, its movement in armored cars, are of little interest to him. To be sure, the remarkable permanence of gold has some economic importance. The flow of capital would be markedly different if every medium of exchange were subject to rapid corrosion. Nevertheless, such matters are not the main concern of the economist, and knowledge of them does not much simplify economic theory.

Psychology, like economics, is a science concerned with the interdependence among certain events rather than with their physical nature. Although there are many disciplines of this sort (classical genetics is another good example), the most prominent ones today are probably the so-called "information sciences," which include the mathematical theory of communication, computer programming, systems analysis, and related fields. It seems obvious that these must be relevant to cognitive psychology, which is itself much concerned with information. However, their importance for psychologists has often been misunderstood, and deserves careful consideration.

Information, in the sense first clearly defined by Shannon (1948), is essentially *choice*, the narrowing down of alternatives. He developed the mathematical theory of communication in order to deal quantitatively with the transmission of messages over "channels." A channel, like a telephone line, transmits information to the extent that the choices made at one end determine those made at the other. The words of the speaker are regarded as successive selections from among all the possible words of English. Ideally, the transmitted message will enable the listener to choose the same ones; that is, to identify each correctly. For practical purposes, it is important to measure the *amount* of information that a system can transmit, and early applications of information theory were much concerned with measurement. As is now well known, amounts of information are measured in units called "bits," or binary digits, where one "bit" is represented by a choice between two equally probable alternatives.

Early attempts to apply information theory to psychology were very much in this spirit (e.g., Miller, 1953; Quastler, 1955), and even today many psychologists continue to theorize and to report data in terms of "bits" (e.g., Garner, 1962; Posner, 1964a, 1966). I do not believe, however, that this approach was or is a fruitful one. Attempts to quantify psychological processes in informational terms have usually led, after much effort, to the conclusion that the "bit rate" is not a relevant variable after all. Such promising topics as reaction time, memory span, and language have all failed to sustain early estimates of the usefulness of information measurement. With the advantage of hindsight, we can see why this might have been expected. The "bit" was developed to describe the performance of rather unselective systems: a telephone cannot decide which portions of the incoming message are important. We shall see throughout this book that human beings behave very differently, and are by no means neutral or passive toward the incoming information. Instead, they select some parts for attention at the expense of others, recoding and reformulating them in complex ways.

Although information measurement may be of little value to the cognitive psychologist, another branch of the information sciences, *computer programming*, has much more to offer. A program is not a device for measuring information, but a recipe for selecting, storing, recovering, combining, outputting, and generally manipulating it. As pointed out by Newell, Shaw, and Simon (1958), this means that programs have much in common with theories of cognition. Both are descriptions of the vicissitudes of input information.

We must be careful not to confuse the program with the computer that it controls. Any single general-purpose computer can be "loaded" with an essentially infinite number of different programs. On the other hand, most programs can be run, with minor modifications, on many physically different kinds of computers. A program is not a machine; it is a series of instructions for dealing with symbols: "If the input has certain characteristics . . . then carry out certain procedures . . . otherwise other procedures . . . combine their results in various ways . . . store or retrieve various items . . . depending on prior results . . . use them in further specified ways . . . etc." The cognitive psychologist would like to give a similar account of the way information is processed by men.

This way of defining the cognitive problem is not really a new one. We are still asking "how the mind works." However, the "program analogy" (which may be a better term than "computer analogy") has several advantages over earlier conceptions. Most important is the philosophical reassurance which it provides. Although a program is nothing but a flow of symbols, it has reality enough to control the operation of very tangible machinery that executes very physical operations. A man who seeks to discover the program of a computer is surely not doing anything self-contradictory!

There were cognitive theorists long before the advent of the computer. Bartlett, whose influence on my own thinking will become obvious in later chapters, is a case in point. But, in the eyes of many psychologists, a theory which dealt with cognitive transformations, memory schemata, and the like was not *about* anything. One could understand theories that dealt with overt movements, or with physiology; one could even understand (and deplore) theories which dealt with the content of consciousness; but what kind of a thing is a schema? If memory consists of transformations, what is transformed? So long as cognitive psychology literally did not know what it was talking about, there was always a danger that it was talking about nothing at all. This is no longer a serious risk. *Information* is what is transformed, and the structured pattern of its transformations is what we want to understand.

A second advantage of the "program analogy" is that, like other analogies, it is a fruitful source of hypotheses. A field which is directly concerned with information processing should be at least as rich in ideas for psychology as other fields of science have been before. Just as we have borrowed atomic units, energy distributions, hydraulic pressures, and mechanical linkages from physics and engineering, so may we choose to adopt certain concepts from programming today. This will be done rather freely in some of the following chapters. Such notions as "parallel processing," "feature extraction," "analysis-by-synthesis," and "executive routine" have been borrowed from programmers, in the hope that they will prove theoretically useful. The test of their value, of course, is strictly psychological. We will have to see how well they fit the data.

The occasional and analogic use of programming concepts does not imply a commitment to computer "simulation" of psychological processes. It is true that a number of researchers, not content with noting that computer programs are *like* cognitive theories, have tried to write programs which *are* cognitive theories. The "Logic Theorist," a program developed by Newell, Shaw, and Simon (1958), does more than find proofs for logical theorems: it is intended as a theory of how human beings find such proofs. There has been a great deal of work in this vein recently. It has been lucidly reviewed, and sympathetically criticized, by Reitman (1965). However, such models will not be discussed here except in passing. In my opinion, none of them does even remote justice to the complexity of human mental processes. Unlike men, "artificially intelligent" programs tend to be single-minded, undistractable, and unemotional. Moreover, they are generally equipped from the beginning of each problem with all the cognitive resources necessary to solve it. These criticisms have already been presented elsewhere (Nisser, 1963c), and there is no need to elaborate them now. In a sense, the rest of this book can be construed as an extensive argument against models of this kind, and also against other simplistic theories of the cognitive processes. If the account of cognition given here is even roughly accurate, it will not be "simulated" for a long time to come.

The present volume is meant to serve a double purpose. On the one hand, I hope to provide a useful and current account of the existing "state of the art." In discussing any particular phenomenon—immediate memory, or understanding sentences, or subception, or selective listening—an attempt is made to cover the significant experiments, and to discuss the major theories. On the other hand, it must be admitted that few of these discussions are neutral. When the weight of the evidence points overwhelmingly in one direction rather than another, I prefer to say so frankly. This is especially because in most cases the indicated direction seems (to me) to be consistent with a particular view of the cognitive processes. Some of the chapters only hint at this theory, while in others it emerges explicitly. When it does, the first person singular is used rather freely, to help the reader distinguish between the facts and my interpretation of them. In the end, I hope to have presented not only a survey of cognitive psychology but the beginnings of an integration.

The title of this book involves a certain deliberate ambiguity. In one sense, "cognitive psychology" refers generally to the study of the cognitive mechanisms, quite apart from the interpretations put forward here. In another sense, "cognitive psychology" is a particular theory to which I have a specific personal commitment. By Chapter 11, it will have become so specific that Rock and Ceraso's (1964) "Cognitive Theory of Associative Learning" will be rejected as not cognitive enough! If the reader finds this dual usage confusing, I can only say that it seems unavoidable. Such double meanings are very common in psychology. Surely "Behavior Theory" is only one of many approaches to the study of behavior, just as "Gestalt Psychology" is not the only possible theory of visual figures (Gestalten), and "Psychoanalysis" is only one of many hypothetical analyses of psychological structure.

The present approach is more closely related to that of Bartlett (1932, 1958) than to any other contemporary psychologist, while its roots are at least as old as the "act psychology" of the nineteenth century. The central assertion is that seeing, hearing, and remembering are all acts of *construction*, which may make more or less use of stimulus information depending on circumstances. The constructive processes are assumed to have two stages, of which the first is fast, crude, wholistic, and parallel while the second is deliberate, attentive, detailed, and sequential.

The model is first elaborated here in five chapters on visual processes. These chapters include an account of the very temporary, "iconic" memory which stores the output of the first stage of construction; a review of various theories of pattern recognition together with relevant data; a specific presentation of the constructive theory as applied to visual recognition; a survey of reading and tachistoscopic word-perception insofar as they are understood; and a discussion of visual memory, imagery, and hallucination. Four subsequent chapters on hearing[1] cover the perception of words, considered in terms of both acoustics and linguistics; various theories of auditory attention, including one which interprets it as a constructive process; the classical "immediate memory" for strings of words; and an account of linguistic structure together with its implications for psychology.

The final chapter on memory and thought is essentially an epilogue, different in structure from the rest of the book. Because of the tremendous scope of these higher mental processes, no attempt is made to cover the relevant data, or to refute competing theories, and the views put forward are quite tentative. Nevertheless, the reader of a book called *Cognitive Psychology* has a right to expect some discussion of thinking, concept-formation, remembering, problem-solving, and the like; they have traditionally been part of the field. If they take up only a tenth of these pages, it is because I believe there is still relatively little to say about them, even after 100 years of psychological research.

There is another respect in which this book may seem incomplete. The cognitive processes under discussion are primarily those of the American adult, or at least of the college student who is so frequently the subject of psychological experiments. Although there will be occasional references to the developmental psychology of cognition, it will not be reviewed systematically. In part, this is because the course of cognitive growth is so little understood. However, even in areas where development is being actively studied, such as concept formation and psycholinguistics, I have not felt qualified to review it.

One last word of explanation is necessary, before concluding an introduction that is already overlong. Many topics that the reader may have expected to find have now been set aside. We will consider neither physiological mechanisms nor information measurement nor computer simulation nor developmental psychology; even remembering and thought are to receive short shrift. Despite these omissions, it must not be thought that the field which remains to be explored is a narrow one. Although the core of the material presented here is taken from within experimental psychology itself, there is extensive use of data and concepts from other fields, including psychiatry and clinical psychology (especially in connection with hallucinations); hypnosis; the social psychology of the psychological experiment; the physiology and psychology of sleep: the study of reading, which too often has been relegated to educational psychology; computer programming; linguistics and psycholinguistics. The reader may hesitate to follow along a path that seems so full of side alleys, and perhaps blind ones at that. I can only hope he will not be altogether discouraged. No shorter route seems to do justice to the vicissitudes of the input, and to the continuously creative processes by which the world of experience is constructed.

---

[1]Sense modalities other than vision and hearing are largely ignored in this book, because so little is known about the cognitive processing involved.

Self-Actualizing People: A Study of Psychological Health

Abraham Maslow

[149][1]
PERSONAL FOREWORD

The study to be reported in this chapter is unusual in various ways. It was not planned as an ordinary research;[2] it was not a social venture but a private one, motivated by my own curiosity and pointed toward the solution of various personal moral, ethical, and scientific problems. I sought only to convince and to teach myself rather than to prove or to demonstrate to others.

Quite unexpectedly, however, these studies have proved to be so enlightening to me, and so laden with exciting implications, that it seems fair that some sort of report should be made to others in spite of its methodological shortcomings.

In addition, I consider the problem of psychological health to be so pressing, that *any* suggestions, *any* bits of data, however moot, are endowed with great heuristic value. This kind of research is in principle so difficult—involving as it does a kind of lifting oneself by one's own norms—that if we were to wait for conventionally reliable data, we should have to wait forever. It seems that the only manly thing to do is not to fear mistakes, to plunge in, to do the best that one can, hoping to learn enough from blunders to correct them eventually. At present the only alternative is simply to refuse to work with the problems. Accordingly, for whatever use can be made of it, the following report is presented with due apologies to those who insist on conventional reliability, validity, sampling, etc.

[153]
GATHERING AND PRESENTATION OF THE DATA

Data here consist not so much in the usual gathering of specific and discrete facts as in the slow development of a global or holistic impression of the sort that we form of our friends and acquaintances. It was rarely possible to set up a situation, to ask pointed questions, or to do any testing with my older subjects (although this was possible and *was* done with younger subjects). Contacts were fortuitous and of the ordinary social sort. Friends and relatives were questioned where this was possible.

---

[1]Since this article has been edited and abridged, readers should note that pages in boldfaced brackets correspond to pagination found in the original article: Maslow, A. H. (1970) *Motivation and emotion.* (2nd ed.). New York: Harper and Row.

[2]That Maslow viewed much, if not all, of his work as research is indicative of the scientific viewpoint he gained while a student of Harry Harlow at Wisconsin.

Because of this and also because of the number of subjects as well as the incompleteness of the data for many subjects, any qualitative presentation is impossible: only composite impressions can be offered for whatever they may be worth.

The holistic analysis of these total impressions yields, as the most important and useful whole characteristics of self-actualizing people for further clinical and experimental study, the following Maslow used:

MORE EFFICIENT PERCEPTION OF REALITY AND MORE COMFORTABLE RELATIONS WITH IT

The first form in which this capacity was noticed was as an unusual ability to detect the spurious, the fake, and the dishonest in personality, and in general to judge people correctly and efficiently. In an informal experiment with a group of college students, a clear tendency was discerned for the more secure (the more health) to judge their professors more accurately than did the less secure students, i.e., high scorers in the S-I test (294).[1]

As the study progressed, it slowly became apparent that this efficiency extended to many other areas of life—indeed *all* areas that were observed. In art and music, in things of the intellect, in scientific matters, in politics and public affairs, they seemed as a group to be able to see concealed or confused realities more swiftly and more correctly than others. Thus an informal survey indicated that their predictions of the future from whatever facts were in hand at the time seemed to be more often correct, because less based upon wish, desire, anxiety, fear, or upon generalized, character-determined optimism or pessimism.

At first this was phrased as good taste or good judgment, the implication being relative and not absolute. But for many reasons, it has become progressively more clear that this had better be called perception (not taste) of something that was absolutely there (reality, not a set of opinions). It is hoped that this conclusion—or hypothesis—can one day be put to the experimental test.

[154] It was found that self-actualizing people distinguished far more easily than most the fresh, concrete and idiographic from the generic, abstract, and rubricized. The consequence is that they live more in the real world of nature than in the man-made mass of concepts, abstractions, expectations, beliefs, and stereotypes that most people confuse with the world. They are therefore far more apt to perceive what is there rather than their own wishes, hopes, fears, anxieties, their own theories and beliefs, or those of their cultural group. "The innocent eye," Herbert Read has very effectively called it.

The relationship with the unknown seems to be of exceptional promise as another bridge between academic and clinical psychology. Our healthy subjects are

---

[1]Numbers in parenthesis indicate reference numbers used by Maslow in the original work.

generally unthreatened and unfrightened by the unknown, being therein quite different from average men. They accept it, are comfortable with it, and, often are even *more* attracted to it than by the known. They not only tolerate the ambiguous and unstructured (135); they like it.

[155] Since for healthy people, the unknown is not frightening, they do not have to spend any time laying the ghost, whistling past the cemetery, or otherwise protecting themselves against imagined dangers. They do not neglect the unknown, or deny it, or run away from it, or try to make believe it is really known. . . .

Thus it comes about that doubt, tentativeness, uncertainty, with the consequent necessity for abeyance of decision, which is for most a torture, can be for some a pleasantly stimulating challenge, a high spot in life rather than a low.

ACCEPTANCE (SELF, OTHERS, NATURE)

A good many personal qualities that can be perceived on the surface and that seem at first to be various and unconnected may be understood as manifestations or derivatives of a more fundamental single attitude, namely, of a relative lack of overriding guilt, of crippling shame, and of extreme or severe anxiety. This is in direct contrast with the neurotic person who in every instance may be described as crippled by guilt and/or shame and/or anxiety. Even the normal member of our culture feels unnecessarily guilty or ashamed about too many things and has anxiety in too many unnecessary situations. Our healthy individuals find it possible to accept themselves and their own nature without chagrin or complaint or, for that matter, even without thinking about the matter very much.

They can accept their own human nature in the stoic style, with all its shortcomings with all its discrepancies from the ideal image without feeling real concern. It would convey the wrong impression to say that they are self-satisfied. What we must say rather is that they can take the frailties and sins, weaknesses, and evils of human nature in the same unquestioning spirit with which one accepts the characteristics of nature.

[156] The first and most obvious level of acceptance is at the so-called animal level. Those self-actualizing people tend to be good animals, hearty in their appetites and enjoying themselves without regret or shame or apology. They seem to have a uniformly good appetite for food; they seem to sleep well; they seem to enjoy their sexual lives without unnecessary inhibition and so on for all their relatively physiological impulses. They are able to accept themselves not only on these low levels, but at all levels as well; e.g., love, safety, belongingness, honor, self-respect.

Closely related to self-acceptance and to acceptance of others is (1) their lack of defensiveness, protective coloration or pose, and (2) their distaste for such artificialities in others. Cant, guile, hypocrisy, front, face, playing a game, trying to impress in conventional ways: these are all absent in themselves to an unusual degree. Since they can live comfortably even with their own shortcomings, these finally come to be perceived, especially in later life, as not shortcomings at all, but simply as neutral personal characteristics.

This is not an absolute late of guilt, shame, sadness, anxiety, defensiveness; it as a lack of unnecessary or neurotic (because unrealistic) guilt, etc. The animal process, e.g., sex, urination, pregnancy, menstruation, growing old, etc., are part of reality and so must be accepted. Thus no healthy [157] need feel guilty or defensive about being female or about any of the female processes.

What healthy people *do* feel guilty about (or ashamed, anxious, sad, or regretful) are (1) improbable shortcomings, e.g., laziness, thoughtlessness, loss of temper, hurting others; (2) stubborn remnants of psychological ill health, e.g., prejudice, jealousy, envy; (3) habits, which, thought relatively independent of character structure, may yet be very strong; or (4) shortcomings of the species or of the culture or of the group with which they have been identified. The general formula seems to be that healthy people will feel bad about discrepancies between what is and what might very well be or ought to be (2, 148, 199).

Spontaneity; Simplicity; Naturalness

Self-actualizing people can all be described as relatively spontaneous in behavior and far more spontaneous than that in their inner life, thoughts, impulses, etc. Their behavior is marked by simplicity and naturalness, and by lack of artificiality or straining for effect. This does not necessarily mean consistently unconventional behavior. If we were to take an actual count of the number of times that the self-actualizing person behaved in an unconventional manner the tally would not be high. His unconventionality is not superficial but essential or internal. It is his impulses, thought, consciousness that are so unusually unconventional, spontaneous, and natural. Apparently recognizing that the world of people in which he lives could not understand or accept this, and since he has no wish to hurt them or to fight with them over every triviality, he will go through the ceremonies and rituals of convention with a good-humored shrug and with the best possible grace.

This same inner attitude can also be seen in those moments when the person becomes keenly absorbed in something that is close to one of his main interests. He can then be seen quite casually to drop off all [158] sorts of rules of behavior to which at other times he conforms; it is as if he has to make a conscious effort to be conventional; as if he were conventional voluntarily and by design.

One consequence or correlate of this characteristic is that these people have codes of ethics that are relatively autonomous and individual rather than conventional. The unthinking observer might sometimes believe them to be unethical, since they can break down not only conventions but laws when the situation seems to demand it. But the very opposite is the case. They are the most ethical of people even though there ethics are not necessarily the same as those of the people around them. It is this kind of observation that leads us to understand very assuredly that the ordinary ethical behavior of the average person is largely conventional behavior rather than truly ethical behavior, e.g., behavior based on fundamentally accepted principles (which are perceived to be true).

Clinical studies of this capacity confirms [159] beyond a doubt the opinion, e.g., of Fromm (145) that the average normal, well-adjusted person often has not the slightest idea of what he is, of what he wants, of what his own opinions are.

It was such findings as these that let ultimately to the discovery of a most profound difference between self-actualizing people and others; namely, that the motivational life of self-actualizing people is not only quantitatively different but also qualitatively different from that of ordinary people. It seems probable that we must construct a profoundly different psychology of motivation for self-actualizing people, e.g., meta-motivation or growth motivation, rather than deficiency motivation. Perhaps it will be useful to make a distinction between living and preparing to live. Perhaps the ordinary concept of motivation should apply only to nonself-actualizers. Our subjects no longer strive in the ordinary sense, but rather to develop. They attempt to grow to perfection and to develop more and more fully in their own style.

PROBLEM CENTERING

Our subjects are in general strongly focused on problems outside themselves. In current terminology they are problem centered rather than ego centered. They generally are not problems for themselves and are not generally much concerned about themselves, e.g., as contrasted with the ordinary introspectiveness that one finds in insecure people. These individuals customarily have some mission in life, some task to fulfill, some problem outside themselves which enlists much of their energies (72, 134).

This is not necessarily a task that they would prefer or choose for themselves; it may be a task that they feel is their responsibility, duty, or obligation. This is why we use the phrase "a task that they must do" rather than the phrase "a task that they want to do." In general these tasks are nonpersonal or unselfish, concerned rather with the good of [160] mankind in general, or of a nation in general, or of a few individuals in the subject's family.

With a few exceptions we can say that our subjects are ordinarily concerned with basic issues and external questions of the type that we have learned to call philosophical or ethical. Such people live customarily in the widest possible frame of reference. They seem never to get so close to the trees that they fail to see the forest. They work within a framework of values that are broad and not petty, universal and not local, and in terms of a century rather than the moment. In a word, these people are all in one sense or another philosophers, however homely.

THE QUALITY OF DETACHMENT;
THE NEED FOR PRIVACY

For all my subjects it is true that they can be solitary without harm to themselves and without discomfort. Furthermore, it is true for almost all that they positively *like* solitude and privacy to a definitely greater degree than the average person.

It is often possible for them to remain above the battle, to remain unruffled, undisturbed by that which produces turmoil in others. They find it easy to be aloof, reserved, and also calm and serene; thus it becomes possible for them to take personal misfortunes without reacting violently as the ordinary person does. They seem to be able to retain their dignity even in undignified surroundings and situations. Perhaps this comes in part from their tendency to stick by their own interpretation of a situation rather than to rely on what other people feel or think about the matter. This reserve may shade over into austerity and remoteness.

This quality of detachment may have some connection with certain other qualities as well. For one thing it is possible to call my subjects more objective (in all senses of that word) than average people. We have seen that they are more problem centered than ego centered. This is true even [161] when the problem concerns themselves, their own wishes, motives, hopes, or aspirations. Consequently, they have the ability to concentrate to a degree not usual for ordinary men. Intense concentration produces as a byproduct some phenomena as absent-mindedness, the ability to forget and to be oblivious of outer surroundings. Examples are the ability to sleep soundly, to have undisturbed appetite, to be able to smile and laugh through a period of problems, worry, and responsibility.

Another meaning of autonomy is self-decision, self-government, being an active, responsible, self-disciplined, deciding agent rather than a pawn, or helplessly "determined" by others, being strong rather than weak. My subjects make up their own minds, come to their own decisions, are self-starters, are responsible for themselves and their own destinies. It is a subtle quality, difficult to describe in words, and yet profoundly important.

The extensive experiments by Asch (20) and by McClelland (326–328) permit us to guess that self-determiners come to perhaps 5 percent to 30 percent of our population depending on the particular circumstances. Of my self-actualizing subjects, 100 percent are self-movers.

Finally I must make a statement even though it will certainly be disturbing to many theologians, philosophers, and scientists: self-actualizing [162] individuals have more "free will" and are less "determined" than average people are. However the words "free will" and "determinism" may come to be operationally defined, in this investigation they are empirical realities. Furthermore, they are degree concepts, varying in amount; they are not all-or-none packages.

AUTONOMY; INDEPENDENCE OF CULTURE AND ENVIRONMENT; WILL; ACTIVE AGENTS

One of the characteristics of self-actualizing people, which to a certain extent crosscuts much of what we have already described, is their relative independence of the physical and social environment. Since they are propelled by growth motivation rather than deficiency motivation, self-actualizing people are not dependent for their main satisfactions on the real world, or other people or culture or means to ends or, in general, on extrinsic satisfactions. Rather they are dependent for their own development and continued growth on their own potentialities and latent resources.

Just as the tree needs sunshine and water and food, so do most people need love, safety, and the other basic need gratifications that can come only from without. But once these external satisfiers are obtained, once these inner deficiencies are satiated by outside satisfiers, the true problem of individual human development begins, e.g., self-actualization.

We must remember that the best technique we know, even though not the only one, for getting to this point of relative independence from love and respect, is to have been given plenty of this very same love and respect in the past.

[163]
CONTINUED FRESHNESS OF APPRECIATION

Self-actualizing people have the wonderful capacity to appreciate again and again, freshly and naively, the basic goods of life, with awe, pleasure, wonder, and even ecstasy, however stale these experiences may have become to others—what C. Wilson has called "newness" (483). Thus for such a person, any sunset may be as beautiful as the first one, any flower may be of breath-taking loveliness, even after he has seen a million flowers. The thousandth baby he sees is just as miraculous a product as the first one he saw. He remains as convinced of his luck in marriage thirty years after his marriage and is as surprised by his wife's beauty when she is sixty as he was forty years before. For such people, even the casual workaday, moment-to-moment business of living can be thrilling, exciting, and ecstatic. These intense feelings do not come all the time; they come occasionally rather than usually, but at the most unexpected moments.

I have also become convinced that getting used to our blessings is one of the most important nonevil generators of human evil, tragedy, and suffering. What we take for granted we undervalue, and we are [164] therefore too apt to sell a valuable birthright for a mess of pottage. . . . Something similar is true for physical health, for political freedoms, for economic well-being; we learn their true value after we have lost them.

THE MYSTIC EXPERIENCE; THE PEAK EXPERIENCE

Those subjective expressions that have been called the mystic experience and described so well by William James (212) are a fairly common experience for our subjects though not for all. The strong emotions described in the previous section sometimes get strong enough, chaotic and widespread enough to be called mystic experiences. . . . There were the same feelings of limitless horizons opening up to the vision, the feelings of being simultaneously more powerful and also more helpless than one ever was before, the feeling of great ecstasy and wonder and awe . . . so that the subject is to some extent transformed and strengthened even in his daily life by such experiences.

It is quite important to dissociate this experience from any theological or supernatural reference, even though for thousands of years they have been linked. Because this experience is a natural experience well within the jurisdiction of science, I call it the peak experience.

[165]
GEMEINSCHAFTSGEFÜHL

This word, invented by Alfred Adler (2), is the only one available that describes well the flavor of the feelings for mankind expressed by self-actualizing subjects. They have for human beings in general a deep feeling of identification, sympathy, and affection in spite of the occasional anger, impatience, or disgust described below. Because of this they have a genuine desire to help the human race. It is as if they were all members of a single family. One's feelings toward his brothers would be on the whole affectionate, even if these brothers were foolish, weak, or even if they were sometimes nasty. They would still be more easily forgiven than strangers.

If one's view is not general enough and if it is not spread over a long period of time, then one many not see this feeling of identification with mankind. The self-actualizing person is after all very different from other [166] people in thought, impulse, behavior, emotion. When it comes down to it, in certain basic ways he is like an alien in a strange land. . . . However far apart he is from them at times, he nevertheless feels a basic underlying kinship with these creatures whom he must regard with, if not condescension, at least the knowledge that he can do many things better than they can, that he can see things that they cannot see, that the truth that is so clear to him is for most people veiled and hidden. This is what Adler called the older-brotherly attitude.

INTERPERSONAL RELATIONS_SA

Self-actualizing people have deeper and more profound interpersonal relations than any other adults (although not necessarily deeper than those of children). They are capable of more fusion, greater love, more perfect identification, more obliteration of the ego boundaries than other people would consider possible. There are, however, certain special characteristics of these relationships. In the first place, it is my observation that the other members of these relationships are likely to be healthier and closer to self-actualization than the average, often *much* closer: There is high selectiveness here, considering the small proportion of such people in the general population.

One consequence of this phenomenon and of certain others as well is that self-actualizing people have these especially deep ties with rather *few* individuals. Their circle of friends is rather small. The ones that they love profoundly are few in number. Partly this is for the reason that being very close to someone in this self-actualizing style seems to require a good deal of time. . . . This exclusiveness of devotion can and does exist side by side with a wide-spreading *Gemeinschaftsgefühl,* benevolence, affection, and friendliness (as qualified above). These people tend to be kind or at least patient to [167] almost everyone. They have an especially tender love for children and are easily touched by time. In a very real even though special sense, they love or rather have compassion for all mankind.

This love does not imply lack of discrimination. The fact is that they can and do speak realistically and harshly of those who deserve it, and especially of the hypocritical, the pretentious, the pompous, or the self-inflated.

THE DEMOCRATIC CHARACTER STRUCTURE

All my subjects without exception may be said to be democratic people in the deepest possible sense. I say this on the basis of a previous analysis of authoritarian (303) and democratic character structures that is too elaborate to present here; it is possible only to describe some aspects of this behavior in short space. These people have all the obvious or superficial democratic characteristic. They can be and are friendly with anyone of suitable character regardless of class, education, political belief, race, or color. As a matter of fact it often seems as if they are not even aware of these differences, which are for the average person so obvious and so important.

They have not only this most obvious quality but their democratic [168] feeling goes deeper as well. For instance they find it possible to learn from anybody who has something to teach them—no matter what other characteristics he may have. . . . It should even be said that my subjects share a quality that could be called humility of a certain type. They are all quite well aware of how little they know then in comparison with what *could* be known and what *is* known by others.

DISCRIMINATION BETWEEN MEANS AND ENDS, BETWEEN GOOD AND EVIL

I have found none of my subjects to be chronically unsure about the difference between right and wrong in his actual living. Whether or not they could verbalize the matter, they rarely showed in their day-to-day living the chaos, the confusion, the inconsistency, or the conflict that are so common in the average person's ethical dealings. This may be phrased also in the following terms: these individuals are strongly ethical, they have definite moral standards, they do right and do not do wrong. Needless to say, their notions of right and wrong and of good and evil are often not the conventional ones.

[169] Self-actualizing people most of the time behave as though, for them, means and ends are clearly distinguishable. In general they are fixed on ends rather than on means, and means are quite definitely subordinated to these ends. This, however, is an overly simple statement. Our subjects make the situation more complex by often regarding as ends in themselves many experiences and activities that are, for other people, only means. Our subjects are somewhat more likely to appreciate for its own sake, and in an absolute way, the doing itself; they can often enjoy for its own sake the getting to some place as well as the arriving. It is occasionally possible for them to make out of the most trivial and routine activity an intrinsically enjoyable game or dance or play.

PHILOSOPHICAL, UNHOSTILE SENSE OF HUMOR

One very early finding that was quite easy to make, because it was common to all my subjects, was that their sense of humor is not of the ordinary type. They do not consider funny what the average man considers to be funny. Thus they do not laugh at hostile humor (making people laugh by hurting someone) or superiority humor (laughing at someone else's inferiority) or authority-rebellion humor (their unfunny, Oedipal, or smutty joke). Characteristically what they consider humor is more closely allied to philosophy than to anything else. It may also be called the humor of the real because it consists in large part in poking fun at human beings in general when they are foolish, or forget their place in the universe, or try to be big when they are actually small. This can take the form of poking fun at themselves, but this is not done in [170] any masochistic or clownlike way. Lincoln's humor can serve as a suitable example. Probably Lincoln never made a joke that hurt anybody else; it is also likely that many or even most of his jokes had something to say, had a function beyond just producing a laugh. They often seemed to be education in a more palatable form, akin to parables or fables.

CREATIVENESS~SA~

This is a universal characteristic of all the people studied or observed. There is no exception. Each one shows in one way or another a special kind of creativeness or originality or inventiveness that has certain peculiar characteristics. These special characteristics can be understood more fully in the light of discussion later in this chapter. For one thing, it is different for the special-talent creativeness of the Mozart type. We may as well face the fact that the so-called geniuses display ability that we do not understand. All we can say of them is that they seem to be especially endowed with a drive and a capacity that may have rather little relationship to the rest of the personality and with which, from all evidence, the individuals seem to be born. Such talent we have no concern with here since it does not rest upon psychic health or basic satisfaction. The creativeness of the self-actualized man seems rather to be kin to the naive and universal creativeness of unspoiled children. It seems to be more a fundamental characteristic of common human nature—a potentiality given to all human beings at birth. Most human beings [171] lose this as they become enculturated, but some few individuals seem either to retain this fresh and naive, direct way of looking at life, or if they have lost it, as most people do, they later in life recover it. Santayana called this the "second naiveté," a very good name for it.

This creativeness appears in some of our subjects not in the usual forms of writing books, composing music, or producing artistic objects, but rather may be much more humble. It is as if this special type of creativeness, being an expression of healthy personality, is projected out upon the world or touches whatever activity the person is engaged in. In this sense there can be creative shoemakers or carpenters or clerks. Whatever one does can be done with a certain attitude, a certain spirit that arises out of the nature of the character of the person performing the act. One can even *see* creatively as the child does.

Furthermore, as we have seen, these individuals are less inhibited, less constricted, less bound, in a word, less enculturated. In more positive terms, they are more spontaneous, more natural, more human. . . . If we assume, as we may from our study of children, that all people were once spontaneous, and perhaps in their deepest roots still are . . . If there were no choking-off forces, we might expect that every human being would show this special type of creativeness (10, 307).

RESISTANCE TO ENCULTURATION; THE TRANSCENDENCE OF ANY PARTICULAR CULTURE

Self-actualized people are not well adjusted (in the naive sense of approval of and identification with the culture). They get along with the culture in various ways, but of all of them it may be said that in a certain profound and meaningful sense they resist enculturation (295) and maintain a certain inner detachment from the culture in which they are [172] immersed. Since in the culture-and-personality literature very little has been said about resistance to molding by the culture, . . . even our meager data are of some importance.

On the whole the relationship of these healthy people with their much less healthy culture is a complex one; from it can be teased out at least the following components.

1. All these people fall well within the limits of apparent conventionality in choice of clothes, of language, of food, of ways of doing things in our culture. And yet they are not *really* conventional, certainly not fashionable or smart or chic.

   But since this tolerant acceptance of harmless folkways is not warm approval with identification, their yielding to convention is apt to be rather casual and perfunctory, with cutting of corners in favor of directness, honesty, saving of energy, etc.

2. Hardly any of these people can be called authority rebels in the adolescent or hot sense. They show no active impatience or moment-to-moment, chronic, long-time discontent with the culture or preoccupation with changing it quickly, although they often enough show bursts of indignation with injustice. All . . . show which might be called a calm, long-time concern with culture improvement that seems to me to imply an acceptance of slowness of change along with the unquestioned desirability and necessity of such change.

   This is by no means a lack of fight. When quick change is possible or [173] when resolution and courage are needed, it is available in these people. Although they are not a radical group of people in the ordinary sense, I think they easily could be. . . . My impression is that they are not against fighting, but only against ineffective fighting.

3. An inner feeling of detachment from the culture is not necessarily conscious but is displayed by almost all, particularly in discussions of the American culture as a whole, in various comparisons with other cultures, and in the fact that they very frequently seem to be able to stand off from it as if they did not quite belong to it. . . . In a word they weigh it, assay it, taste it, and then make their own decisions.

   Detachment from the culture is probably also reflected in our self-actualizing subjects' detachment from people and their liking for privacy, which has been described above, as also in their less than average need for the familiar and customary.

4. For these and other reasons they may be called autonomous, i.e., [174] ruled by the laws of their own character rather than by the rules of society. It is in this sense that they are not only or merely Americans, but also to a greater degree than others, members at large of the human species.

   In summary the perennial question, "Is it possible to be a good or healthy man in an imperfect culture?" has been answered by the observation that it *is* possible for relatively healthy people to develop in the American culture. They manage to get along by a complex combination of inner autonomy and outer acceptance that of course will be possible only so long as the culture remains tolerant of this kind of detached withholding from complete cultural identification.

The Imperfections of Self-Actualizing People

The ordinary mistake that is made by novelists, poets, and essayists about the good human being is to make him so good that he is a caricature, so [175] that nobody would like to be like him. The individual's own wishes for perfection, and his guilt and shame about shortcomings are projected upon various kinds of people from whom the average man demands much more than he himself gives. . . . Our subjects show many of the lesser human failings. They too are equipped with silly, wasteful, or thoughtless habits. They can be boring, stubborn, irritating. They are by no means free from a rather superficial vanity, pride, partiality to their own productions, family, friends, and children. Temper outbursts are not rare.

[176] Even their kindness can lead them into mistakes, e.g., marrying out of pity, getting too closely involved with neurotics, bores, unhappy people, and then being sorry for it, allowing scoundrels to impose on them for a while, giving more than they should so that occasionally they encourage parasites and psychopaths, etc.

Finally, it has already been pointed out that these people are not free of guilt, anxiety, sadness, self-castigation, internal strife, and conflict. The fact that these arise out of nonneurotic sources is of little consequence to most people today (even to most psychologists) who are therefore apt to think them *un*healthy for this reason.

What this has taught me I think all of us had better learn. *There are no perfect human beings!* Persons can be found who are good, very good indeed, in fact, great. There do in fact exist creators, seers, sages, saints, shakers, and movers. This can certainly give us hope for the future of the species even if they *are* uncommon and do *not* come by the dozen. And yet these very same people can at times be boring, irritating, petulant, selfish, angry, or depressed. To avoid disillusionment with human nature, we must first give up our illusions about it.

VALUES AND SELF-ACTUALIZATION

A firm foundation for a value system is automatically furnished to the self-actualizer by his philosophic acceptance of the nature of his self, of human nature, of much of social life, and of nature and physical reality. These acceptance values account for a high percentage of the total of his individual value judgments from day to day. What he approves of, disapproves of, is loyal to, opposes or proposes, what pleases him or displeases him can often be understood at surface derivations of this source trait of acceptance.

Not only is this foundation automatically (and universally) supplied to *all* self-actualizers by their intrinsic dynamics (so that in at least this respect fully developed human nature may be universal and cross-cultural); other determiners are supplied as well by these same dynamics. Among these are (1) his peculiarly comfortable relationships with reality, (2) his *Gemeinschaftsgefühl*, (3) his basically satisfied condition from which flow, as epiphenomena, various consequences of surplus, of wealth, overflowing abundance, (4) his characteristically discriminating relations to means and ends, etc. (see above).

One most important consequence of this attitude toward the world [177]—as well as a validation of it—is the fact that conflict and struggle, ambivalence and uncertainty over choice lessen or disappear in many areas of life. Apparently much so-called "morality" is largely an epiphenomenon of nonacceptance or dissatisfaction. Many problems are seen to be gratuitous and fade out of existence in the atmosphere of pagan acceptance. It is not so much that the problem is solved as that it becomes clearly seen that it never was an intrinsic problem in the first place, but only a sick-man-created one, e.g., card-playing, dancing, wearing short dresses, exposing the head (in some churches) or *not* exposing the head (in others). . . . Not only are such trivialities deflated; the process also goes on at a more important level, e.g., the relations between the sexes, attitudes toward the structure of the body and toward its functioning, and toward death itself.

The pursuit of this finding to more profound levels has suggested to the writer that much else of what passes for morals, ethics, and values may be the simple by-products of the pervasive psychopathology of the average.

[178] The topmost portion of the value system of the self-actualized person is entirely unique and idiosyncratic-character-structure-expressive. . . . They are more completely individual than any group that has ever been described and yet are also more completely socialized, more identified with humanity than any other group yet described. They are closer to *both* their species-hood and to their unique individuality.

THE RESOLUTION OF DICHOTOMIES IN SELF-ACTUALIZATION

At this point we may finally allow ourselves to generalize and underscore a very important theoretical conclusion derivable from the study of self-actualizing people. At several points in this chapter—and in other chapters as well—it was concluded that what had been considered in the past to be polarities or opposites or dichotomies were so *only in less healthy people.* In healthy people, these dichotomies were resolved, the polarities [179] disappeared and many oppositions thought to be intrinsic merged and coalesced with each other to form unities.

In this, as in other ways, healthy people are so different from average [180] ones, not only in degree but in kind as well, that they generate two very different kinds of psychology. It becomes more and more clear that the study of crippled, stunted, immature, and unhealthy specimens can yield only a cripple psychology and a cripple philosophy. The study of self-actualizing people must be the basis for a more universal science of psychology.

AFTERWORD

What is one to think after reading several competing theories about psychology? The following poem by John Godfrey Saxe (1882) provides an interesting perspective:

It was six men of Indostan
    To learning much inclined,
Who went to see the Elephant
    (Though all of them were blind).
That each by observation
    Might satisfy his mind.

The *First* approached the Elephant
    and happening to fall
Against his broad and sturdy side,
    At once began to bawl:
"God bless me but the Elephant
    is very like a wall!"

The *Second* feeling of the tusk
    Cried, "Ho what have we here
So very round and smooth and sharp?
    To me 'tis mighty clear
This wonder of an elephant
    Is very like a spear!"

The *Third* approached the animal,
    And happening to take
The squirming trunk within his hands,
    Thus boldly up and spake:
"I see," quoth he, "the Elephant
    Is very like a snake!"

The *Fourth* reached out his eager hand,
    And felt about the knee.
"What this wondrous beast is like
    Is very plain," quoth he;
"'Tis clear enough the Elephant
    Is very like a tree!"

The *Fifth,* who chanced to touch the ear,
    Said: "E'en the blindest man
Can tell what this resembles most;
    Deny the fact who can,
This marvel of an Elephant
    Is very like a fan!"

The *Sixth* no sooner had begun
    About the beast to grope,
Than seizing on the swinging tail
    That fell within his scope,
"I see," quoth he, "the Elephant
    Is very like a rope!"

And so these men of Indostan
    Disputed loud and long,
Each in his own opinion
    Exceeding stiff and strong
Though each was partly in the right,
    And all were in the wrong!

    This poem raises exciting questions for the field of psychology. Upon reflection, two come immediately to mind: (1) is there part of the elephant that is yet to be discovered? and (2) is it possible to develop a theory that covers many parts of the elephant? History shows us that the answer to the first question is yes. One can cite with some irony the major developments of the 19th and 20th centuries as examples. In the 19th century, psychologists discovered that physiological disorders could have a psychological basis, and in the 20th-century, psychologists have discovered the physiological basis for many psychological disorders. One new frontier, or part of the elephant, might be the creative integration of psychological and physiological knowledge. Richter's (1957) fascinating article concerning the sudden death phenomenon, for instance, represents an intriguing speculation about the physiology of hope. More recently, Pennebaker (1988) and his colleagues have documented the physical benefits of keeping a journal concerning psychologically distressing events.

    Regarding the second question, psychologists of the 1960s and 1970s would have despaired at the idea of an integrative scheme appearing on the horizon. Yet, one could make a case that cognitive theory might be the first integrating system for psychology. Certainly, cognitive theory has dramatically influenced the way contemporary psychologists view learning, memory, language, social psychology, psychotherapy, and personality theory. We are, perhaps, on the verge of becoming a paradigmatic science. This is, of course, speculation. Even if impossible, this quest is worthwhile. The history of psychology is important because it both informs us about our inherited knowledge base and points the way to what potentially could be known. It is an exciting state of affairs to know there are vast continents yet to be explored. Aristotle was right, human nature is to know.

REFERENCES

Pennebaker, J. W., Khecolt-Glaser, J. K., & Glaser, R. (1988). Disclosure of traumas and immune function: Health implications for psychotherapy. *Journal of Consulting and Clinical Psychology, 56,* 239–245.

Richter, C. P. (1957). The phenomenon of sudden death in animals and man. *Psychosomatic Medicine, 19,* 191–198.

Saxe, J. G. (1882). *Poetical works.* Boston: Houghton Mifflin, pp. 111–112.

INDEX

Abnormal, perfection in the, 279-280
Acceptance, self-actualization and, 304-305
Active agents, 307-308
Adaptation, striving as ultimate, 278-279
Adler, Alfred, 12, 267-268, 277-290, 293, 309
Adler, H.E., 39
Adolescent Aggression (Bandura & Walters), 202
Agassiz, 114
Aggression, 202
    delayed imitation of, 220
    imitative, 222-223, 224
    instigation of, 219-220
    models of
        film-mediated, 215-227
        reality-fictional stimulus dimension of, 216
        sex of child and sex of, 223-224
    predisposition to, 224
Aggression: A Social Learning Analysis (Bandura), 202
Albert, R.S., 216
Alienists, 135
Alimentary (food) reflex, 159
Allen, G.W., 113n
Allport, Gordon W., 8n, 230
American Psychological Association, 134
Analogy in psychology, 181
Analysis, testing of, 88
Analytic introspection, 85
Angell, Frank, 84, 115
Angell, James Rowland, 123-130, 178
Anger, 88-89
Animal Intelligence (Thorndike), 156
Animals
    association in, 173, 174
    memory in, 175
    vision in, 187-188
Animal spirits, 23, 24
Anna O (Bertha Papenheim), 246
Anokihin, P.K., 154n
Ansbacher, H.L., 268
Ansbacher, R., 268
Apes, intelligence of, 238-244
Apperception, schema of, 281-283
Applied (practical) psychology, Watson on, 186
Appreciation, freshness of, 308
Archetypes, 273-277
Aristotelian paradigm, 3, 7n
Aristotle, 98n
"Artificially intelligent" programs, 299
Art of Travel: Shifts and Contrivances Available in Wild
    Countries (Galton), 96
Asratyan, E.A., 154n

Association(s)
    in animals, 173, 174
    of ideas, 65
    laws of, 72
    permanence of, 175
Associationists, 116, 117
Astronomy, Ptolemaic vs. Copernican, 1-2, 3, 4
Auditory cognition, 295
Avenarius, 91
Averages, constant, 78-80
"Axes of bias," 9n

Baars, B.J., 291n
Babkin, B.P., 154n
Baird, J.W., 92
Baldwin, Mark, 91, 178
Bandura, Albert, 202-203, 215-227
Beagle, H.M.S., 95
Beck Depression Inventory (BDI), 134
Behavior, 294
Behaviorism, 12-13, 201-227, 296
    antecedent influences, 154-176
        Pavlov, 154-155
        Thorndike, 155-157
    of Bandura, 202-203
    consciousness and, 181-184
    on memory, 189
    of Skinner, 201-202
    of Watson, 177-200
Behavior of Organisms, The (Skinner), 202
Beitrage zur Theorie der Sinneswahrnehmung (Contribu-
    tions Toward a Theory of Sense Perception)
    (Wundt), 57
Bell, Alexander Graham, 133
Benedict, Ruth, 293
Berkowitz, L., 216
Bernheim, 256
Beyond Freedom and Dignity (Skinner), 202
Beyond the Pleasure Principle (Freud), 247
Bias, axes of, 9n
Binet, Alfred, 131-132, 134-144
Binet Simon Scale & Its Developments (Binet & Simon),
    134-144
Biological Principles (Woodger), 9n
Bits (binary digits), 298
Bjork, D.W., 201
Blin, Dr., 135, 138
Blueler, Eugene, 266
Boakes, R., 155n, 157
"Bobo doll" study, 203
Bodily process, mental process and, 89

Body-mind duality. See Mind-body duality, 324
Boodoo, G., 134n
Boring, E.G., 38n, 40, 56n, 57n, 83n, 84, 85, 90-93, 132n, 291
Bottome, P., 267n
Bouchard, T.J., 134n
Boykin, A.W., 134n
Boyle, Robert, 21
Brain
    animal spirits in the, 23
    soul and, 25-26
Brain-experiences, 118
Breuer, Josef, 246, 248, 250-252
Brewer, C.L., 177n
Briefer Course, The (James), 114
Brody, N., 134n
Brome, J., 265n
Brücke, Ernst, 246
Bruner, J.S., 8n
Brunswik, E., 8n, 9n
Buckley, K.W., 177n, 178, 179
Building by chimpanzees, 242-243
Burghölzli, 266
Burnham, J.C., 156n

Calkins, 115
Cattell, James McKeen, 91, 132-134, 145-153
Ceci, S.J., 134n
Channels, 298
Chaplin, J.P., 5n
Charcot, Jean Martin, 246, 255-256
Charles I, King of England, 20
Children
    aggression. See Aggression
    measurement of development of intelligence in, 138-139
    problems of labeling, 132
Chimpanzees
    building by, 242-243
    intelligence in, 240-241
Christina of Sweden, Queen, 20
Classes, 237
Classical conditioning, 155
"Classical Introspection" (Boring), 90-93
Classification, 63-64
Cocaine, Freud's research on, 246
Cognition, 117
Cognition and Reality (Neisser), 292
"Cognitive Approach, The" (Neisser), 294-301
Cognitive Psychology (Neisser), 292
Cognitive theory, dynamic theory vs., 296
Cohen, D., 177n, 178
Cohen, E.D., 265n
Collective unconscious, 266, 275-277
Color vision, Young-Helmholtz theory of, 39, 42-48
Communal life

as absolute truth, 283-284
    necessity of, 284
Community, mental, 70
Comparative Individual Psychology, 280
Computer-man parallel, 297
Computer programming, 298-299
Conceptions and Methods of Psychology, The (Cattell), 145-153
Concerning Memory (Über das Gedächtnis) (Ebbinghaus), 58
"Conditioned Emotional Reactions" (Watson & Rayner), 191-200
Conditioned reflex, formation of, 166-167
Conditioned Reflexes (Pavlov), 155, 158-170
Conditioned responses, detachment or removal of, 199
Conditioning
    classical, 155
    operant (instrumental), 156, 202
Conduct of Human Understanding, The (Locke), 21
Conscious elements, 87
Consciousness, 2, 86, 176, 180
    behaviorism and, 181-184
    chemistry of, 85
    functionalism and, 127-128, 129
    functions in, 270-273
    Jung on, 269-273
    search for origin of, 181-182
    states of, 125
Contributions Toward a Theory of Sense Perception (Beitrage zur Theorie der Sinneswahrnehmung) (Wundt), 57
Conversion, hysterical, 254
Conversion disorder, 246
Copernican paradigm, 1-2
"Co-Relations and Their Measurement, Chiefly from Anthropometric Data" (Galton), 104-112
Cousin, Victor, 7n
Creativeness, self-actualization and, 311-314
Crisis, 4
Culture, independence of, 307-308
Current science, 291-317
    Maslow, 292-293
    Neisser, 291-292

Dallenbach, Karl M., 84, 85
Dalton, 103n
Damaye, M., 135-136
Darby, C.L., 226
Darwin, Charles Robert, 94-95, 96, 98-104, 154n
Darwin, Erasmus, 94
Darwin, Robert Waring, 94
Darwinian movement, 182
Deduction, 10
Defence reflex, 159

Delayed imitation, 220

Democratic character structure, self-actualization and, 310

Descartes, Rene, 19-20, 21, 22-28

Description, explanation vs., 64

Detachment
  of conditioned emotional responses, 199
  self-actualization and, 306-307

Development of intelligence in child, measurement of, 138-139

Dewey, John, 178, 278

Dichotomy resolution, self-actualization and, 315

Dieterici, C., 46

Discourse on Method, The (Descartes), 20

Discrimination between means and ends and between good and evil, self-actualization and, 310-311

Distal stimulus, 295

Dogmatism, 4

Dollard, J., 203, 226

D'Omalius d'Halloy, M.J., 101

Donaldson, H.H., 178

Doob, L.W., 226

Double personality, 254

Drugs, psychology of, 186, 187

Dualism, 61

Duncan, C.P., 226

Dynamic theory, cognitive theory vs., 296. See also Psycho-analysis

Ebbinghaus, Hermann, 57-59, 71-82

Economics-psychology parallel, 297

Ectopsyche, 271, 274

Effect, law of, 156

Ego (self), 116, 234
  acceptance of, 304-305
  Jung on, 270

Eidola, 294, 296

Elementalism, 85n

Elemente der Psychophysik (Elements of Psychophysics) (Fechner), 58

Elementism, 90-91

Eliot, Charles William, 114

Ellenberger, H.F., 245n, 265n, 266n, 267n

Emery, F.E., 216

Emotion, experience of, 87

Emotional transfers, 197

Empathy, 287-288

Empirical psychology, 62, 67
  varieties of, 63

Empiricism, 9, 10, 11

Enculturation, resistance to, 312-313

Endopsyche, 271

Environment, independence of, 307-308

Epstein, Raissa, 267

Eroféeva, Dr., 168

Errors, Law of, 80-82

Essay Concerning Human Understanding, An (Locke), 21, 29-37

Eugenics, 96, 133n

Evans, R.B., 178n, 201n, 265n

Evans, R.V., 83

Existential psychology, 92

Experience, 60
  mystic, 308-309
  peak, 308-309

Experiencing subject, 60

Experimental method, 70

Experimental observation, 68-69

Experimental psychology, 70, 148
  Cattell on, 150

Experiments, 68
  Cattell on, 150

Explanation, description vs., 64

Explanatory psychology, 64

Faculty-psychology, 64

Fancher, R., 38n, 56n

Fear, 200

Fechner, Gustav Theodor, 39-41

Feeling, 271-272
  intuition vs., 272

Feshbach, S., 216

Film, aggressive models from, 215-227

Fjeld, H.A., 226

Food (alimentary) reflex, 159

"Forgetting of Foreign Words" (Freud), 260-264

Form-quality, 233

Franklin, Benjamin, 21

Fraulein Elizabeth case (Freud), 246

Free association, 246

Freedom reflex, 167

Freeman, L., 246n

Freke, Dr., 102

Freud, Jacob, 245

Freud, Sigmund, 245-264, 268

Freudians, 200. See also Psychoanalysis

Frolov, Y.P., 154n

Fromm, Eric, 293

Frost, Carl, 201

Functionalism, 12-13
  antecedent influences
    Darwin, Charles Robert, 94-95
    Darwin, Erasmus, 94
    Galton, 96-97
  consciousness and, 127-128, 129
  development and founding, 113-130
    James, 113-116
  legacy of, 131-153
    Binet, 131-132
    Cattell, 132-134

Functionalism, *(Cont.)*
  psychophysics and, 127-129
  structural psychology vs., 124-127
  Watson on, 184
Fundamentals of Psychology (Grundzüge der Psychologie)
    (Ebbinghaus), 58
Furomoto, L., 115n

Galilean mode of thought, 7n
Galton, Francis, 94, 96-97, 104-112, 131, 133, 149
Gannt, W.H., 154n, 155
Gaukroger, S., 19n
Gemeinschaftsgefühl, self-actualization and, 309
General Problems Selection 1 Gestalt Theory (Wertheimer),
    230-238
Genius, heritability of, 96
Geocentric theory, 1
Geoffroy Saint-Hilaire, Isidore, 99, 102
Gestalt psychology, 12-13, 228-244
  fundamental "formula" of, 232
  fundamental question of, 235
  mind-body problem and, 235-236
  of Wertheimer, 228-230
Gibbons, Alice, 114
Giurgiea, C.E., 154n
Glaser, R., 317n
Goble, F.G., 292n
Goethe, 99n
Goldstein, Kurt, 293
Goleman, D., 291n
Goltz, 121
Good-evil discrimination, self-actualization and, 310-311
Goodman, Bertha, 293
Grant, Professor, 100
Grundzüge der Psychologie (Fundamentals of Psychology)
    (Ebbinghaus), 58

Haldemar, Professor, 100
Hall, C.S., 247
Hall, G. Stanley, 114
Halpern, D.F., 134n
Hamilton, Alexander, 21
Hamilton Dickson, J.D., 112
Hannush, M.J., 178n
Harlow, Harry, 293
Heart, movement of, 22-23
Heliocentric theory, 1
Helmholtz, Hermann von, 38-39, 57, 58n
Henle, M.E., 230n
Henri, Victor, 132
Henslow, John Stevens, 95
Herbert, Dean, 103
Herbert, W., 100
Hereditary Genius (Galton), 96
Herschel, John, 103

Hicks, D.J., 215n
Hillex, W.A., 12-13
Historical Introduction to Modern Psychology (Murphy),
    8n
History of psychology, 1-18. See also Prescriptions of psy-
    chology
  scientific progress, 1-3
Hoffman, E., 267n, 268, 292n
Hoffman, P., 247
Hollender, M.H., 246
Hooker, Dr., 104
Horney, Karen, 293
Hothersall, D., 56n, 57n, 132n, 201n
Hubert, H., 275
Hume, D., 237
Humor, sense of, 311
Hunt, William Morris, 113
Huston, A.C., 216
Hutchins, 12
Huxley, T.H., 104
Hypnoidal states, 254
Hypnosis, repression and, 258
Hysteria, 249-255
Hysterical conversion, 254

Ickes, Mary, 178
Ideas, 64
  associations of, 65
  attribution of nature of things to, 65
Identification, 288
Idiography, 9
Imageless thought controversy, 228-229
Imitation, delayed, 220
Imitation of Film-Mediated Aggressive Models (Bandura,
    Ross, & Ross), 215-227
Imitative aggression, 222-223, 224
Immediate experience, 60
  psychology as science of, 62, 63
Independence of physical and social environment
  self-actualization and, 307-308
"Individual Psychology of Alfred Adler, The" (Adler), 277-
    290
Induction, 10
Information theory, 298
Innate notions, 29-37
  existence of, 21
  in the mind, 31-37
Innate potentiality, 287
Inner perception, introspection vs., 91
Inner sense, 59, 60
  psychology of, 62, 64
Innocent eye, 303
Instinct, 119
"Instincts and Their Vicissitudes" (Freud), 295
Institute for the Experimental Study of Medicine, 155

Instrumental (operant) conditioning, 156, 202
Intellectualistic psychology, 64-65
Intelligence, 121
    of apes, 238-244
    in child, measurement of development in, 138-139
    subnormal, 135
Interactionists, 147
Interest, social, 287-290
    empathy, 287-288
    innate potentiality, 287
    other-directedness, 288-290
    universality of, 290
Interpersonal relations, self-actualization and, 309-310
Interpretation of Dreams, The (Freud), 246
Introspection, 59, 62, 180
    analytic, 85
    behaviorist critique of, 183-184
    constraints on, 92
    inner perception vs., 91
    memory and, 92
    usefulness of, 92-93
Intuition, 236, 272-273

James, William, 113-122, 148, 156
Janet, P.M.F., 266
Joncich, G., 155n
Jones, E., 245n
Jones, Harold E., 179
Jones, Mary Cover, 179
Jones, W.T., 9n
Journal of Psychology and Physiology of Sense Organs
    (Zeitschrift für Psychologie und Physiologie der Sinnesorgane), 58
Jung, C.G., 265-267, 269-277

Kanfer, F.H., 226
Kant, Immanuel, 38, 237
Kenny, D.T., 216
Keyserling, Count, 103
Khecolt-Glaser, J.W., 317n
King, D.B., 228n
Koch, A.M., 226
Koch, Sigmund, 5n
Koenigsberger, L., 38n
Koffka, Kurt, 229, 293, 295
Köhler, Wolfgang, 229-230, 291, 293
König, Arthur, 46, 58
Krawiec, T.S., 5n
Krestovnikov, 166
Kuhn, T.S., 1, 2, 3, 4, 5
Külpe, Oswald, 90, 91, 92, 93, 228

Labeling children, problems of, 132
Ladd, Geo. T., 118n, 122
Lamarck, J.B., 98

Language, 284-285
La psychologie individuelle (Binet & Henri), 132
Leahey, T.H., 85n
Learning
    observational, 202
    overt performance vs., 225
Leary, D.E., 113
Lecoq, M., 103
Le Farge, John, 114n
Legal testimony, 187
Leibniz, G.W. von, 7n
Levin, H., 216, 226
Lewes, 121
Lewin, Kurt, 7n, 8n
Lewis, D.J., 226
Ley, R., 229n
Libido, Jung on, 266
Liebmann, 122
Lindzey, C.S., 247
Linnaeus, 152
Little Albert study, 192-200
Locke, John, 20-22, 29-37
Loeb, Jacques, 178
Loehlin, J.C., 134n
Logic, 284-285
"Logic Theorist" (program), 299
Lotze, Hermann, 132
Lövaas, O.J., 216, 224
Love, 200, 286
Lovejoy, A.O., 10n
Ludwig, Karl, 154
Lyle, J., 225

McBrearty, J.F., 226
Maccoby, E.E., 216, 226
McGuire, W., 266
Mach, 91, 146, 228
Maddocks, M., 114n
Madigan, S., 115n
Madison, James, 21
Mahaffey, J., 19n
Man-computer parallel, 297
"Manual of Physiological Optics, A" (Helmholtz), 42
Marston, A.R., 226
Martin, H.N., 122
Marx, M.H., 12-13
Maslow, Abraham, 291, 292-293, 302-317
Materialistic psychology, 61
Matter-mind distinction, 146. See also Mind-body duality
Matthew, Patrick, 100
Mauss, M., 275
"Meaning and Problem of Psychology, The" (Titchener), 86-90
Means-ends discrimination, self-actualization and, 310-311
Measurement, Cattell on, 151-152

Measuring Scale of Intelligence, use of, 143-144
Mechanical materialism, 61
Mechanism-vitalism dichotemy, 9
Mediate experience, 60
Memory, 117
    in animals, 175
    behaviorist approach to, 189
    dependencies of, 72-73
    Descartes on, 28
    introspection and, 92
    knowledge of
        deficiencies in, 73-74
        enlarging, 74-82
    manifestations of, 71-72
    numerical measurements for contents of, 75-77
Memory a Contribution to Experimental Psychology
        (Ebbinghaus), 71-82
Memory Observed (Neisser), 292
Mental elements, 87, 88
Mentality, means and ends in, 120
"Mentality of Apes, The" (Köhler), 238-244
Mental Life of Monkeys and Apes: A Study in Ideational
        Behavior (Yerkes), 244
Mental process, 86
    bodily process and, 89
    description and explanation of, 89-90
Mental products, 70
Mental sciences, 60
Mental testing, 133
Metaphysical psychology, 61, 67
Method(s), 14-15
    of natural science, 74-75
    of psychology, 67-70
Methodological subjectivity-objectivity, 10
Meyers, 113n
Miller, George, 9, 291
Miller, N.E., 203, 226
Mind, 86
Mind-body duality, 20, 25, 62
    Fechner on, 40
    Gestalt theory and, 235-236
    interaction in, 27
    psychophysics and, 53-54
    Titchener on, 89
    Watson on, 185
Mind-matter distinction, 146
Minister of Public Instruction, 134-135
Modeling, 202
    of aggression, 215-227
Modes of thought, Galilean and Aristotelian, 7n
Molarism, 11
Molecularism, 11
Monadology, 61
Monism, 10, 61
Morgan, Lloyd, 175

Motivation and Emotion (Maslow), 293
Motor reflex, 159
Mowrer, O.H., 216, 226
Müller, G.E., 90, 92
Müller, Johannes, 47
Munsterburg, Hugo, 115
Murphy, G., 8n
Murray, Henry, 8n
Muscles, movement of, 23-24
Mystic experience, self-actualization and, 308-309

Naiveté, second, 312
Nathanson, Amelia, 245
Naturalness, self-actualization and, 305-306
Natural process, 68
Natural science, 60, 67-68
    method of, 74-75
Nature, acceptance of, 304-305
Naudin, 103
Neisser, Ulric, 131n, 291-292, 294-301
Nerve-physiology, 119
New Essays Concerning Human Understanding
        (Leibniz), 7n
New Introductory Lectures on Psychoanalysis (Freud), 247
New psychology, 56-82
    Ebbinghaus, 57-59
    Wundt, 56-57
Newton, Isaac, 21
Nomotheticism, 9, 12

Objectivity, 10
Objects of experience, 60
Objects of nature, 68
Observation, 68, 70
    experimental, 68-69
    pure, 69-70
Observational learning, 202
Occupation, social ties through, 285-286
O'Hara, R., 115n
Oken, Lorenz, 39
On the Psychology of the Unconscious (Jung), 266
"On the Rate of Transmission of the Nerve Impulse"
        (Helmholtz), 48-52
Operant (instrumental) conditioning, 156, 202
Operationalism, 7
Opthalmosope, 39
"Origin and Development of Psychoanalysis" (Freud),
        248-260
Origin of Species (Darwin), 95, 98-104
Other-directedness, 288-290
Others, acceptance of, 304-305
Outline of Psychology (Titchener), 85
Outlines of Psychology (Wundt), 59-70
Overt performance, learning vs., 225
Owen, Professor, 101-102

Papenheim, Bertha (Anna O), 246
Paradigm, 3-4
   Aristotelian, 3, 7n
   guidance function of, 4-5
   Ptolemaic, 1-2, 3, 4
   shifts in, 2
Parallelism, 147, 185
Parker, E.B., 225
Passions
   principal effect of, 27
   seat of, 26
Passions of the Soul, The (Descartes), 20, 22-28
Pavlov, Ivan Petrovitch, 154-155, 158-170, 201
Peak experience, 308-309
Pearson, Karl, 146
Peckler, M.A., 228n
Pennebaker, J.W., 317
Perceived Self, The (Neisser), 292
Perception, self-actualization and, 303-304
Perfection, striving for, 277-280
Perloff, R., 134n
Perry, 113n
Personality, double, 254
Personal unconscious, 274
Pflüger, 121
Philosophical influences, 19-37
   Descartes, 19-20
   Locke, 20-22
Philosophy of Nature (Oken), 39
Phi phenomenon, 229
Physicalism, 7
Physics
   paradigmatic shifts in, 2
   psychology and, 91
Physiological influences, 38-55
   Fechner, 39-41
   Helmholtz, 38-39
Physiological psychology, 70, 84
Physiologische Psychologie (Wundt), 148
Physiology, 63
Popular Science Monthly, 133
Potentiality, innate, 287
Powell, Baden, 103
Practical applications, 152-153
Practical (applied) psychology, 186
Prejudgments, 7n, 10
Prescriptions of psychology, 3-16
   borrowings from other disciplines, 11-12
   in contrasting pairs, 6, 9
   criteria for, 7
   dominant and counterdominant, 9-10, 13-14
   orientative character of, 8-9, 12
   philosophical roots of, 11
   as prejudgments, 10
   schools of, 12-13

   Zeitgeist and, 14
Principles of Behavior Modification (Bandura), 202
Principles of Psychology, The (James), 114, 116-122, 148
Privacy, need for, 306-307
Problem centering, self-actualization and, 306
Process(es)
   bodily, 89
   mental, 86, 89-90
   psychical, 61
   Titchener's definition of, 86
Productive Thinking (Wertheimer), 230
Program analogy, 299
Programming, computer, 298-299
Province of Functional Psychology, The (Angell), 123-130
Proximal stimuli, 295
Psychical experience, nature of, 62
Psychical processes, 61
Psychoanalysis, 12-13, 245-264
   of Adler, 267-268
   of Freud, 245-247
   of Jung, 265-267
Psychological Corporation, 134
Psychological Types (Jung), 266
Psychology
   analogy in, 181-182
   definitions of, 59
   empirical, 62, 67
   existential, 92
   experimental, 70, 148
      Cattell on, 150
   explanatory, 64
   general forms of, 60-67
   history of, 1-18
      scientific progress, 1-3
   intellectualistic, 64-65
   lack of unity in, 5
   materialistic, 61
   metaphysical, 61, 67
   methods of, 67-70
   parallels with economics, 297
   physics and, 91
   physiological, 70, 84
   practical applications of, 152-153
   practical (applied), 186
   prescriptions of, 3-16
      borrowings from other disciplines, 11-12
      in contrasting pairs, 6, 9
      criteria for, 7
      dominant and counterdominant, 9-10, 13-14
      orientative character of, 8-9, 12
      philosophical roots of, 11
      as prejudgments, 10
      schools of, 12-13
      Zeitgeist and, 14
   problem of, 59-60

Psychology (*Cont.*)
  in relation to other disciplines, 67
  scope of, 116-122
  social, 70
  spiritualistic, 61, 116
  Titchener's definition of, 86
  voluntaristic, 64, 65
"Psychology: A Prescriptive Science" (Watson), 2-16
"Psychology as the Behaviorist Views It" (Watson), 178, 180-191
Psychometrics, 131-134
  Binet and, 131-132
  Cattell and, 132-134
Psychopathology of Everyday Life, The (Freud), 246
Psycho-physical materialism, 61
Psychophysics, 40, 52-55
  functionalism and, 127-129
  mind-body duality and, 53-54
  outer and inner part of, 54
Ptolemaic paradigm, 1-2, 3, 4
Pure observation, 69-70

Rafinesque, 100
Rage, 200
Raney, S., 228n
Rationalism, 9, 10, 11
Raynor, Rosalie, 178-179, 191-200
Read, Herbert, 303
Reflex
  conditioned, 166-167
  defense, 159
  definition of, 164
  food (alimentary), 159
  freedom, 167
  motor, 159
  salivary, 159
  secretory, 159
Reflex acts, 119
Regression, 109
Removal of conditioned emotional responses, 199
Repression
  Freud's concept of, 257-258
  hypnosis and, 258
Research, constancy of conditions requisite for, 77-78
Resistance
  to enculturation, self-actualization and, 312-313
  Freud's concept of, 257
Revolutions, scientific, 1, 3, 4
Richter, C.P., 317
Riopelle, A.J., 226
Rising Curve, The (Neisser), 292
Roazen, P., 247
Ross, B., 113
Ross, D., 203, 215-227

Ross, S.A., 203, 215-227
Ruger, G.J., 156
Rules, 284-285
Russell, Bertrand, 19
Rychlack, J.F., 246

Salivary reflex, 159
Santayana, G., 312
Saxe, John Godfrey, 315
Schaaffhausen, Dr., 103
Schaef, R.W., 228n
Schema of apperception, 281-283
School Achievement of Minority Children, The (Neisser), 292
Schramm, W., 225
Schuman, 229
Science, Titchener's definition of, 87
Science and Human Behavior (Skinner), 202
Scientific progress, 1-3
Scientific revolutions, 1, 3, 4
Scott, F.J.D., 178n
Sears, R.R., 216, 226
Sechenov, 154n
Sechrest, L., 226
Second Essay (Renouvier), 114
Second naiveté, 312
Secretory reflex, 159
Self (ego), 116, 234
  acceptance of, 304-305
  Jung on, 270
Self-actualization
  acceptance and, 304-305
  creativeness and, 311-314
  democratic character structure and, 310
  detachment and, 306-307
  dichotomy resolution and, 315
  discrimination between means and ends and between good and evil and, 310-311
  freshness of appreciation and, 308
  gemeinschaftsgefühl and, 309
  imperfect, 313-314
  independence of physical and social environment and, 307-308
  interpersonal relations and, 309-310
  mystic experience and, 308-309
  naturalness and, 305-306
  peak experience and, 308-309
  perception and, 303-304
  problem centering and, 306
  resistance to enculturation and, 312-313
  sense of humor and, 311
  simplicity and, 305-306
  spontaneity and, 305-306
  values and, 314-315

"Self-Actualizing People: A Study of Psychological Health" (Maslow), 302-317
Self-boundedness, 289
Self-Efficacy: The Exercise of Control (Bandura), 203
Self-enhancement, striving for, 280
Sensation(s), 53-54, 183-184, 271
    attributes of, 92
    stimulus and, 54-55
Sensationism, 91
Sense of humor, self-actualization and, 311
Sense-perception, 59
Senses, 24
Shakow, D., 57n
Siegel, A.E., 216
Signalization, 164-165
Simon, T., 131n, 132, 134-144
Simplicity, self-actualization and, 305-306
Skinner, Burrhus Frederick, 21, 201-202
Social embeddedness, 283-286
Social Foundations of Thought and Action (Bandura), 202
Social interest, 287-290
    empathy, 287-288
    innate potentiality, 287
    other-directedness, 288-290
    universality of, 290
Social Learning and Personality Development (Bandura & Walters), 202
Social Learning Theory (Bandura), 202
Social psychology, 70
Social ties, 285-286
Society, 286
Sokal, M.M., 132n, 230
Some Experiments on Animal Intelligence (Thorndike), 171-176
Some Thoughts Concerning Education (Locke), 21
Soul
    actions of, 28
    brain and, 25-26
    functions of, 25
    James on, 116-118
    power of, 27-28
Soul-body duality. See Mind-body duality
Species, transmutation of, 94
Spencer, Herbert, 102
Spiritualistic psychology, 61, 116
Spontaneity, self-actualization and, 305-306
"States of consciousness" doctrine, 125
Statistical techniques, Galton and, 96, 97
Steinbruner, John, 215n
Sternberg, R.J., 134n
Stimulus-error, 92
Stimulus/stimuli
    distal, 295
    proximal, 295
    sensations and, 54-55

Striving
    for perfection, 277-280
    for self-enhancement, 280
Strong, Edward K., 133
Structuralism, 83-93
    functionalism vs., 124-127
    of Titchener, 83-85
    Watson on, 184
Studies in Hysteria (Freud & Breuer), 246
Stumpf, 90, 228
Subjectivity, 10
    uniqueness and, 280-283
Sublimation, 259-260
Subnormal intelligence, 135
Syllogisms, 237
Synthesis, 88

"Tavistock Lectures, The" (Jung), 269-277
Test-Book of Psychology (Titchener), 84
Testimony, legal, 187
Testing, mental, 133
Thema, 8n
Thematic Apperception Test (TAT), 134
Thinking, 271
Thomas, R.K., 154n
Thorndike, Edward Lee, 115, 133, 155-157, 293
Three Essays on Sexuality (Freud), 247
Threshold phenomena, 234
Thumb sucking, 199-200
Titchener, Edward Bradford, 2, 8n, 21, 56n, 57, 83-85, 86-90, 91, 92, 184, 293
"Two Essays Upon Dew and Single Vision" (Wells), 99
Two Treatises on Government (Locke), 20-21

Über das Gedächtnis (Concerning Memory) (Ebbinghaus), 58
Unconscious, 254
    collective, 266, 275-277
    Jung on, 269-270, 274
    personal, 274
Understanding, Locke on, 29-37
Unger, 103n
Uniqueness, subjectivity and, 280-283
Universality
    of social interest, 290
    of striving, 278
Urbina, S., 134n

Values, 272
    self-actualization and, 314-315
Varon, E.J., 131n
"Vestiges of Creation," 100

Violet, 45
Vision
    in animals, 187-188
    color, 39, 42-48
Visual cognition, 295
Vitalism, 235
Vitalism-mechanism dichotomy, 9
Voluntaristic psychology, 64, 65
Von Baer, 104
Von Buch, 100
Von Ehrenfels, 228, 233

Wagner, Rudolph, 104
Walden Two (Skinner), 202, 204
Wallace, Alfred Russel, 95, 104
Walters, R.H., 202, 225, 226
Warden, C.J., 226
Washburn, M.F., 83, 84
Washburn, Margaret, 133
Washington, George, 21
Watson, Jim (son), 178n
Watson, John Broadus, 2, 21, 93, 177-200, 201, 293
Watson, R.I., 2-16, 265n
Weber, E.H., 39
Wechsler Adult Intelligence Scale (WAIS), 134

Wechsler Intelligence Scale for Children (WISC), 134
Wedgewood, Emma, 95
Wedgewood, Susannah, 94-95
Wehr, G., 265n
Wells, W.C., 99
Wertheimer, Max, 93, 228-230, 244, 293
Whitehead, A.N., 10n
Will, 307-308
Windholz, G., 154n, 155n
Wissler, Clark, 133
Wolpe, J., 21n
Woodworth, Robert S., 57n, 115, 133, 156
Worf, T.H., 131n
Work of the Principle Digestive Glands, The (Pavlov), 155
Wundt, Wilhelm, 56-57, 59-70, 83, 84, 90, 91, 133, 148, 150

Yerkes, R.M., 244
Young, Thomas, 39, 43, 44, 46, 47
Young-Helmholtz theory, 39, 42-48

Zeitgeist, 14
Zeitschrift für Psychologie und Physiologie der Sinnesorgane (Journal of Psychology and Physiology of Sense Organs), 58

CREDITS

Chapter 1 Watson, R.I. Psychology: A Prescriptive Science. *American Psychologist*, 22, 435–444. Copyright © 1967 by the American Psychological Association. Reprinted by permission.

Chapter 2 Descartes, R. (1931). The Passions of the Soul. In E.S. Haldane & G.R.T. Ross (Trans.) *Philosophical Works of Descartes.* (Rev. ed.) Vol. 1, pp. 329–427 excerpted. New York: Dover. Reprinted by permission of the publisher. Locke, J. (1690). *An Essay Concerning Human Understanding.*

Chapter 3 Helmholtz, H. (1850). *On the Rate of Transmission of the Nerve Impulse.* Helmholtz, H. (1912). A Manual of Physiological Optics. In B. Rand (Ed.) *The classical psychologists.* (pp. 571–581). Fechner, G. (1859). Excerpt from *Elements of Psychophysics* by David H. Howes and Edwin G. Boring, translated by Helmut E. Adler, copyright © 1966 by Holt, Rinehart and Winston. Reprinted by permission of the publisher.

Chapter 4 Wundt, W. (1907). *Outlines of Psychology.* Leipzig: Englemann, pp. 1–18. Ebbinghaus, H. (1964). *On Memory: A Contribution to Experimental Psychology.* (H.A. Ruger and E.E. Bussenius, Trans.) New York: Dover. Reprinted by permission of the publisher.

Chapter 5 Titchener, E.B. (1897). *An Outline of Psychology.* (2nd ed.) New York: MacMillan, pp. 1–25. Boring, E.G. A History of Introspection. *Psychological Bulletin,* 50, 169–189, pp. 171–175. Copyright © 1953 by the American Psychological Association. Reprinted by permission.

Chapter 6 Darwin, C. (1859). *The Origin of the Species.* Galton, F. (1888). Co-Relations and Their Measurement, Chiefly from Anthropometric Data. *Proceedings of The Royal Society of London,* 15, 135–145.

Chapter 7 James, W. (1890). *Principles of Psychology.* New York: Holt, pp. 1–11. Angell, J.R. (1904). The Province of Functional Psychology. *The Psychological Review,* 14, pp. 61–91.

Chapter 8 Binet, A. and Simon, T. (1905). *Sur la necissite a etablis un diagnostic scientific des etate inferieurs de l'intelligence. L'Anee Psychologique,*

11, 163–190. (Kite, (1916) Trans. *The development of intelligence.* Baltimore: Williams and Wilkins.) Binet, A. and Simon, T. (1908). *La development de l'intelligence chez les infants. L'Anee Psychologique,* 14, 1–94. (Kite, (1916) Trans. *The development of intelligence.* Baltimore: Williams and Wilkins.) Cattell, J.M. (1904). The Conceptions and Methods of Psychology. *Popular Science Monthly,* 66, 176–186.

Chapter 9 Pavlov, I.P. (1927). *Conditional Reflexes.* Translated and edited by G.V. Anrep, pp. 17–32. Reprinted by permission of Oxford University Press. Thorndike, I.P. (1898). [Monograph supplement]. *Psychological Review,* 2(8). (Excerpted).

Chapter 10 Watson, J.B. (1913). Psychology as the Behaviorist Views It. *Psychological Review,* 20, 158–177. Watson, J.B. and Rayner, R. (1920). Conditioned Emotional Reactions. *Journal of Experimental Psychology,* 3, 1–14.

Chapter 11 Skinner, B.F. (1976). *Walden Two.* Pp. 36–53. Reprinted by permission of Prentice-Hall, Inc., Upper Saddle River, NJ. Bandura, A., Ross, D., and Ross, S.A. Imitation of Film Mediated Aggressive Models. *Journal of Abnormal and Social Psychology,* 66, 3–11. Copyright © 1963 by the American Psychological Association. Reprinted by permission.

Chapter 12 Wertheimer, M. (1938). Gestalt Theory. In W.D. Ellis, Ed., *A Source Book of Gestalt Psychology,* pp. 1–11. Routledge. Reprinted by permission. Köhler, W. (1925). The Mentality of Apes. Pp. 1–2, 9–10, 139–141, 276–279. Routledge. Reprinted by permission.

Chapter 13 Freud, S. (1910). The Origin and Development of Psychoanalysis. *The American Journal of Psychology,* 21, pp 181–198. Freud, S. (1914). *Psychopathology of Everyday Life.* A.A. Brill, trans. New York: Mentor.

Chapter 14 Jung, C.G. The Tavistock Lectures. In *Collected Works.* (Vol. 18). Pp 5–45. Copyright © 1935, 1950 by Princeton University Press. Reprinted by permission. Adler, A. Excerpted from *The Individual Psychology of Alfred Adler* by Heinz L. Ansbacher and Rowena R. Ansbacher. Copyright © 1956 by Basic Books,